ROANOKE COUNTY PUBLIC LIBRARY
VINTON BRANCH LIBRARY
300 S. POLLARD STREET
VINTON, VA 24179

'80s Action Movies
on the Cheap

NO LO
PROPERTY OF
ROANOKE COUNTY LIBRARY

D1235487

0 1197 0845178 4

'80s Action Movies on the Cheap

284 Low Budget, High Impact Pictures

DANIEL R. BUDNIK

McFarland & Company, Inc., Publishers
Jefferson, North Carolina

LIBRARY OF CONGRESS CATALOGUING-IN-PUBLICATION DATA

Names: Budnik, Daniel R., 1973– author.
Title: '80s action movies on the cheap : 284 low budget,
high impact pictures / Daniel R. Budnik.
Other titles: Eighties action movies on the cheap
Description: Jefferson, N.C. : McFarland & Company, Inc., Publishers, 2017. | Includes index.
Identifiers: LCCN 2017002718 | ISBN 9780786497416 (softcover : acid free paper) ∞
Subjects: LCSH: Motion pictures—Reviews. | Motion
pictures—Catalogs. | Low budget films—Catalogs.
Classification: LCC PN1998 .B785 2017 | DDC 791.43/75—dc23
LC record available at https://lccn.loc.gov/2017002718

BRITISH LIBRARY CATALOGUING DATA ARE AVAILABLE

ISBN (print) 978-0-7864-9741-6
ISBN (ebook) 978-1-4766-2687-1

© 2017 Daniel R. Budnik. All rights reserved

*No part of this book may be reproduced or transmitted in any form
or by any means, electronic or mechanical, including photocopying
or recording, or by any information storage and retrieval system,
without permission in writing from the publisher.*

Front cover: Poster art for the 1987 film
American Ninja 2: The Confrontation (Cannon Films/Photofest)
Back cover images © 2017 iStock

Printed in the United States of America

*McFarland & Company, Inc., Publishers
Box 611, Jefferson, North Carolina 28640
www.mcfarlandpub.com*

This book is dedicated to Madelynn Fattibene,
my sweet wife, my love, my life.
Thank you for all your support.
And thank you for putting up with me when I dressed as a ninja
and ran around the backyard scaring squirrels.

Special Thanks

To Fred Adelman of the eternal exploitation movie website *Critical Condition*. Fred has an incredible collection of movie memorabilia, including posters, ad mats and VHS tapes from all over the world. The illustrations in this book are taken from his collection. Back in 1994, my first piece of published writing was in a print issue of *Critical Condition*. It was good to work with him again. Thank you, Fred.

To the Margaret Herrick Library. A fantastic resource of rare cinema-related materials. Scouring their vaults sent me looking for movies I'd never heard of. Plus, I learned One Great Fact from their files: Christopher Walken was originally set to star in *River of Death*. Could you imagine that?

To Eddie Brandt's Saturday Matinee in North Hollywood. They are one of the best video stores in the United States. Quite a few of the films in this book were rented from there.

Table of Contents

Introduction

I ended up watching a lot more cock-fighting than I ever expected. It happens, I guess. One goes into a project not sure of what to expect. I didn't realize how much fun the *American Ninja* movies were. I didn't know how crazy Indonesian action films were. I certainly didn't know that the Swedes made ninja movies. I should have seen all this cock-fighting coming. This book travels to assorted spots in the world to examine the large (but similar) landscape of action films through the 1980s. So, although I expected to hear that same group of English dubbing artists that one encounters in non–English films of this time period, I didn't expect the cockfighting.

I can't say I'm a fan. It also brings up a strange association. A movie that has one car chase may have a shootout or a fistfight. It's the same thing with, say, a slapstick comedy. There may be a thrilling madcap chase followed by a pie fight. It's associative. Someone tuning into an action film is probably going to want to see a gunfight, followed by a car chase and so forth. But what does it say about what the filmmakers think of me when they associate my watching their film with an urge for cockfighting?

One doesn't necessarily have to love all the tropes of a genre to enjoy it. In the 1980s, quite a few comedies were notorious (*Stripes, Summer Rental, National Lampoon's European Vacation*) for spending their first hour just goofing around with no particular storyline and then, suddenly, in the last half-hour a story comes out of nowhere. I was never a fan of that. *Summer Rental*, in particular, is quite funny and charming until the big boat race. Then, it becomes just okay.

So, there's nothing to lead me to believe that I need to love everything within action films to love action films. Heck, I'm also not a fan of the sexual assaults against women in these movies, which are generally used as the excuse for a revenge plot in which some big guy goes crazy and starts shooting everything. For me, a grand action film is one that has charming characters (sometimes they can be tough guys, too), a minimum of plot and strong action set pieces throughout. *Action U.S.A.* is an almost-perfect example. *American Ninja 2* is another. And that doesn't get us out of the "A's."

I also love my action films batshit crazy or super-weird. (Hello, anything directed by Arizal or *The Courier of Death*.) But that's a different kind of film; those films may not always succeed as "action" films but they may entice and pull the viewer along in different ways. The opening scene of *American Hunter* where the guys in the skyscraper are interrupted by a car flying through their window is exciting and crazy. The Courier in the previously mentioned film is just a bit too goofy-looking to be the kick-ass action hero that he's supposed to be.

Keep me excited and on the edge of my seat. Or keep me confused and amazed. That's what I want from an action film. Boredom is not going to work. And too many shots of guys in long shot firing guns that cut to long shots of guys falling down dead can work for John Woo but can get deadly dull after a time. There are a lot of films like that in this book.

My purpose in exploring this area of film is because, to me, the 1980s was the true birth of the action film as we know it today. The films of Stallone, Schwarzenegger, Norris and others set the big blockbuster tone that action films exhibit at the box office in our times. In a bit, I'll discuss action (and adventure) films of prior decades. But, for now, it's the big name stars coupled with the blockbuster mentality that arose out of films like *Jaws* and *Star Wars* in the second half of the 1970s that led to big, big action films.

And all big successes lead to knockoffs, rip-offs and odd follow-ups. The 1980s was the original decade of the slasher film and following all the children of Michael Myers, Jason Voorhees and Freddy Krueger is a fascinating journey. Well, following the children of Indiana Jones and Rambo is just as fascinating. Watching the Indonesian take on Rambo or the Italian version of the Vietnam War (which can be as odd as their version of the American Old West) can really discombobulate a viewer as they watch something that was so specific to American culture, get moved around and twisted about. The clothes are there but it's not the same person inside.

As with horror films, action films were helped along incredibly by the advent of home video. Companies like Action International Pictures and PM Entertainment (most of their product was made in the 1990s) thrived on low-budget mostly action films direct for the home video market. And there are plenty of other films in here that got very limited (or no) theatrical release. There are even a few shot-on-video films in here. Ingenuity knows no bounds.

Then, there are the legion of "ninja" films made by Godfrey Ho and Joseph Lai in the late 80s. Ho and Lai were known for their cut and paste style of filmmaking, in which they would acquire the rights to a random Asian film, the genre was irrelevant, and insert newly shot footage of Australian actors dressed as ninjas. They would completely rewrite the soundtrack of the acquired film to get it to sync with what the ninjas were doing and saying. Every one of their films is a semi-surreal, semi-incoherent adventure. They capitalized on the popularity of ninjas, a word which appeared in the title of all their films, but the original film, which made up the bulk of the movie, had nothing to do with ninjas. It was hucksterism at its absolute finest. You

will encounter quite a few of their films in this book. Warning: Incoherence Abounds!

When *Terminator 2: Judgment Day* (1991) came out, action films changed. Although in that film most of the digital effects involve the T-1000, the action scenes are generally shot for real; it was the ability to now use CGI that made everyone an action star. As the 1990s went on, the action star on the big screen faded because Keanu Reeves was now an action star. Tom Cruise was now an action star. An era ended.

Each year is given its own chapter. Each chapter begins with a brief rundown of the biggest moneymaking movies of that year and the biggest (and/or most influential) action-adventure films of that year. Then, within each year, the movies are arranged alphabetically.

The Keystone Cops may have started it all back in the second decade of the 20th century. From the mind of Mack Sennett, they were a group of wacky cops that sped through the streets, hung from cliffs and generally got involved in super silent craziness to the delight of audiences. The Cops were apparently quite well loved because they appeared in many two-reel silent comedies. But, as far as I know, they were never really the stars of anything. A regular two-reeler would go along and climax in the need for cops and the Keystone Cops would be called in. They're entertaining to watch now—although the comic action in Buster Keaton, Harold Lloyd and Laurel and Hardy films is much funnier.

Alongside the comic action, they had the cowboy shoot-'em-up pictures. Those were filled with lots of shootouts and fistfights and chases on horses. They're quite an energetic bunch of movies. And, in certain ones, you can sense the spirit of the modern-day action film. In particular, some of the early 1930s (sound now) John Wayne pictures like *Haunted Gold* and *Telegraph Trail*. They have a certain *joie de vivre* that is almost exhilarating. And, apparently, it's helped along by the fact that in some of them, there's silent film footage of another cowboy star for the stunt and riding scenes. But, throughout a lot of the 1930s and 1940s and 1950s, action was confined to madcap comic endings for films or for Westerns or for jungle films like the Tarzan series or the Saturday morning serials.

Alongside some of the more action-packed Westerns, the serials provided the most straightforward full-on action folks could see back then. That was the point. It was something to keep the kids riveted to their seats before the first feature. In their 15-to-30-minute chapters, fighting and shooting and chasing around could begin at the drop of a hat. This sort of Pure Action was mainly thought to be made for kids.

Then, in the 1950s, they put a lot of oil on a bodybuilder and Hercules hit the screen. Tons of sequels and rip-offs followed, most of them from Italy, most of them looking fairly epic. These are the peplum films. Peplum means "tunic." Guys in tunics and togas, alongside beautiful women, fighting evil tyrants, sorcerers, moon men, monsters. Years later, *Conan the Barbarian* kicked off the 1980s and a whole different world full of peplum-adventure films. Films that no longer were set in a strange mythological past but that might be in our future or on another planet. But the meandering and mostly entertaining sword-and-sandal pictures of the late 1950s were there first. Italians also gave us Spaghetti Westerns, which were shot in such an epic fashion that it was almost impossible to tell what they represented. Italian filmmakers were using the iconography of classic Westerns without actually having been part of the culture that settled that vast landscape. The violence increases here. Some of these films are very dark. And everything got much longer. Honestly, however, the influence of the Spaghetti Western is not so much on action films but on all future Westerns, which would, generally, become more introspective and less action-filled.

Then we got the James Bond films and all the secret agent films that followed in their wake. The early Bonds, especially *Dr. No, From Russia with Love* and *Goldfinger,* are more spy thrillers than action films. After the 1960s, the films become more action-oriented with the huge set pieces taking over some of the movies. Around the world, but mainly from Italy, spy rip-offs followed (sometimes using the lead guys from peplum films). *Lightning Bolt, Operation Double 007* (with Neil Connery, Sean's brother) and the charmingly titled *Danger!! Death Ray* did their variations. And series like Matt Helm and the two Derek Flint films kept the action coming with a great sense of 1960s camp and style.

In the late 1960s and 1970s, there weren't many action films, per se. There were thrillers, detective movies and cop films that had action set pieces in them. *Bullitt* and *The French Connection* are said to have the best car chases ever, but one would be hard-pressed to call them action films as we know them. Sam Peckinpah's *The Wild Bunch* has several scenes of absolutely brilliant action but is more of a dark character study than action. Films of this era would have sudden bursts of action in and amongst the storyline, character studies or, in some cases, comedy. Richard Rush's *Freebie and the Bean* has two of the best car chases I've ever seen but it's mostly a screwy, breaking-all-the-rules comedy. Even Robert Altman's wonderfully weird *Brewster McCloud* has a strange car chase. (On a side note: Italians took movies like *The French Connection* and *Dirty Harry* to heart and the Poliziotteschi genre was born. These were tough, sometimes semi-coherent films about cops breaking all the rules and getting the job done. They were generally pretty violent and usually contained some sort of action scenes. One of the best, *The Violent Professionals,* has two absolutely thrilling car chase sequences.)

Another brand of action coming from Asia began to appeal to a lot of people: the karate–kung fu films made in China and Hong Kong. They were dubbed and sent to theaters for B-movie–style runs. The top purveyor of this brand of fighting, Bruce Lee, only made four completed kung fu films but they're all classics. When he died, a hole was left in the land of martial arts cinema. Out of that grew a new genre: Brucesploitation. Even though Bruce died in the mid–1970s, these subsequent films (with stars such as Bruce Li and Bruce Le) kept going into the 1980s. This book covers a few of them. But, keep in mind, that's a subgenre ending rather than, say, Namsploitation (the use of the Vietnam War for action entertainment purposes).

At this point in time, "action" films were as individual as horror films were. Anything goes. Action was part of the package. Not all of it. It was the blockbuster film mentality that made action films more about action. One can see it grow in leaps and bounds if one watched the original *Star Wars* trilogy. *Star Wars* came out in the U.S. in the summer of 1977 and was, obviously, huge. The interesting thing about the film is that as much as it's remembered as being an action-packed thrill ride, things are calm for the first half. The movie is assembling the characters and putting the story into motion. It's the second half that has the thrills, spills, light saber fights and spaceship battles.

The Empire Strikes Back mixes it up a bit. While it brings the characters and their development to the forefront, the action kicks in much quicker, as befit a film following on from *Star Wars*. People want more action, more excitement. So, in the first hour, we get the fight with the AT-ATs in the snow and the awesome chase through the asteroids with the Millennium Falcon. Then the epic light saber battle to close it out.

By the time of *Return of the Jedi* in the summer of 1983, the face of action had changed. The set pieces come quite regularly, from the fight over the Sarlacc pit to the speeder bike chase to the epic conclusion (three battles going on at once). There's the way the action film developed. People wanted it louder and faster and more action-packed. Filmmakers were willing to give it to them, sometimes at the expense of all logic and sense. But that could be part of the fun.

The 1980s hit and money was on everyone's minds. And the big action films came pouring out of the gates. This book has approximately 284 reviews of low-budget (and a few not-so-low-budget) action-adventure films from the 1980s. It covers theatrical releases from all around the world and quite a few direct-to-video releases. Each review has the English title (sometimes the non–English title also), followed by director, writer, producer and cast members. This is followed by the review. Basic plots appear within the reviews. Spoilers have been kept to a minimum although sometimes they are necessary.

Think of this book as an alternate journey through a big, bright, loud decade worth of films. A journey filled with many trips to Vietnam, many tough cops, stars like Williamson, Rothrock and Dudikoff, stars like Joey Johnson, locations around the world, guys that look like Indiana Jones but are not, guys that look like Rambo but are not and more ninjas than you ever imagined you'd see in not only this life but the next. There will be shooting. There will be wrecked cars. There will be crazy stunts. Give a big Reb Brown scream and hold on tight.

A few notes:

(1) This book also includes "adventure" films, sort of modern-day peplum films, most of them coming off the back of *Conan the Barbarian*. These are generally set in the distant past or the post-apocalyptic future or in some sideways world. I differentiate "adventure" from "action" because "adventure" usually involves a lot of action but the plots are usually meandering along in a quest fashion. So, in general, there's plenty of peril within each individual fight scene. But, also, a lot of walking around. (See Ator films.)

(2) Hong Kong films are only touched on here. During the 1980s, through the work of John Woo, Tsui Hark, Ringo Lam and Jackie Chan, Hong Kong action cinema was making the world a more exciting place. Whether it was through elaborate balletic gunfights, action scenes that made your jaw drop or watching Jackie Chan fall from a clock tower and drop to the ground three stories below in one continuous take, the Hong Kong films are as exciting to watch as silent comedies. They were creating a whole new world and raising the bar. These films have been covered heavily in other books. They will be mentioned but not dwelt on.

(3) I tried to be as thorough as I could. I tried to find as many movies from this time

period as possible. But, sometimes, the fates were against me. I found the McNamara Brothers' second film *Dragon Hunt,* but came up short on their first one, *Twin Dragon Encounter*. In a similar fashion, *American Force 2* and *3* were easy to find. Part 1, however, I could not locate. Maybe the Second Edition.

(4) Each section begins with a rundown of the most popular movies and TV shows of that year. That is followed by major news events and a short list of the bigger action films released in that time.

1980

Highest grossing films in the U.S.
1. *The Empire Strikes Back*
2. *9 to 5*
3. *Stir Crazy*
4. *Airplane!*
5. *Any Which Way You Can*

Highest rated TV shows in the U.S.
1. *Dallas*
2. *60 Minutes*
3. *The Dukes of Hazzard*
4. *The Love Boat*
5. *Private Benjamin*

Big historical events
Winter Olympics, U.S. victory in hockey
John Lennon assassinated
Ronald Reagan elected president
Pac-Man video game released
Mount St. Helens erupts
"Who Shot J.R.?"

Action movies
The Empire Strikes Back, Smokey and the Bandit II, Flash Gordon, The Octagon, Mad Max, The Big Brawl

Challenge of the Tiger

Director: Bruce Le
Screenplay: Bruce Le, Fan Poon
Producers: Dick Randall, Leung-On Cheng, Bruce Le
Cast: Bruce Le (Huang Lung), Richard Harrison (Richard Cannon), Wang Jang Lee (Comrade Yang), Nadiuska (Maria), Bradford Harris (Leopard)

The formula for a drug that will make all men sterile is stolen from Spain. CIA agents Huang Lung and Richard Cannon track it all the way to Hong Kong, fighting all sorts of crazy people along the way. Huang and Richard are good pals. Huang is very dedicated and a kung fu master. Richard is more interested in the ladies. Together they make the perfect team to Challenge the Tiger!

Bruce Le is a great fighter. In this one, he gets lucky because groups of thugs throw themselves his way. He even has a bullfight ring scene where he takes on a bull! That's good kung fu. Harrison is a fine fighter too but he is presented as more of a lover than a fighter. There's some fun comedy moments between the two of them and the fights are strong and exciting.

In this semi straightforward kung fu film, Le seems to have (apart from his name) shed the Bruce Lee exploitation feel and simply made his own action film. With that bull scene and the way Richard's character is treated, he's clearly having more fun than Bruce seemed to have in his films. And the plotline is nice and screwy. It feels a bit like a variation of the story for *Three the Hard Way*, except the focus is not race but the sterilization of men. There are occasional moments when things turn odd. They seem to have producer Dick Randall stamped all over them.

Those bits mainly involve all the naked ladies. It's pretty astounding when we go to Richard's estate for the first time at the start of the movie. There are large groups of topless (sometime naked) ladies just hanging around. They swim. They lie out in the sun. They play tennis topless. Yes, that's possibly a miscalculation on someone's part. The topless tennis player is a beautiful woman and she has a lovely chest. In slo-mo, bouncing all around, however, it ends up going from erotic to amusing. Slo-mo will do that.

A few of the leading women kind of look the same, or maybe they were the same and this reviewer lost track. A woman who fools around with Richard is shot. But then, one of the main terrorists is a lady who looks an awful lot like the lady who got shot. Frankly, there was some confusion. But maybe that was the point. This is made by the same gaggle of guys who gave us *The Clones of Bruce Lee* so all of this could be a way of keeping the suspense going: by completely confusing the viewer. (Or Dick Randall really had a type.)

Challenge of the Tiger features a brief cameo appearance by Jack Klugman and Jane Seymour. It's at some sort of sporting event where Le is seen talking to them. Is this the only kung fu film that Klugman did? It's an unexpected appearance and the celebrities don't seem to be telling Le to hit the road and stop putting them in his movie. So that's good.

The Clones of Bruce Lee

Director: Joseph Kong

Producers: Dick Randall, Chang Tsung Lung

Cast: Dragon Lee (Bruce Lee 1), Bruce Le (Bruce Lee 2), Bruce Lai (Bruce Lee 3), Bruce Thai (Chuck Lee), John Benn (Prof. Lucas), Bolo Yeung (Trainer)

This film is a Dick Randall–influenced morass. "Morass" is generally used in a bad way. But, for *The Clones of Bruce Lee*, it's only semi-bad. This is the ultimate in Bruceploitation concepts while not quite being the best in that strange film genre. (Possibly *Fist of Fury, Touch of Death*?) In this movie, Bruce Lee has just died of a heart attack. The Special Branch of Investigations contacts the presiding doctor and gets a sample of Bruce's DNA. Three clones are created. (This reviewer is a little unsure as to who "Chuck Lee" was in the film.) The clones, named Bruce Lee 1, Bruce Lee 2 and Bruce Lee 3, are played by three of the major

RICHARD HARRISON
BRAD HARRIS
BRUCE LE
DICK RANDALL

CHALLENGE OF THE TIGER

Bruce impersonators of the time, Dragon Lee, Bruce Le and Bruce Lai. Although they all make Bruce noises and Bruce faces, they don't look the same, which shoots the whole clone thing in the foot.

The movie is a series of unconnected events. Prof. Lucas brings the clones to life. Then, the SBI man sends them on adventures. Bruce Lee 1 goes to a film production company that smuggles gold and beats up a lot of people. There are some dubbed chats between the producer and the director that have the sort of circular goofiness that the best odd dubbing in these films has. ("We should shoot him on camera." "No, we shouldn't shoot him on camera. But that's a good idea." "I think it's a good idea." "Just because we won't use that idea doesn't mean it's not a good idea. [Pause] Shoot him on camera. That's a good idea.") Then Bruce Lees 2 and 3 go to Thailand to stop a mad inventor and his "bronze men" (guys in their underpants who have been painted bronze). When the bronze men are punched, there is a metal sound. (The way they get rid of these guys is awesome.) The film ends with the professor trying to take over the Bruce Bunch. There is a fight with Bolo Yeung, death rays and a very ugly man.

Randall puts his trademark on the film during a scene where Bruce Lee 3 and, I think, Chuck Lee watch some women playing on the beach. Six or seven completely naked women frolic around, giggle a lot and oil up their boobs. They grab a random guy on the beach and leap all over him. Apart from their being

naked ladies, there isn't much explanation for them given. A little later, more naked women show up. No one kept it quite as gratuitous as Dick.

This reviewer wishes that he could say that *The Clones of Bruce Lee* is all-out awesome. The premise is. The dubbing certainly is. Watching the set-ups for the action film are amusing to anyone who has worked in film. ("Okay. You two in this shot. Give me some high kicks!") The professor is a hilarious creation. The ending is super-perfunctory. The naked ladies are lovely. And the clones are covered in so much oil, it seems like a possible aftereffect of the cloning process. But, unfortunately, the fighting lets the film down. There's a lot of it. Some of it is very good. It is, however, endless. Apart from the "bronze men" fighting, by the end, interest had waned. But there's almost always a little bit more silly dubbing and odd plotting on the horizon. If one can just hold on.

WATCH THE REAL BRUCE LEE DESTROY HIS CLONES IN THE GREATEST DEATH FIGHT EVER!

"THE CLONES OF BRUCE LEE"
THE FURY OF LEE TIMES THREE!

Enter the Game of Death aka
The King of Kung Fu

Directors: Kuo-Hsiang Lin, Joseph Velasco
Screenplay: Kwon Yong
Producer: Robert Jeffery
Cast: Bruce Le (Chang), Bolo Yeung (Yang See), Steve James (Martial Artist)

Enter the Game of Death is very good Brucesploitation, as opposed to really crazy Brucesploitation, like *The Clones of Bruce Lee* and *Fist of Fury, Touch of Death*. As in *Game of Death*, Bruce Le as Chang must ascend a tower filled with kung fu masters, one on each level. He faces off against a black martial artist (in this case it is the always awesome Steve James). They even dress Chang like Bruce Lee and have him do a lot of Bruce Lee–style faces throughout. It really is amazing, the number of Bruce Lee imitators and imitation films.

The movie is set in China during the run-up to World War II. Important Chinese documents are hidden in the Tower of Death and the Japanese are after them. Chang is chosen by the government to go the Tower. But first Chang fights about ten guys (including Bolo Yeung) in the forest. Then he fights in the ring. Then he has another forest fight. Now Chang can start fighting people in the Tower. There are some political machinations that happen first. And they're not terribly interesting. But once the Tower is entered, things get really fun.

Chang goes from level to level (although it feels more like room to room) and fights a wacky group of guys. There's one guy in all brown who looks sort of like Kung Fu Jack Black. There is the obligatory guy with the long white hair. Then there is the snake guy. There are lot of snakes in his room. He's nuts for them! He throws them at Chang. At one point, he bites the head off of one and squeezes the blood out of it like water from a hose. Suffice it to say, Chang makes his way through these guys. Eventually, he has a big fight with Steve James in a field, much of it in slo-mo. Really, the movie's about fighting.

Bruce Le is quite good. When he was able to shed the shtick he's doing here, like in *Challenge of the Tiger*, he makes a fine movie. He's certainly not as charismatic as Bruce Lee was but he's a great martial artist and he knows how to keep the film moving. *Enter the Game of Death* does sometimes get a bit bogged down, partially because, apart from the snake guy, the fights don't have that much variation. After a while, this reviewer found himself thinking "Oh, no, are they going to smash into that rack of candles?" or "Look out for that post." Especially when everything goes super slo-mo.

Half the time, these films have slo-mo in them. It doesn't seem to make sense. They shot the scene and then, because it's in slo-mo, they're determined to use it. Slo-mo usually means that the viewer can see more clearly when a punch or kick doesn't land right. That's a distraction.

Enter the Game of Death is fun kung fu. It is pure exploitation of Bruce Lee's name. Oddly enough, it is actually exploiting something that was exploitation. *Game of Death* was cobbled together after Bruce's death. *Enter the Game of Death* adds on to that.

The Exterminator

Director, Screenplay: James Glickenhaus
Producer: Mark Buntzman
Cast: Robert Ginty (John Eastland), Christopher George (Detective James Dalton), Samantha Eggar (Dr. Megan Stewart), Steve James (Michael Jefferson), Patrick Farrelly (CIA Agent Shaw), Tony DiBenedetto (Chicken Pimp)

The all-exploitation version of *Death Wish* hits us hard with Robert Ginty (from *The Paper Chase*) as John Eastland, Vietnam vet, who goes after criminals roaming the streets of New York City in assorted violent ways. He becomes known as the Exterminator and, according to a random reporter, he's doing a better job of cleaning up the streets than the cops are. Christopher George is the tough cop trying to catch him. Samantha Eggar is a doctor who keeps examining the brutally beat-up bodies of the people that the

Exterminator attacks. And Tony DiBenedetto plays the Chicken Pimp. (Don't ask.)

Writer-director Glickenhaus goes right for it. The opening sequence is a Vietnam battle that starts with a beautifully filmed explosion and a man flying through the air. Soon after, Eastland and his pal Michael Jefferson (played by the eternally awesome Steve James) are captured by Vietcong. We witness a horrible decapitation. Very surprising and very real. But our guys escape. Fast-forward to the modern day (1980) and things start to go wrong. Glickenhaus doesn't goof around here. A bunch of thugs attack Eastland and Jefferson. Jefferson is paralyzed in a brutal fashion. That begins Eastland's crusade.

There is a tendency to make Eastland out to be a crusader who has a flame thrower. Early on in the film, he does torture a gang member with a flame thrower. But he really uses a variety of weapons, including an industrial-strength grinder. He dangles a mob boss over it as he gets information from him. Then he lowers the mob boss in. *That's* a spicy meatball! The Exterminator doesn't screw around. Eastland is calm, cool and collected throughout, even when he's going to meet the Chicken Pimp.

Ginty never ever seems less than completely sincere no matter what happens. Every time he encounters some sort of strange perversity or horrific event, he acts heartbroken. It's astounding to watch. Charles Bronson gets pissed and kicks ass. But, before Eastland kicks ass, he always seems so sad-dened by what's going on in the world. He pauses and then he kicks the ass. That's why, in the end, Christopher George's character doesn't fully go after him (in a sad ending) because Eastland is doing good. He's helping people by tearing up the bad and bringing in the justice.

An exploitation journey through a magical revenge land, *The Exterminator* gives us what we want: hurting jerks. It's an entertaining, sleazy and gory film that's quite enjoyable. All we need is a souped-up garbage truck.

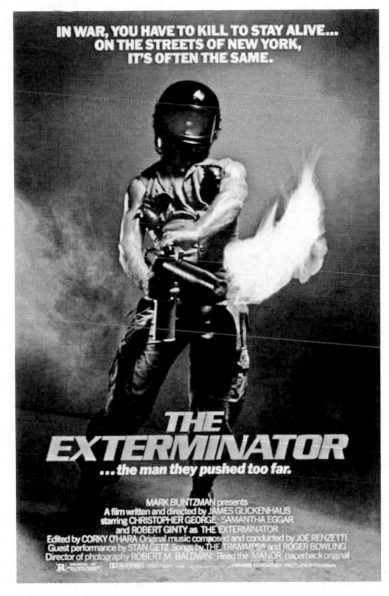

Fist of Fear, Touch of Death

Director: Matthew Mallinson
Screenplay: Ron Harvey, Matthew Mallinson
Producer: Terry Levene
Cast: Bruce Lee (Himself), Fred Williamson (Hammer—The Ladies Man), Adolph Caesar (The TV Reporter), Ron van Clief (The Boxer), Bill Louie (Kato #2), Aaron Banks (The Promoter)

Felt Forum, 1979, World Karate Championships. The purpose? To find the successor to Bruce Lee. I am unsure of the provenance of this competition and don't know how they got the go-ahead to bestow that title. But it happened. I just watched it. After several rounds of Brucesploitation in my life, *Fist of Fear, Touch of Death* is the most hilarious. The film follows a TV reporter as he moderates this martial arts competition. This is intercut with footage of interviews with Bruce (that are always dubbed wrong), interviews with other martial artists and a long, long section purporting to be the Story of Bruce Lee. It's all hilarious. Thank God for Fred Williamson, the one person who seems to be taking none of this seriously.

This film reminded me of *Game of Death*, *Overlords of the UFO*, *The Force on Thunder Mountain* and *Devil Monster*: It's a mix of chicanery on top of lies piled on hilarity, all scrambled together with actual footage from this competition. It's almost indescribable. One must see it to properly appreciate it. But here's some description, which may go some way towards putting the reader in the right frame of mind.

The TV reporter starts by showing us the venue and some early fights. Then he interviews promoter Aaron Banks, who says that Bruce Lee was murdered by the Touch of Death. There's more fighting. Everyone mistakes Fred Williamson for Harry Belafonte. Then the reporter is shown interviewing Bruce (with completely mismatched shots) about Bruce's secrets. Whatever Bruce is saying in the interview is not what the voice on the soundtrack is saying. There's something hilariously perverse about taking footage of a man who had been dead for seven years and inserting fake platitudes into his mouth.

That middle section of the film that tells the Story of Bruce Lee is from an Bruce film made when he was very young. The filmmakers have completely dubbed over it with their own story. Sort of like the extended *Jimmy the Boy Wonder* animated sequence. Bruce loves karate. People keep telling him not to do it. He does it. There are many references to his grandfather, a samurai. But as Bruce and his family are Chinese and samurai were Japanese, I'm not sure how that would work. Sort of like Lee Van Cleef being the only white ninja from *The Master*, one imagines. Oh, and Grandfather is represented by footage from an old kung fu movie.

After this very lengthy section, which is presented as a special treat for the audience rather than as a huge chunk of space being taken up, the tournament continues. Sometimes what we see on screen matches what the announcer says, sometimes not really. Williamson is interviewed and says that the whole "Finding a new Bruce Lee" thing is nonsense. The reporter says that's what the people want.

There is a category of film I call Sheer Audacity films. Films where one sits and watches amazed at what they're being made to view. *Devil Monster* is one: a 66-minute film with over a half-hour of stock footage. *Night of Horror* is another: a horror movie where, literally, nothing happens. *Fist of Fear, Touch of Death* is a third. Its mix of exploiting a real-life celebrity, goofy dubbed scenes and decent martial arts make it one for the books. Personally, I loved it.

Hawk the Slayer

Director: Terry Marcel
Screenplay: Terry Marcel, Harry Robertson
Producer: Harry Robertson
Cast: Jack Palance (Voltan), John Terry (Hawk), Bernard Bresslaw (Gort), Ray Charleson (Crow), Patricia Quinn (Woman), Morgan Sheppard (Ranulf)

This sword-and-sorcery adventure, direct from England, has, as its main theme, a very funky disco number. *Hawk the Slayer* starts rather regally with Voltan (Jack Palance) killing his father over some sort of mystical gewgaw. As Dad dies, Hawk, the youngest son, arrives. Dad gives Hawk the last Elven Mindstone, which, when placed in the hilt of the Mindstone Sword, gives the wielder great power. Then, if the viewer has kept up with all that, the credits begin and the disco kicks in. The viewer immediately feels a little wary.

Now it is 1980. At the start of the year, disco is all the rage. At the end, it's a laughable fad that has passed its sell-by date. Using disco prominently in 1980 is like doing a hair metal album in 1991, for release in early 1992. When you start, you're hip. When it gets presented, it's laughable. Poor *Hawk*. Not sure why they didn't just stick with a symphonic score. (Hawk's theme is very disco-based.) Then they shoot themselves in the foot again. After the credits, a man with a bad wound winds up at a nunnery. The nuns tend to him … and all this viewer could think of was the nunnery in *Monty Python and the Holy Grail*. I find no sign that *Hawk the Slayer* is a comedy. It is very, very serious.

Is it very, very good? Well, it is a lot of fun. Hawk assembles a group of warriors, including a big guy, an elf who is a master archer, a witch named Woman and a filthy guy whose purpose I forgot. They are going to free an abbess that Voltan has kidnapped and free the world from Voltan. Voltan, horribly burned on one side of his face, wears a metal mask covering that portion. The rest of the face is pure Palance, giving it the finest sneer and growl he can.

John Terry does a fine job as the hero, Hawk. He spends much of his time standing around as that Mindsword flies in and out of his hand. The rest of the cast is made up of British movie and TV actors. If you're a fan of *Doctor Who*, you can spend a lot of time spotting folks who look very familiar and some who will make you say "Isn't that … hmmm … who *is* that?" That's fun.

Hawk the Slayer is, like most films in this book from 1980, not actually part of the full-on 1980s world of action. It seems to belong to a slightly earlier era, an era that knows all the Conan-esque tropes but hasn't gotten its action heroes and its action cinema to follow. So *Hawk* meanders a bit and takes a lot of time (around 50 minutes) assembling the troops. Most of the time the film is entertaining. Plus, the final fight scenes are entertaining. The mix of funky synth music and decent actors giving it their all elevate the movie. Palance slicing the ham is amusing. And the title is great. It's definitely worth a viewing. Plus, there's every good chance that repeated viewings might reveal it to be pure genius. Might.

Intrepidos Punks

Director: Francisco Guerrero
Screenplay: Roberto Marroquin
Producer: Ernesto Fuentes
Cast: El Fantasma (Tarzan), Juan Gallardo, Ana Lura Pelueo, Princess Lea (Fiera), Martha Elena Cervantes, Alfredo Gutierrez

Tarzan, a Lucha Libre tough guy, is in charge of the Intrepidos Punks, a rather crazy gang of punk bikers (many with Mohawks) terrorizing the Mexican countryside. A huge Amazonian woman named Fiera and another smaller, rather zaftig woman named Panther spend their days worshipping Satan, having orgies and generally screwing up people's lives. Why? Because they want to. Is there any way that Marco and the other special agents can stop them?

Intrepidos Punks is freakin' nuts. Tarzan wears his modified wrestler's mask and leads his group of punk bikers down all sorts of avenues. They buy drugs from a fat mobster. The women dress as nuns and rob a bank. Fiera, pretending to be a Mexican variation of a Tupperware lady, goes into the home of one of the officers. The bikers kidnap all the cops' wives and aren't very nice to them. (Sexual assault is also a big thing here.) They are generally a really nasty gang.

But there's a slight goofiness to all of it. Tarzan is a bit too much of the lucha libre wrestler. He rants about Satan and sex and drugs. But, one really wants to see some ropes thrown up around him and to have the Blue Demon show up. Every time Fiera and Panther are together, this reviewer kept thinking of a *Sabado Gigante* sketch that went horribly wrong. The bikers are *so* nasty, it ends up being amusing after a while.

At first, the violence and the nasty bikers can be a bit rough. Then the movie leavens some of it by cutting to Marco and super square cops. There is a long sequence where two cops pretend to be ranchers trying to buy drugs from the fat gangster. It goes on so long that one forgets all about the punks and thinks they're watching a semi-mediocre Mexican cop film.

Intrepidos Punks may be a perfect approximation of what Mexican punks and bikers were like. But the combo of Mohawks with bikes and the very 1960s-sounding fuzz guitar soundtrack (mixed with a rather metal theme song for the gang) makes it seem like they're channeling *The Warriors* along with the Hell's Angels. But then they dress as nuns. And then there's Tarzan. The local culture, and what the culture brings to their own movies, begins to seep into the framework of *Intrepidos Punks*. That's what makes it interesting.

Oddly enough, for a film that alternates boring police with punk biker atrocities with orgies, the ending is fairly conventional. The police attack the gang at their hideout, which is, basically, the outdoors. It seems like it should have had a crazier ending but that's how it went. It's not specifically setting itself up for a sequel. But maybe all one has to do is wait a bit.

The Last Hunter

Director: Antonio Margheriti

Screenplay: Dardano Sacchetti

Producer: Gianfranco Couyoumdjian

Cast: David Warbeck (Capt. Henry Morris), Tisa Farrow (Jane Foster), Tony King (Sgt. George Washington), Bobby Rhodes (Carlos), Margi Eveline Newton (Carol), John Steiner (Major Cash)

The Last Hunter takes place during the Vietnam War. It's an Italian film so it's not made by a country that actually fought in the Vietnam War. It's made by a country that really enjoyed a few films about the Vietnam War, specifically *Apocalypse Now* and *The Deer Hunter*. It was directed by the great and mighty Antonio Margheriti who hopped all around the genres, ripping off this and that. He has said that when he made *The Last*

Hunter, he didn't want it to be dour like those other movies. He wanted to make a fun Vietnam War film. But he ended up sticking a little too close to his forebears to make something really fun.

Capt. Henry Morris (David Warbeck) is sent deep into enemy territory to take out a pirate radio station. The station constantly broadcasts the voice of a woman delivering anti-war propaganda that the American soldiers can hear. Along the way, Morris picks up war photographer Jane Foster, played by Tisa Farrow. So it's that Warbeck-Farrow team-up that the world always wanted to see. Every group of American soldiers that Morris encounters is semi-lethargic or semi-crazy. Will he ever get to the radio station? What will he find there?

There are bursts of action across *The Last Hunter.* They're pretty fun. But there aren't nearly enough of them. The film is trying to emulate the big Vietnam dramas up to this point. It also wants to have fun. But "fun" for Margheriti seems to involve burned-out soldiers doing stupid things, lolling around and trying to rape Jane again and again. After a time, Morris was waiting at one camp for so long that this reviewer couldn't remember what was going on any more. If the director was trying to make this fun, he should have tried to make it fun. As it stands, it teeters very close to dull.

Because Dardano Sacchetti wrote this, there are several logic-defying moments that may leave average viewers scratching their heads. Some of the dubbed dialogue is as weird as anything in an Italian horror movie of the time. Warbeck's voice is dubbed by someone else, which is too bad. To top it all off, the climactic reveal of the radio station involves a twist that comes right out of Loopy Town. When a movie throws in an extraneous flashback to slow down its already slow running time, the flashback will probably mean something somewhere. But what it means in this movie is just nonsense. It doesn't fit in with the Vietnam world apart from the fact that it is very silly.

The Last Hunter is one this reviewer can't really recommend. It is an attempt at doing a Fun Vietnam Drama but it's not that much fun. Warbeck and Farrow do their best but the action never quite takes off. The movie just sort of sits there.

Super Fuzz

Director: Sergio Corbucci

Screenplay: Sergio Corbucci, Sabatino Ciuffini

Producer: Maximillian Wolkoff

Cast: Terence Hill (Dave Speed), Ernest Borgnine (Sgt. Willy Dunlop), Julie Gordon (Evelyn), Joanne Dru (Rosy Labouche), Marc Lawrence (Torpedo)

Super Fuzz is a movie that I watched maybe 20 twenty times when I was young. HBO seemed to play it constantly, and it was sheer joy. A Florida cop who gets caught in some sort of atomic blast finds that he has super power as well as telekinetic and psychic powers. Alongside his partner, he gets mixed up with a counterfeiter named Torpedo and a Hollywood star named Rosy Labouche. Along the way, they get involved in all sorts of zany shenanigans in a very silly film.

Director Sergio Corubucci also helmed the original *Django.* He doesn't seem like the natural choice for a slapstick comedy, but he gets the action scenes right and the slapstick works like a charm. There is a joyous scene in a small house where Speed beats up three thugs. And Ernest Borgnine really goes for it. Borgnine at his zaniest is great fun. Mixed in with all of that is Mr. Terence Hill. He's well known around the world for making around 20 movies with Bud Spencer. Their films are usually action-comedies and quite a lot of fun. I don't know why Spencer wasn't involved in *Super Fuzz* but Borgnine is the perfect replacement.

The movie gets by because inventive things are constantly going on. Speed is being sent to the electric chair for having killed Dunlop. As he strolls to the chair (after eating a lot of beans), he reminisces about the past few weeks. Very quickly, he gets his powers and begins to use them. He moves a truck and a manhole cover with his mind. He can see through walls when people are committing crimes. He runs really fast all over the place. He makes a crowd at a stadium disappear so he can smooch his sweetie Evelyn. He catches a bullet in his mouth. He falls out of a very high window and lands on his feet, perfectly fine. There is one drawback to it all: His power vanishes when it is involved with something red. Apart from that, he's pretty amazing.

I was a little worried about returning to this film for the first time since childhood. It still holds up, it still works. Mainly because it is a fun film. Even the criminals have a lovely goofiness to them that makes the film a smooth 90 minutes of cinema. To date, there is no digital release of the film. That's too bad. This is the sort of film that a whole family could watch and enjoy.

Plus, let's not forget two awesome things. One is the giant bubblegum balloon at the end. The other: It has one of the best theme songs ever, "Super Super!" Whenever the song kicks in, I want to stand up and do some good old-fashioned chair dancing. Why was there no *Super Fuzz 2*?

1981

Highest grossing films in the U.S.
1. *Raiders of the Lost Ark*
2. *On Golden Pond*
3. *Superman II*
4. *Arthur*
5. *Stripes*

Highest rated TV shows in the U.S.
1. *Dallas*
2. *60 Minutes*
3. *The Jeffersons*
4. (tie) *Joanie Loves Chachi, Three's Company*

Big historical events
Assassination attempt on President Reagan
Assassination attempt on the pope
Wedding of Charles and Diana
AIDS is diagnosed
Personal computers are introduced

Action movies
Raiders of the Lost Ark, Superman II, Cannonball Run, For Your Eyes Only, Clash of the Titans, Tarzan, the Ape Man, Excalibur, Escape from New York, Nighthawks, Dragonslayer, Legend of the Lone Ranger, Comin' at Ya

Enter the Ninja
Director: Menahem Golan
Screenplay: Dick Desmond, Mike Stone

Producers: Menahem Golan, Yoram Globus
Cast: Franco Nero (Cole), Sho Kosugi (Hasegawa), Susan George (Mary-Ann Landers), Christopher George (Charles Venarius)

This is the big one. The touch paper for the big ninja excitement that sent the world spinning. The film that kicked Cannon Films into high gear as Super Action filmmakers of the 1980s. This is the film that brought Sho Kosugi to the world's attention and led to many more ninja films (probably about half of them made by Godfrey Ho and Joseph Lai). This is the film that brought the word "ninja" to everyone's attention. *Enter the Ninja*. I just wish this was a great film.

Cole is a white guy with a big mustache. He's also a ninja. After finishing up his ninja training, he goes to visit some friends in the Philippines. They have crops which are being threatened by a businessman named Venarius who wants their land. Venarius has lots of thugs on his side. He also has a guy with a hook for a hand. Eventually, he has Hasegawa, a ninja who trained with Cole. This isn't going to end well.

The best director of any of the Cannon ninja movies was Sam Firstenberg. As mentioned elsewhere, it takes a knack to shoot action well. Anyone can point a camera at something and let it happen. But, to make it really take off, it's a combination of the action in front of the camera, camera placement, camera movement and editing. *American Ninja* and *American Ninja 2* are great examples of this. Unfortunately, Golan chose to direct this film himself. Honestly, he's not the sharpest action director.

The ninja scenes, and the fight scenes in general, should be exciting, breathtaking and trend-setting. They're not. They're thoroughly average. Golan did a much better job with all the musical numbers in his wonderfully weird mystical rock musical *The Apple*. Maybe it's Franco Nero? He doesn't seem terribly convincing as a ninja. When Kosugi does his stuff, Nero looks stodgy. The mustache isn't helping. Not to say that the film doesn't have excitement. The guy with the hook is pretty great. It's just not superb excitement.

And that always feels odd. When you sit down to watch a groundbreaking film in any genre, you expect it to be fantastic in every way. When it turns out to be kind of mediocre, there's kind of a sinking feeling. Here, it's the fact that Nero is meant to be our main ninja. Then the international cast and the post-dubbing make it feel like an Italian knockoff of a ninja film rather than "the Big One." Then, when the action doesn't live up to what one has seen in other, later films … things feel weird.

Enter the Ninja is worth a viewing. But it is not the best ninja movie. Frankly, it's a little lacking all the way around. When Kosugi shows up, things pick up a touch but it's a little too little, a little too late.

For Y'ur Height Only

Director: Eddie Nicart
Screenplay: Cora Caballes
Producer: Dick Randall
Cast: Weng Weng (Agent 00)

Agent 00 hits the streets of the Philippines (hard!) to track down a scientist kidnapped by the evil Mr. Giant. He has all the latest gadgets, including a pair of X-Ray specs, and he can take down an army of thugs ready to wallop him into next week. Of course, the ladies love him. They can't stop wondering about him and kissing him and wanting to be near him. Agent 00 loves the ladies so the feeling is mutual. Can he rescue the scientist and save the free world? One caveat: Our hero is played by Weng Weng, who is not quite three feet tall. When he presses himself up against a door, he is directly beneath the doorknob.

For Y'ur Height Only is hilarious and entertaining, and just when you think that it's running out of steam, 00 straps on a jetpack and goes flying through the air. Weng has a cool bowl haircut, a sense of style that makes all the chicks stand up and notice and a way with a swift kick to the crotch that makes him the best. He is dubbed throughout with a slightly high-pitched, squeaky voice, which is really amusing.

One of my favorite films is Doris Wishman's *Double Agent 73*, a super-cheap intrigue-filled adventure that takes place mainly in what is probably Doris' house and in her neighborhood. There are no fancy cars or exotic locations. It's James Bond done almost the way a child would do it. Now, in *Double Agent 73* (starring the 73-inch-chested Chesty Morgan), there is very little sense of comedy. *For Y'ur Height Only*, however, is pure out-and-out comedy with thrills, sort of like a Jackie Chan film. Add in the theme music, which is a bit of *For Your Eyes Only* played over and over, along with the dubbing, and a masterpiece of oddball action cinema presents itself.

The dubbing is the real hero of the film. If it had been dubbed in any sort of straight-ahead manner, this film would have been interminable. But everyone in the dubbing bay seems to have been goofing around, and it makes the film a joy. There are many great lines. ("Don't be a nosy parker, Paco. Or you could wake up dead."). There are many great voices. (The man who runs the gold company has one of the best dubbed voices ever.) And the scene where 00 gets all his gadgets is absolute high hilarity. Weng Weng says nothing while his chatty boss hits the heights of the hilarity meter again and again.

The film is joy. It is filled with very entertaining action, mainly between a three-foot

tall man and regular-sized guys. It is funny and silly and so weird that the average viewer will want to immediately show this to everyone he knows. The tone of the film can be summed in a scene where a group of Mr. Giant's thugs drive around in a beat-up blue car when they're off duty. They're just looking for some off-the-clock thuggery. It's all great.

The Last Chase

Director: Martyn Burke
Screenplay: C.R. O'Christopher, Roy Moore, Martyn Burke
Producer: Herb Abramson
Cast: Lee Majors (Franklyn Hart), Chris Makepeace (Ring), Burgess Meredith (Capt. Williams), Fran Rosati (Endora)
The Last Chase is a title that is kind of fun to mull over. What might the Last Chase be? What vehicles would it involve? Well, director Martyn Burke clues us all in. The Last Chase will involve a Porsche Formula 1 race car and a phantom jet speeding across America. The

car will have Lee Majors and Chris Makepeace in it. The jet will be flown by Burgess Meredith. Maybe not the first thoughts the average viewer had for the last chase but that's how it goes down.

In the future, oil is gone. People walk everywhere or take government-supplied public transport. The government is very totalitarian. Franklyn Hart simply doesn't fit in. He was a race car driver before the oil went. Now he has a job talking to students about what he used to do and how it's obsolete in the perfect society they're now in. No one really cares and he hates doing it. One day, with a student named Ring stowing along, he hops in his old Porsche and takes off—the first car on the road in decades. Hart is going to the West Coast where people aren't under government control. But the government has a trick up their sleeves. The last of the jets, flown by Meredith, is sent to destroy the Porsche. The chase is on.

The Last Chase is old-school action with

several big exciting moments mixed in amongst a lot of character development. The government officials are the worst kind of government officials, 100 percent bureaucrat. The type that believes that the rules, as written, are the society. And the people within are only as good as their following of the rules.

It's an odd movie because this chase is big and important. But, until the end, there's no fanfare. Because there is no one else out on the road. Just one car and an occasional jet. It's a silent, epic, almost Western chase. And it's all the better for it. Then there is the oddness of a regime promoting environmentalism through totalitarianism. And our hero is a man who wants to take out one last fossil fuel–burning, polluting vehicle.

The Last Chase is just one step above a TV movie, which is not an insult. If you can catch a widescreen copy, do so. The scope of the Porsche on the road works better. This film is good. It's not fist-pumping, adrenaline-rush good. Simply good.

Lovely But Deadly

Director: David Sheldon

Screenplay: Patricia Joyce, David Sheldon

Producers: Doro Vlado Hreljanovic, David Sheldon

Cast: Lucinda Dooling (Mary Ann Lovitt), John Randolph (Franklin Van Dyke), Mel Novak (Warren Lang), Susan Mechsner (Suzie), Richard Herd ("Honest Charley" Gilmarten)

Mary Ann Lovitt (known as "Lovely") goes back to high school to find the pushers who killed her brother. Along the way, she gets in some kung fu fights, locker room fights, shootouts, big action scenes with speedboats and other shenanigans. Some fit the tone of the "woman seeking revenge" theme and some are straight out of some sort of goofy '70s exploitation moonshine picture or something. It gives *Lovely But Deadly* an odd, but mostly amusing, feel to it.

The high school is out of a cheerleader film from the '70s but without a lot of the T&A. The football players are addicts but no one cares because they're the football players. There are drug addicts everywhere. Only Lovely seems capable of standing up and fighting for what is right. As she investigates, the drug ring extends to several wealthy men, including one who throws big, decadent parties. One party ends with Lovely fighting a cheerleader on the buffet table. Wacky goons show up and kidnap Lovely. The goons also steam a student to death in a scene that feels more than a little out of place.

In true exploitation fashion, the mood will shift from wacky (the music will tell the viewer so) to violent and unpleasant. L.D. Foldes is listed as providing the story for this film, and that's sort of a trademark of his late '70s and early '80s films: no concept of how the tone of a film should go. *Lovely But Deadly* keeps diving headlong into different spaces. It'll give the viewer some sort of Cinematic Whiplash. And, half the time, Lucinda Dooling (Lovely) looks a bit like she's goofing around so it's tough to figure out what to think.

There is a bunch of fighting. Lovely knows kung fu and is ready to use it. The fight scene at the end is down by some docks, so there is a big speedboat chase. All the drug dealers in the world are stopped. Hooray! Well, actually, the closing credits roll as one of the thugs who was involved in the speedboat chase sits dazed on the shore. Where is this film going? Where did it come from? Who knows?

This is from the same sort of world as *Malibu High* but it was the early '80s now. The form of this sort of movie was slowly changing. The free-for-all drive-in movie style that the '70s embraced was passing away. *Lovely But Deadly*, while enjoyable, is schizophrenic, to say the least. There's only one director listed but the film's style changes so much there could be ten directors involved. There are certainly a lot of characters. And sometimes it does become tough to gauge who is who as the film burns towards its ending. Lovely does save the day. Now this reviewer needs some sort of neck brace and a massage.

Mad Foxes

Director: Paul Grau
Screenplay: John R. Woodhard, Paul Gray
Producer: Erwin C. Dietrich

Cast: Jose Gras (Hal Walters), Laura Premica (Silvia Godo), Andrea Albani (Babsy), Peter John Saunders, Brian Billings

John R. Woodhard writes a good script. Trust me. *Mad Foxes* is one of the nuttiest films ever. It's action. It's sexploitation. It's revenge. It's got the most full-frontal male nudity the average viewer will see outside of a gay porno. The movie begins with our hero driving his kick-ass Corvette Stingray hard and fast through crowded city streets to the tones of Krokus's "Easy Rocker." And it ends with the Stingray flying along the road to the tune of Krokus's "Celebration." A man is castrated and has his penis shoved into his mouth. A man on the toilet is blown up when a grenade is dropped into it. The movie takes two or three minutes of running time to show a couple of professional dancers at a hip club dancing to 1950s-type music. A man is stabbed in the face with huge garden shears. A virgin is violated on the street outside the swinging club. Nazi bikers. Nude people wandering around a street. There's a kung fu vs. Nazi fight in an amphitheater. And it's topped off with dubbing that includes the dubbing artists constantly running over one another's lines. This is a great film.

Mr. Walters, some sort of rich Spanish guy, drives a Stingray. He's taking an underage virgin to a hip club. He falls afoul of some Nazi bikers. He is beaten and his date is sexually assaulted. Walters hires kung fu guys to beat up the bikers. Then revenge begins. And it goes to the countryside where the bikers kill Walters' family, back to the city where Walters takes the bikers out one by one.

There is no proper way to critique this film. It hops from genre to genre but makes its base in an action-revenge-type film. One that just happens to have a lot of naked men in it. This movie comes from a place where nothing that resembles regular storytelling exists. Life is just not something that comes near *Mad Foxes*. Dancers dance. Bikers bike. Kung fu fights rage. People are here—then they're over here! Nazi women whip Nazi men. Long sequences of screwing around overwhelm the film. Walters' boring family is killed.

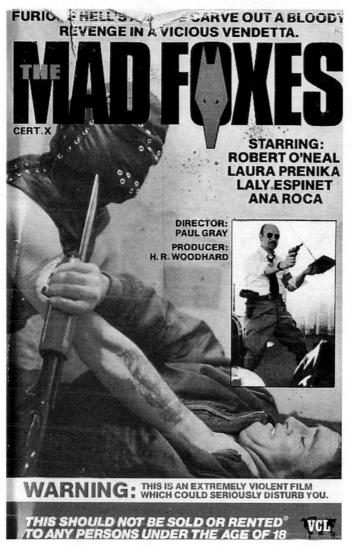

FURIO... HELL'S... CARVE OUT A BLOODY REVENGE IN A VICIOUS VENDETTA.

MAD FOXES

CERT. X

STARRING:
ROBERT O'NEAL
LAURA PRENIKA
LALY ESPINET
ANA ROCA

DIRECTOR:
PAUL GRAY
PRODUCER:
H. R. WOODHARD

WARNING: THIS IS AN EXTREMELY VIOLENT FILM WHICH COULD SERIOUSLY DISTURB YOU.

THIS SHOULD NOT BE SOLD OR RENTED TO ANY PERSONS UNDER THE AGE OF 18   VCL

Weapons of Death

Director, Screenplay: Paul Kryiazi

Producer: Richard H. Sydel

Cast: Eric Lee (Eric), Bob Ramos (Curt), Ralph Castellanos (Bishop), Louis Winfield Bailey (Carter), Gerald Okamura (Chong), Nancy Lee (Angela)

It's very nice to watch a film that surprises you. One goes into every film hoping to have a great time, get carried away, experience exhilaration. Experience something. Many times, nothing happens. One comes away with a shrug, sometimes barely remembering what happened in the film. When a film sneaks up on you and is just a good film, that's cool. I didn't expect a whole heck of a lot from *Weapons of Death* but it's a charmer with some fun fight scenes ... not the best fight scenes but they have an energy to them. And a film with just enough character and incident to make it 90 minutes well spent.

In San Francisco, a young woman is kidnapped by a very large gang of kung fu fighters and a couple of random guys. They demand a ransom from her family. Her brothers and a few other fighters team up and head out to the woods to get her back. Eventually, their estranged father joins in and emotions run high. The girl keeps escaping from her kidnappers and getting caught again. Family secrets are revealed, bikers are beaten up and ... does it end in victory for good or is this one all about evil? Watch and see.

Weapons of Death starts out with a brawl in a bar. One of our lead bad guys recruits another man to help with the kidnapping. Then the movie gets into a series of fights, angst-

Look, this film is nuts. It's also not for the children. If one enjoys a film that has no logic, not even internal logic, and seems to be going out of its way to offend but really isn't all that offensive, just kind of silly, then *Mad Foxes* is the movie for you. I was a little unsure whether or not to include it in this book. But at its base, it's an action-revenge film. At its heart, it is about jerks committing violence against one of the most hilariously high-falutin heroes around. That's what makes it go here. Hop all the genres you want. I recognize an action film when I see it. I don't care how many wieners go flapping around in the breeze.

filled family moments and the scene with the bikers. The movie is just okay but then there's that scene with the bikers. That's where it sort of all turned for me. There were weapons of death, lots of crossbow action. There were kung fu shenanigans but that biker fight…

The fight scene could have used a few more cuts, slightly better camera angles. But it is robust. Basically, the man who was recruited in the bar, Carter, is trying to recapture Angela, the daughter. She accidentally wanders into a meeting of a biker gang. Carter shows up and tries to get her out of there. That doesn't work so the fighting commences. Carter lays waste to the whole batch of them.

But it's not beautifully-set-up-and-timed laying waste. It's kind of sloppy and kind of haphazard. It's a bit tough to describe. It's just a free-for-all that's thrown at Carter and he wins. The closing moments of the fight sum it up. Carter is on a hill. The fattest biker tries to chase him up it. Carter picks up an abnormally large boulder and throws it at the biker, who falls. All in one shot. It's pretty great.

Just to be entertained is all a viewer asks for, most of the time. The filmmakers here go that extra mile. They make the movie a little bit less obvious than one expected. That works. It's fun. And one gets to see that fat guy hit with a boulder. Victory for everyone.

1982

Highest grossing films in the U.S.
1. *E.T.*
2. *Tootsie*
3. *An Officer and a Gentleman*
4. *Rocky III*
5. *Porky's*

Highest rated TV shows in the U.S.
1. *60 Minutes*
2. *Dallas*
3. (tie) *M*A*S*H*, *Magnum, P.I.*
5. *Dynasty*

Big historical events
"Thriller" released
Falkland Islands invaded

Action movies
Rocky III, 48 Hrs., First Blood, Firefox, Conan the Barbarian, The Sword and the Sorcerer, Tron, The Road Warrior, Death Wish II, Silent Rage, Forced Vengeance, Megaforce, Fighting Back, Penitentiary II

Ator the Fighting Eagle
Director, Screenplay: Joe D'Amato (as David Hills)
Producer: Alex Sussman
Cast: Miles O'Keeffe (Ator), Sabrina Siani (Roon), Ritza Brown (Sunya), Edmund Purdom (Griba), Laura Gemser (Indun)

Every good epic begins somewhere. Along those same lines, epics that aren't quite as good have to begin somewhere too. Enter Ator. He is a pure, straight-up Conan the Barbarian rip-off from the good people of Italy. Ator is big and buff. He's in love with his sister who is not really his sister. She gets kidnapped by a bunch of jerks who have something to do with a Spider God. Ator trains and trains and becomes the buff, all-knowing super-fellow who will dominate … well, at least the sequel.

Miles O'Keeffe is pretty buff. He's a handsome guy with excessively big hair who is on the side of right. That's what we want in a hero. He's got it in spades. Hail, Ator! This film came out not too long after *Conan* so the rip-off wheels were spinning fast in the mind of Joe D'Amato (AKA David Hills). (Neither of those names are his real name.) So, what the speedy production means is that there are sequences of idyll in the beginning and scenes of Ator and his gang wandering around that seem like filler. They're sort of nebulous, bordering on uninteresting. But then, the fights start.

The action, thank goodness, is where the film comes to life. Not that the action is up to the quality of the fighting in *Conan*. It's all a little lackadaisical, like a lot of Italian action.

There doesn't seem to have been enough time to shoot the action scenes with style. So everyone gets in front of the camera and flails around and does their thing. Then—it's over. There are fights with all sorts of standard warriors. Fights with shadowy men. And a fight with a giant spider. That's the spider god right there.

In fact, the sequences near the end with the Spider worshippers are a bit creepy in that way that anything involving a giant spider is. There's no getting around the fact that all a filmmaker has to do is just show a portion of a practical giant spider and the imagination (well, this reviewer's anyway) will do the rest. The image of a giant, hairy beastie works almost anywhere. The limited giant thing that Ator battles works nicely too.

All of this chatter is in aid of the fact that *Ator* isn't a great movie. The synth score does its best to keep everyone thrilled. Miles is wooden but he's charming wood. The story is a series of meandering set pieces that ends when the film reaches the 90-minute mark. Sabrina Siani is as beautiful as always. Can't take that away from her. But the film really isn't that great. It is exciting enough to watch and enjoy, however. The second film has more of a push to its narrative. The third film is quite weird. And the fourth film seems to have been made by seven-year-olds. But all that Ator *is,* starts here. If one wants to spend the day with a charming but semi-mediocre hero, begin here.

Battletruck

Director: Harley Cokliss
Screenplay: Harley Cokliss, Irving Austin, John Beech
Producers: Lloyd Phillips, Rob Whitehouse
Cast: Michael Beck (Hunter), Annie McEnroe (Corlie), Bruno Lawrence (Willie), John Bach (Bone), John Ratzenberger (Rusty)

Combine a post-apocalyptic setting with beautiful New Zealand locations and a giant truck ... what is before your eyes? Why, it's *Battletruck*. A pretty entertaining post-apocalyptic movie about people trying to survive, the jerks they meet, the man named Hunter who might save them all ... and one big-ass truck.

Wow, New Zealand really looks like a beautiful place. Look at the scenery throughout this film. There is a scene where the bad guy, Bone, is standing with a henchman on some sort of giant outcrop of rock. Far below, the viewer can see his cronies causing trouble. The landscape stretches off into the distance and it's all so beautiful. It's not endless desert or quarries. It's rolling hills and beautiful valleys and ... it's beautiful.

The filmmakers decided to make this action-filled film in the middle of all this beauty. Nothing wrong with that. The action is well-done. The truck is awesome. Hunter is an okay hero. One never quite warms up to him, which is the point. But one never fully engages with him either, which is too bad. He's not helped by the main heroine of the film, Corlie. Corlie is a bit overwrought throughout. This can work to a film's advantage. But when the viewer wants at times to reach through the screen and give her a bit of a slap to calm her down, then maybe it isn't going that great.

Bone and his band of jerks are sufficiently jerky enough to make the viewer await, anxiously, Hunter kicking their asses and, possibly, blowing up their Battletruck. There is a peaceful commune, surviving after the nuclear war. Bone and his henchmen pull up and tell them that he is in charge and if they don't like it, they'll be shot. For some reason, Bone is annoying and worthy of a punch in ways that some of the other *Road Warrior*–inspired villains are not. There is nothing camp or goofy about Bone. He is simply a jerk with a gun and a big truck full of guys.

Hunter does his job. He may be a little bland but when the action gets rolling, it goes down hot in *Battletruck*. One would hope that a film with this name wouldn't let anyone down in the battle and truck department. A filmmaker wouldn't name their film *Deadly Donut* if there was nothing deadly in the film and it lacked a donut. It's common sense. For some reason, this reviewer thinks that New Zealanders have a good deal of common sense. But don't hold me to that.

Battletruck is very derivative and only occasionally rises to an exciting place outside of all the other films of this sort, like in the big battletruck-filled finale. But if the viewer likes post-apocalyptic fun, this does everything one would expect it to and leaves a warm, fuzzy feeling. Plus, the film is set in New Zealand. By the end, one has almost completely forgotten the endless quarries and random woods of its Italian brothers.

The Beastmaster

Director: Don Coscarelli

Screenplay: Paul Pepperman, Don Coscarelli

Producer: Paul Pepperman

Cast: Marc Singer (Dar), Tanya Roberts (Kiri), Rip Torn (Maax), John Amos (Seth), Josh Milrad (Tal)

Dar can befriend the animals. He's out to return to the home of his father and destroy the evil wizard Maax. Along the way, and travelling with a bird, a tiger and two ferrets, he assembles a merry band, including Tanya Roberts as a hot slave girl, a young boy and the dad from *Good Times*. Do they have enough gumption and power to overthrow Maax? One imagines they might.

Don Coscarelli is the man behind *The Beastmaster*. He has directed several films that, around these parts, give anything else he directs an automatic Interest Factor. He made the *Phantasm* films and *Bubba Ho-Tep* and an all-time favorite of this reviewer, *Kenny & Co.* So if he wants to make an epic sword-and-sorcery film, I'm on board. The film itself is a good time. It has an epic sweep as Dar is shown commanding the animals. Then he moves across the landscape trying to save the land from evil.

Marc Singer is a suitably buff hero. This is a year or so before he became a less buff but still heroic guy in the *V* miniseries and series. Tanya Roberts is as beautiful as always. John Amos is suitably powerful and tough. Rip Torn is nasty. The animals are fun and funny. And they're also very heroic when they need to be. The film is, perhaps, a little too long (almost two hours). There are a lot of brief encounters, like with the bird creatures that devour men, and the encounter with the jerks who put leeches into people's ears. Not all of the lit-

The epic adventure of a new kind of hero.

Broadcast Premiere!

MARC SINGER
TANYA ROBERTS THE
BEASTMASTER

FRIDAY'S 8 O'CLOCK MOVIE 11 Alive
WPIX

tle side vignettes are interesting. Every once in a while, one wishes that the film would speed up. It's interesting but not quite as interesting as it seems to think it is.

I always have the same thought when watching this movie: *The Beastmaster* and *Manimal* never teamed up. Could you imagine the excitement if they had? Dar meeting up with Dr. Chase and stopping evil. They could have done a *Beastmaster 2* thing and sent Dar to our world. Glen A. Larson would have had a field day with it. Well, I think it would have been fun. Unfortunately, *The Beastmaster* isn't terribly well-regarded and *Manimal* is considered a bit of a joke. (Seriously, they put the show up against *Dallas* in the first half of the 1980s. Is it any wonder *Manimal* got cancelled after eight episodes?)

The Beastmaster definitely has its charms and is worth a viewing. Everyone does their jobs. It only occasionally looks a bit cheap. But that never really gets in the way. The adventures of Dar would continue for two more films and a brief TV series but they would never be as much fun as they are here.

Ferocious Female Freedom Fighters

Director: Jopi Burnama
Screenplay: Deddy Armand, Joey Gaynor
Producer: Dhamoo Punjabi
Cast: Eva Arnaz (Bambi), Barry Prima (Barney), Leily Sagita, Wieke Widowati

This Indonesian action movie is about a group of women wrestlers who begin fighting back against jackass males in Indonesia. Eventually they begin to fight bigger and crazier foes. There are conspiracies everywhere. Most people are awful. The movie,

however, always remembers to stop for some more wrestling. It almost becomes a Mexican lucha libre film.

The actual film is fine. It's Indonesian 1980s action, so it's got verve, some good fighting, the occasional crazy moment and an overuse of every guy, except the hero and the main villain, being a crazy rapist. All of that is par for the course. But what one version of this film has is a specifically goofy soundtrack ladled over it by Troma. Both versions are kind of goofy but the Troma version really goes for it.

And the Troma version is fine. There are some good jokes in there. You'll laugh. I did. But it didn't stick with me and the occasional straining to be funny left me a little cold. I will take my Indonesian action films straight,

please. The film in its original form (but, obviously, dubbed in English) is decent. The script is by Deddy Armand whose name is on several wonderfully odd films. Mainly ones directed by Arizal. Deddy seems to be on his game here.

The movie is basically women fighting guys, then women wrestling each other. It's never "what the hell?" crazy like, say, *Final Score* or *The Stabilizer*. You can't have it all. The women fight well. The guys gets their asses handed to them on a regular basis. Good stuff.

It might be time for someone to write a tome on wrestling around the world. The ladies wrestling here look a lot like the lucha libre ladies except they don't wear the masks and they don't seem to take on the more elaborate personalities. But they pack a wallop. And the movie does that thing that many of their Mexican counterparts do where the main plot ends … and then we return for one more wrestling match. Sure, why not?

Ferocious Female Freedom Fighters is a mouthful of a title to say and to type. The movie is okay. If you're in the mood for semi–no holds barred Indonesian action, you could do better. But this isn't bad.

The Great Skycopter Rescue

Director, Producer: L.D. Foldes

Screenplay: L.D. Foldes, Henry Edwards, Tony Crechales

Cast: Aldo Ray (Sheriff Burgess), William Marshall (Mr. Jason), Terry Michos (Jimmy Jet), Paul Tanashian (Will), Russell Johnson (Prof. Benson), Terri Taylor (Susie), Maria Rebman (Karen)

Sometimes you just can't get your action movie started.

All the elements are in place but things just aren't igniting the way they should. There is the big businessman, Mr. Jason (played by William Marshall). He's got some bikers on his payroll that he wants to send to a small town. The bikers are going to do some terrorizing. Why? Oil. Jason has the sheriff (played in a lopsided manner by Aldo Ray) under his thumb. Two young men, Jimmy and Will, want to restore the peace with the help of two young ladies, Karen and Susie. Everything is in place. So, why does it feel like Mr. Foldes' movie never begins?

Foldes directed the horror film *Don't Go Near the Park* which has a tremendously com-

The Cannon Group, Inc. presents A Star Cinema Production of a Lawrence D. Foldes film "THE GREAT SKYCOPTER RESCUE" Starring ALDO RAY • WILLIAM MARSHALL • TERRY MICHOS Introducing PAUL TANASHIAN as Will and RUSSELL JOHNSON as Professor Benson Produced and Directed by LAWRENCE D. FOLDES • Written by LAWRENCE D. FOLDES, HENRY EDWARDS and TONY CRECHALES • Executive Producer GEORGE FOLDES

Printed in USA

plicated opening series of sequences. In fact, it's almost 20 minutes before the film gets to the present day and the heroine's journey proper begins. *The Great Skycopter Rescue* is a variation on that theme. There is a threat from bikers. Yes, much of the time they're driving around shoving ice cream into people's faces down at the Foster's Freeze. But occasionally (in this family-friendly movie), they pull a woman's top off and go back into an alley with her. The sexual assault is a Foldes theme. It happens in *Park* and it's not pleasant there either. Everyone has their strange habits and peccadillos. Sometimes we are made to watch.

Will and Jimmy spend most of their time screwing around. Jimmy was a DJ, specializing in dressing as an astronaut for some reason that probably made sense at the end of the '70s but is lost on a modern world. Will is just kind of creepy. He has a "skycopter," a very loud minicopter that flies around a lot in the movie. A lot. It certainly is pretty watching it fly around. There are a lot of beautiful landscapes to see. But that shouldn't be the point of this film, which presents itself (via publicity) as action.

It's not. It almost is. It seems to be action from another era. The 1970s. When action films were lazier and shit happened when shit happened. Will and Jimmy get around to meeting up with the professor and getting some explosives. And they throw some explosives at the bikers from a great height and the movie ends. But it's all so leisurely. With possibly one too many breaks for disco dancing.

The film is professional-looking. It's well put-together. It's just not very much fun. Two dudes hanging around. At one point, they're on Will's couch and Will has his shirt off. But they like girls! Really, they do! And they dance with ladies. And Aldo Ray stumbles around. And William Marshall sits at a table and acts. And the skycopters fly. And there isn't really a rescue. That could be called false advertising but it would require too much energy.

Hunters of the Golden Cobra

Director: Antonio Margheriti (as Anthony M. Dawson)

Screenplay: Tito Carpi; Original Story: Tito Carpi, Gianfranco Couyoumdjian

Producer: Regal Films

Cast: David Warbeck (Bob), Almanta Suska (June), Alan Collins, John Steiner (Dave)

The time is the 1940s. The place is the Philippines. Two soldiers, Bob and Dave, are sent deep into the jungle to find the Golden Cobra, which will help ease unrest amongst local tribes. June, a young woman who may or may not have a twin worshipped by the Golden Cobra tribe, joins them, along with a scraggly old guy who seems to have his own agenda. Taking a long look at his unkempt appearance, one could imagine that he certainly has his own smells. As the movie goes along, shooting, car-chasing and derring-do in lava-filled caves take over. Yes, Antonio Margheriti has hired David Warbeck again and then watched *Raiders of the Lost Ark* another time.

The thrills and shenanigans add up to a rousing good time here. Warbeck's character, Bob, is less thrilled with the adventure than he will be in their next team-up, *Ark of the Sun God*. Bob and Dave are shown in a pre-credits sequences trying to catch a traitor. The traitor's plane crashes in the jungle. Dave is okay but Bob ends up with a poison dart in his chest, floating down the river on some bamboo shoots. A touch of animosity has arisen between the two gentlemen. Dave is a chipper Colonial Brit. Bob, after the river sojourn, is seen dirty and tired, moderating a cockfight in Manila.

The prologue is lengthy, setting up Bob's bravery and courage. And paralleling that with Dave's strange "pip pip cheerio"–type character who always comes out unscathed while Bob ends up getting shot at and flailing above lava. The main portion of the film is quite a bit like all the other 1980s Indiana Jones rip-offs. There is a government meeting where we learn all we need to know. Then the group is off to the jungle. The action and thrills are okay for an Italian rip-off such as this. There's never anything that's stand-on-your-chair rousing but also nothing as odd as the toy car chase we find in *Ark*.

The film culminates inside a massive

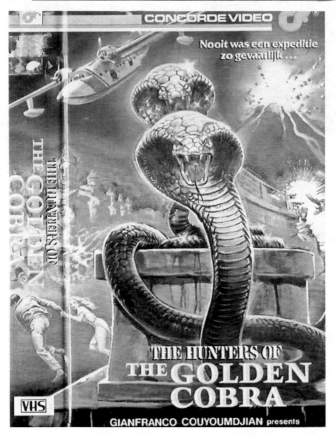

cave with a stone snake mouth spewing lava, an altar and the golden cobra. It's a big lava-filled set (and model). And it works. It's sufficiently epic and overwhelming and only (right around the stone snake's head) looks a bit like a carnival prop that's been repurposed. Bad guys receive their comeuppance. It does get a bit hairy with all that lava floating around, but good guys make it out alive.

This is not the best of the Indiana Jones rip-offs. Both *Ark of the Sun God* and *Warriors of Atlantis* are more fun and exciting. But *Hunters* has David Warbeck being heroic and moves at a decent pace. If you've watched the other ones, try this one. If you're a lava fan, so much the better.

The Impossible Kid

Director: Eddie Nicart
Screenplay: Greg B. Macaberta
Producer: Twinkle
Cast: Weng Weng (Agent 00), Romy

Diaz, Nina Sara, Tony Carreon, Ben Johnson, Rene Romero

Weng Weng is back. God is the best!

Agent 00 returns in *The Impossible Kid*, another completely crazy Filipino action film. He may be a little under three feet, but that means he's right at groin level. He has a black belt. Your nuts are his. Again and again, the men of the Philippines present their junk to Agent 00's fast feet. *For Y'ur Height Only* was the sort of film that one couldn't imagine being topped. Well, *The Impossible Kid* may not have all the novelty of *Height* but it fixes up some of the problems of that movie.

The *Impossible Kid* bad guys are the dumbest guys ever. They can't stop laughing, and eventually it becomes pretty infectious. Especially when they've captured Agent 00 and put him in a bird cage. They throw him in a lake, laughing the whole time as the score, which sounds a hell of a lot like the *Pink Panther* theme, plays again and again. There's a better flow to this movie than *Height*. The plot is stronger. Terrorists threaten a group of very wealthy men. 00 seems to get in more fights here. There are more women who fall in love with him. And there is a sequence where he is practicing karate as a woman watches and a beautiful love theme plays. All A+ behavior in a screwball movie.

They didn't give Weng Weng the high-pitched, goofy voice that he got in *Height*. It's more adult. When he flashes his badge and says "Interpol," it can take the viewer by surprise. But then a bartender tries to throw him out because he thinks 00 is a kid. It all comes around, right back to crazy behavior. There aren't any lines as good as "You got a bug in your hair." But the dubbing is just as loopy as in *Height*. There are some moments, like 00 leaping from a hotel room using a sheet as a parachute. He lands in a pool where a big guy holds him, laughing, and wondering where this little man came from. Scenes like that (and 00 driving his very tiny motorcycle down the street) are pure goofballery. 00, however, kills a lot of people. So the director must be applauded for keeping all this insanity kind of light.

00 gets a lot of ladies. The Filipino women really go nuts for him. He kicks so much butt throughout the movie that one pretty much has to fall in love with him. And there is a woman in the movie named Chicklet. That's the actress' name. Why hasn't there been a mega-super HD release of Weng Weng's movies? Films from the Philippines weren't kept in the best shape so there probably exist video masters only. Surely this is why time machines need to be invented. So someone can go back to the early 1980s and retrieve the negatives of these films.

Joyous. Big-hearted excitement from action films favorite little guy. Rock on, 00!

Kill Squad

Director, Screenplay, Producer: Patrick G. Donahue

Cast: Jean Glaude (Larry), Jeff Risk (Joseph), Jerry Johnson (K.C.), Bill Cambria (Alan), Francisco Ramirez (Pete), Marc Sabin (Arthur), Gary Fung (Tommy), Cameron Mitchell (Dutch)

Patrick G. Donahue is a Renaissance man in the land of action and stunts. As the credits indicate, he writes, directs, produces, does stunts and acts. He has his own stunt team, Stunts Nor-Cal. And he's made a number of films in the vicinity of San Jose, California, including the very odd *Parole Violations*. If *Kill Squad* is anything to go by, people in San Jose must spend the majority of their time stepping over beaten bodies and smashed cars. This film is absolutely loaded to the gills with them.

A man named Dutch and his gang of burly jerks cripple an Vietnam vet named Joseph and kill Joseph's wife. Joseph, from the confines of his wheelchair, re-forms his Vietnam squad of fighters to take down Dutch. All members of the Kill Squad, led by the super-cool Larry, know the latest and greatest fighting techniques, circa 1982. One of them is a nunchaku master. Another spins switchblades around. One of them is strong like the mighty bull. Another is a goofball, which is not as painful as some of these other techniques, but never knock goofy. The squad begins a hunt for Dutch. But someone is hunting the Squad. Stand up straight and throw your recliner out the window. *Kill Squad* has just arrived to kick your ass.

This is a film that takes place just the other side of the Looking Glass. A place called Action Earth. It looks like our Earth but there a few fundamental differences. On Action Earth, all conflicts, ranging from the heights of war to a debt of one dollar to the simple troubles of the All American Pimp, are resolved through fistfights. Or kung fu fights or the use of hand-held weaponry and, in a very few cases, guns. There is no diplomacy unless diplomacy is defined as "punching your fellow man at the slightest provocation." On Action Earth, that is the exact definition.

Kill Squad takes place in the California section of Action Earth. The rules of the world are this: Guys come to your house and punch you. They leave. You get some friends together and find those guys. You punch them. Rinse and repeat. The squad is assembled in this way. The first ambulatory member of the squad is shown beating up some people in a tool and die factory. Joseph sends him to find another member, who is tearing up a car and beating up some people. The car wrecker knows where the next member is located. They find the next member doing something that ends in fighting. Eventually, the squad is assembled.

Their mission involves going from place to place looking for Dutch and beating up people. The most entertaining place they visit is an "abandoned ranch" where about a dozen cowboys live with their gals and horses. Would that ranch be "abandoned" if, in fact, a dozen people or more live there? In Action Earth, it doesn't matter. All scenes are a fight (or, in one case, a car chase) or a linking scene that will take us to a fight. That's *Kill Squad*. All the while, vaguely disco-ish music plays.

Plot holes and odd dubbing of all the characters may spread a thick lather over the movie, distracting those viewers who need some sort of logic or who need their characters to sound like they're saying what they're supposed to be saying. But the true test of an action films like this (that trades in fight scene after fight scene) is: How are the fight scenes? The answer is: pretty darn good. They range from slightly awkward to well-choreographed. And there are a lot of them. Mr. Donahue knew what he wanted his film to be: fights. On Action Earth, fights are as common as flies. With gleeful relish and beautiful abandon, *Kill Squad* pits a group of good guys against a group of bad guys in a world where He Who Punches Harder Wins. This is a fun film.

If the constant fights should become monotonous, go out in the street and punch a friend. It can be a real relief.

The New Barbarians aka Warriors of the Wasteland

Director: Enzo G. Castellari
Screenplay: Tito Carpi, Enzo Girolami
Producer: Claudio Grassetti
Cast: Timothy Brent (Scorpion), Fred Williamson (Nadir), George Eastman (One), Anna Kanakis, Thomas Moore

2019 AD. This movie takes place after the nuclear holocaust. Out in the wastelands. Various groups of people are trying to stay alive. In true jackass fashion, a bunch of asshats called the Templars, led by a crazy man named One, are driving around killing everyone they find. Mainly because they are crazy. A guy named Scorpion (Timothy Brent) and his pal (Fred Williamson) come to the rescue.

If there is no love in your heart for Italian post-apocalyptic movies, at least tune into *The New Barbarians* so you can enjoy the kick-ass rotating propeller thing hooked up to the side of a car that cuts a guy's head off. It's brilliant.

This one is a winner. It's well-paced. It's exciting. The viewer gets to like Scorpion. He's not an anti-hero. He's simply a good guy. He helps out a young lady with huge hair. His best friends are a little kid and Fred Williamson. Even though the Templars constitute two dozen nuts (including a beautifully coifed gentleman named Shadow), it's pretty obvious that Scorpion is going to kick all their asses.

This film is of the fun post-apocalyptic variety. There are good guys and bad guys. The bad guys are very bad. The good guys save the day. The action is well done. Some great futuristic car chases. A lot of shooting. Some hand-to-hand fun. Some surprising moments here and there. This one would make a fun double feature night with *Endgame*. Both are entertaining films set after the apocalypse.

There's good use of quarries and industrial centers in this film. Well, who doesn't love a good quarry? One would like to think that all the quarry chases were done in the same spot just slightly redressed. And that could be true.

One is played by George Eastman, as crazy-looking as ever. He's great as a strange Messiah-esque leader. He is taking revenge on the world that caused the apocalypse by killing everybody. It's not the smartest idea but then he's crazy. Shadow is a bit more in control. But when let loose, he gets pretty nuts too.

There may not be any one post-apocalyptic *Road Warrior* rip-off to see first. But *The New Barbarians* keeps it simple, piles on the thrills, adds a few moments of absurdity and has a hero named Scorpion.

1990: The Bronx Warriors

Director: Enzo G. Castellari
Screenplay: Dardano Sacchetti, Elisa Livia Briganti, Enzo G. Castellari
Producer: Fabrizio De Angelis
Cast: Mark Gregory (Trash), Vic Morrow (Hammer), Fred Williamson, Christopher Connelly

In 1990, the Bronx is a no man's land, a wasteland of assorted gangs and crazy people. An heiress to a munitions corporation runs away to the Bronx. Hammer, a mad police officer, is sent to get her back. It's up to Trash, the head of the biker gang known as the Riders, to protect her. The viewer enjoys a high-energy, slightly mental Italian rip-off of *The*

1990: THE BRONX WARRIORS · A Film Produced by FABRIZIO DE ANGELIS · Starring VIC MORROW · CHRISTOPHER CONNELLY
FRED WILLIAMSON · MARK GREGORY · with STEFANIA GIROLAMI · Screenplay DARDANO SACCHETTI · ELISA LIVIA BRIGANTI · ENZO G. CASTELLARI
Directed by ENZO G. CASTELLARI · © 1983 DEAF INTERNATIONAL FILM s.r.l. **R** UNITED FILM DISTRIBUTION COMPANY

ing. Except when he's punching someone or throwing something. He likes doing that.

The film spends quite some time setting up the world and the situation. Hammer is gradually introduced and, yes, he is a nutjob. Vic Morrow pulls out all the stops. There are many shootouts, fist-fights and plenty of people dying. There's never a lot of blood. Most of it is yelling and falling and dying. It is almost as cartoon-like as some of the gangs.

Halfway through, the heiress is kidnapped by a rival gang. Trash has to proceed across the Bronx, encountering gang after gang. At the same time, Hammer is setting little traps to cause unrest among the gangs. It all ends with flame throwers and screaming. It does not end well.

1990: The Bronx Warriors is a straightforward, entertaining romp through the Italian mind. Trash is a good-looking, rock-hard slab of granite. The gangs are definitely colorful and entertaining. It's a movie that keeps the pace going and occasionally dips into the darkness. But, generally, it's a romp. Director and co-writer Enzo G. Castellari always shoots a good action scene. The widescreen photography is great. There are some nice compositions and some interesting ideas framed within the shots.

But, really, is there a lot of violence? Is there good action? Well, it's not as good as *The Warriors* but I have watched it more often than *Escape from New York*. Depending upon the viewer's preferences, adjustments can be

Warriors with a touch of *Escape from New York* thrown in.

The exteriors are in New York City and some very rundown streets somewhere or other. These places give the feel of a post-apocalyptic landscape that simply didn't have an apocalypse. Like *The Warriors*, each gang has a theme. Bikers, Broadway dancers, pimps in Cadillacs, zombies. The only one who seems to have any sort of deep thought processes is the buff, Ramones-esque Trash. But he's a bit too enigmatic for his own good so it's not always easy to gauge what he's think-

made from there. The sequel *Escape from the Bronx* is, in this man's eyes, better. Trash as a loner is more fun than Trash in a gang. He just seems like he should be a loner. Unless the gang helps him out with conditioner and shampoo. The man has beautiful hair.

Ninja Strikes Back

> *Director:* Bruce Le, Joseph Velasco
> *Screenplay:* Joseph Velasco
> *Producer:* Dick Randall
> *Cast:* Bruce Le (Bruce), Wong Ching-Li (Ron), Harold Sakata (Sakata), Andre Kobb, Chick Norris

The ninjas from a less extravagant Godfrey Ho film come up against the non-disappearing power of kung fu master Bruce Le in *Ninja Strikes Back*. The ninjas don't actually show up until over halfway into the movie but that doesn't mean their power isn't felt. The final battle between Bruce and Ninja takes place in a huge Roman amphitheater. It's a good fight (although Bruce's walk up to the ninja is a little lengthy) and almost justifies the crazy location. This is not the craziest Bruce Le–Dick Randall concoction but it's not normal, that for sure.

Bruce was a criminal but he's left the gang behind. They kidnap the daughter of an ambassador in Rome, taking her to Hong Kong. Bruce is called up to bring her back. Really, though, all he wanted to do was spend some time with his girlfriend in Rome and maybe get married. Stuff goes wrong.

Let's get this out of the way right now: Since this is a Dick Randall film, is there a lot of gratuitous nudity? Yes, yes, there is. The normal topless ladies by the pool. The ambassador's daughter is tied topless to the mast of a

boat. And there is a scene with a lesbian porno being shot. All gratuitous, all completely expected. No one ladles out ladies quite like Randall. Randall is in the movie as the ambassador. He has appeared in his movies before but in this one he's not a sleazy jerk. Congratulations, Mr. Randall.

Ninja Strikes Back is one of those films that just barely keeps its grasp on coherency. The plot is technically straightforward: ambassador's daughter kidnapped. Bruce is sent after her. But then Bruce's sister is kidnapped. The ninjas show up and they begin disappearing and acting in supernatural ways that don't

completely jive with the way the more natural fighting in these sorts of kung fu films occur.

The fights, as always, are energetic. And Bruce has fun with them. When he is fighting the ninjas, there's an element of humor. Bolo Yeung and Oddjob from *Goldfinger* show up. The latter has a killer bowler hat and an actual golden hand. The James Bond music starts playing and it all gets a little nutty.

Ninja Strikes Back is certainly not the best of these types of kung fu films. *Challenge of the Tiger* is more fun. *The Clones of Bruce Lee* is nuttier. But this one has ninjas in it. They are always fun and almost always goofy.

Nomad Riders

Director, Screenplay: Frank Roach
Producer: Stephen Fusci
Cast: Tony Laschi (Steve Thrust), Wayne Chema (Grenades), Marilyn McCormick (Marlo), Richard Kluck (Cannibal), Ron Gregg (Crud), Frank Roach (Mr. Vacci)

This book continues to stand by the theory that Steve is the best name for an action hero. It's a take-charge name. It's got a v that really seems to ground this single-syllable excitement in a hard reality. It's also heroic. Say it out loud five times and everything will be all right.

If the action hero of a film is named Steve, and his last name is Thrust, then that might be the best action film hero ever. *Nomad Riders* presents us with Mr. Thrust as action hero. He's a little nebbishy. He's a little bland. The ladies love him but there's never a lot of evidence for why, precisely. Except for his name and his take-no-prisoners attitude towards life. Steve Thrust is here.

A bad man named Mr. Vacci has sent three crazy thugs to kill Thrust's wife and child. They succeed. Thrust goes on the revenge warpath. No scuzball or dirtbag is safe. Thrust will take them all down, and then he'll get to Vacci. He'll do whatever it takes.

Hire informants. Punch informants in the head. Threaten other informants. In this world, there are three types of people: informants, thugs and Steve Thrust. Oh, there's also a redheaded female cop (played by the heroine of Roach's *Frozen Scream*) who Thrust takes to the heights of passion and back. It's only natural.

Nomad Riders is a lot of fun. It's got Thrust in front. It also spends a lot (a *lot*) of time with some strange bikers, the Nomad Riders. They party and drink. They blow up a portable potty. They drive their bikes through the home of an elderly woman enjoying an issue of *Playgirl* with Paul McCartney on the cover. The movie spends as much

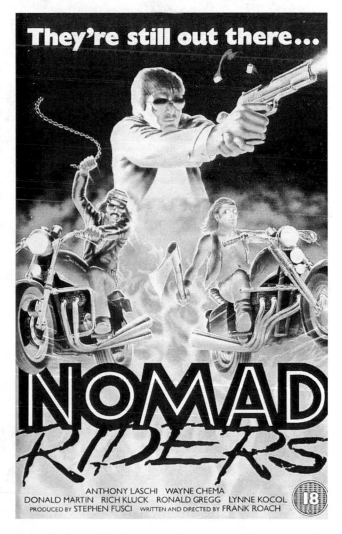

They're still out there...

NOMAD RIDERS

ANTHONY LASCHI   WAYNE CHEMA
DONALD MARTIN   RICH KLUCK   RONALD GREGG   LYNNE KOCOL
PRODUCED BY STEPHEN FUSCI   WRITTEN AND DIRECTED BY FRANK ROACH

time with them as it does with Thrust and his revenge plot. It is cool how the Riders don't care about Thrust when their job is done for the day. They just want some prime party time. Thrust cares about nothing but taking down the Riders and Vacci. Eventually, they converge.

The film is pretty straightforward entertainment with the addition of some tangents, including a very long party with the Nomad Riders. Some strange patrons in a biker bar are given a lot more screen time than they should. There are just enough tangents to make one think that this might become some sort of Robert Altman–esque ensemble piece. But it doesn't do that. The viewer wants some shooting, fighting, exploding, chasing, thrusting—that's the purpose of *Nomad Riders* And, Frank Roach (who also plays Vacci) gives the viewer what they want.

Put your trust in the power of Thrust, Steve Thrust. He will make everything all right. Yes, there may be many bodies in his wake. But everything will be all right.

One Down, Two to Go

Director, Producer: Fred Williamson

Screenplay: Jeff Williamson

Cast: Jim Brown (J), Fred Williamson (Cal), Jim Kelly (Chuck), Richard Roundtree (Ralph), Paula Sills (Teri), Laura Loftus (Sally), Joe Spinell (Joe Spangler)

One Down, Two to Go is sort of the sequel to *Three the Hard Way* (1974), a wonderful, weird black action film featuring Jim Brown, Fred Williamson and Jim Kelly kicking a lot of white people's asses. It's a bit of a country-spanning epic that turns almost sci-fi with its explanations in the end. Then the

main guys made *Take a Hard Ride*, a spaghetti Western with Lee Van Cleef. So when a viewer gets to *One Down, Two to Go,* he expects super-cool dudes kicking a lot of white guy behind and sleeping with a lot of white women. "I may not know kung fu but I'm an expert in gun fu." One would not be wrong.

The movie is about a big martial arts tournament. Participant Chuck is there with Ralph, his manager. After Chuck wins, there is some chicanery involving Joe Spinell (frankly, when isn't there?) and a man named Rossi. Chuck is wounded. Cal and J (Jim Brown) are called in to commence the major round of ass-kicking. The majority of the film

is Cal and J going from place to place, asking people questions and then beating them up. Whether Fred and Jim are beating people up or saying "To hell with it!" and pulling a gun, they're awesome. The lack of Jim Kelly is a little sad but he's there for the first half-hour or so. Richard Roundtree doesn't do much but his presence is felt.

As far as the action goes, the movie begins with quite a bit of great martial arts in the ring. Then there are a few fights out in the world. After Cal and J show up, things really take off. As in many of the black action films from the 1970s, the action is fun but never fully, truly exciting. It's all cool but never "Wow!" if that makes any sense. The actors are giving it their all so I would hazard a guess that it's the direction, mixed with the editing. The camera isn't always in the right place to maximize some of the fights and shootouts. Sometimes the editing is just a split-second off on either side of the shots. It's not a deal-breaker. The film still can be enjoyed.

One Down, Two to Go has the feeling of an era ending. A feeling of folks being re-assembled one last time to kick ass the way they used to. When Fred and Jim show up, it is a fantastic moment. They are in charge and oh-so-cool. But not having Jim Kelly there makes things feel a little off. Kelly was the slightly more crazy side of things with his huge Afro and *Enter the Dragon* lineage. It's sad that he kind of leaves the movie before the actual action begins. That might be the end of the era right there. The other two, however, do not go down.

She

Director, Screenplay: Avi Nesher
Producer: Renato Dandi
Cast: Sandahl Bergman (She), David Goss (Tom), Quin Kessler (Shandra), Harrison Muller, Jr. (Dick), Gordon Mitchell (Hector)

She has a sequence where the main characters have to cross a bridge guarded by a very weird man named Xenon. If you attack him with a sword and cut off his arm or head, another version appears. So, eventually, one gets attacked by a squad of this one weird man.

That's fun. But as She approaches the bridge, the strange man is singing the theme song to *Green Acres*, doing both Oliver and Lisa's voices. *She*, you've won this reviewer over.

This film is a post-apocalyptic adventure set in Year 23 After the Cancellation. It is filled with *Conan*-style high adventure, some very entertaining moments and satire. It has a score by Rick Wakeman and songs by Motorhead and Justin Hayward. It has vampire people at a party, weird monks worshiping a weirder man named Godan and it has She, played by Sandahl Bergman. She seems a bit more square than everyone else in the film but it lends just enough gravitas to what is, essentially, a strange, almost Monty Python–esque comedy with action.

I enjoyed *She*. The credits state that it is "suggested" by the H. Rider Haggard novel. And that's right. Avi Nesher has made a film riffing on assorted madcap situations that one would normally see in a post-apocalyptic film. By calling the film *She*, Avi gave it a certain cachet that it wouldn't have had if it had just been about some blonde woman sword-and-sorcering her way around the countryside.

There are torture scenes. A scene involving a strange, foppish man who imprisons our heroes in pendulous, plastic-covered prisons. The rock ratchets up on the soundtrack when it needs to, which anticipates some of the '80s Italian horror films that would use heavy metal-hard rock in such a way (*Demons* is a good example). It makes the film, set in a post-apocalyptic world, alternately hipper and less hip. Hipper because they are rocking out. But slightly less hip because of the dating inevitability of the music.

She is a fun film that caught me off-guard. I expected a rather humorless, straightforward, aimless ramble through post-apocalyptic societies. That's technically what it is. But minus the humorless portion. Sandahl is a beautiful She. The guys are good-looking. The bad guys are sufficiently awful. And the monstrous, weird things are doing their jobs. This one is worth watching. It is a bit overlong for what is, more or less, a series of hit-or-miss sketches. It has the feel of the concurrent TV show *Wizards and Warriors*, with boobs instead of Jeff Conaway.

The Sword and the Sorcerer

Director: Albert Pyun

Screenplay: Albert Pyun, Tom Karnowski, John V. Stuckmeyer

Producers: Brandon Chase, Marianne Chase

Cast: Lee Horsley (Prince Talon), Kathleen Beller (Alana), Simon MacCorkindale (Prince Mikah), George Maharis (Machelli), Richard Lynch (Cromwell), Richard Moll (Xusia)

The most profitable independent film of 1982, *The Sword and the Sorcerer* grossed around $40 million. It is probably the best film made by the prolific Albert Pyun, whose output generally ran to the slightly bland side of things. As if, possibly, he didn't or couldn't care about what was going on. In this film, however, Pyun keeps things moving and fun. It's like a slightly less epic version of *Conan the Barbarian* where the main hero isn't as cool as Conan but there's an element of gory sleaze that keeps creeping in.

The plot itself is pretty epic, structured like a smaller-scale version of a series of adventure-fantasy books. An evil leader, Cromwell, summons a demon called Xusia to help him win over everyone. Talon, a prince from a conquered country, grows up to be a warrior. Talon returns to Cromwell's kingdom to save the day. There are a lot of other elements, many of them involving demons and giant snakes and ladies with nice behinds being oiled. It's all part of the mélange of the film.

There is plenty of action, sword fighting, fistfighting, pyroballistic chicanery and so forth. But there's also a sleazy side, especially when Talon is storming through a harem of lovely topless ladies. There's a gory side with Xusia engaging in several really gross activities, like rising out of the insides of a man. This all means that while the film is a good swashbuckling time (which the music will insist

upon), there is a darkness that makes it ostensibly more "adult" than an Errol Flynn–style adventure or something one could bring the whole family to. *The Sword and the Sorcerer* really is a fantasy adventure for grown-ups. It's the sort of film that a kid would watch and be slightly scarred for life.

But that's not a bad thing. Scarring kids with crazy adventure, boobs and gory demons isn't the worst profession to have. Pyun is up for the task. The film does have a lushness to it. This wasn't made on the cheap. (And, even if it was, so what?) It seems almost legit. Then the boobs show up and it takes on a bit of a Cannon film feel. There is, however, nothing at all wrong with this. The viewer is meant to be experiencing a world. And that's what the movie gives us.

The Sword and the Sorcerer is a very entertaining movie, released in the immediate wake of *Conan the Barbarian*. The only regret is that the announced sequel *Tales of the Ancient Empire* did not come out until decades later.

They Call Me Bruce?

Director, Producer: Elliot Hong
Screenplay: David Randolph, Elliot Hong, Johnny Yune, Tim Clawson
Cast: Jonny Yune (Bruce/Joon/Grandfather), Margaux Hemingway (Karmen), Raf Mauro (Freddy), Pam Huntington (Anita), Martin Azarow (Big Al)

Bruce Lee was the cultural touchstone, in the western world, for all things karate and kung fu. When he died, he left a big hole, which has never really been filled. Jackie Chan got close but he really goes in a totally different direction. (Best example is gauged by the fact that guys who love Bruce love the fact that he kicks ass completely. Whereas Jackie is all about jumping around and spinning and flipping. I once watched *First Strike*'s ladder fight with a co-worker at a video store and even though Jackie was doing crazy shit, the co-worker shrugged it off: "If he were Bruce, or even Steven Seagal, he'd just stand there and pound the shit out of them." I tried to explain that this was different but it didn't work. Some guys seemed to be bothered by

Jackie because he wasn't about just kicking ass.)

Many Bruce Lee impersonators appeared. Some of them, like Bruce Li, were quite good but they were all impersonators. That's where *They Call Me Bruce?* comes in. Joon, the lead character, isn't even Chinese, he's Korean. But all white people think Asians look the same so everyone calls him Bruce. In fact, this review will call him Bruce. Bruce is not a fighter, although he worships Bruce Lee (and Rocky). But he keeps getting involved in fights where, mainly through accident, he comes out on top. This is a comedy and it's a pretty good one.

The film feels like it might have gone a little further towards the *Airplane!* route but it stays relatively grounded in reality. Bruce is not a fighter but he's willing to go along with whatever stereotypes the film has for him. (And, it has plenty for everyone else, including Italians.) Bruce's thing is misquoting commercials. ("I once got run over by a Toyota. Oh, what a feeling.") and telling jokes in an innocent way that, maybe, too many people laugh at onscreen. Johnny Yune is charming though. The supporting cast, including Margaux Hemingway, seems game for whatever.

The film feels like it might be a kung fu film but then it becomes a road film. Bruce and a mob assistant are sent across the country to deliver "flour" (cocaine) to other mobsters. Bruce doesn't know this. He just wants to get to New York City where he will meet the lady that his grandfather told him to meet when he died. Along the way, he gets in a lot of almost-fights and makes a lot of friends.

They Call Me Bruce? was a minor box office hit. This was the time of movies like *Airplane!* and all the other parodies and it fit right in even though it is less of a parody and more of a film about people reducing others to stereotypes. The mobsters, and many others, can't tell Joon from Bruce. But Bruce doesn't mind because it gets him to New York City. And Johnny Yune has some very funny moments. The hot tub gag and the nunchucks as chopstick gags are still funny so many years later.

Tiger Joe

Director: Antonio Margheriti
Screenplay: Tito Capri
Producer: Gianfranco Couyoumdjian
Cast: David Warbeck (Tiger Joe), Annie Belle (Kia), Tony King (Midnight), Alan Collins (Lenny), Giancarlo Badessi (Bronski)

Quick note: The name Giancarlo Badessi is a great name for a guy in an action film. Bronski isn't much of an action film guy but that name…

Tiger Joe is a David Warbeck, gun runners in the Cambodian jungles, fighting guerrillas kind of movie directed by the mighty Antonio Margheriti. Joe's plane crashes in the jungle. He and his pal Midnight get captured by guerrillas, a really nasty bunch. They'll kill anybody. Soldiers, old people, women, children. Doesn't matter. The guerrillas themselves are a hazily sketched bunch but, just keep in mind, they are jackasses. Joe and Midnight are joined by some friends (including Bronski) and much jungle chaos ensues. There is shooting, fistfighting, snakes and panther attacks. All the elements one would need to construct a classic.

But *Tiger Joe* isn't a classic. It kind of goes along and does its business. Sometimes it's pretty exciting. There are several great scenes set on bridges, including some under-the-bridge stuntwork which is awesome. There's lots of shooting, especially in the final sequence with Joe and Midnight trying to stop the crazy guerrillas on a beach. But, unfortunately, the characters are blanks. Normally, the dubbing in these films doesn't bother me. For some reason, however, the dubbing in *Tiger Joe* distanced me from the film. It's neither very good nor very funny. It's just bland and disconnected from the images.

And this film needs to have that emotional attachment, because it's not an epic war movie or an Indiana Jones rip-off. It's about a couple guys, helping out a bunch of innocent folks. Joe falls in love. Midnight shoots a lot of people. And the heart isn't there. When the dubbing decides to go silly, it's always at the wrong moments. When Midnight is shot dur-ing the final shootout, he asks, "Why me?" And it seems funny and inappropriate as he and Joe are at a gun boat shooting rows of guerrilla soldiers down. It tries to be about these people fighting this nameless, faceless evil. But it doesn't quite accomplish what it sets out to do.

Tiger Joe meanders when it should be on point. There should be a feeling of growing tension and suspense as they proceed through the jungle. But it really feels like the director lost the script somewhere in the quicksand and is stringing together bits and pieces. Then the film cuts to a city where Bronski and another guy decide to head into the jungle to find Tiger. Like the similar cuts to New York City in films like *Cannibal Ferox*, the film droops and loses its momentum. Then the film has its poignant bits. Joe refers to causes. Everybody has causes. That's probably true. But the guerrillas cause seems to be shooting everybody. Does "causes" work as reasoning when the enemy seems to be just insane?

This is a little bit too much criticism for a film called *Tiger Joe*. The action is decent but it really is kind of a meanderer from scene to scene. If you like Warbeck, tune in. If you need to see all the action movies ever made, tune in. It's okay. Just nothing all that fantastic.

2020: Texas Gladiators

Director, Producer: Joe D'Amato (as Kevin Mancuso)
Screenplay: Alex Carver
Cast: Harrison Muller (Jab), Al Cliver (Nisus), David Stephen (Catch), Peter Hooten (Halakkon), Sabrina Siani (Maida)

Post-apocalyptic films always imagine the worst in people. Rarely does one encounter a hippity-hoppity good time post-apocalyptic number. Although, most of the time, the political leaders and the people who initiated the nuclear holocaust are long dead. The people one meets in these movies are regular folks (sometimes soldiers) out to survive. That involves a lot of death and destruction. When groups work together and try to survive through peaceful means, that simply means that, at some point in the near future, violent people will take things away from them.

2020: Texas Gladiators is a great title. The film itself is a pretty good post-apocalyptic free-for-all. A group of people tries to make their way in the desolate landscape. Strange bikers and odd Nazi-esque gentlemen who form the New Order and are led by the Black One (a white guy dressed all in black) take it all away from them. There is a lot of violence, implied rape and general unpleasant behavior. This one is on the darker end of the Italian spectrum.

As with a lot of these films, there's never a feeling that the terrible, inhuman behavior is being either condoned or accepted by the filmmakers. They are making a rip-off of *The Road Warrior* and they are following what that film did, the best that they can. No need to judge the film harshly or put it down. It's just doing its job.

A hairy man and a beautiful woman have a child. Then the bad guys show up. No one can leave anyone alone. Broken families abound. Broken bodies litter the landscape. And there's always the Black One with his black leather outfit and his scads of troops. If one isn't so thrilled with that, they can spend time marveling at the odd structure of the film, which seems to take quite some time to make it to the actual point it needs to be at with the decimated community and the broken families.

The film starts with a segment involving crazed punks assaulting nuns. Then a group of hairy guys come in and kill the punks. One of the hairy guys (actually the one hairy guy who is not hairy, if that makes sense) assaults a blonde. She is rescued and tells the lead hairy guy about a better place he could be. Then the film jumps to the community.

Within minutes of that, the bad guys attack. It's a whirlwind that leads the viewer to think, several times, that the plot is upon them. But it takes a while. It takes a lot of characters. And, for a film that is a kinda straightforward post-apocalyptic rip-off, that strange structure adds something extra to the first half. A little extra bit of wonder to the outcome of this adventure.

2020: Texas Gladiators is not the best of the post-apocalyptic Italian yarns but it has a lot of action. So that's worth the time spent.

1983

Highest grossing films in the U.S.
1. *Return of the Jedi*
2. *Terms of Endearment*
3. *Flashdance*
4. *Trading Places*
5. *WarGames*

Highest rated TV shows in the U.S.
1. *Dallas*
2. *60 Minutes*
3. *Dynasty*
4. *The A-Team*
5. *Simon & Simon*

Big historical events
Star Wars defense plan announced
Sally Ride is the first woman in space
Cabbage Patch Kids are huge
Mr. T enters our pop culture world

Action movies
Return of the Jedi, Octopussy, Sudden Impact, Superman III, Never Say Never Again, Blue Thunder, High Road to China, Krull, Lone Wolf McQuade, 10 to Midnight, Smokey and the Bandit III

Ark of the Sun God aka Sopravvissuti della citta morta

Director: Antonio Margheriti
Screenplay: Giovanni Simonelli
Producer: Giovannu Paolucci
Cast: David Warbeck (Rick Spear), Susie Sudlow (Carol), Jon Steiner (Lord Dean), Alan Collins (Beetle)

Rick, a treasure hunter, is hired to find the Scepter of the Sun God, which is located in the Tomb of Gilgamesh. Cult members are also after the Scepter, and they will stop at nothing. Car chases, foot chases and crazy *Raiders of the Lost Ark*–style cliffhanger adventures abound. Also, Rick drinks a lot of rum. Antonio Margheriti knows how to keep this sort of film fun. It's pure *Raiders* rip-off but it's a good time.

The film is set in Istanbul, so it has a nice international flavor. Rick is tricked into becoming a part of this expedition with his girlfriend Carol and two strange men, Beetle and Mohammed. Prince Abdullah has an endless supply of men that he sends after Rick to stop him from getting to the tomb. The tomb is identifiable from the air by a swastika-shaped mountain. All this is lathered on top of a couple high-speed car chases that involve the use of toy cars for some of the larger stunts.

These Italian action films, with their post-dubbed action and over-complicated plots, can induce a strange dream-like state in certain viewers, especially this reviewer. *Ark of the Sun God* is watched all the way through and images stand out: Rick and Carol leaving a boat at the start to the strong funky theme song. The strange car chases. The really cool, low-rent temple that they invade in the end. The swastika mountaintop. Rick drinking all that rum. But when the movie ends, there is a remembrance of very little. Just those images. That makes for an interesting viewing experience.

When one can't remember what the heck just happened, that brings the viewer back. Returning to the film to try to gauge what was happening. Who are Beetle and Mohammed? Why are some of the chases occurring?

The moment the nighttime car chase begins, the action is running high! Intercutting the actors in the cars with the toy cars tearing through the streets. High-tension music pounds away! And then the cars start to move a little too quickly. They make slight movements (especially while going through the air and hitting the ground) that cars can't actually make. Physics comes into play here. During the second car chase, in the desert, it's more pronounced. And the viewer begins to stare intently at the scenes, wondering if the cars are being pulled along or if someone is pushing them hard into frame. The questions keep coming, especially during moments

when real stunt cars are mixed in with the toy cars.

Ark of the Sun God will keep you asking questions. It's a little dull. It takes forever to get to the desert. But David Warbeck is charming and questions like "Why those damn toy cars?" will keep you coming back for more. The realization that there are other Italian films like this is just like Christmas.

Conquest

Director: Lucio Fulci
Screenplay: Gino Capone, Jose Antonio de la Loma, Sr., Carlos Vasallo

Producer: Giovanni D. Clemente

Cast: George Rivero, Andrea Occhipinti, Conrado San Martin, Violeta Cela, Jose Gras Palay

This film is an Italian-Spanish-Mexican co-production. That's not something we see every day. It's also a sword-and-sorcery film from the strange hand of Lucio Fulci. Fulci directed films for decades in Italy. He did giallo films (*Don't Torture the Duckling*), comedies (*Dracula in the Provinces*) and straight-up horror (*Zombie* and many others). Here he is trying sword and sorcery, which requires an adept hand at action.

One of Fulci's trademarks, in my opinion, is that there are times when his ideas behind a scene or a story seem to come from another world. His *City of the Living Dead* is a good example of this. From the scene of the young woman vomiting out her insides to the strange climactic freeze frame, Fulci either has such an individual vision that it comes from another place or he was making it all up as he went along. Maybe both. *Conquest* is one of the nuttiest films in a nutty filmography.

Ilias is the young warrior. Maxz is the older warrior. Ocron is the evil sorceress. She is nude. She wears a head-covering gold mask. And she's nude. But that was already mentioned. Ilias is on a young warrior's journey. Maxz is just kind of hanging out and being nice to animals. Ocron is after Ilias' magic bow, which fires magical arrows. Some of her wolf-men henchmen fire arrows too. Those arrows are scratched onto the film. It worked back in the silent era and it works here.

Actually, harkening back to the silent era may be the best way to watch this film. The silent era had a great sense of excitement and achievement as the realm of film was new. People were still learning. *Conquest* feels like that. From its odd story arc involving Ilias, to the protracted sequence involving an ill Ilias oozing pus from assorted pustules on his leg. Then there's the odd use of constant, thick mist in the film. Fulci seems to have either never seen a sword-and-sorcery film or he was trying to reinvent the genre. But his main definition of reinvention is odd characters, weird monsters, clumsy fights and a smoke machine. So many scenes are drenched in mist, it makes you think the film is set in another world. It's like this world is on fire all the time and no one knows how to put out the flames. Ilias and Maxz remain constantly shrouded in smoke. As their characters are a little dippy, that's kind of fun. But it's the most obvious example of insanity in very weird film made by a man who made many weird films.

Deathstalker

Director, Producer: James Sbardellati (John Watson)

Screenplay: Howard Cohen

Cast: Richard Hill (Deathstalker), Barbi Benton (Codille), Richard Brooker (Oghris), Lana Clarkson (Kaira), Victor Bo (Kang), Bernard Erhard (Munkar)

Deathstalker begins in a much more serious way than its sequel. Deathstalker, a muscular, not-terribly-talkative swordsman prone to sexual assault, is told by a witch that he must find a chalice, an amulet and a sword. Munkar the Magician has two of them. Deathstalker heads to Munkar's kingdom, gets involved in a big tournament to find the best warrior and sees a lot of naked women. A lot. One of them is Barbi Benton. Another is Lana Clarkson. Frankly, he's not having a rough time of it.

Deathstalker was the first of Roger Corman's

1980s sword-and-sorcery movies. In the wake of *Conan the Barbarian* and *The Sword and the Sorcerer*, Corman sent his crew to Argentina to tell the derivative, violent and kinda sleazy story of Deathstalker. It was popular. They made it cheap (but not as cheap as, say, the Ator films). It pulled in almost 12 million bucks. That's why there are four of them.

After watching this film, I firmly believe that what *Deathstalker* brought to sword and sorcery was the unabashed celebration of beautiful naked ladies everywhere. Benton is nude a lot. She has a harem. They're pretty nude. Clarkson's character, Kaira, doesn't really wear a top much. And she is well-endowed in the area of boobs. It's no wonder Deathstalker gets so horny when he's out there. And the ladies seem to be feeling what he's feeling, quite a bit of the time.

This film is just loaded with nudity and sexing around. In fact, it is almost the point of the film. There is one moment where Kiara shows up at a campfire with her, well, boobs out. Even Deathstalker's mouth drops open. That cuts to the model of Munkar's castle. The camera pans up a phallic turret-like area and then the viewer is back in the harem. More naked ladies. This is the sort of film that would probably have (actually, probably has) twisted around the minds of more than one young man (and probably several young women) who came upon it late at night.

At one time, sword and sorcery was for kids. There could be violence and some sexiness. Many of the series like Gor and Conan did have more adult bits in them. But kids went to see, say, *The Golden Voyage of Sinbad* or the peplums of the 1950s and 1960s. But

Conan, very specifically, made it more "adult" and then *The Sword and the Sorcerer* followed that up. It seems as if *Deathstalker* took the "adult" portion very seriously and almost made a sex film.

Endgame

Director, Producer: Joe D'Amato (as Steven Benson)

Screenplay: Alex Carver

Cast: Al Cliver (Shannon), Moira Chen (Lilith), George Eastman (Karnak), Jack Davis (Prof. Levin), Al Yamanouchi (Ninja)

It is May 10, 2025, and the apocalypse has hit. But it's okay! Things are a bit desolate and there are some mutants. But as long as the average person keeps off the street at night,

...beginn... berleben...

Al Cliver
Laura Gemser
George Eastman
Mario Pedone
und Gordon Mitchell

– DAS LETZTE SPIEL MIT DEM TOD –

Kamera: Federico Slonisco · Herstellungsleitung: Helen Handris · Produktion: FILMIRAGE Rom/Los Angeles
Regie: STEVEN BENSON

TIVOLI

things aren't bad. The newest excitement, a show called Endgame, involves three bounty hunters trying to catch someone between 22nd and 33rd street in New York City. Today's hunted is a man named Shannon. *Endgame* shifts from coverage of the game to Shannon being recruited to get a group of mutants (humanity's future) the hell out of New York. The Security Service doesn't want this happening.

Has anyone mentioned that this is another Italian post-apocalyptic film? And it's as entertaining as the others. There is satire, with the bounty hunting game being sponsored by Life Plus, some sort of high-protein energy tablet that makes you a "man among men." A drink that brings you strength. There's a lot of great action, from the game itself to protecting the mutants. There are psychic moments, strange blind monks and a great climactic scene that begins with the psychic sentence "Tommy, can you hear me?" The film is around 95 minutes long, which might be a touch too long. But mostly it's fun.

The fact that the hero, Shannon, is not a loner out there in the wasteland, but a TV star, known for a violent reality show, gives it a rather modern (well, first half of the 21st century) twist. The addition of the always scary George Eastman as Shannon's biggest rival, Karnak, adds to the excitement. Eastman is always kind of scary, even when he's not supposed to be. Ninja, an Asian fighter, is along to protect the mutants.

Some of the post-apocalyptic films are downers. Some are kind of goofy. Some are entertaining action films. This one is in the third category. There's a real excitement to the final minutes. The final shot is straight out of *Rocky III* but it's cool.

This is a favorite post-apocalyptic film of mine. The satire, the shifting of the storylines, the movement from the city to the deserted countryside, Shannon kicking ass and Lilith being psychic. This one works and is an entertaining evening's viewing. Team it up with one of the *Bronx Warrior* films or, maybe, *Warrior of the Lost World*.

Escape from the Bronx

Director: Enzo G. Castellari
Screenplay: Enzo G. Castellari, Tito Carpi
Producer: Fabrizio De Angelis
Cast: Mark Gregory (Trash), Henry Silva (Floyd Wangler), Valeria D'Obici (Moon Gray), Antonio Sabato (Dablone)

Trash has returned. He's no longer part of the Riders from *1990: The Bronx Warriors*. In fact, all the colorful gangs from the first film now live underground. A corporation is evacuating the Bronx and sending everyone to New Mexico. They plan on leveling the whole thing and making it a wealthy person's paradise. Contrary to popular belief, the Bronx inhabitants aren't being sent to New Mexico to live. They're being burnt alive. Trash, and a few friends, take exception to this.

In the sheer wonderful chaotic traditions of Italian rip-off cinema, *Escape from the Bronx* is not a continuation of the *Warriors* riffs of the first film. It goes off on its own. This one is mainly about shooting members of the Disinfestation Annihilation Squad (DAS). Trash, a reporter, a strange ordnance expert named Strike and his son storm around the Bronx shooting silver-suited DAS employees while deftly avoiding flame throwers and bullets.

This is one of those "rows of guys being shot, flailing and falling" kinda movies, and Castellari is a master at those. Much like there is a neverending supply of Vietcong to shoot in movies like *War Bus* and *Strike Commando*, there is a neverending supply of silver-suited men to take out here. And it's fun to watch. Maybe it goes on a little too long but it sustains itself most of the way. There are several underground side trips where the viewer sees the remnants of the gangs from the first movie. (Frankly, if the viewer hasn't seen the first movie, this group of costumed goofs is hilarious and rather confusing.) The leader of the gangs, Dablone, is boisterous and Italian and a lover of life. His scenes bring an extra verve to a film that is mostly people shooting other people.

Mark Gregory is great, as always, as Trash. He has a stone face a lot of times but the viewer knows what he's been through. He's hiding his emotional side. And, he still looks like a post-apocalyptic member of the Ramones. Henry Silva is suitably nuts as Floyd Wangler, head of the DAS. Several Italian actors who appeared in the first film have different roles here, which gives *Escape from the Bronx* an odd ensemble feel. And the dubbing crew, as familiar to viewers of this type of movie as Grandma and Grandpa, are back on board.

How is the action? It's Castellari. It's good and just varied enough so that it doesn't start to strain until near the end. The film leaves its ending open. The DAS may be in a shambles, but does that mean the corporation is done with its rascally behavior? I thinks not. Unfortunately, Trash never returned. *The New Barbarians* is sometimes called the third in the *Bronx* trilogy. It's post-apocalyptic and Trash-less. Mark Gregory did appear later in the 1980s in the *Thunder Warrior* trilogy. Maybe that's Trash gone Southwest? Did he take the corporation up on the New Mexico thing? Maybe it was a compromise? Sort of a "We'll send you to New Mexico if you just stop killing all our employees."

Exterminators of the Year 3000

Director: Jules Harrison
Screenplay: Elisa Briganti, Dardano Sachetti, Jose Truchado Reyes
Producer: Camillo Teti
Cast: Robert Jannucci (Alien), Alicia Moro (Trash), Alan Coloins (Papillon), Luca Vententini (Tommy), Fred Harris (Crazy Bull)

Well, they can't all be good. One has to know that. When so much time is spent ripping off (or emulating) other films, there's bound to be one that gets too close and ends up looking a bit foolish because it can't replicate the thrills and spills and excitement of the original. *The Road Warrior*, I would like you to meet ... *Exterminators of the Year 3000*.

Exterminators (which is all–Italian, all the time) is about a post-apocalyptic future world where water and oil are scarce. A group

of nice people try to transport said liquids across a desert area. They enlist the help of a man named Alien, kind of a rugged outsider with his own agenda, but also kind of nice. He drives a rig through portions of the film. He's sort of Mad Max meets B.J. McKay (*B.J. and the Bear*). Tommy, a little kid, befriends Alien. There's chaos on the open road with a gang of thugs called the Exterminators, led by a man named Crazy Bull.

Alien has an ex named Trash. If that makes you want to start rewatching *1990: The Bronx Warriors*, you would be forgiven. An old man with old technology hides in a cave, with beer. Tommy gets an arm pulled off when the Exterminators draw and quarter him. But it's a robotic arm. The old man soups it up and it's better than ever. Those are some nice asides. But the rest is a lot like a much cheaper, less imaginative, less epic version of *The Road Warrior*. Watch the two side by side and see how alike they are.

It's too bad that *Exterminators* is so close because it has the charms of any film that rips off another film so slavishly. Watching the *Road Warrior*–style chases and thinking "Why isn't this bigger?" There are lots of vehicles. They're constantly moving. The direction and editing aren't inept. But *Road Warrior* had those grand moments where the camera went overhead. And there were grand helicopter shots of all these vehicles speeding along the road. In the midst of all the close-up action and crazy stunts, the overhead shot would establish where everyone was in relation to everyone else and give a strong feel for all the spatial relations and makes this chase epic.

Exterminators keeps everything too close during these scenes. The camera sees the trucks tooling along but there's never the epic moment, never the moment where the whole empty landscape is shown with nothing but these vehicles and their drivers fighting for their lives. It's almost as if the director was afraid to show too much of the area because there was another *Road Warrior* rip-off shooting about a half mile away and they didn't want their chases to cross.

Actually, that sounds completely right. That's why the chases are less epic. And that's funny.

Fireback

Director: Teddy Page
Screenplay: Timothy Jorge
Producer: Silver Star Film Company
Cast: Richard Harrison (Jack Kaplan), Mike Monty (Duffy Collins), Gwendolyn Hung (Eve), Ann Milhench (Diane), Jim Gaines (Digger)

The one-man-army gun: OMEGA. It does everything. It fires harpoons and missiles and regular bullets and it slices and dices and … who knows? It really does a lot of shit. Munitions expert Jack Kaplan (Richard Harrison with a kick-ass mustache) demonstrates it for a bunch of soldiers. Something goes wrong and Kaplan ends up accused of crimes he did not commit.

The film devotes an inordinate amount of time to Kaplan trying to reunite with his estranged and hot wife. There is a sequence where he tells someone all the ways he's tried to get her back and the viewer sees little vignettes of him giving her gifts, touching her back and so forth. It's really quite amusing. Back when *The Electric Company* was teaching me about parts of speech, it would use this very simplistic style to get a point across. Here it seems like someone seriously misjudged the age group of the viewers.

A huge force of law enforcement officials comes after Jack Kaplan. I can't fully remember why. But it all culminates in a huge shootout at an old building where Kaplan ends up dressed as a ninja. It's odd.

Many of the Filipino films reviewed for this book are a bit on the matter-of-fact or dull side. They have their charms, they do their thing, but they're not great. Not like the Indonesia films that operate on a different level. Well, this Silver Star production is almost Indonesian. I don't know if that's a good thing to say but it makes for a very fun film, albeit a little dull here and there.

Fireback exists in a hazy post-dubbed dream state where men frame other men to steal their wives and then forget to fill the viewer in on anything happening until it's much too late. A film where Kaplan is defending himself against dozens of guys and yet has time to stop for a flashback to a time when he made out with his wife by the pool. A film that does not stop to give itself time to think about things like coherence because craziness is a hell of a lot more fun.

I don't want to make *Fireback* seem like more fun than it is. It's a good action film with an almost Godfrey Ho touch of madness. One that has escaped our world and exists "somewhere else." This reviewer has been hanging out there for a while. Sometimes men kill. Sometimes they shoot. Sometimes they scream. There are also ladies in bikinis, so tell your friends.

Gold Raiders

Director, Producer: P. Chalong
Screenplay: Carl Wingard
Cast: Robert Ginty (Mark Banner), Sarah Langenfeld (Cordelia Dubois), Sombat Krung Ron, Manop Noppol Reed, Dusty Rhodes, Thai General Pichai Vasnasong

Gold Raiders starts off with too much exposition. A thousand gold bars are hijacked and taken to Laos; they're on a plane that is shot down in the jungle. A band of intrepid gold raiders, led by Mark Banner and Cordelia Dubois head out to get them back. There are evil soldiers, evil local people, caves filled with bats, lots of shooting and, yes, star Robert Ginty's Missile Motorcycle that flies. *Megaforce,* you got nothing on the Gint!

This film feels like two movies crashed into each other. There's the gold raiders portion of the movie, with all sorts of derring-do and adventure. A motorcycle with missiles riding along a tightrope. Stuff like that. Banner and Dubois once had an affair. There's an underwater frogmen spear gun fight scene like a much smaller version of the climax to *Thunderball.*

Mixed in with that is a film about Communist vs. capitalists; a sister and a brother keep meeting up and arguing about these issues. There's also a thread about the military treating the indigenous people as primitives and a whole lot of Thailand-related stuff that semi-overwhelms the film at points. It's about 108 minutes long, much longer than many of the films in this book. So maybe the point was not the action. Maybe it was piggyback for other issues. Maybe.

The action is pretty good. Ginty looks a little odd throughout, as if someone who didn't like him did his hair and makeup. Sarah Langenfeld, who plays Cordelia, is not very attractive except in a scene where she gets all wet. The Thai actors fare much better although the dubbing doesn't do them any favors. There is a lot of shooting and a lot of talking about doing things, which doesn't always quite translate into doing things.

I don't know where they came up with the idea for the Missile Motorcycle but it's fairly wacky. It runs on crystal something-or-other, like a spaceship, and it has six missiles. It can fly when it's got a hang glider attachment on it. Maybe this was a device that they gave to Ginty to keep him calm after he read the schizophrenic script.

Gold Raiders has its moments, but at the end, it does something that films like this shouldn't do. The raiders begin getting killed and it all ends with an impassioned "Was it worth it?" followed by images of the dead raiders on-screen during the credits. Don't pull nonsense like that, movie. You're a fun movie about gold raiders. You can't carry the weight of an ending like that.

Hercules

Director, Screenplay: Luigi Cozzi
Producers: Menahem Golan, Yoram Globus
Cast: Lou Ferrigno (Hercules), Sybil Danning (Ariadne), Brad Harris (Augias), Ingrid Anderson (Cassiopea), William Berger (King Minos), Mirella D'Angelo (Circe)

The Labors of Hercules, as told by Luigi Cozzi and starring Lou Ferrigno, sounds like it could be one of the best movies ever. When one adds on the fact that Cozzi seems to be channeling his earlier epic *Starcrash* as much as any sword-and-sorcery movie, it becomes

even more probable that this will be the best movie ever. At the end of the day, yes, this *is* the best movie ever, apart from *Starcrash* and maybe *Hercules II* and a few others. Cozzi's endless and boundless energy is amazing. The film is a constant series of inventive sequences. Many times, the effects let everyone down a bit, but the honest feel of people giving it their all exists.

Hercules is a fantastic movie in more ways than one. It opens with around five minutes of wonderfully portentous narration about the creation of the universe. We meet the Greek Gods, who hang out on the moon. Then we meet Hercules (Ferrigno), a superhuman created to help protect humanity. By the end, you will believe that he can save the world. Especially when he flings a log from the Earth to the moon. When sharp blades hit his legs and shatter. When he throws a stone out of a citadel and the stone is tied to a chariot and he and Circe, the siren, ride the chariot around the world. Hercules also separates the land masses of Europe and Africa. He's good.

The evil King Minos and the evil Ariadne are all about giving Princess Cassiopea trouble. Luckily, she has Hercules on her side. Hercules has awesome pecs. Sybil Danning has awesome pecs. It all depends upon what sort of pecs one wants to spend their time looking at. Hercules cleans a stable and fights the Hydra. He fights huge biomechanical beasts. He beats up a bear. All to try and get to and save his beloved Cassiopea. As in *Clash of the Titans*, the gods watch from on high, or the moon, and argue with one another. The gods do look like they escaped from an Abba video but they're still the gods and they deserve our respect.

The movie ends in Atlantis where King Minos is using science to try to destroy the gods. The narrator returns wondering if evil will triumph over good and generally being a downer. But Hercules is still alive and well so I don't think there's much of a chance of evil taking over here. *The Adventures of Hercules* is a bit crazier than this movie, especially in the metaphysical ending which needs to be seen to be believed, if not understood. This film is a little more straightforward but only as straightforward as one can imagine the mind of Luigi Cozzi, who seems to be a grown man who retains every single crazy shred of imagination he had as a child. And, at his best, he brings them to the big screen for us to drink in and enjoy. It's too bad we never got a Pec-Off between Ferrigno and Danning, though. That would have been kick-ass.

Jungle Warriors

Director, Producer: Ernst R. Von Theumer
Screenplay: Robert Collector, Ernst R. Von Theumer
Cast: Nina van Pallandt (Joanna Quinn), Paul L. Smith (Cesar Santiago), John Vernon (Vito Mastranga), Alex Cord (Nick Spiloto), Sybil Danning (Angel), Woody Strode (Luther), Marjoe Gortner (Larry Schecter)

Just because a film seems to have everybody in the world in it is no guarantee of quality. Look at that cast. Everyone you want to know is in this film. Some are only in a few scenes, others are in it a lot. There may not be enough Marjoe Gortner in the film but that could be said to be true of so many movies. Even though all these stars top-load the movie, *Jungle Warriors* (until the action at the end) seems determined to be as dull as possible.

In fact, for some time it's tough to gauge what kind of film this is meant to be. John Vernon goes to see Paul L. Smith deep in the jungle. It's all about drugs. Marjoe is leading a group of fashion models into the jungle for a very European, 1980s-style photoshoot. (There is a montage.) There is some espionage. Suddenly Marjoe is gone and the fashion models are being held captive. I'll be damned, I must have blinked. What the hell happened to Marjoe? Did they kill him? Did somebody kill Larry Schecter? He was there and then Paul L. Smith was there playing a suave South American drug lord with Sybil Danning as his wife. And one can't help but think that this must be a parody.

Never argue with a man named Ernst R. Von Theumer. The name is altogether too regal and slightly sinister. Ernst is probably a kick-ass guy. But be on your guard. So one doesn't want to put down *Jungle Warriors* for being a rather lifeless action film (until the end) that sort of meanders about for quite some time. But one can ask, "Ernst, what were you doing with this film? Seriously."

When the movie is in the final stretch, we get some decent action. Oddly enough, it becomes a variation on *Hell Squad*. The fashion models who suddenly become commandos and take out all the bad guys. Fighting within the ranks of the drug runners leads to some action too. But the film doesn't have the slightly dippy, almost surreal feel of *Hell Squad*. The gals become commandos simply because they get handed guns. It's fun to watch but none of the fashion models are the big stars. So the film has the feel of the director using the stars all he can but then discovering that there is an ending looming and he doesn't have the stars quite as much as he'd like. He piles on the fashion models who weren't all that interesting in the first place. It's nice to have some action but it feels a little strange.

Jungle Warriors is not a very good film. But it does have jungle in it. They don't rip the viewer off there. It also has some Gortner. That's always worth some time.

The Last Ninja

Director: William A. Graham
Screenplay: Ed Spielman
Producer: Anthony Spinner
Cast: Michael Beck (Kenjiro Sakura), Anny Kwan (Noriko Sakura), John McMartin (Mr. Cosmo), Mako (Aitaro Sakura), Richard Lynch (Dr. Gustav Norden)

The Last Ninja is one of the few made-for-TV movies in this book. It's the story of Sakura, an art dealer who may be a super white ninja. Mr. Cosmo tries to convince Sakura to help free some hostages in a high-rise building that have been taken prisoner by a group of international terrorists led by the scary Richard Lynch. It looks like it was a pilot for a show that never went to series. Too bad; it might have been an interesting series. It doesn't have the full-on crazy ninja action of a Sho Kosugi film or *Ninja Mission*; it's calmer and more thoughtful, with rounds of kick-ass thrown in.

Sakura is trained by his adoptive father in Japan how to be an ninja. If this were made one year later, *The Karate Kid* would be a definite influence. As it stands, it's just using the standard martial arts master-student scenes. And Mako is a very entertaining teacher.

As the film progresses, and Sakura goes to the building to save the day, the flashback sequences match up with the scenes we're seeing; for example, when Sakura falls from the side of the building, it is intercut with young Sakura learning about hanging from stuff and gaining upper arm strength. It's an interesting idea. One wonders if episodes of the show would have done the same sort of thing. (The TV series *Psych* shows scenes from its heroes' childhoods that relate to the episode). The intercutting with the hostages keeps the tension up because Lynch always looks like he's going to jump off the screen and punch the viewer in the mouth.

The Last Ninja is a pretty entertaining variation of the ninja movies from that era. Its action is well shot. The camera is always in the right spot. The actors are uniformly strong. It's recommended.

Metalstorm: The Destruction of Jared-Syn

Director: Charles Band

Screenplay: Alan J. Adler

Producers: Alan J. Adler, Charles Band

Cast: Jeffrey Byron (Dogen), Tim Thomerson (Rhodes), Mike Preston (Jared-Syn), Kelly Preston (Dhyanna), R. David Smith (Baal)

A sci-fi epic from the folks at Empire Pictures—and in 3-D.

Set on a desert world named Lemuria, *Metalstorm: The Destruction of Jared-Syn* is about a good guy named Dogen trying to catch a bad guy named Jared-Syn. Dogen meets up with the rascally Rhodes, the lovely Dhyanna—and Richard Moll as Hurok (in the first of Moll's shaven-headed roles).

This movie starts off strong with a lot of *Road Warrior*–esque vehicles and some sort of sky bike flying around. Tim Thomerson shows up and that's generally a sign that something fun will happen. But then there's a lot of talk of soul stones and the One-Eyed civilization and a lot of areas that one must keep out of and a lot of names that, frankly,

got rather silly. At least Dhyanna is pronounced *Diana*. It's only when one sees the spelling that they groan.⁻

Somewhere within the film, director Charles Band and his friends do the thing that would blight *The Phantom Menace* several years down the line. *Metalstorm* has too many dumb sci-fi names, too many vague sci-fi concepts and too much story. Not enough plot. The movie should have kept the story simple: galactic cop hunting for bad guy. But it gets out of hand. And there's so much that needs explaining. When it should have focused on the joy of throwing 3-D junk around, it instead spends a lot of time explaining the rules of nomads fighting. And talking about the soul stones...

It seems to be setting things up for a series of films (the ending certainly is) that never happened. So one learns a lot, a *lot*, about this world and its people and its customs and the movie never gets down to the brass tacks of just having fun and bringing up the action.

Mission Thunderbolt

Director, Screenplay: Godfrey Ho
Producers: Joseph Lai, Betty Chan
Cast: Jonathan Stierwald, Chan Wai Man, Steve Daw, Chan Kun Tai, Summer Dora, Tina Matchett, Philip Ko, John Ladalski

There are two gangs here, the Scorpions and the Serpents. Someone is causing trouble between them. A trio of people are killing off gang members. An Interpol agent is after someone called the Panther. At one point, in a club, the band sings Toni Basil's "Mickey," which is awesome. One of the assassins, a lovely blonde, uses razors. A lot. She jabs a bunch of blades into the top of one guy's head, which looks really painful. A crazy one from the Ho-Lai estate. *Mission Thunderbolt's* got a lot of great action and that's cool. It's also got semi-coherence, which is cool too.

This one has more craziness in the plot than some of the others. The Phoenix, the Panther, the Scorpions, the Serpents, Hercules, the this, the that. A woman gets dragged around in a lobster trap. And my heart goes with it.

The Interpol guys have boring conversations about nothing in particular. A naked woman hangs out in a sauna. She's sweaty!

A review of a film like this might end up as nothing but a description of the plot. That's not necessarily a bad thing. Sometimes the loopiness can make a viewer gasp over and over. There's a bit in a junkyard (I *think* it's a junkyard) that is pretty fine. So the film does have moments that are actually like—wow, this is good. Then the film throws in some of the goofy dubbing that we all love and steals music from somewhere that it shouldn't. The use of Pink Floyd in these movies (not necessarily this one) presumably precludes these coming out on beautiful DVD sets. So we are stuck with what we can see on VHS. This subgenre within a subgenre makes life better.

Mission Thunderbolt succeeds in having the most coherent title of all of these films. It actually makes sense, although there should probably be a colon in between the words. One wonders about the moviemakers' grasp of the English language. I like to think that the English dubbing artists, who already seem to be having a great time, named these things and made them as lusciously loopy as possible. So many movies, so little time.

Prisoners of the Lost Universe

Director: Terry Marcel
Screenplay: Terry Marcel, Harry Robertson
Producer: Harry Robertson
Cast: Richard Hatch (Dan), Kay Lenz (Carrie), John Saxon (Kleel), Peter O'Farrell (Malachi), Ray Charleson (The Greenman), Dan Abraham (Shareen), Kenneth Handel (Dr. Hartmann)

Dr. Hartmann has invented some sort of technological device that sends him, news reporter Carrie and regular guy Dan to the Lost Universe, a post-apocalyptic, *Conan the Barbarian*–style world ruled over by the evil Kleel. There are more kicks to the crotch, *boing!* noises and goofy green guys than are found in a lot of other Lost Universes. It's almost a parody world, sort of like from the TV show *Wizards and Warriors*. Kleel, as played by John Saxon, is sufficiently jerky. Dan and Carrie make a fun couple. Throw in a thief named Malachi and a couple of hot broads and you've got a decent afternoon's entertainment.

Prisoners of the Lost Universe is the much calmer version of the sort of *Road Warrior–Conan* rip-offs that one normally finds around here. It was made for cable television and so it has the 1983 TV limitations (quick shooting schedules and limited budgets). It seems like it's a bit more about having fun and goofing around than others. I wouldn't call this a parody. "A sci-fi romp" would be more appropriate. And it's not what one might call an "action" film. It's more of an "adventure" film from a bygone era, throwing in some moments of comedy. More ambition would have been a definite plus, especially as it was made for cable. You'd think the early 1980s cable networks would have gone for a more gung-ho approach. They don't. So one must adjust his expectations. Or keep the focus on the awesomeness of Richard Moll.

Kleel is a decent villain. But John Saxon plays this type of character in his sleep. He never seems that threatening. A few of the set pieces are fun, like Dan's fight with the really big guy with metal nuts. The dead returning to life and attacking is great. But the end just sort of occurs. Actually, the beginning is like that too. It just sort of happens. A couple of characters appear, they get thrown together and suddenly they are in the Lost Universe.

Prisoners of the Lost Universe is fun but it's not essential. Regardless of how many green men they had. Regardless of how many low-growly speeches John Saxon gives. And regardless of how much Richard Hatch they include.

Raiders of Atlantis aka The Atlantis Interceptors

Director: Ruggero Deadato
Screenplay: Robert Gold, Vincent Marino
Producer: Regency Productions
Cast: Christopher Connelly (Mike Ross),

Tony King (Washington), Ivan Rassimov (Bill Cook), Gioia Scola (Dr. Cathy Rollins)

Non-stop shooting. Rows of people with their bodies jerking and falling to the ground. Followed by 15 minutes of sci-fi *Raiders*-style excitement and then it's all over. That is *Raiders of Atlantis*. Ruggero Deadato, director of *Cannibal Holocaust*, doesn't do things by half measures. When a group of mercenaries and some scientists go to an island populated by Atlanteans with guns who want to take over the world, shooting happens a lot. It begins early in the film and never stops.

That's not necessarily a bad thing. Shooting the hell out of people is something that Italian action films of the 1980s really became expert at. Throw in the pseudo–sci-fi element and there before the viewer is a film filled with almost everything an action film lover could want. Except it does become a little tiresome.

Mike and Washington (aka Mohammed) are the two main guys. No-nonsense Vietnam vets who shoot more people in this movie than the Allied forces did in World War II. Deadato presents the Atlanteans almost in the style of *The Warriors* here, which means the film is a bit of everything that was percolating around at that time. That makes it fun. Whether or not the viewer gets a bit worn out by the constant shooting is a personal preference. *The Bronx Warriors* has an absolutely amazing amount of shooting but looking at Trash is fun. This one almost lost me.

Every once in a while, a bit of an emotional attachment can be a nice thing. Other times, turn off the mind and let the crazy begin. Deodato faked the viewer out with the overwhelming intensity of *Cannibal Holocaust*. This one is just about fun. If one were to replace the bullets with pies, this would be a comedy classic. Mercenaries shoot people until a strange, almost *Logan's Run*–esque group of aliens arrive, and then the movie enters the realm of Indiana Jones. Can you pay homage to everything in one film? Deodato really pulls out all the stops.

Action with no redeeming qualities beyond the shooting of people and crazy violence. It's something to get behind.

Rescue Team

Director: Jun Gallardo
Screenplay: Don Gordon Bell, Carl Kuntze
Producer: Silver Star Film Company
Cast: Richard Harrison (Burton), Romano Kristoff, Don Gordon Bell, James Gaines, Michael James, Carol Roberts

In *Rescue Team*, a bunch of soldiers led by the mighty Burton (Richard Harrison) are sent into the jungle to rescue an officer named Coleman. Burton's ragtag bunch is very similar to a lot of other ragtag bunches I've encountered. The Burton character is pretty funny. He drinks a lot, especially while bowling, and he says a lot of great stuff. As he's with a naked woman, he says "Mmm, you smell so good … and you taste good too." Now, maybe that's not terribly funny but the way he is dubbed is. It's very matter-of-fact. A scene where he gives a list of swear words to a Vietnamese soldier is also pretty great.

The film is standard Filipino action of the time, which means it's semi-crazy, overwrought, hilariously dubbed and features that one kind of large older guy who is in many of these films. (He is the one who gets kidnapped in *For Y'ur Height Only*.) In this film, he is dubbed with a pretty entertaining voice. It sounds like someone is occasionally running their finger across his lips as he talks. It's great.

For Burton and his team (Larry Greene, Harry Thomas, William Rogers, Franco Mancini), things don't go smoothly. They shoot a lot of people. But the best stuff in this is Harrison when his character is drinking and when they go to one of those great dance clubs that always seem to pop up in these films. There are a lot of booby traps in the film and at the club there are variations of booby traps, if you get my meaning.

From bowling to disco to jungle shootouts (no cockfighting!), *Rescue Team* does everything a film like this normally does, no better, no worse. It is almost a comforting film in that Harrison isn't going to let you down. He's not that kind of guy. He's more fun when he's fighting with ninjas but it's tough to argue with the silliness of this film. The ending, which almost comes out of nowhere, is quite good. And the film ends on a freeze frame which is either genius or some sort of error

CANNON INTERNATIONAL
presents

Rescue Team
™

RICHARD HARRISON

ROMANO KRISTOFF   DON GORDON BELL
CAROL ROBERTS   JAMES GAINES
MICHAEL JAMES   MIKE COHEN   MIKE MONTI
TONY McQUEEN

Music by PATRICK WALES   Story & Screenplay by CARL KUNTZE & DON GORDON
Directed by JOHN GALE

©MCMLXXXIV CANNON INTERNATIONAL

or there was something wrong with my VHS tape. It's tough to tell sometimes.

Revenge of the Ninja

Director: Sam Firstenberg
Screenplay: James R. Silke
Producers: Menahem Golan, Yoran Globus
Cast: Sho Kosugi (Cho Osaki), Keith Vitali (Dave Hatcher), Virgil Frey (Lt. Dine), Arthur Roberts (Braden), Mario Gallo (Caifano), Grace Ferrare (Cathy), Kane Kosugi (Kane)

Ninjas are not all evil. Cho Osaki says this near the beginning of *Revenge of the Ninja,* and he's right. Ninjas can get a pretty bad rap. Cho is played by Sho Kosugi (credited as Black Ninja), star of *Enter the Ninja.* This film is sort of a follow-up to that one.

When Cho's family is massacred by ninjas, he leaves Japan with his good American friend Braden. Cho brings along his mom and his son Kane, both of whom have some pretty kick-ass martial arts skills. Cho and Braden open a gallery that will deal in Japanese art. Braden is teamed up with a mobster named Califano. The art will contain heroin. And things won't get better from here. Mobsters shoot and fight. A rogue ninja starts killing mobsters. Cho ends up in the middle of all of it.

The film begins with the massacre in Japan. Lots of innocent people are killed by ninjas before Cho and Braden kick their asses. The setting shifts to America and, for 20 or 25 minutes, the plot builds up. Then the fighting begins. Almost the entire second half is fight after fight, or a buildup to a fight. Hell, even Mom and little Kane get a fight!

Any time you see director Sam Firstenberg's name in the credits, you know that the fighting will be good. And in *Revenge of the Ninja,* it is. From a knockdown drag-out fight in an alley that spills out onto the road to a playground brawl to the final rooftop Good Ninja vs. Bad Ninja tussle, they are exciting and well-put together. The actors are fine. No one really stands out too much. The little kid is fun. Sho is fine, but a little stiff.

This film is never too far from a rousing bit of action. Take a deep breath and get ready to immerse yourself. The boys at Cannon refuse to let the viewer down. It's not in their nature. This film has all the ninja action a viewer could want. Good ninja-filled action. That's something to look forward to.

Rush aka *Blood Rush*

Director, Screenplay: Anthony Richmond
Producer: Marcello Romeo
Cast: Conrad Nichols (Rush), Laura

Trotter (Carol), Rita Furlan (Lorna), Brigit Pelz, Richard Pizzati (Steel)

Welcome back to the post-apocalyptic Earth. This time all the vegetation is gone. A man named Rush is protecting the remaining piece of vegetation on Earth. Unlike most of the Earth's inhabitants, he is not contaminated with radiation. He is a good man, alone, out there doing his thing. Then a jerk named Yor and a bunch of other people catch him and make him a slave. Rush works with a bunch of other slaves, including a nice gal named Carol. Eventually there is rebellion and a lot of shooting. It's goofy and it's semi-incoherent but it is, in fact, a *rush*.

Like the other post-apocalyptic Italian action films, *Rush* has got a lot of excitement and some strange twists and turns. It has a bit of originality (the vegetation storyline) alongside moments that are shameless rip-offs of other films. But *Rush* somehow feels a little less chintzy than the others. The action feels a little bigger. Maybe the fact that so much of it makes little sense had my mind reeling. Tough to say. Regardless, this is a fun one.

It gets tough to differentiate some of these films after a while. The same actors show up over and over. They're dubbed by the same people. Most of them look like they were shot in the same area. With such a limited number of locations, it's tougher to differentiate these films. Post-apocalyptic rip-off is post-apocalyptic rip-off. There's not much to set them apart. But *Rush* comes at us with solid action and those weird moments.

Rush writer-director Anthony Richmond tells a story that has been told before and makes it worth watching. And the action is strong. No reason to be ashamed of putting this one in a triple feature alongside some of the other greats from this genre.

Stryker

Director, Producer: Cirio H. Santiago
Screenplay: Howard Cohen
Cast: Steve Sandor (Stryker), Andria Savo (Delha), William Ostrander (Bandit), Michael Lane (Karvis)

Water is power.

Everyone can agree that *The Road Warrior* is an awesome film. Especially Cirio H. Santiago and Howard Cohen, who made *Stryker*. All the *Road Warrior* elements are here. The loner with a bit of an attitude. The crazy-looking bad guys. The nice people who want to live.

It is post-apocalypse. It hasn't rained in a very long time. All the bad guys seem to be after a woman named Delha, who has more water than everyone else. Where is it coming from? Stryker joins the fray with his friend Bandit to protect Delha. The issue of the water becomes bigger. The evil, hook-handed Karvis gets involved. Eventually all is made clear but not before a lot of fighting and a lot of pygmy gibberish is heard.

Like a lot of the *Road Warrior* rip-offs, this one doesn't have the epic scale. But *Stryker* is fun. It's got good action. A nasty bad guy, Karvis, with a group of jerks who follow him around being nasty as well. Stryker is cool. He's even got a backstory with Karvis that means Stryker is going to have to kill Karvis in the end. One of the big plusses of this movie is that it's only about 82 minutes long. It comes in, does its business and is gone before the viewer can wonder if there's another post-apocalyptic film they could be watching.

My favorite element of the movie is the music. There's piano, synths and drums with the occasional bit of electric guitar looping around. Stryker's theme is particularly striking with the piano playing an incessant beat as the drums pound behind it. Then, during the opening action scenes, the synths are laid on super-thick—the sort of synths one would hear in a mid–'70s horror film like *The Redeemer* or *The Child*. It feels futuristic, which I really like. There are sequences where the drums just play and play. At one point, it's presented as "Everyone getting into their vehicles" music and it's quite charming. Then that theme appears again at the end and makes the viewer smile. This is a great score, one worth hearing outside of the context of the film.

There's lots of action in *Stryker* from top

to bottom. There may be better ways to spend 82 minutes but none quite as fun. Santiago made a no-nonsense actioner that is good for anyone, like this reviewer, who enjoys seeing what the future of mankind will be like. (Hint: It begins with a mushroom cloud.)

Thor the Conqueror

Director: Tonino Ricci
Screenplay: Tito Carpi
Producers: Roberto Poggi, Marcello Romeo
Cast: Conrad Nichols (aka Bruno Minniti) (Thor), Maria Romano (Ina), Christopher Holm (Etna), Malisa Longo (Slave Girl), Raf Baldassarre (Gnut)

Thor the Conqueror begins as it will go along: kind of stupid. In the opening sequences, a bunch of people in prehistoric UGG boots fight each other randomly. As this happens, a deep voice intones, "In the Age of Someone at the Dawn of Something, some guy who is son of somebody will give birth to Thor the Conqueror!" or something like that. (There's a guy named Gnut. I remember that.) My eyes glazed over and then my mind went hazy. In fact, it went so hazy that in the next scene, when a man is attacked and killed by a bunch of strange-looking fellows, I thought, "Oh no, they killed Thor!" But I think they killed his dad. I think. From that point on, luckily, it's just a series of Thor-related adventures with his Magic Owl Man buddy.

The first big adventure is fighting a bunch of cannibals and rescuing a woman. She's not the sharpest knife in the drawer but neither is Thor. What advice does the Owl Man have for Thor regarding ladies? "Make her lie down and play with her. What else is she good for?" Things don't go well with him and the lady. More adventure awaits.

There are strange, bouncing images of skeletons and ghoul faces in a cave. And virgin warriors, a group of women who don't fight that well and wear wicker baskets on their heads. The look is not without its charms. Thor even gets a virgin warrior to wander along with him for a while. But what will happen when he enters the Land of the Unknown? And where exactly is Gnut hiding?

Thor the Conqueror wallows in its own stupidity. That's not bad. It can be annoying, the misogyny is not a thrill but these were different times. (Actually I'm not sure what time this is set in.) From its ridiculous hero to an awful cannibal tribe to the bombastic score that goes epic when there's nothing epic happening on screen, the movie is 90 percent good, ten percent bad. Most of the ten percent is that asshat Owl Man narrator but he comes and goes.

The Throne of Fire

Director: Franco Prosperi
Screenplay: Giuseppe Buricchi, Nino Marino
Producer: Ettore Spagnuolo
Cast: Sabrina Siani (Princess Valkari), Pietro Torrisi (Siegfried), Harrison Muller (Morak/Belial), Beni Cardoso (Azira)

The Throne of Fire is a *Conan* rip-off from Italy. Elements of it add up to early 1980s excitement—elements such as the synth score and Sabrina Siani, for example. The film itself feels more like a peplum from the late 1950s. It has a bit less gore and violence. There's no sex, apart from some smooching and the opening impregnation bit but that's handled tastefully. And the film has that meandering feel that many of the older peplum have. Not to put the film down, however. It has its charms.

Belial (basically, Satan) rapes a woman in order to sire his offspring Morak. Morak (who looks like Belial) is destined to sit on the Throne of Fire, which actually sets people on fire if they're not supposed to sit on it. Morak must kill the king and marry Princess Valkari. Then he sits on the throne and takes over the world! A young man, Siegfried, is destined to stop him. A series of fights and captures and escapes, with a side visit to the Well of Madness, ensue. Sabrina Siani spends the movie in a sort of loincloth bikini thing, which should reaffirm anyone's faith in humanity.

Morak is a great villain. Early on, talking to his mother, his voice is dubbed in an odd sing-song fashion that seems amusing in a snide Bond villain way (but is probably unintentional). His mother says, "You will kill the king and marry the princess." Morak repeats that in a bouncy sort of manner. Then she says something like, "You will have to kill women and children, babies." "I will kill women and children." The dubbing is alternately hilarious and a bit chilling because he does all these terrible things. The best moment is when his mother says that he must sit on the Throne before "The Day of the Night in the Day." Morak replies, very quickly and incredulously, "The Day of the Night in the Day?"

In true B-movie hero fashion, Siegfried and the princess are less interesting. There is a section where Siegfried becomes invincible, like Siegfried from Wagner's "Ring Cycle." That's cool. But then the movie doesn't allow him much time to enjoy the power before Morak stops him. That's too bad.

The princess kicks ass and looks great doing it. The story runs in circles. She is captured and Morak demands she marry him. Siegfried arrives and he is captured. He is thrown in the Well of Madness where he becomes invincible. Then he frees the princess … and they get captured again. They escape and plan a big offensive with a neighboring village … but they get captured again. There's a possibility that the film just had the one castle location and couldn't go too far away. It does make the structure a bit repetitive but Morak is evil enough to carry you through.

Thunder Warrior aka *Thunder*

Director, Producer: Fabrizio De Angelis
Screenplay: Fabrizio De Angelis, Dardano Sacchetti
Cast: Mark Gregory (Thunder), Bo Svenson (Sheriff Cook), Raymond Harmstorf (Deputy Henson), Valeria Ross (Sheila), Antonio Sabato (Thomas)

In Arizona, Navajo warrior Thunder returns to town after a period of absence. Very quickly, the law gets in his way. The bank puts up funds to excavate a sacred Native American burial ground. Some hick construction workers beat the crap out of Thunder

and leave him for dead in the desert. Now Thunder is pissed. But since he is played by Mark Gregory, his "pissed" face looks like his other faces.

Thunder Warrior is sort of a *First Blood* variation with a Native American warrior hunted by tons of white guys. Almost all the white guys are jerks. They kill an old Indian gentleman and kidnap Sheila, Thunder's gal— and almost sexually assault her. But Thunder has it under control. He can punch with the best of them. Hide like a chameleon. He is one hell of an expert with the bow and arrow. The sheriff (Bo Svenson) and his jerks don't stand a chance.

The film begins very quickly. Within 15 minutes, Thunder has no recourse but to fight back. Unfortunately, the film hasn't yet fully explained who Thunder is or what he was doing before the movie started or why he acts as he does. The assumption is that he is protecting his tribe. That is all that is needed. Very few white people here are worth anything. From the sheriff to the construction workers to a random lady who mutters, "Why don't they stay on their reservations?," the racist angle of the movie kicks in fast. With a film like, the viewer wants to see crackers shot up … and fast.

I like Mark Gregory. His inability to show an emotion is not that much of a liability when he's trying to be stoic, as he is here. But the film introduces a reporter and a local radio DJ who are on Thunder's side. Their goal is to "make him a hero." (In fact, there's a closing moment with two little kids playing cowboys and Indians. The white boy who is playing Thunder yells, "Thunder will never die!") But the whole Make Him a Hero thing is done too casually and kind of ineptly. It seems like lip service.

The film does two odd things in its second half. When the manhunt begins in earnest and the reporter starts his vague crusade, Thunder vanishes from the film for about 15 minutes. At first, it seems like suspense building but then one wonders where the heck the hero went. The other thing is, the deputy, one of the two most heinous people in the film, is shot with arrows in the arm. The last time the viewer sees him, he's practicing his shooting. And that's it. He gets no real comeuppance.

Thunder Warrior brings up issues of race and equality and heritage. But really doesn't give a crap. It simply wants to ape *First Blood* and, possibly because it's Italian, uses the Native Americans and their culture so casually and strangely that the film almost becomes surreal.

Treasure of the Four Crowns

Director: Ferdinando Baldi

Screenplay: Lloyd Battista, Tony Anthony

Producers: Tony Anthony, Gene Quintano

Cast: Tony Anthony (Striker), Ana Obregon, Gene Quintano, Jerry Lazarus, Francisco Rabal

Several cinematic threads combine and entangle here:

(1) Everybody loved *Raiders of the Lost Ark*. That meant lots and lots of rip-offs.

(2) Around 1982, 3-D came back into the world of films.

(3) Tony Anthony and Gene Quintano struck it big with *Comin at Ya!*

Comin' at Ya! was a 3-D Western that was about throwing all kinds of junk in the faces of audience members wearing cardboard glasses. The film did quite well, so Anthony and Quintano decided to make another 3-D extravaganza. The rather crazy *Treasure of the Four Crowns* used a bit of *Raiders of the Lost Ark* mixed with a heist film.

Anthony plays fortune hunter Striker, a man of adventure hired to break into a strange cult's castle and steal two of the four crowns. The power of the Treasure related to the Four Crowns is immeasurable and mystical and as weird as everything else in this strange movie. It begins

with Striker engaged in a 20-minute-long extension of the opening scene in *Raiders*. Striker avoids everything Indiana Jones did, plus some crazy dogs and two giant flaming balls. The sequence exists solely to throw stuff at the audience. The fact that it goes on and on and on, never taking a break from throwing objects in the viewer's faces, makes it audaciously wild.

Then for 40 or 45 minutes, Striker learns about the crowns, the cult and assembles his team of motley (rather drunk) misfits-experts to help him get the treasure. This segment of the film continues to throw stuff in faces. There's a sequence with the Key to the Crown.

TREASURE OF THE FOUR CROWNS

It flashes and flies all around the room. The whole film seems to have been made with no regard to anything but what can be waved at the camera.

The final half-hour is the group breaking into the fortress, and things get crazier. Lots of flailing and waving things around. When the crowns' power is activated, shit gets really weird. There is a face-melting scene (*a la Raiders*) that goes on for ages. The man's face melts and falls apart endlessly. Striker's head spins around about ten times. Those are just two of the 100 nutty things that happen in the last reel.

The 3-D format is rarely used as gleefully as it is here. Setting aside all sense of taste or decorum, the makers of *Treasure of the Four Crowns* gave the world one of the goofiest, zaniest and "most 3-D" of all 3-D movies. The filmmakers don't care if wires are visible or something clearly looks fake. Not important! Wave it at the camera and get ready to watch everyone duck out of the way.

Yor, the Hunter from the Future

Director: Antonio Margheriti

Screenplay: Robert D. Bailey, Antonio Margheriti

Producer: Michele Marsala

Cast: Reb Brown (Yor), Corinne Clery (Ka-Lan), John Steiner (Overlord), Carole Andre (Ena), Luciano Pigozzi (Dag)

Yor, the Hunter from the Future starts with the kick-ass theme song "Yor's World." It's very European, which fits the very Italian nature of the film. Reminiscent of "Flash's Theme"

from *Flash Gordon,* it has an epic feel to it with a big rousing chorus that has many voices singing at once. But it's missing Freddie Mercury's flair and it's missing the big Brian May guitar tone. But it's fun and feels a little dumb. That sums up this movie perfectly. Antonio Margheriti strikes again with another odd number that seems to float right outside of the area where humanity is able to make sense of things.

Yor is played by Reb Brown, who is A-1 tops over in this neighborhood. This is his most naked role that I know of. Yor is an Conan-esque blond tough guy who wanders

He is from a future world. Trapped in prehistoric times. Searching for his past.

A hunter of incredible power and strength.

In his quest for his origin, he and the woman he loves must fight hostile tribes. Battle deadly beasts. And try to survive the violent forces of a newly born Earth.

YOR
The Hunter from the Future

around with a gal named Ka-Lan and a guy named Dag. They get into skirmishes with all sorts of strange Conan-type monsters. There are dinosaurs and albino-ish guys. Yor meets a woman and falls in love with her and then she's dead in a few minutes. Yor is captured by a post-apocalyptic guy called the Overlord, and Yor turns out to be the…

I will stop there. Suffice it to say, in the last half-hour of the film, it shifts into a post-apocalyptic adventure. In fact, the whole film has an odd epic feel to it. It shifts from event to event like many of these films. But it doesn't move *towards* anything. Conan has a quest. Ator has quests. But Yor just kind of does his business and suddenly becomes part of a bigger epic. There's a reason for this.

Apparently, *Yor, the Hunter from the Future* was edited from a much larger Italian miniseries. In that form, the film makes more sense. The plot thread with the woman that Yor falls in love with, before she promptly dies, seems odd. One imagines that this may have been an episode edited down. Yor might have met this woman at the start and then lost her in the end. The encounter with the post-apocalyptic society may have been the ending of the penultimate episode. A cliffhanger that changed the whole direction of the series.

Well, it makes some sense. Or it makes more sense of a movie which is well-meaning and pretty entertaining. As it's Italian, Reb is dubbed. So there's no odd shrieking and his big smiles look strange when the voice is not there. But Margheriti shoots a decent action scene and he made a great miniseries (probably). And that miniseries became a film that is, frankly, silly but not without its charms.

Young Warriors

Director: L.D. Foldes
Screenplay: L.D. Foldes, Russell W. Colgin
Producers: Russel W. Colgin, L.D. Foldes, Victoria Paige Meyerink
Cast: Ernest Borgnine (Lt. Bob Corrigan), Richard Roundtree (Sgt. John Austin), Lynda Day George (Beverly Corrigan), James Van Patten (Kevin Corrigan), Anne Lockhart (Lucy)

Tone problems galore. That might be the problem with the entire oeuvre of Lawrence D. Foldes. *Don't Go Near the Park* slips from gory horror to TV movie dramatics to themes of incest all set to music that would have followed Cannon around throughout the 1970s. *The Great Skycopter Rescue* seems like a light-hearted romp until one woman is violently beaten and another is taken to the side of a burger joint for some sort of activity that involves evil.

Young Warriors starts off like an after-school special from the Underworld. A bunch of cool guys graduate from high school in Malibu. When they're in college Kevin's sister is sexually assaulted and killed. The cops don't accomplish much. So Kevin and his friends become vigilantes who travel with a toy poodle. The film starts with endless screwing around in bars and libraries and lots of leering at young women. Then it gradually becomes darker and more unpleasant, until there is no hero and it's all so ambiguous that one wishes it was a little shorter than its 104 minutes.

In this film and some of Foldes' others, there seems to be an attitude towards women verging on "they are slabs of sexy meat." Linnea Quigley pops up for ogling purposes. There's nudity and a lot of leering. It's strange to watch a film about a young man trying to avenge his sister's violent rape and murder that pretty much treats all the women as meat. There's sort of a Boys Only feel to a lot of this movie, which leaves an odd aftertaste. It feels like a personal attitude that becomes part of the film, infecting it.

And what's with that poodle? Yes, it is funny watching vigilantes driving around with a white poodle in between them. But did anyone really think that the poodle would live? It's brought along so it can get killed. Why bring it in the first place? Are toy poodles known for their hunting and fighting abilities?

Young Warriors' action has a strange nastiness to it. The Malibu rich boy vigilantes take out the bad guys with no problem. But it all feels like some sort of wish fulfillment. And not always good wish fulfillment.

1984

Highest grossing films in the U.S.
1. *Beverly Hills Cop*
2. *Ghostbusters*
3. *Indiana Jones and the Temple of Doom*
4. *Gremlins*
5. *The Karate Kid*
6. *Police Academy*

Highest rated TV shows in the U.S.
1. *Dynasty*
2. *Dallas*
3. *The Cosby Show*
4. *60 Minutes*
5. *Family Ties*

Big historical events
PG-13 created in response to *Gremlins* and *Indiana Jones and the Temple of Doom*
Indira Gandhi is killed
Los Angeles Summer Olympics

Action movies
Beverly Hills Cop, Indiana Jones and the Temple of Doom, The Karate Kid, Romancing the Stone, Red Dawn, The Terminator, Conan the Destroyer, Missing in Action, Supergirl

Ator 2: The Blade Master

Director, Screenplay: Joe D'Amato
Producer: John Newman
Cast: Miles O'Keeffe (Ator), Lisa Foster (Mila), Charles Borromel (Akronos), David Brandon (Zor)

The Geometric Nucleus is nothing to screw around with. It's powerful and it's shiny. And evil Zor, with his bird-like hat and fantastic facial hair, is after it. Akronos, the man who created the Nucleus, sends his daughter Mila for some assistance. She is to bring Ator and his assistant Thong. They must protect the nucleus. Lucky for everyone, Ator is as buff and smart and beautifully coiffed as ever.

The first *Ator* was a lot like every other sword-and-sorcery movie that flowed out in the wake of *Conan*. In general, it felt a bit pat, going through the motions. *Blade Master* is more about one tough guy getting in a lot of sword fights with assorted bands of bad guys. Then fighting a giant snake and building the world's first hang glider. It's one of those sequels, like *The Godfather: Part II*, that is able to improve upon the original because the initial exposition, the origin story as it were, is out of the way. In the Land of Ator, the origin story is ripped off from someone else's origin so having that behind us is a good thing.

As in *Ator*, Joe D'Amato brings the same sort of energy to action scenes mixed with an odd laziness to the whole adventure. A fight scene begins with mad men dressed as samurai-kabuki dancers. The tension is high. The excitement builds. And then D'Amato shoots the scene in a style that is never terribly exciting. It never grabs the viewer downstairs and whips him around the room. Action scenes require a special skill. Just because D'Amato makes them, doesn't mean he's great at them. *Blade Master* has a ton of fight scenes of all varieties so, although they're not great, at least they're numerous.

Zor is a very funny-looking villain. Ator's hair is a mile high. That's a combination of evil vs. good right there. Both villain and hero are both kind of ponderous guys. Zor has the slinky almost effeminate nature of many of the low-budget baddies. Ator is proud and strong and likes to pontificate when given half a chance. He's the perfect all-around warrior.

Bruce's Fist of Vengeance

Director: Bill James
Screenplay: Bugsy Dabao, Bill James
Producer: K.Y. Lim
Cast: Bruce Le (Peter), Romano Kristoff (Miguel), Jack Lee (Jack), Manny Luna, Eve Wong, Carla Reynolds (Miriam)

Jack has a book of Bruce Lee's karate secrets. He goes to Hong Kong to fight in a tournament with his friend Peter. Jack and Peter's girlfriend Miriam are kidnapped by a bunch of jackasses who want the book. Peter beats up a lot of people to get his friends back and protect the book. He also goes to see a cockfight. Possibly several cockfights. Welcome, *Bruce's Fist of Vengeance,* to the hallowed halls of Brucesploitation.

By 1984, this subgenre should have been at an end. In Hong Kong, filmmakers John Woo, Jackie Chan and Tsui Hark were re-imagining what action films could do. Then this film appeared. There are big pictures of Bruce Lee everywhere. There's some film footage of him. There's Bruce Le up to the same old shenanigans. As the film goes along, it becomes more like *Challenge of the Tiger* and a little less reverential to Lee. But there's always his ghost hanging over the production, making it feel exactly like the exploitation film it is.

Le is fine, but still not much of an actor. He gives the fighting his all. At one point, as he's putting on pants, he uses his behind to take an attacker down. The final fight in a fountain is knockdown, drag-out … but it's a little dull. By that point, the energy has waned a bit. There is also a bit of a problem with the direction. On more than one occasion, a punch or kick misses (but

it gets a sound effect, as though it had connected). That's some bad direction there. One must learn where to place the camera.

Then there's the cockfighting. Peter takes Miriam there, and the camera sits on the ground as two roosters tear each other up. There is even some slo-mo. People cheer and cheer. Bets are placed. Peter and Miriam have a lot of fun. And it's all pretty grotesque. Most

of these films that revel in their cockfighting show a bunch of grubby spectators, usually in an alley or warehouse or something, but *Bruce's Fist of Vengeance* takes us right into an epic stadium filled with people watching two enraged roosters ripping at each other. The movie was going okay up until that point.

The dubbing might all be done by the same three people, regardless of how many characters there are. I'm not over the moon about this movie.

The Courier of Death

Director, Producer: Tom Shaw
Screenplay: Ron Schmidt

THE COURIER OF DEATH
Starring JOEY JOHNSON with BARBARA GARRISON   JOHN BENNETH   DIANA BAUER
REBECCA STEELE   LEO GOSSEN and JAMES JAMESON as the Colonel
Produced and Directed by TOM SHAW   Screenplay by RONALD SCHMIDT
Story by TOM SHAW

Cast: Joey Johnson (Joey), Mel Fletcher (Carver), Diana Bauer (Nancy Neuberger), Joan Beckerich (Julie Blackman)

The Courier of Death feels like a labor of love from Mr. Tom Shaw. A man with a dream to make a kick-ass action film about an Army vet who has settled down and become a courier. But it's the sort of courier work that involves a lot of shooting and people dying. A bunch of thugs working for an even nastier thug announces that the guys are transporting $76 million. That's a lot of freaking money for two guys to carry around. It doesn't matter if they wind up in Portland, Oregon (where much of the movie was shot), which is supposed to be a nice place to live. Never send two guys in a regular van to deliver $76 million.

Joey saves the money but loses his best friend and humiliates the mob guys. So, they kidnap and kill his wife. Revenge! It's going to be one of those sorts of movies. Except it's not quite. Soon after the revenge plotline begins, Joey is contacted by an Army sergeant who convinces our hero to go after a gang led by a mob guy. Then plotlines begin to get lost. People get shot and it can be tough to remember why they're being shot. Joey spends a bunch of time hunting for a guy who I couldn't place. The person that seemed to be the big bad mob guy might actually be someone else. And it might all tie in with the revenge plotline. Ladies and gentleman, this reviewer got a little lost. And he loved it.

The Courier of Death made me think of the slasher film *Graduation Day*. The slasher genre has rather strict tropes, but *Graduation Day* keeps wandering off. The person that one thinks will be the Final Girl vanishes for almost all the killings. Characters like the principal and his secretary take up long portions of the film, but, they have nothing to do with the slasher plotline. *The Courier of Death* does a similar thing with action, except it keeps the main character. Story-wise, it keeps moving from one area to another. Action Couriers! Revenge! Mob stuff! Revenge (?)! Mob stuff!

When a movie's intentions are tough to pin down and yet it satisfies all the qualifications of its genre, then it's a success. And remember: A confusing success is still a success.

Deadly Impact

Director, Producer: Fabrizio De Angelis

Screenplay: Dardano Sacchetti, Fabrizio De Angelis

Cast: Bo Svenson (George Ryan), Fred Williamson (Lou), Marcia Clingan (Kathy Heller), John Morghen (Al), Vincent Conte (Kurt)

In Las Vegas, a couple set up an elaborate scam to bilk the slot machines out of tons of money. But some vicious thugs, Al and Kurt, get wind of this and want the loot. Car chases ensue. Sometimes they become helicopter chases. Officer George Ryan and his pal Lou go after Al and Kurt in a movie that has a definite "buddy picture" vibe. But not quite, as Fred Williamson sort of vanishes from the film for long stretches. However, Bo Svenson holds strong on his end and director Fabrizio De Angelis pulls out all the stops with the action.

The action is a bit sporadic but when it does begin, they are the sort of chase sequences that go on for half an hour and remain entertaining. Yes, it takes some time to get to the first chase. There is a lot of set-up with the couple and their ill-gotten winnings. Then time spent with Al and Kurt. Then George and Lou get involved in their first car chase and things pick up.

I want to say that the car chases may have been modeled on Richard Rush's *Freebie and the Bean*. They don't have the sort of immediate visceral impact but they are kind of crazy. On more than one occasion, a car flies through the air an incredible distance in slow motion and it's funny. And it's great. The first car chase goes on and on and it's good. It ends up with them chasing the perp across a roof.

Deadly Impact has some character development. It gives Bo a back story. Fred's character doesn't have much but he shows up and is cool. Even the bad guys are given some sort of attempts at development. They cook up

some clever plots to kill George and Lou and everyone stays on their toes. The film spaces the action sequences very well. There is another chase just at the point where you're starting to think "I could use another chase right about now." There's one that makes the viewer think, "Did they have permission to just go wild throughout the streets of Phoenix? This is crazy." It all ends with a big helicopter chase, flying through downtown Phoenix and ending up in the desert.

I can't say that *Deadly Impact* is a great movie but, action-wise, it's got a lot of it and it's all pretty darn exciting. Throw in Fred and Bo and it's even more fun.

Death Raiders

Director: Segundo Ramos
Screenplay: Larry Dolgin
Producer: Emperor Films International, Inc.
Cast: Johnny Wilson, George Pallance, George Regan, Ramon Zamora, Robert Lee, June Ariston

In the Philippines, a man named Karamat kidnaps a governor and his daughter and a bunch of others. A team called the Death Raiders is assembled and sent after them. The film is filled with lots and lots of shooting and shooting. There is the occasional kung fu fight and fistfight interspersed but, mostly, it's about the shooting. And Karamat arguing with his son, which is a little dull.

Death Raiders is a very serious film about this group of Special Operation guys going into the countryside on their mission. Except when it's a little silly, like in the disco scene and the scene set in the brothel. One can enjoy watching an old man in his tighty whities running down the hall away from the Raiders. It makes for a strange tone in the film because the humor is intentional. (Or it seems that way.) But that's mixed in with lots of violence and all the attempted rapes. I was surprised that there wasn't a cockfight thrown in but you can't have it all.

The film has great action. The Death Raiders are a sharp bunch. They've got it under control. Even when they stop to fool

around with ladies, the action is strong. But some of the side stuff isn't as hot. Karamat's son is not thrilled with what his dad is doing, all that kidnapping and such. Dad even whips the boy in public. In the end, Son and Mom help out the Death Raiders. None of that is very interesting, especially when intercut with shooting, running through caves and discotheque scenes. They should stick do what they do best. All that shooting.

Death Raiders has the usual gang of goofball dubbing artists. It's always interesting to hear their voices. No matter where one goes in the world during this era, there are those same voices. I don't know who they are, but they are friends to me.

I don't know if all *Death Raiders* prints are like this but in the one I watched, the Death Raiders are saving the day and suddenly, abruptly, the film just ends. It's a little odd. But, hey, better to end on a high note than to leave everyone wishing that your movie would be over with.

The Dungeonmaster aka Ragewar

Directors: Dave Allen, Charles Band, John Carl Buechler, Steven Ford, Peter Manoogian, Ted Nicolaou, Rosemarie Turko
Screenplay: Allen Actor, Dave Allen, Charles Band, John Carl Buechler, Jeffrey Byron, Peter Manoogian, Ted Nicolaou, Rosemarie Turko
Producer: Charles Band
Cast: Jeffrey Byron (Paul Bradford), Leslie Wing (Gwen), Richard Moll (Mestema) X-CaliBR8 is X-CaliGREAT!

Ragewar (my favorite title) is a not-quite-anthology film from the realm of Charles Band's Empire Pictures. It's about a man named Paul Bradford who is pulled into another dimension to face off against Mestema, who is also the Devil. Mestema is very impressed by Paul's use of computers, especially a semi-artificial intelligent thing called Cal. Mestema holds Paul's girlfriend Gwen captive and declares that Paul must accept seven challenges.

Each challenge scene has a different director, although they generally don't look all that different from one another. But they are vastly entertaining and the segments in caves feature more fake rocks, frozen or otherwise, than you've ever seen before. And that includes any and all episodes of *Doctor Who*. Plus, Richard Moll is Mestema. He has hair and he is cool as hell.

The seven challenges and what they feature are as follows:

- Ice Gallery! Paul and Gwen fight the Frozen Dead! Including Jack the Ripper!
- Demons of the Dead! Paul fights undead soldiers and meets a demon named Ratspit!
- Heavy Metal! Paul fights the band W.A.S.P. at a concert! Blackie Lawless = scariest part of the movie.
- Stone Canyon Giant! David Allen's great stop-motion animation brings a giant to life!
- Slasher! A mini-slasher where Paul has one hour to save Gwen!
- Cave Beast! There's a beast! In a cave! Not all is as it seems…
- Desert Pursuit! Mad Max! With Paul and Gwen!

Imagine a TV show like *Knight Rider* or *Automan*. Take seven or eight episodes of a show like that and smash them down into a 78-minute film, where the last six minutes are credits. Add an unrelated opening pre-credit bit with a naked lady and zombies. Now include Blackie Lawless. Well, that's *The Dungeonmaster*. An extremely entertaining anthology film that gives the viewer everything they could want from this sort of film. (Not all sections are action-related.) Empire Pictures was a lot more interesting than Full Moon.

The Executioner Part II

Director: James Bryan
Screenplay, Producer: Renee Harmon
Cast: Chris Mitchum (Roger), Antoine John Mottet (Mike), Renee Harmon (Celia Anhurst), Aldo Ray (Police Commissioner), Bianca Phillipi (Laura)

Confession: I love the films of James Bryan. Whether I'm watching his early, very odd sex films like *The Dirtiest Game in the World* or the comedy of *Boogie Vision* or the hilarious insanity of one of my all-time favorites *Don't Go in the Woods*, Bryan's sensibility is one I really enjoy. His strange sense of humor permeates all of his films. The sort of humor that makes the viewer pause and wonder if the filmmaker is fooling around or is in on it. Bryan is in on it. His films may be very low-budget and the budget may hamper certain elements *of* these films, but he's got his own style and it's always visible.

Now team Bryan with German-born Renee Harmon, who has her own very distinct style (not to mention a very thick accent), and you've got the Laurel and Hardy of low-budget exploitation pictures. *Lady Streetfighter* may be the epitome of their collaboration. *The Executioner Part II* has a plot that gets a little over-complicated with too many characters, odd sound editing and varying volume levels, action scenes that are kind of awkward and throwaway lines that will make you laugh out loud. Renee produces, writes and co-stars in this film as a TV reporter. Bryan directs it all like a mad god high up in the Hollywood Hills.

In Los Angeles, crime is rampant. Gangs roam the streets. Drug pushers reign supreme. The police commissioner is useless. There is only one good cop, played by Chris Mitchum. His daughter Laura, with the help of a very funny friend, is getting into drugs and prostitution. A TV reporter is nosing into everyone's business. But there is hope: The Executioner, a Vietnam vet who has gone vigilante and likes dropping hand grenades down people's pants. The underworld is frightened. The police are embarrassed. The cop's daughter just wants some cash for coke.

The sound design is unusual. No room tone. Abnormal pauses between sentences. A gun that, when fired, says the word "Bang!" instead of making a gunshot sound. And, as mentioned, the volume is all over the place. The viewer never knows when a scene begins, what exactly the sound is going to do. That's exciting. Throw in some library music that appeared in Bill Rebane's *Invasion from Inner Earth* and you have an amazing curiosity of an action film from two great exploitation filmmakers.

This is a film that, even when it's slow, keeps things happening. The very long fist-fights are reminiscent of brawls in the 1960s *Batman* TV show (without on-screen sound effect words like BAM!) because people just punch and punch and there's no sign of who is winning until the fight is over. Then, whoever Destiny chose to win has won. All hand grenade explosions are rendered by the same stock footage that changes the aspect ratio on the VHS tape. Aldo Ray appears briefly in mismatched close-ups that seem to go out of their way to prove that he is not with the other actors. It all ends in a strange free-for-all with swords and explosions and the Executioner being nuttier than ever.

This motion picture is a pure example of Insane Cinema, a film that you can't imagine actual people making but they did. I met James Bryan. He's very nice. If none of this is enticement for viewing, there is one obvious moment that may pull a reticent viewer in: Where is *The Executioner*, the original? At first, I thought this film was meant to be a fake sequel to *The Exterminator*. But it is actually a sequel to the Sam Wannamaker film *The Executioner* from 1970 starring George Peppard. It's true. James Bryan says so on the DVD.

Exterminator 2

Director: Mark Buntzman
Screenplay: Mark Buntzman, William Sachs
Producer: William Sachs
Cast: Robert Ginty (John Eastland), Deborah Geffner (Caroline), Frankie Faison, Mario Van Peebles (X)

John Eastland, the man with the flame thrower, is back! This time he's souped up a garbage truck with guns and armor. A strange gang led by X (Mario Van Peebles) kills John's girlfriend (after crippling her) and John's best friend. What can John do but exterminate? There's also some Italian mob guys with drugs. But, mainly this is a lot like the first *Exterminator,* just a little more out of control.

Robert Ginty is back and he looks kind of odd here. The big cheeks of *Warrior of the Lost World* are not around yet. He looks slightly aloof from the proceedings. But the power of Peebles (X) keeps it real. It's a very idiosyncratic gang he has. Sort of taken from *The Warriors.* The scene where they kill the man on the subway tracks while carrying torches is some sort of beautiful scene of trash art. The other characters are there to fill in the blanks in a vigilante movie. This is really X vs. the Exterminator. And only one man will survive!

In "The Exterminator" he made the streets of New York safe. All has been quiet...until now!

THE CANNON GROUP, INC. presents ROBERT GINTY in a GOLAN-GLOBUS / MARK BUNTZMAN film EXTERMINATOR 2 • DEBORAH GEFFNER • FRANKIE FAISON and MARIO VAN PEEBLES as "X" Executive Producers MENAHEM GOLAN and YORAM GLOBUS Music by DAVID SPEAR Edited by BOB BALDWIN Produced by MARK BUNTZMAN and WILLIAM SACHS Written by MARK BUNTZMAN and WILLIAM SACHS Directed by MARK BUNTZMAN

CANNON RELEASING CORPORATION   R   EXTERMINATOR 2

Exterminator 2 is very entertaining. It's not as sleazy as the first film. It kind of lightens up a bit. It throws in some breakdancing and a scene with a man on roller skates dancing around. It has a score (synth-heavy) that is alternately moody, wonderful and sometimes silly, as if all this wasn't being taken as seriously as the first film. But most of it works. The action scenes are great. The killer garbage truck is awesome. Whenever Eastland dons that helmet and puts on the flame thrower, it kicks ass. It still seems like an overly violent way to kill but it is really quite satisfying.

This book is not condoning vigilantism with a flame thrower. Merely stating that it looks cool.

The cops are not an element in this film. They pop up now and again, but the main focus is the Exterminator against this gang. They're a more interesting gang then the one in *Death Wish 3*. A scene where a couple walk down the sidewalk and a gang member roller skates by, grabs her and disappears down an alley happens so fast and unexpectedly that it's sort of silently brilliant. Why haven't other films thought of that?

The thought of there being an *Exterminator 3* is a fun one. But R. Ginty died of cancer in 2009, so that won't happen. They might remake it but they probably shouldn't. The saga of one of the finest rip-off vigilantes draws to a close. In the final shot, John sets down his fire equipment and walks towards a bright light. The symbolism has been noted.

The Final Executioner

Director: Romolo Guerrieri
Screenplay: Roberto Leoni
Producer: Lucia Appignani
Cast: Harrison Muller (Erasmus), Marina Costa (Edra), William Mang (Alan Tanner), Woody Strode (Sam)

The Final Executioner meshes post-apocalyptic shenanigans from 100 other films with a bit of *The Most Dangerous Game* alongside *The Running Man* and *Endgame*. After 90 or so minutes, there is some passable action mixed in with a few odd moments that are al-most par for the course for Italian rip-offs like this.

After the apocalypse, there are two groups: the wealthy who were unaffected and everyone else who are mutated by radiation. (But the movie doesn't really show this. The wealthy dress like characters from *The Road Warrior*. All of the extras seem to have a wardrobe that makes you suspect the wardrobe people telling them to "bring their own clothes.") The wealthy play a game, which they call "The Hunt": They hunt down anyone who isn't wealthy.

They've dressed "the wealthy" like the crazy people from other films of this sort. So it took some time for it to sink in that these were the ones with the money. The one time we see the Hunt, it involves a bunch of extras running through a quarry getting shot. It's not much of a hunt. Yes, one of the hunters, Erasmus, uses a sword. But everyone else sits some distance away and shoots. There's no urgency. Even when they rape and kill a woman and then hunt her husband Alan, there's no urgency.

Alan escapes, trains with Woody Strode and returns for revenge … still no urgency. It's just one event after another and the whole thing kind of goes on until a demand for understanding in the end that feels as contrived as using sexual assault as a plot point. Which is something that one gets really tired of seeing, by the way, as these films go on. Whenever one of these Italian films has a violent sexual assault in it, there's never any feeling at all with it. It's just a cliché being used (like a prologue in a slasher film set years before the body of the film) to move one plot point on to the next. But they're using rape to forward their plot. Not a classy idea. To add confusion, the Wealthy have a mind machine that puts thought on screen. One jackass turns on the machine and thinks about the rape for five minutes so we get to see it over and over. Got it! They are decadent and sleazy! The point was made some time ago.

This is a completely average film with occasional shining moments of action but nothing else. It completely fails to create the world that it says exists in its opening minutes.

Final Mission

Director: Cirio H. Santiago

Screenplay: Joseph Zucchero, J.M. Avelcana

Cast: Richard Young (Deacon), Christine L. Tudor, John Dresden, Jason Ross, Kaz Garas

Deacon is a tough cop. He was a tough Marine. Fighting in Vietnam. He makes an enemy of a fellow soldier in Laos. In 1984 Los Angeles, it comes back to haunt him. His wife and son are killed. Deacon heads to a nearby small town to find the killer. But first he has to face the sheriff, a ton of thugs and, almost out of nowhere, tons of soldiers. When will it end? And does this really need to be his ... *Final Mission?*

Cirio H. Santiago strikes again with his mostly high-octane style of action. Not a lot of finesse. Not a lot of high-tension excitement that pulls the viewer in and carries them to another plane. But solid storytelling (derivative but solid) and good action make the film worth a watch. Deacon is a bit of an ass but

once they kill his family, you're on his side. The sheriff (who is the bad guy's brother) gets to bypass some standard stereotyping and not be a full-on jerk. He loves his brother but he knows his brother has done wrong. However, he will protect his brother.

Final Mission is like all the Santiago films: entertaining but never overwhelmingly so. And, of course, there are boobs. Lots of women getting their boobs out. Even when it doesn't seem terribly essential to the plot, the boob count stays high here. It seems like all the standard Santiago elements are mixed together into a fragrant pot here. With two added elements:

(1) The music. I'm not sure I've ever heard a more empathic film score. And that's counting any film that John Williams has ever scored and all the films from the 1990s that had blazing techno-industrial scores. (Plus, *Scream for Help.*) The orchestra rises up high and makes all the action scenes rousing and brilliant, except when they're not. Then they

end up looking overdone, which happens on more than one occasion. The music is so loud and over-the-top that it must have been a conscious decision. Then there's the theme song, "Always on My Mind"—not the Willie Nelson song. This one is straight from the Foreigner playbook and it's cool. It pops up several times.

(2) The ending. Deacon is on the hunt for a while, then *he* becomes the hunted and the film becomes a *First Blood* variant. The final 15 minutes involve Deacon on a hill with weaponry shooting waves of soldiers coming at him. The very ending is either a big copout or the perfect ending for this type of film. (Think a variation of *Deadly Prey*'s ending.) The film is good but that ending is fantastic.

Final Mission is solid. It has a lot of action (including a cool chase along some bridges). And it has a decent plotline. Nothing spectacular but definitely fun.

Furious

Directors, Screenplay, Producers: Tim Evritt, Thomas Sartori

Cast: Simon Rhee (Simon), Arlene Montano (Kim Lee), Howard Jackson (Howard), Phillip Rhee (Master Chan), Mika Elkan (The Sorcerer), Bob Folkard (Mongol Leader), Jon Dane (Dale), Joyce Tilley (Donna), John Potter (Doug)

Things to clue a viewer into how awesome and how weird *Furious* is going to be:

(1) The Mongol Leader in the opening scene is played by someone who screams "Canuck!"

(2) The Mongol Leader's war cry is the Mackenzie's Brothers theme from SCTV.

(3) The lead guy has three friends he fights with. Their names are Dale, Donna and Doug.

(4) A sorcerer shoots chickens from his hands.

(5) The tagline of the movie is "Karate heroes fight aliens for control of the astral plane!"

No shit. *Furious* is awesome. As the credits roll, a man's hands do tricks with tarot cards. Then a helicopter shot over vast, rolling hills as Mongol warriors chase a woman with a magic spinning tusk. The woman, Kim Lee, is killed. Her brother Simon wants to avenge her. With the help of Master Chan, Simon goes on a journey and encounters a lot of people. He's joined by his Three D friends and fighting breaks out all over. There's a weird New Wave band playing in a room. Lots of guys with dark glasses in white jumpsuits hang around. Voices speak to Simon in echoes and whispers. Then that damn sorcerer starts shooting chickens from his hands. It makes no sense and that's all right with me. In the end, it is all something about aliens; a pig makes an appearance in a heartbreaking scene. (Sort of.)

Simon Rhee is one of the best-known Hollywood stunt performers and has been for decades. He's charming in this movie. Possibly a bit too stoic for his own good. But he definitely knows how to fight. Many of the fight scenes are actually quite good. Unfortunately, the camera isn't always in the right spot so the fights aren't always as exciting as they should be. Plus, there are a lot of fights. The last half hour is mainly one big series of fights. And the movie is only 71 minutes long.

There are a lot of random chickens in the movie. This is not the place for spoilers. But the use of the chickens does make some sort of sense in the end. *Furious* relies more on images and movement and fighting and constant classical music than anything else.

Hell Riders

Director: James Bryan

Screenplay: James Bryan, Renee Harmon

Producer: Renee Harmon

Cast: Adam West (Dr. Dave), Tina Louise (Claire), Renee Harmon (Knife), Russ Alexander (Snake)

The makers of *The Executioner Part II* are back with another round of violence and strange human behavior. This film is set in a ghost town where people spend a lot of time hanging out at a diner. A group of crazy bikers, the Hell Riders, arrive and havoc ensues. Tina Louise plays a Las Vegas prostitute and Adam West plays the local doctor. So not only does the viewer get another dose of Harmon-Bryan goodness but West and Louise have joined the fray.

Hell Riders isn't as immediately crazy-looking as past Harmon-Bryan collaborations. There is sync sound. There are actors who are recognizable and (unlike, say, Aldo Ray) seem to be incorporated into the movie. The weirdness of this movie sneaks up on the viewer. It sneaked up on me; I had to watch it three times before I got it. This film is akin to Renee Harmon's shot-on-video *Night of Terror*: It looks like a regular, sort of bland shot-on-video from the mid–80s, but things get crazier as it goes along. *Hell Riders* starts crazy. It just sort of looks normal.

The thing that made me giggle throughout is the diner in the ghost town. People hang out and chat. The sheriff stops by. Everyone knows one another. They talk about work, etc. But it's a ghost town. They live on a single Old West street, *a la* every cheap Western (and some not-so-cheap). They live, in effect, on a set. But they act like they're hanging out at a small town diner. People mention that it's a ghost town but no one acts that way. The juxtaposition of these two elements make for strangeness in all of these scenes that is never really addressed. It just is.

The bikers are alternately threatening and very silly. When they get a chance, sexual assault seems to be a favorite pastime. However, they also goof around when they get to the diner. One of them actually turns to the camera and tips his hat to us. Then there is Knife (played by Harmon). She almost always come across like she's acting. There's a glorious self-consciousness about her that is even more accentuated with her thick accent and strange behavior as a Hell Riders member.

The action is more energetic than in previous Bryan-Harmon films. That doesn't necessarily mean that it's better. But there's a lot more stunt work and a lot more action. Here and there it all bogs down because there's no real plot, just a bunch of bikers threatening people. They leave the ghost town. Then they come back and threaten some more. They

might be the most incompetent biker gang around. But they seem like they're having a good time being rude and gross. There's a preacher guy with a naked woman on a leash.

Hell Riders gets better on repeated viewings. It's no Bryan-Harmon classic but, it's got that wonky, off-kilter charm that all their films have. As if the inhabitants of Venus have been sending us their VHS tapes.

The Last Mercenary aka *Rolf*

Director, Screenplay: Marlon Sirko
Producer: Metheus Films
Cast: Tony Marsina (Rolf), Kelly Nicols (Joana), Tony Raccosta, Louis Walser

Rolf was once a mercenary with a group of real jerks who destroyed an African village. That event has left scars all over Rolf. He has more heart-to-heart talks with his girlfriend and gets close to tears more often than any mercenary in cinema history. When his mercenary pals come to him demanding he fly some drugs around for them, Rolf says no. Things go bad. For a while this film becomes *First Blood* but it never really settles on one film.

Rolf is kind of gross and rather sleazy. It's also filled with a lot of action and a Rambo-style sequence where our "hero" goes after his mercenary friends after they go after his woman. (Sexual assault as entertainment and used as the basis for revenge became a tiresome, lazy trope after a while.)

The movie starts with Rolf being harassed by police (and includes a very long flashback where Little Rolf watches his mom die from an overdose). The police hassle Rolf. Shit is involved (literally). Then the mercenaries show and the film becomes something else for a while. Kudos to the casting department for coming up with a batch of the ugliest, sleaziest guys around! Rolf kicks some ass and hangs from a cliff for a while. Although the Rambo portion feels like it should be the end, there's still another 10 to 15 minutes of movie.

Rolf feels like it was made by a bunch of filmmakers who had a template to follow but kept sleazing off to one side or another. They couldn't limit themselves to one path for their movie. It makes the movie schizophrenic and it feels a bit longer than it is. But it also makes for the sort of movie that one can return to (when in a sleazy mood).

Because *Rolf* seems to be doing its own thing, it sticks in the memory a bit longer than some of the other films of this sort. Having never been a mercenary, I can't speak to whether or not this is the sort of thing that happens to mercenaries on a regular basis. One tries to lead a better life but keeps seeing flashbacks to a massacre that one was a part of. And this film has a real weird scene when the mercenaries are tearing apart the African village.

One of them calls for target practice. So they begin throwing an African child into the air and shooting him, like skeet shooting. He goes up. Pow! Pow! He comes down. He goes up. Pow! Pow! Back down. Who came up with this idea? And is he in prison? Luckily, Rolf puts a stop to it. It's one more thing he'll end up crying about. But that's our Rolf.

Malibu Express

Director, Screenplay, Producer: Andy Sidaris

Cast: Darby Hinton (Cody Abilene), Sybil Danning (Contessa Luciana), Art Metrano (Matthew), Shelley Taylor Morgan (Anita Chamberlain), Brett Clark (Shane), Niki Dantine (Lady Lillian Chamberlain), Lynda Wiesmeier (June Khnockers)

This is the first of 12 films Andy Sidaris sent to the world of video. Films filled with action, explosions, hunky guys, beautiful women, gunplay, strange plot turns and some of *the* most convoluted set-ups in the world of action. Films also loaded with playful references to themselves. Films loaded with so much innuendo that Benny Hill might have requested they be toned down a touch. They are a little ponderous, here and there, a little too obvious at times, but they are films that are, at their base, simply fun. Not something you'd show Grandma (unless she's a bit pervy), but great for an evening with friends or if you're just feeling down.

Malibu Express also holds the distinction of being the naughtiest episode of *Magnum P.I.* ever.

The star is Darby Hinton, playing private detective and playboy Cody Abilene. Cody lives on a yacht, the *Malibu Express*, and he has a glorious mustache which makes him the alternate version of Tom Selleck. The one who doesn't mind showing you his ass or putting a bunch of large boobs in his face. But this movie is an elaborate (possibly overelaborate) mystery. Cody doesn't quite have the charm of a Selleck and the movie is pitched as an erotic detective journey. It's also a Class A hoot.

There are more beautiful women in this movie than can be reasonably counted. (Literally. I have a notebook here where I got up to eight and gave up.) Cody is of the thinner buff variety and there are several really big, beefy guys. Then you get Art Metrano, right before playing Mauser in the *Police Academy* films. He may not be hunky but he's not without his charms. Then, you get Sybil Danning at her most overwhelming. Mr. Sidaris knows how to stack them.

The plot is (and this would be much more pronounced in later films) alternately very straightforward and way too complicated. The constant flow of lovely naked bodies always very clearly expresses what's going on. A chauffeur videotapes dalliances with everyone in the mansion where Cody is investigating. That's straightforward. Sybil Danning's character is after some government secrets. But, then the plotlines begin to accumulate. Scene after scene introduces new characters and new situations until, when you think about it, the whole thing seems crazy. Next we meet the Huffingtons, a crazy trio who keep forcing Cody to drag race them. Then there's the transvestite husband of one of the women at the mansion. And because it's a mystery at heart, it can't resolve everything until the end.

The end provides a good time: a big car chase and shootout, followed by Cody assembling everyone on his yacht to reveal the killer of the chauffeur, which was actually a minor point in the film but that's not a complaint. The killer reveal doesn't quite resolve everything but it is the point where the movie ends. It's a good point because the one problem with the film is all the plot stopping and starting means that there's absolutely no pace to it. Sidaris would correct that as his series of films went on. But this one feels like a bunch of isolated incidents that last for 101 minutes. Some with shooting, some with a character called June Khnockers (she has large breasts). If the viewer can get lost in the world of the film, it's not really a problem. But it means that the film feels much longer than it is.

If one, however, takes this film as an all-inclusive action–T&A extravaganza, then it doesn't really matter how long it feels like it takes because it has almost everything.

The Manhunt

Director, Screenplay, Producer: Fabrizio De Angelis (as Larry Ludman)

Cast: Ethan Wayne, Ernest Borgnine, Bo Svenson, Henry Silva

In this movie, Ethan Wayne (John Wayne's son) plays a character who could be related to Dusty Farlow on *Dallas*: a lonely guy wandering the prairies. He comes up against trouble and that trouble has three names: Ernest Borgnine, Henry Silva and Bo Svenson. Start running, boy.

Ethan has two lovely horses. He stops at a watering hole … but it's Borgnine's watering hole and trouble ensues. Ethan is accused of stealing the horses. He cannot provide a receipt. Within minutes of screen time, he's in a maximum facility prison doing a year and a half. And all he wants to do is find the guy who sold him the horses. He's treated awfully in prison, so what can he do but break out and go after justice? If he gets caught again, he'll break out again for more justice.

The Manhunt is as slightly askew as almost everything with Fabrizio De Angelis's name on it. The film begins with a horse race that doesn't seem to tie in with the remainder of the film as there are horses but no more horse races. Ethan is a free man wandering around and then he finds himself in prison very quickly. There is an assumption of how powerful Borgnine's ranch owner is without

actually telling the viewer. And there is an assumption that Ethan's character is correct and is being treated badly before we even learn who he is. The movie bypasses the moments of logic and moves directly into the story portion of it and revenge begins!

It's not a bad evening's entertainment if you don't mind going immediately from the opening to the revenge. We don't actually see Ethan before he is wronged so we're never quite sure if he stole the horses or not. But, frankly, it's pretty obvious that he is a good guy who has gotten the short end. The way he launches into Action is a good sign. The first time he does, when Borgnine's men attack him, things go into momentary slo-mo and he throws everyone around. It's great.

This film isn't quite an action film except when our hero fights. Then it is clearly in the land of action. The other actors have a good time. The film itself moves slowly from bit to bit and there's a strange thing it does where Ethan escapes and then gets captured again and then escapes again. Odd structures are a De Angelis trademark. Silva, Borgnine and Svenson are fun and the ending is semi-surprising. Or at least I thought it was.

Ninja Busters

Director: Paul Kyriazi

Screenplay: Sid Campbell

Producer: Carlos Navarro

Cast: Eric Lee (Chic), Sid Campbell (Bernie), Gerald Okamura, Carlos Navarro, Nancy Lee, Frank Navarro

Two doofuses, Chic and Bernie, join a martial arts school after getting beat up by thugs at the wharf warehouse where they work. Their boss is a crook. They want to learn to defend themselves but, mainly, they want to score with chicks. They spend three years at the school becoming masters … and then all hell breaks loose. The bad guys have hired ninjas. Somehow Chic and Bernie and all their pals wind up fighting ninjas and gangsters and other jerks.

The two stars, Eric Lee and Sid Campbell, are karate grandmasters. The film is a goofy comedy, sort of *a la They Call Me Bruce?* but without the comedy stylings of Johnny Yuen. Everyone in the film is charming and is clearly having a good time. But one can write as many jokes as one wants but there is such a thing as comic timing. Lee and Campbell goof around ... a lot ... but rarely are they funny. Some of that is down to Campbell's script. A few of the jokes are older than vaudeville and untrained comic actors can't bring life to them. Some of the jokes may or may not actually be jokes. It's tough to tell as everyone goofs so much.

This means that as an intentional comedy, it never works. People put too much ham into their performances. Plus, there are a lot of people that speak in heavily accented English, some Chinese, some Japanese, some Hispanic ... some a little vaguer. It can be very tough for people who don't speak English well to emote properly. When the dialogue is not the best, it can be very tough. And, pound for pound, *Ninja Busters* has more awkward scenes between people who don't always seem to know what they're saying than any other movie I've seen.

The fighting is pretty exciting. There's no forward momentum to the film. So nothing builds as it goes. The first 45, 50 minutes are training sequences and jokes, including a series of montages that almost overwhelm the film. One montage is fine. Two montages mean there's an error in the storytelling somewhere. Once all this is done and the training has passed, the fighting begins, and there's a lot of it. It's never killer. It's not Bruce Lee or Jackie Chan excitement. But everyone carries themselves well, except for maybe the ninjas who are fairly awful throughout.

Ninja Busters is full of charm and, in its second half, full of fighting. It feels like a bunch of folks who love their karate getting together to make a goofy movie about these two guys making good. It's fairly obvious that Lee and Campbell are clearly very good at fighting, long before the three years are up. (That's another strange point about the film: It jumps ahead three years in about ten minutes. The reason why is semi-funny but it's a jarring leap in time.) There are also too many

characters. It's semi-boring but fun to watch when it works.

Ninja III: The Domination

Director: Sam Firstenberg
Screenplay: James R. Silke
Producers: Menahem Golan, Yoram Globus
Cast: Sho Kosugi (Yamada), Lucinda Dickey (Christie), Jordan Bennett (Secord), Dale Ishimoto (Okuda), James Hong (Miyashima), David Chung (Black Ninja)

If ninjas are such an indestructible force, why do hordes of them always get beaten up in movies? Specifically bad ninjas. Think of all the times an army of ninjas has rushed the good guys and gotten the crap kicked out of them. *Ninja Busters*, anyone? Why is it that only the main bad ninja in any film seems to be decent? Well, *Ninja III: The Domination* gives us a bad ninja who is nigh-on-indestructible. The result: one of the best sustained action sequences in 1980s action cinema.

In the opening reel, a ninja attacks a bunch of golfers. It escalates from some basic fighting to an army of police officers swarming him and he escapes again and again and it keeps building and building. There's no one better to direct it than Sam Firstenberg, who had just done some brilliant work in *Breakin' 2: Electric Boogaloo*. This sequence is superb. From the initial guy the ninja kills to the incredible number of bullets they fire into him at the end ... superb.

Then Lucinda Dickey arrives and she's awesome. She plays a telephone linewoman who gets possessed by the ninja and begins taking care of his old business. When she's not doing that, she teaches aerobics, dances in her apartment, pours V-8 on her chest and listens to Uriah Heep (we don't hear Heep but there's an album of theirs in her collection). Consider this film a mix of *Poltergeist* with *Demon Witch Child* alongside a lot of action and Sho Kosugi.

The *III* in the title creates slight confusion. First there was *Enter the Ninja*. *Revenge of the Ninja* is *II*. Not sure why this was *III*. I remember being confused by that at a young age, and unsuccessfully trying to find the first two. But Cannon Films kind of always did their own thing. And if *Empire of Ash* could be reissued as *Empire of Ash II* with absolutely no changes, then the Ninja Conundrum can be figured out.

During the possession scenes, there are a lot of lasers playing on Lucinda Dickey's face. There is a lot of flying sword action. Then the fight scenes kick in and it becomes another movie, and it's all great. One cannot argue with the mix of every great thing that 1984 had to offer humanity. This is certainly the best of the three ninja movies. It flows better than the other two. It dispenses with the wooden Franco Nero. It takes the ninjas to a supernatural plane just as it opens with that rousing golf course sequence.

My background is horror movies, so anything riffing on supernatural horror and also filled with action and ninjas and Dickey will naturally be the best around. It's my favorite Sho Kosugi film. All the elements combine to make for a perfect good time. *Ninja III* does everything it needs to do, does it well and then kicks your ass again.

The Ninja Mission

Director: Mats Helge
Screenplay: Matthew Jacobs
Producer: Roger Lunden
Cast: Christofer Kohlberg (Mason), Hanna Pola (Nadja), Bo F. Munthe (Hansen), Curt Brober (Markov)

Mason, a Swedish CIA agent, and his band of men are sent into Russia to bring back a research scientist and his daughter so that World War III won't begin. They will gladly break into the nuclear-related facility where the professor is being kept. It should be easy because Mason and his men are ninjas and this is *The Ninja Mission*. The finest ninja movie ever made in Sweden.

Seeing ninjas brawl in the snow is a treat. A lot of times they are in cities, woods, deserts or at pagodas of some sort. Here there is a lot of snow fighting. There is a lot of gunplay. This film is loaded with more shootouts and more car chases than the average ninja film.

The closing action sequence (breaking out the professor) is a hilariously violent shootout in a factory using exploding darts and random sprays of poisonous gas. (In one scene, a man is hit with the gas and vomits inside his gas mask. Not pleasant.) People are blown apart. Bodies pile up. Can the ninja save the day and avert World War III? Probably. They are ninja, after all.

On top of that, the filmmakers made the professor's daughter Nadja a pop singer. She sings a tune in a nightclub while wearing leather pants and a see-through mesh top. The song has the line "Baby, you ran away from me." No way, Nadja. All of us want to stay close. Throw in a bit of political intrigue and you find yourself wishing that there were more Swedish ninja films.

This film is violent, crazy and very, very entertaining. The incongruity of the ninjas in Sweden (and the snow) adds a bit of wonder. Especially because the ninja seen here aren't nearly as articulate in all ways of fighting and weaponry like their Japanese counterparts. They look like decent fighters who happen to be dressed in all black. One wonders if the moviemakers were fully sure what ninjas were. But if the viewer has seen the director's *Hills Have Eyes*–esque *Blood Tracks*, which features a heavy metal band, then you'll know that he doesn't seem to understand what constitutes heavy metal music.

The professor hides the code for some sort of nuclear fission something-or-other in the text of a romantic novel. That's a good idea. But he doesn't know that the Communists (who he thinks are from the UN) have flown him from Russia *back* to Russia, instead of Sweden. The man with the most elaborate code ever has no sense of direction. It's okay, professor. Ninjas are on the way.

The Ninja Mission has action and violence a-plenty plus the occasional contemplative moment that reminds a viewer that this was made in the same country as Ingmar Bergman's films. And it has dubbed voices that range in accent from American to Swedish to English to Australian. It has it all. Thank you, Sweden. Thank you kindly.

Ninja's Force

Directors: Teddy Page, Romano Kristoff
Screenplay: Romano Kristoff, Ken Watanabe

Producer: Regal Films

Cast: Romano Kristoff (Kenzo), Mike Monty, Jeselle Morgan, Ken Watanabe, Gwendolyn Hung

Filmmaker Teddy Page developed across the 1980s. Watch *Ninja's Force* and then watch *Phantom Soldiers*. Both are crazy action films filled with gore, violence and random nudity. Both of them have plotlines that border on the ludicrous. (Actually, *Ninja's Force is* ludicrous.) Both seem to come from another world. But *Phantom Soldiers* has an eeriness and urgency to it. It also has decent character development and several clever moments. *Ninja's Force* is a laugh riot that may make you wet your pants.

A top secret government formula is stolen by ninjas. The government has to go to Japan to get another ninja to kill *those* ninjas and get the formula back or destroy it. They bring in Kenzo, a Japanese ninja played by Romano Kristoff, and he kills a lot of people and beds some lovely ladies. It all ends in a big ninja sword fight with strangely inappropriate slow motion.

Yes, this one is goofy. The dubbing is some of the most hilarious in a genre filled with hilarious dubbing. They play Kenzo as being a very sophisticated, honorable ninja. But he doesn't look that way. It can be tough to stifle the giggles. At the start of the film, several young ladies keep giggling about the ninjas and their dubbing seems like it was done by two (possibly one) woman as she was walking from one end of the studio to the other.

There are lots of fights, including several that are sped up. Kenzo rescues a woman in an alley and takes the first guy down in fast motion, which is either an error or some crazy ninja skill. But, as it causes the person he's fighting to speed up too, it's tough to say. Kenzo has a scene where he is sneaking around a bad guy's living room. He keeps popping up in different spots saying, "I'm over here now" and there's something about the confused bad guy, the voice of Kenzo and his popping up throughout this very 1984 room that is funny.

Ninja's Force is dumb all the way around.

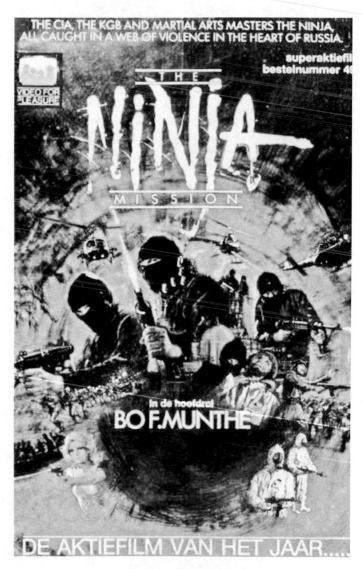

But there's enough good dumb stuff to keep you tuned in. If you know Page's later work, this one might blow your ninja-loving mind.

Raw Courage

> *Director, Producer:* Robert L. Rosen.
> *Screenplay:* Ronny and Mary Cox
> *Cast:* Ronny Cox (Pete), Art Hindle (Roger), M. Emmet Walsh (Col. Crouse), Lois Chiles (Ruth), Tim Maier (Craig)

Three guys, including Ronny Cox, go for a run in the desert, where they are "captured" by a survivalist group led by Col. Crouse. Crouse's group consists of a bunch of folks with guns training for the upcoming Communist invasion. The relationship between three guys just trying to run through the desert and the survivalists does not go well. Roger, one of the runners, is killed. The film becomes about Pete and Craig trying to get out of the desert before this crazy bunch gets to them. It's very well done.

Raw Courage takes place in the desert with its vast vistas and the occasional big hill or mountain. So there aren't a lot of places to hide and it's mighty desolate. The survivalists have vehicles and provisions. The guys are running through the desert. It's sort of a high desert version of *Deliverance.*

There are enough variants in the incidents to keep the film interesting. Some of the runners' activities are interspersed with flashes to their home lives. Pete tends to ignore his family. Craig has an overbearing dad. The flashes end up doing less than what they seem intended for but they're not a bad idea. They give the backstory to the characters, which is nice. It seems like there should be more of a link between what we see happening and the flashes, but there isn't quite.

Raw Courage gets more bloody as it goes along. The two runners are very vulnerable, in their running gear and with very few provisions. The para-military nuts are nutty, ready to go ballistic as soon as the joggers fight back and accidentally kill one of their own. One imagines they'll make a great fighting force.

There was a brief run of survivalist-type movies during the '80s, including one called *The Survivalist*. The Reagan years, the Cold War and the possibility of all-out nuclear war created a pre-apocalyptic cinematic thread. This one goes right-wing military group extreme big-time. The best of these movies was probably Michael Ritchie's *The Survivors* in which Walter Matthau and Robin Williams go nuts in the woods. But Ronny Cox and pals pull off a good one here. *Raw Courage* is exciting and dark and, best of all, intelligently made.

Raw Force

> *Director, Screenplay:* Edward Murphy
> *Producer:* Frank Johnson
> *Cast:* Geoff Binney (Mike), Jillian Kessner (Cookie), John Dresden (Jon), Jennifer Holmes (Ann), Hope Holiday (Hazel), Cameron Mitchell (Capt. Dodds)

One doesn't need to know Edward Murphy to know that he is an awesome human being. I have no idea what else Mr. Murphy did with his life, but he made *Raw Force* and for that, I'd like to invite him to dinner at my house. Its mix of kung fu, cannibal monks, zombies, Cameron Mitchell, naked ladies and action make it one of the wackiest films in this book. It's a genre-hopper that refuses to keep its focus at any point.

Somewhere off the California coast, Warrior Island is populated with monks and zombies. There's a man with a thick German accent and a Hitler mustache. Young women are constantly being brought to the island for unsavory purposes. The Burbank Kung Fu club end up on the island. Cannibal Monks Meet the Burbank Kung Fu Club! Life will never be the same.

The film has quite a bit of action. Long stretches of it are shooting and kung fu and just great violence. But there are also long stretches of wacky comedy with Cameron Mitchell as a sea captain arguing with a woman who conducts a tour. In another part of the movie, Club members go to a strip joint. At other times, everyone just hangs around and talks about life. I wonder if those scenes could have been ad libbed or if they were in the script. Part of my mind says ad lib, but another part really hopes that Mr. Murphy's script is filled with every line spoken here.

The movie does hop the genres. At its heart, it is a crazy kung fu film, but it takes time out for some shooting and some horror moments. There's also a lot of nudity in *Raw Force,* and it's of the lingering variety. No boob goes unleered.

This film is pretty awesome. It teeters right on the border between professional and amateurish. That includes the acting and the fighting. The fact that the heroes are specifically identified as being from Burbank is a joke that I enjoy.

Mr. Murphy, the offer still stands. I want to hear all about Cameron Mitchell, the cannibal monks and all those naked women. I imagine the stories will be kick-ass.

Savage Streets

Director: Danny Steinmann
Screenplay: Danny Steinmann, Norman Yonernoto
Producer: John Strong
Cast: Linda Blair (Brenda), John Vernon (Underwood), Robert Dryer (Jake), Johnny Cenocur (Vince), Linnea Quigley (Heather)

How nasty are the people in *Savage Streets?* Well, one character tells another, "Go fuck an iceberg." The person asked to have sex with the frozen water is a jerk named Jake. Jake is the head of a bunch of thugs who drive around in a convertible. The person who says it to him is John Vernon playing Principal Underwood. This film is hard-boiled when the principal goes at people with lines like that. In fact, everyone in the film is hard-boiled and bad-ass and nasty except for Heather, who is a deaf mute. One gets the feeling that if Heather could hear and speak, she'd be as unpleasant as everyone else.

Welcome to the cinema of Danny Steinmann! Steinmann made two other well-known 1980s films, both horror: *The Unseen* and *Friday the 13th: A New Beginning.* (The closing sequence of *Savage Streets* shows off his horror side with the Relentless Jake attack.) *Unseen* and *New Beginning* are both good films, both misanthropic and rather hateful. The *Friday the 13th* film uses that Steinmann streak to its advantage because Jason is there to kill all these unpleasant people. (It is the film in that franchise that has the largest body count.)

Savage Streets is set in Los Angeles, more or less suburbia. There are Girl Jerks and Guy Jerks. The difference is that, until the end, the Guy Jerks play for keeps. The gals fool around with the guys' car. The guys sexually assault Heather in a rest room at school. Then one of the gals is thrown off a bridge. Brenda (Linda Blair), the head gal, isn't very nice but she's less mean than the guys and eventually she takes revenge.

The film is professionally made. At times it feels like it might become a fun teen film, but then it just becomes nasty. Everyone is unlikable so it's impossible to root for anybody. Two things that bothered me: (1) The gang (apart from one guy) is supposed to stay off the school grounds, but they are there constantly! Doesn't the sight of four "punked-out" guys sitting on the bleachers attract any attention? (2) This movie takes place in one of those worlds where the police don't arrive until everything is done. A gal is thrown off of a bridge in the middle of Los Angeles and there's no one around? Where *is* everyone?

The revenge sequence at the end is satisfying. It would be more so if the viewer liked Brenda but she's as mean as everyone else. And there's the Lopsided Revenge Film problem. Watching the guys be awful for an hour doesn't quite equate to watching them get killed in a few minutes. The balance is off. Only Jake's killing is really satisfying.

The Stabilizer

Director: Arizal
Screenplay: John Rust, Deddy Armand
Producers: Dhamoo, Gobino, Raam Punjabi
Cast: Peter O'Brian (Peter), Craig Gavin (Greg Rainmaker), Gillie Beanz (Sylvia), Harry Capry (Capt. Johnny), Dana Christina (Christina)

When a movie begins with a motorcycle driving through the front window of someone's home, one should sit up and pay attention. When the film is directed by Arizal, director of the awesome *Final Score*, then one should move to the edge of one's seat. And when Peter, the Stabilizer, arrives with his huge mullet and his ability to over-laugh at things, you are off the seat and on the floor. *The Stabilizer* is here. Indonesia will never be the same.

Greg Rainmaker is evil. He is trying to obtain a narcotics detector to help put other big drug dealers out of business. Rainmaker kidnaps Prof. Provost, who has his own narcotics detector. Peter and some other folks, including the professor's daughter Christina,

go after Rainmaker and his endless supply of thugs. Car chases, kung fu fights, free-for-alls, shootouts—this movie has them all. Like Arizal's previous films, it's all about the quantity, the quality isn't so high here. But once the gang climb into a speedboat and get in a semiautomatic shootout with guys on the shore, all bets are off. Focus on the good guys and hope they win the day.

The dubbing is boisterous and silly throughout. Rainmaker is a hilarious mob boss–type guy who seems to kill more of his own guys than the good guys. Peter and his sidekick have a lot of loud laugh moments over things that don't always make much sense. There is a Stabilizer theme song with a violent, pounding drum machine beat that plays over the credits. This song will rock you hard. There are several moments of geek behavior. And not charming (or profitable) *Big Bang Theory* geek behavior.

The Stabilizer is a crazy, fluid film gaily prancing (with violence) from one shootout to the next. The excitement never stops. When it does, there are usually boobs involved.

The Warrior and the Sorceress

Director: John Broderick

Screenplay: John Broderick, William Stout

Producer: Frank K. Isaac, Jr.

Cast: David Carradine (Kain, the Dark One), Maria Socas (Naja the Sorceress), Luke Askew (Zeg the Tyrant), Anthony De Longis (Kief), Harry Townes (Bludge the Prelate), Guillermo Marin (Bal Caz)

The back of Shout! Factory's *Warrior and the Sorceress* DVD has this to say: "Kain (David Carradine) was once an exalted warrior-priest but now wanders the planet Vra as a mercenary sword-for-hire. In the small village of Yam-A-Tar, he finds two vicious clans struggling for power, and he becomes embroiled in the treachery and battles, the mighty wizardry and rampant debauchery." I watched the movie and for some reason about half of that description went completely by me. I thought the film was a post-apocalyptic thing where people had sort of regressed to medieval times.

Well, I went back and re-watched the movie. It is in fact what the blurb says it is as far as planets and villages (although every time I read that paragraph, I think "If I never had to watch another one of these movies with all the silly names, I'd be a happy man"). The film also brings in a bit of *Yojimbo*. Kain gets between the two clans fighting over a well. This planet has two suns and that area only has the one wellspring. Kain begins playing one clan off of the other through chicanery. At some point, he starts working with Naja the sorceress. Naja's big thing is that she wears a small thong and pretty much nothing else for the entire movie. You will get to know Naja's breasts.

The tone of the movie falls somewhere between the first two *Deathstalker* films. It's not a joke film but there are some silly moments. There's a goofy guard. There's the fact that Carradine is playing a character named Kain. (If you've seen *Kung Fu*, you'll know what I mean.) There are a lot of silly masks and goofy people running around. There is an alternately terrifying/ridiculous multi-tentacled monster that I loved. *And* it's got a lot of violence, much of it on the gory side. There is a sequence where Zeg has a woman drowned for sport. Everybody gets blood all over them. Kain strangles a four-breasted woman doing an exotic dance.

I wasn't particularly enamored with it. I found it kind of dull and with no forward motion to the plot. There were some clever moments, some decent performances and some good fighting. Writing about *The Warrior and the Sorceress*, however, makes me want to watch it again. It's kind of a nutty-ass film, buoyed by Carradine's calm performance and the constant nudity of the Sorceress. Some

films are multi-layered. I may be returning to the planet Vra shortly.

Yellow Hair and the Fortress of Gold

Director: Matt Climber
Screenplay: John Kershaw, Matt Climber
Producers: John Ghaffari, Diego Sempre
Cast: Laurene Landon (Yellow Hair), Ken Roberson (Pecos Kid), Cihangir Gaffari (Shayo Teewah), Luis Lorenzo (Col. Torres), Claudia Gray (Grey Cloud)

Yellow Hair is an exotic young woman in Mexico with the Pecos Kid. They are looking for a temple filled with gold, guarded by a group of Indians. The Indians have a habit of dipping people into a lake of molten gold and then pulling their golden heads right off. Yellow wants to learn about her parents, who had something to do with the gold. Pecos, a bit of a rascal, just wants the gold. A crooked colonel with an army of troops are also after the gold.

I'm not sure that I've figured out the cinema of Matt Climber. From *The Black Six* to *The Witch Who Came from the Sea* to *Butterfly,* each time I see one of his films I end up being taken slightly aback. There is talent here, real talent, but to what purpose? *The Black Six* is straight-up good times blaxploitation but it stars NFL players as its tough guys. So the action is never anything other than kind of obvious and the film is constantly drawing attention to itself. *The Witch Who Came from the Sea* is a weird film about a repressed woman, a legend of a witch and some castrations. The tough football guys she attacks seem to be a response to *The Black Six* in some way. *Butterfly* is Pia Zadora at her zenith.

Yellow Hair looks like it should be a fun Indiana Jones rip-off but it's very idiosyncratic. It's filled with action and adventure—bar fights, stagecoach chases, shootouts and other sundries from the action film catalogue. But the film does something odd and endearing although it prevents it from having a proper ending, which it kind of needed. The film begins with a crowd in a theater sitting down to watch this movie. The movie is presented as one chapter in a longer serial. The main characters are all given fun captions that describe them to the crowd and people are heard cheering or hissing. This is all fun.

Then the movie itself becomes more of an old-style Western serial with a bit more violence, T&A and gore than one would expect from the 1930s or 1940s. And the film never provides the thrills that one might hope for from an Indiana Jones–type film. Yellow Hair and the Pecos Kid argue a lot. They've known

each other since childhood so it's more banter but still one hoped that the film would have a bit more kick to it.

Matt Climber tells some strange stories. *Yellow Hair and the Fortress of Gold* is one of them. But this one has fun locations, some interesting characters, some fine action and a general sense of humor about itself. That's all good stuff. This is not one to hunt for (unless one is really interested in Matt Climber) but it's worth watching.

1985

Highest grossing films in the U.S.
1. *Back to the Future*
2. *Rambo: First Blood Part II*
3. *Rocky IV*
4. *The Color Purple*
5. *Out of Africa*

Highest rated TV shows in the U.S.
1. *The Cosby Show*
2. *Family Ties*
3. *Murder, She Wrote*
4. *60 Minutes*
5. *Cheers*

Big historical events
Dynasty's wedding terrorist attack cliffhanger finally beats *Dallas*
Glasnost and Perestroika
New Coke
"We Are The World"
First Internet domain name is registered

Action movies
Rambo, Rocky IV, Jewel of the Nile, Spies Like Us, View to a Kill, Mad Max Beyond Thunderdome, Commando, The Last Dragon, Code of Silence, Year of the Dragon, Invasion U.S.A., Death Wish 3, Remo Williams, Missing in Action 2, Red Sonja

Alien Warrior aka *King of the Streets*
Director: Ed Hunt
Screenplay: Ed Hunt, Rueben Gordon, Steven Schoenbeerg, Barry Pearson

Producers: Ed Hunt, Takox Bentsvi
Cast: Brett Clark, Pamela Saunders, Reggie DeMorton

King of the Streets is a better title than *Alien Warrior*. The protagonist is actually more of an Alien Peacemaker. Sent from his home planet to find and stop a Great Evil, this Alien Warrior comes to Earth. The Great Evil portion of this is all rather vague. He's not specifically after bringing down the world's most evil person. In the opening Earth scenes, he wanders the streets of Los Angeles looking for the Great Evil. Eventually, he finds it in the persona of Mr. 1, a pimped-out gent who sells drugs, keeps some prostitutes and is constantly killing his competition. Alien Warrior meets Mr. 1 and learns that this man, in the sweet car with the sweet ladies, is the self-proclaimed greatest evil. Alien Warrior meets people in the neighborhood and begins to rally them onto the side of good. It all moves towards a final confrontation with Mr. 1 and his minions.

Ed Hunt had previously directed *Bloody Birthday* (a slasher about three killer kids) and *The Brain* (a giant killer brain eats people). He seemed to specialize in genre films with a slight skew to them. *Alien Warrior* is no different. This film brings us a strange alien who appears out of nowhere, defeats the evil and then leaves, which gives the film a disconnected feel. The viewer knows that, although he is saving us from the Great Evil, he's really doing it so he can assume power on his home planet. It's a bit self-serving.

Alien Warrior is very pious, very calm as he spouts his words of wisdom. He clearly feels that he is much better than the humans. He has some magical powers but they're a little sketchy. In the end, he shimmers half-in, half-out of existence in a wonderfully uncomplicated and unexplained way. It just happens. That's how he defeats the Great Evil. He's one of those great alien characters who keeps coming up with life-saving powers and abilities right when he needs them.

Mr. 1 and all the thugs are presented in a very realistic fashion. They shoot groveling minions in toilets. They hang out with topless, drugged out prostitutes. They hurt everybody.

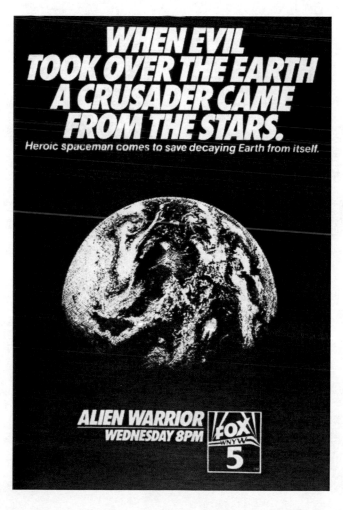

WHEN EVIL TOOK OVER THE EARTH A CRUSADER CAME FROM THE STARS.

Heroic spaceman comes to save decaying Earth from itself.

ALIEN WARRIOR WEDNESDAY 8PM FOX WNYW 5

So the contrast of Tough Thug action mixed with sci-fi otherworldliness is like watching an extra-terrestrial Mickey Rooney announce that we're putting on a big show in the barn as he levitates the animals out and implants lines inside everyone's minds. The dichotomy makes the whole film exist on two different planes, which keep crashing into one another.

Luckily, all of this is fast-paced and well done. If Alien Warrior's piousness took over or if Mr. 1's sleaze overwhelmed, this wouldn't be fun to watch, unless you were in a dark and sleazy mood. Ed Hunt seems to be taking it very seriously. But then Mr. 1 leaps out of his Rolls-Royce dressed only in his underpants and starts shooting people. That's funny! That's the two sides of *Alien Warrior* colliding in a spray of entertainment.

The great David L. Hewitt did the main title design.

American Commandos
aka *Hitman*

Director: Bobby A. Suarez

Screenplay: Ken Metcalfe, Bobby A. Suarez

Producer: Just Betzer

Cast: Chris Mitchum (Dean Mitchell), John Phillip Law (Kelly), Franco Guerrero (Somsak), Robert Marius (Brutus), David Brass (Chandler), Kristine Erlandson (Lisa)

Two things immediately jump to your attention as you start watching *American Commandos*.

(1) There is one funky-ass synth score playing over the opening credits. There is a shot of an American squad from Vietnam. The synths play, sort of doing a 1970s thing. But the player seems to have some troubles and notes seemed to be missed or played wrong.

(2) Chris Mitchum plays a character who goes off to work and has his house attacked. His wife and child are killed, just like in *Final*

Score and possibly other Chris Mitchum films. All I could think was that, in real life, Mitchum must have been continually happy to get home from work and discover his family had not been killed during the day.

Soft Delights is the name of the massage parlor in Thailand where all the guys go before heading into the jungle to destroy the Golden Triangles, the biggest heroin pushers and distributors anywhere.

Mitchell's family is killed by a bunch of jerks high on heroin. At first, Mitchell goes after the local jerks. Eventually, and somehow, he ends up in Asia, with his old commando pals, going after the main gang. Things go from a semi–*Death Wish* vibe to a huge, crazy "Commandos in the Jungle Shooting Tons of Army Guys" adventure.

Chris Mitchum is not the best of actors but he seems game for any craziness that comes along. John Phillip Law doesn't show up for a while but he's always welcome. The action is plentiful and well done. At one point, the commandos (known as the Rat Bastards back in Nam) drive a huge kitted-out truck through the bad guys. It even contains a bulletproof motorcycle that Mitchell rides out of the back. It's awesome.

If you like women, you may not be so thrilled on this film. There's a lot of sexual assault, slapping women around and generally treating them like garbage. This is a real "Guy's Film" and so one should wander in at their own risk. I don't know why they had to keep bringing this element in. But, then I'm not Bobby A. Suarez. He definitely has his own plans for things.

American Commandos is entertaining. It starts off going in on direction and then shifts sharply in another. The second one has that huge building called Soft Delights. I can go for that.

American Ninja

Director: Sam Firstenberg

Screenplay: Gideon Amir, Avi Kleinberger

Producers: Menahem Golan, Yoran Globus

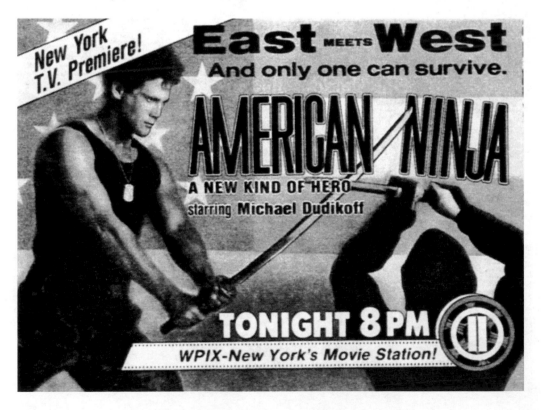

Cast: Michael Dudikoff (Pvt. Joe Armstrong), Judie Aronson (Patricia Hickock), Steve James (Corp. Curtis Jackson), Guich Koock (Col. Hicock), John Fujioka (Shinyuki)

In the first two minutes of *American Ninja*, Michael Dudikoff's Joe refuses to play a game of hacky sack. If that's not enough to get the viewer on his side, ten minutes later he's fighting a phalanx of ninjas to save a hot girl. If that doesn't convince the viewer, then remember that Dudikoff can be called up and sent to individuals' houses to kick individuals' asses. If one doesn't believe in the power of this ninja in America, watch Joe kick ass all throughout this extremely joyous slice of mid–1980s action.

Golan, Globus, Firstenberg, Dudikoff. The Fantastic Four of Action Cinema? Possibly. They gave us this strong, fast-paced, funny and fun movie set in the Philippines. Private Joe is a loner in an Army platoon. He saves the colonel's daughter and they fall for each other. As this romance develops, Joe gradually makes pals with the soldiers. Jackson becomes his BFF. They gradually uncover the smuggling of American weapons by a nasty criminal, his ninja army and a man on the base. All hell breaks loose every 10 to 15 minutes.

Although the fight scenes are as serious as a piano dropping on a dog, *American Ninja* itself is having fun. The scenes with Joe and Patricia are charming in a way that scenes between two good-looking people who have some chemistry always are. There is an officer who always seems to end up getting dumped on. Mixed in with the deadly ninjas and the corrupt Army officials, these scenes gives the film a lighter feel that works to the picture's benefit.

That lighter tone works because the action is good. Dudikoff is very convincing as a ninja. Firstenberg knows how to handle action scenes. There are several in here, including the opening convoy hijack attempt, a brawl in a warehouse and the closing sequence, which are really well-shot, well-edited and exciting.

Joe is given a mysterious background that has points of light poked into it as the viewer learns how this white guy became a ninja. It works nicely because it feels a bit like an origin story trope. But it runs parallel to the story of evil that develops throughout the movie. Sometimes it seems surprising when a low-budget film tells a story well, the way it'd be told in a much larger action film. *American Ninja* works because it keeps humor and humanity balanced with copious amounts of ninjas flipping around and giving hell to other ninjas. Dudikoff is cool and Judie Aronson is hot. Watch this today.

Blackfire

Director: Teddy Page
Screenplay: Teddy Page, James Gaines
Cast: Romano Kristoff (Blackfire), Jim Gaines, Ray Vernal, Anthony Carreon, Charlotte Maine

Blackfire is a *First Blood* rip-off. The movie starts in Vietnam, during the war. A group of crazy American commandos wipe out some Vietcong. Eventually two of them, including our hero, wind up under the command of a weapons smuggler. A woman snoops around, learning things she shouldn't. There are corrupt government officials. There is a lot of very loud library music. (Someone made a lot of great money off of the soundtrack for this film.) But eventually *Blackfire* comes together and makes sense.

Not really. Everyone learns that our main man is Blackfire, a special ops sort of guy. He's tortured by the local government but ends up beating the crap out of all of them. Then, 70 minutes into this 85-minute film, Blackfire straps on the big guns and puts on the headband and it becomes a Rambo knockoff. But a pretty darn amusing one. For around 15 minutes, Blackfire shoots and shoots and shoots everything in sight. He has a big knife that he occasionally uses to slit throats. Mainly, though, he looks like Rambo and shoots every single bad guy who has ever bothered him for, apparently, the entirety of his life. It seems to be very cathartic for him.

Blackfire is an okay film. For the first 70 minutes, it goes along with only an occasional burst of energy. A lot of time is spent on general military protocol in Vietnam, which may be interesting to certain viewers but leaves something to be desired in an action flick.

More so than other rip-offs, this one seems to know where it wants to go but simply takes too long to get there. A film like *Strike Commando 2* shifts and moves between the movies it is ripping off. Many of the post-apocalyptic rip-offs just bide their time from one *Road Warrior* lift to another. *Blackfire* feels like it was always meant to be a Rambo-type rip-off but whoever wrote the script simply put too much plot into it before the Rambo section. It's an interesting miss but one worth watching.

The Blind Warrior

Director: Ratno Timoer
Screenplay: Piet Burnama
Producers: Subagio S., Gope T. Santani
Cast: Advent Bangun (Barda), Enny Beatrice (Sirimbi),

Indonesian films will drive you to madness. *The Blind Warrior* will lead you there.

In a village ruled by the evil Raden Parda, he treats everybody terribly and mistreats young virgins. Barda enters the village and, though blind, kicks all the asses of all the local bad guys. He also falls into Hell at one point. He fights about 30 swordsmen at one time and he's great. He's sort of like Zaitochi the Japanese blind swordsman except in a much sillier film.

The Blind Warrior is so much fun. It rises from the strange imagination of Indonesian filmmakers and seems to have no story ties to anything that a Western viewer might have seen. While the story itself is kind of standard, it's all about the weird details—first off, the blind man who whoops the behinds of all these bad guys. In one scene, he is in a field and wave after wave of guards rush him with swords and he casually repels them all. He may be blind but he has the eye of the tiger.

There are decapitations in this film that are just incredible. One guy is decapitated and keeps running with his sword. There are several brilliant decaps here along those lines. Barda has a pet monkey that doesn't really do anything. One thinks a pet monkey would do more. I'm trying to avoid making this review a list of crazy stuff that happens in this film. Sometimes movies are like that. They're not good or bad, per se. They're simply nuts. They're filled with all sorts of original, endearing business that makes the viewer want to cheer for the imagination (or film-sanctioned insanity) of the filmmakers.

The Blind Warrior is one of the wildest and most colorful and joyously weird Indonesian films I have ever seen. There are beautiful women, guys with great beards and mustaches and so many fight scenes. Plus a blind man at the center of it all, kicking ass but always in a slightly goofy way. At least Zaitochi looked good when he did all the things he did. Barda sometimes looks like he might be getting some help from a few incompetent guardsmen.

Make this film your own. It is crazy and wonderful and full of fantastic action.

Blood Debts

Director: Teddy Page
Screenplay: Timothy Jorge
Cast: Richard Harrison (Mark Collins), Mike Monty (Bill), James Gaines (Peter), Ann Milhnech (Liza), Ann Jackson (Yvette Collins)

Blood Debts has the best closing 30 or so seconds ever in a film. Better than the twist at the end of *Criminally Insane*, more awesome than the closing minutes of *It's A Wonderful Life*. Mark Collins, the hero, saves the day and sorta *loses* the day in the same shot. And it is glorious. The rest of the film is not as good as those moments, but it has a hell of a lot of great stuff in it.

The daughter of Vietnam vet Collins (Richard Harrison) is raped and shot by a bunch of jerks. There is some wonderfully awful dubbing between the daughter and her boyfriend, who is also killed. We see these guys leering and then it all happens. No setup, no shading, no nothing. Just the events occurring. The matter-of-fact *mise en scène* of Teddy Page is strong. Collins is wounded by the jerks and laid up in the hospital. When

Blood Debts is nuts. Teddy Page and Richard Harrison together seems to almost guarantee goofiness. The dubbing is some of the funniest this side of *For Y'ur Height Only*. A cop with strange lower teeth is dubbed in the most halting and humorous matter I've ever heard. Mark just has one damn thing after another happen to him. Harrison keeps the same determined, possibly slightly bored look on his face throughout. The fight scenes range from entertaining (the closing one) to rather sloppy (one involving Collins fighting a purse snatcher. As with many of these Philippines films, sexual assaults happen a lot. Collins is the only guy in the film who seems to have a normal sexual relationship. Every other guy is (pretty much) a rapist. What's the matter with guys in the Philippines?

Sloppy fighting, incoherent, random, Bizarro World plotting, goofy acting and dubbing straight out of *What's Up, Tiger Lily?* insure that *Blood Debts* is the sort of debt you won't mind paying.

The Bounty Hunters aka Revenge of the Mercenaries

Director: Bruno Pischiutta
Cast: Ian McPhail, Jon Austin, Robin Atha

he's released, he goes after the killers vigilante-style, hunting them down in seedy bars, in alleyways. Then the film pulls a little twist out of the realm of *The Star Chamber* or, maybe, *Magnum Force* and goes off in a different direction. Collins' wife is kidnapped by a businessman and his gang. They are super-vigilantes who now force Collins to go on "hits" for them along with a blonde with great legs who used to be a mob hitwoman. After a few hits, Mark gets pretty sick of this crap ... and, again, revenge is taken.

Located in Hamilton, Ontario, Emmeritus Productions flooded the home video market with a slew of direct-to-video, mostly shot-on-video films in the second half of the 1980s. ("Shot directly on video exclusively for the videophile" is printed on their VHS boxes.) The films ran the gamut from the conspiracy thriller *Mark of the Beast* to the almost disturbing cop film *Blue Murder* to the High-Rise-Computer-Goes-Crazy epic *The Tower*. The productions range from professional-looking (*The Tower*) to rather amateurish

(*The Bounty Hunters*). Several of them, such as the one currently being reviewed, are entertaining because they're just plain nuts.

Vietnam vets Ralph and Terry are called to Toronto for a covert mission. They are to kidnap a crazy man named Tom, guilty of multiple murders in the U.S., and sneak him across the border so the U.S. government can arrest him. Apparently Our Heroes have done this sort of bounty hunter thing before and they get a kick out of it. They locate the fugitive (now a photographer), who holds semi–Satanic ceremonies in a large garage. With some assistance, they put Operation Kidnap the Crazy Guy into effect.

That's the very basic storyline of this film, which clocks in at just under an hour. But, in a film like this, the basic storyline means nothing. The true joy is in the details. The film contains six subplots that complicate matters to the point of distraction:

(1) There's a Vietnam scene at the beginning which is pretty irrelevant.

(2) A woman named Janet helps the hunters. She spends a lot of her time fake-seducing Crazy Tom. Janet never quite gels with the story itself.

(3) The bounty hunters call in another woman at the last minute who contributes approximately zero to the proceedings.

(4) Two hair salon employees are tricked into being part of Tom's ceremony. Much time is spent with them.

(5) Tom gets assistance from a woman with an Eastern European accent who has some sort of past with a brothel.

(6) There is a long section with a mall security guard and two friends of the hair salon employees discussing what the hair salon gals went through.

The film seems determined to go off on as many tangents as possible, which does something interesting to the overall layout of the film: It stops this action film from becoming an action film. Whenever it builds to a point (like the kidnapping scene) where the action should kick in, a subplot appears. All tension drains away, replaced by scenes that seem like they should have been left on the cutting room floor.

The hunters kidnap the nutty guy in a scene that starts in the middle and seems to end too soon. Then, instead of watching them heading to the border, the movie takes a different tack: It cuts to the scene with the security guard and the friends of the hair salon employees. Basically, when suspense should be at its height, viewers instead find themselves watching a guy they've never seen before talking to two people about two characters who weren't that interesting. It goes on and on and achieves nothing, except taking up time.

Maybe that was the purpose; maybe the director was more interested in everything going on around the bounty hunters. Maybe the director was trying to do something experimental with narrative. Maybe this is an alternate cut of a far more entertaining movie. There are no answers forthcoming. Those borders are closed.

City Limits

Director: Aaron Lipstadt
Screenplay: Don Opper
Producers: Rupert Harvey, Barry Opper
Cast: James Earl Jones (Albert), Rae Dawn Chong (Yogi), Robbie Benson (Carver), Kim Cattrall (Wickings), John Stockwell (Lee), Darrell Larson (Mick)

Sometimes one can watch a film and see the ambition, see the work that went into it. One senses that this was a labor of love for the folks involved, working hard to get their vision out into the world. One can't help but appreciate the effort. Appreciate the film but not actually enjoy it. In 1982, Aaron Lipstadt and Don Opper made *Android* with Klaus Kinski, a charming, well-done sci-fi film with a wonderful human side. The sort of film that sneaks up on you, give you some entertainment and perhaps makes you ponder human relationships for a while. It was a lovely debut. So what would the guys do next?

City Limits is the answer to that question. A post-apocalyptic *Road Warrior-Logan's Run* variation that is not very much fun. It's more action-oriented than *Android*, and the action is okay, but there are many more characters and locations and a lot (a *lot*) of plot. The whole enterprise seems to go a little south. Although the plot makes sense, it's not terribly interesting. The human factor from the previous film is lost in a bunch of gang members dressed like the cast of *The Warriors*. The charm is missing. That is too bad.

City Limits is set in a grim future where there aren't a lot of older folks. A young man named Lee heads from the desert to Los Angeles to join a gang called the Clippers. He gets involved in a war between the Clippers and another gang, the DAs. Kim Cattrall works for an evil corporation headed by Robbie Benson. There's fighting back and forth and the gangs eventually join forces. There's a long sequence with James Earl Jones playing an old guy in the desert. There's a big ending where the gangs storm the corporation.

But none of it is terribly effective. Something went really generic with *City Limits*. The action isn't the most exciting, but there are very few directors who can make action really exciting. There are some good actors here. But they're kind of dull, except Rae Dawn Chong who has a sparkle in her eye. And the plot is just a little overcomplicated. They should have taken a page from the Italian post-apocalyptic playbook and either kept it simple or made it crazy. The plot is not much fun.

Which is the downfall of *City Limits*. It tries hard but it's just not very entertaining. One can applaud the makers of *Android* for trying something completely different from their first film. It's too bad it simply isn't that interesting.

Cocaine Wars

Director: Hector Olivera
Screenplay: Steven M. Krauzer
Producers: Alex Sessa, Roger Corman
Cast: John Schneider (Cliff), Kathryn Witt (Janet), Royal Dano (Baily), Federico Luppi (Gonzalo)

Roger Corman throws his hat into the action ring. He also throws in John Schneider and a lot of cocaine. *The Dukes of Hazzard*

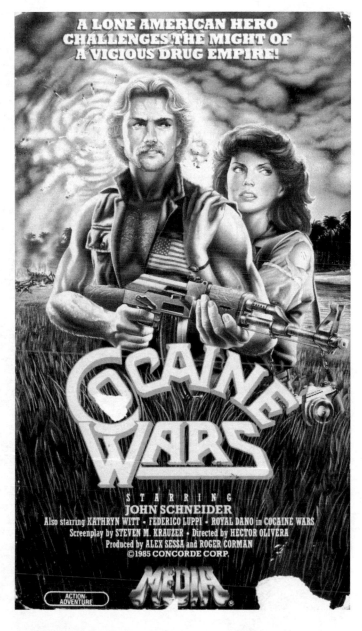

ended and Schneider hopped on the Corman bus for a movie filled with drugs, torture and a lot of polo. *Cocaine Wars* is all about tough, cop action. Cliff, a DEA agent, tries to overthrow a drug ring. Along the way, he falls in love and receives some dental torture. Basically, it's an "undercover partner gets killed, cop goes to get revenge" film.

A completely average B-actioner of the time period, it has car chases, shootouts and fistfights. And it's all fine. It's heavy on the South American drug-running angle, which is one I don't derive much entertainment value from. But folks seem to enjoy it. There's always something extra-sleazy about the Latin American-South American drug cartel–type stuff that always seems to preclude me being terribly entertained.

Schneider gives it his all. The Dukes had ended earlier that year so an Argentinian-American co-production involving Roger Corman probably seemed like an awesome thing to do. So, why couldn't one of the Duke Boys be a kick-ass machine for justice? I wonder why they didn't ask Tom Wopat along. Maybe they did. He and Sorrell Booke were probably doing summer stock somewhere in Maine.

Cocaine Wars comes alive when they're torturing Cliff. Those are the scenes that really seem to reverberate in my mind. The one that involves dental torture, in particular, is a tough one to think about. The polo sequences linger in the mind too. The head drug guy loves polo so that's where he and Cliff meet up. That's also where Cliff meets with his lovely lady.

Some films don't stick in the mind. It's almost like the film dares the viewer to retain

images of it in their mind. Generic, nondescript films that could use the touch of crazy that, say, the Italians would bring to something like this. Or even, a bit of the amateur to it. *Cocaine Wars* needs a touch of that. It is a thoroughly low-budget professional production and it thoroughly does not stick in my mind. Not even a scorching love scene with one of the Duke Boys keeps it there.

Deadly Prey

> *Director, Screenplay:* David A. Prior
> *Producer:* Peter Yuval
> *Cast:* Ted Prior (Mike Danton), Cameron Mitchell (Jaimy's Father), Troy Donahue

(Don), Fritz Matthews (Thornton), David Campbell (Col. Hogan), Dawn Abraham (Sybil)

In 1983, the Prior brothers, David and Ted, made the shot-on-video slasher *Sledge Hammer*. That film, like this one, featured David in charge of writing and directing and buff Ted as star. But their hearts always seemed to be into the action, with Tough Ted taking off his shirt and crushing people or shooting them. *Deadly Prey* is a fiercely primitive version of what action films are like when everything goes out the window except the action. That is why it is such a fun film.

One morning, Vietnam vet Mike Danton is kidnapped from right outside his house. He is taken to a mercenary training camp where they try to hunt him down like an animal. But it's not going to be that easy because Mike is a John Rambo–style killing machine. They can rape and kill his wife. They can shoot his father-in-law. They can torture him. Nothing stops Mike Danton. Even the fact that all he's wearing in the woods is a little pair of gray underpants, no shoes and an awesome mullet. Once a killing machine, always a killing machine.

Deadly Prey starts with men chasing another man though the woods and shooting him. Within ten minutes, Danton is being chased through the woods in a mix of *First Blood* and *The Most Dangerous Game*. There is an energy and a verve to the film. It slows down here and there to give some background but never for long. Action is the keyword. Whether it's one-on-one fighting or a series of Rambo traps spread throughout the woods, it's all here. And, it's all slightly amateurish in the best possible way.

A man sees a gun on the leafy ground. He picks it up. Danton's hand shoots out of the leaves and grabs him. That tops the "man stopping under one of a thousand trees and getting jumped on by Rambo" trick. How did he get himself buried so perfectly? He's just under leaves. Wouldn't someone walking over him have thought "Hey! There's a guy underneath these leaves!" Another man stops to take a sip of water at a small pond. There is

clearly a man under the water. Danton awkwardly comes out of the water and grabs the guy. Again, how did he know this guy would stop here? How long was he holding his breath? A million questions can be asked. But that's against the spirit of this film.

Deadly Prey starts a ball rolling right after the opening credits. It's a synth-fueled, Prior-powered film that picks up more speed as it goes. Everything that happens builds towards the next thing that happens or towards Danton's rage. There's no time to stop. Even his wife's father doesn't get a name, just "Jaimy's Father." Why? Because there's no time for names. Keep it rolling! Yes, there are a few too many scenes in Colonel Hogan's tent. Yes, some of the post-dubbing is distracting. But this film is about holding on and enjoying moments of action that will make the viewer cheer alongside slightly goofy moments that don't quite work. But, at 85 minutes, there is nothing to begrudge *Deadly Prey*. It is Neanderthal filmmaking but that is not a bad thing.

Deadly Trigger

Director, Screenplay, Producer: Joe Oaks
Cast: Judy Landers (Ruth Morrison), Audrey Landers (Polly Morrison), Harry Wolf, Joe Martinez, James McCartney, Jan Fedder

Only a heartbeat away: That's where Heaven is if you trust the Landers sisters. Welcome to *Deadly Trigger*, a shot-on-video adventure made specifically for Audrey and Judy's fans in Germany. They play hot singing sisters who go to Koln and get roughed up and assaulted by a gang of jerks. The head jerk has a father who is well-connected so he goes free. But, justice comes around…

More or less. The whole thing feels a little off. The Morrison sisters are attacked almost immediately and Ruth has a series of injurious mishaps befall her that are almost Wile E. Coyote–esque. Within minutes they go from promising singing stars to one of them being crippled for life and the other working in a bank. The film keeps cutting away to the head jerk continuing to be a total jackass, raping, robbing, killing—I don't understand German law.

Somewhere along the way, the Landers sisters, especially Judy, begin to have less and less to do. Audrey falls in love with the head cop and has a couple make-out sessions with him. Then the sisters try to frame the criminal, the final chase begins and the Landers sisters more or less vanish from the movie as they chase this guy by car, motorcycle, helicopter, etc. The film hadn't quite been an action film up to this point but now it is.

When it becomes an action film, the Landers sisters got left at home. Which is probably for the best. Without them involved, why would anyone watch this? Apart from me. I'll watch anything. It's just a strange vehicle for them, especially Audrey, who played Afton Cooper, Cliff Barnes's love interest, for four seasons on *Dallas*. (She returned in the continuation TBS series.) *Dallas* was the #1 (sometimes #2) TV show in America during that time period. Judy was in some movies (*Stewardess School*) and appearing here and there so one can see her being in *Deadly Trigger*, but Audrey? It would be like Larry Hagman leaving his role as J.R. and immediately starring in a Ted V. Mikels film. The weird thing is, the girls are clearly speaking English in the film but their voices are dubbed. Which means the German cut would have had dubbed voices and the English cut did too. I love the Landers Sisters but I am confused.

Deadly Trigger is a little loopy, a little dull, a little dumb but worth your time.

Dog Tags

Director, Screenplay: Romano Scavolini
Producers: Alain Adam, Dalu Jones
Cast: Clive Wood (Cecil), Mike Monty (Capt. Newport), Baird Stafford (Ron), Robert Haufrecht (Willy)

Watching all of these action movies can be exhausting. One can endure only so many car chases and shootouts and fistfights. When they are incompetent, it can be a real hoot; when they are well done, it is exhilarating. But, on average, the films in here are entertaining for what they are: low-budgeters that are generally ripping off something or other. Sometimes to a hilariously obvious extent.

Things that are said and done in these films are said and done because the bigger films did them. Any political, social or economic commentaries are generally there for the same reason that the heroes in *Road Warrior* rip-offs are loners and the heroes in *First Blood Part 2* rip-offs can rig such ridiculous traps … that's what the source material did.

Dog Tags is from Romano Scavolini, maker of *Nightmare* (AKA *Nightmares in a Damaged Brain*). It even features *Nightmare*'s killer Baird Stafford. It also features a format that is more novelistic than filmic: *Dog Tags* is broken into several parts with a prologue and an epilogue. (*Nightmare* was divided into sections by the days it covers.) *Dog Tags* seems far more serious than any of the other Namsploitation films. In fact, this isn't even 'sploitation.

A chopper containing top secret government files has gone down in the Vietnam jungles. A shifty man named Capt. Newport sends a bunch of tired and wounded soldiers to retrieve them. Things don't go well. The men are exhausted and they have no idea why they are being sent back into enemy territory. They begin to die, generally horribly. They are attacked by the Vietnamese a lot.

The whole film is grim, especially a scene involving the removal of a gangrened leg. It shows us what war does to men and what governments will do to protect their secrets. Like *Nightmare*, it is just a bit darker and smarter than all the other films around it. The characters are a little bit sharper. One doesn't want to see them suffer and die, but the viewer knows that this is what's going to happen. There's a good subplot involving them helping a little boy who may—or may not—actually be setting traps for them.

In the end, the difference between a fun film and a darker, more real, one comes down to moments. There is a scene where a woman is bathing in a lovely river. She goes under the water. It's very tranquil. When she comes back up, there is a loop of wire wrapped around her neck, and a mine attached to the wire rises too. This sort of thing pops up in other movies of this sort. But the way it's shot, the character and other characters' reactions to the situation make *Dog Tags* more real and charged than others. Of course, what it gains in realism and grim behavior, it loses in fun.

Gymkata

Director: Robert Clouse

Screenplay: Charles Robert Carner; Based on the novel *The Terrible Game* by Dan Tyler Moore

Producer: Fred Weintraub

Robert Clouse, the director of *Enter the Dragon,* takes Olympic gymnast Kurt Thomas and pits him against a swarm of men dressed kind of like ninjas in the ancient European village of Parmistan. Kurt, with the assistance of a Parmistan princess, is trying to win something called the Game. It all has to do with the United States trying to get a strategic location for the Star Wars Defense program. A very athletic man, Kurt twists and turns and spins with the best of them. Luckily for the U.S., gymnastics translates smoothly into action in a way that, say, curling might not.

Clouse. Thomas. Principal photography in the country formerly known as Yugoslavia and on the Adriatic Sea. Big Australian stuntman Richard Norton. Buck Kartalian. Sundry and diverse threads that interweave to give the action film lover 90 minutes of pure excitement.

The film begins with Thomas engaged in gymnastics and then dives right into the mission. No stopping to build Kurt's character. All you have to know is that he is brave, strong, good with a spinning kick and, at certain angles, he looks like MacGyver. Those traits are all we need for the perfect Action Man. Sent to Parmistan, he comes in contact with Richard Norton, who is not nice. He also meets the head of Parmistan (Kartalian, star of *Please Don't Eat My Mother* and the Wolfman on TV's *Monster Squad*).

The Game is exciting. Kurt's fighting skills are never in question. During a scene in a mental institution, a pommel horse sits in the middle of a square; when Kurt is attacked by a crowd, he uses it to kick the heck out of everyone. Acting-wise, he's a little wooden, but it works for his character. Although gymnastics lends itself to some fun fight scenes, there are moments when all the spinning and flipping becomes a liability.

More than once Kurt is being chased by thugs down a thin Parmistan alley, when he leaps up and grabs a bar conveniently stretching between the buildings. Unlike Jackie Chan, who might do the same thing, but remain in fight mode as the thugs rush, Kurt needs to do a couple acrobatic 360s to build up his kicking strength. The thugs rush him, but not too fast because the gymnast requires a moment to gather momentum. It doesn't

A NEW KIND OF MARTIAL ARTS COMBAT! THE SKILL OF GYMNASTICS. THE KILL OF KARATE.

GYMKATA

A FRED WEINTRAUB PRODUCTION "GYMKATA"
Starring KURT THOMAS · TETCHIE AGBAYANI · RICHARD NORTON · EDWARD BELL   Associate Producer REBECCA POOLE
Screenplay by CHARLES ROBERT CARNER Based on the novel "The Terrible Game" by Dan Tyler Moore Produced by FRED WEINTRAUB
R   Directed by ROBERT CLOUSE

happen often, and when it does it's kind of charming. Almost like the bad guys don't want to take advantage of Kurt needing a moment. It's quite considerate of them. Not all hired thugs and mercenaries are low on manners.

The Game itself involves a lot of running through woods and cornfields, scaling mountains and crossing crevasses by treacherous hand-only rope bridges. The rules change several times so the viewer is never quite sure what will happen next. This certainly keeps things tense. In the final fight in the asylum, the contestants head through the building and beat up any insane people who get in their way. There are a lot of insane people in Parmistan. Maybe it's not as idyllic as they pretend.

Gymkata is full of action. It has a charming star. It doesn't stop for any character bits. It has that nice mid–80s, post–*Rocky IV*, post–*Rambo: First Blood Part 2* jingoism to it. And obviously, it's all a little absurd. You may find yourself laughing at certain moments, but the laughter does not take away from the excitement.

Never underestimate entertainment like this, especially when kickass gymnasts are involved. Have you seen *Mr. T: The Animated Series*? Use an episode of that as a chaser before watching *Gymkata*. A great evening awaits.

Hell Squad aka
Commando Girls

Director, Screenplay, Producer: Kenneth Hartford

Cast: Bainbridge Scott (Jan), Glen Hartford (Jack), Tina Lederman, Maureen Kelly, Penny Prior, Walter Cox (Jim), Jace Damon (Mark), Marvin Miller (The Sheik),

Cannon Films and Kenneth Hartford had a dream. Hot women with guns shooting terrorists. It is not known if Cannon and Hartford came up with the ideas separately or whether a meeting of the minds revealed similar dreams. But Hartford got a hold of a script and ran with the concept. *Hell Squad* is the result.

The Hell Squad is a group of tough ladies with guns, leather boots and attitude. These highly trained broads set out to rescue Jack, the kidnapped son of an ambassador in the Middle East. A terrorist regime has taken the idealistic young man hostage and, according to this movie, only the Hell Squad can save him. The women, individually, aren't given any specific traits. They were all showgirls, so they can sing and dance. Only the lead, Jan, is given a name that is repeated. She is also the one who gets naked often. There is a price to pay for loss of anonymity.

A series of sequences involves the girls shooting all sorts of terrorist types. Then they retire for the night to the hotel hot tub. Every once in a while they do some dancing, because they're undercover as dancers in a club. But the dancing takes second place to the shooting because the terrorists want the codes for the dreaded Neutron Bomb.

Hell Squad doesn't take itself all that seriously. The gals get a wacky training sequence, which is sort of like *Private Benjamin* but with more jiggling. They shoot a lot of people. The movie alternates hot tub, mission, hot tub, mission and so on for quite some time. I was invested in it. The missions they go on don't seem to bring them any closer to finding the kidnapped guy, but they're fun. Gals with guns is iconography the planet Earth should get behind.

The action scenes are never quite as exciting as they should be. And the movie is repetitive. But it's got a brio to it, a gusto—a refusal to stop when, for example, they don't have two radiation suits for a scene at an atomic testing site and so they use one radiation suit and one yellow contamination suit instead. Why not? If you only have one gal who will appear topless, use her. Show those boobs.

Toward the end, the gals are captured by the terrorists and chained up while wearing their lingerie. There is a fat white guy playing a sheik and a wacky scene with a tiger. In the closing sequence, the villain is unveiled in the style of *Scooby Doo*. And it is hilarious.

Hercules II aka The Adventures of Hercules

Director, Screenplay: Luigi Cozzi

Producers: Menahem Golan, Yoram Globus

Cast: Lou Ferrigno (Hercules), Milly Carlucci (Urania), Sonia Viviani (Glaucia), William Berger (King Minos)

When a sequel opens with several minutes of action highlights from the first film, it's a sign that one (or more) of several things happened: The filmmakers loved those scenes and wanted the

viewers to see them again; it is a sort of recap from the first film, sans dialogue; it's an easy way to add more action to the movie; or it's filling out a movie that ran short. In *The Adventures of Hercules*, it might have been all four of these things. But the first *Hercules* was so much fun, it primes the viewer for yet more enjoyment.

Hera and several gods have stolen Zeus' seven thunderbolts and hidden them around the world. Hercules (Lou Ferrigno), joined by several lovely ladies, goes after them. There are undead fighters, giant scorpions, wizards and, as unbelievable as this may sound, a final fight in outer space. When the fantasy of

Conan the Barbarian meets the sci-fi crazy of *Starcrash,* nothing will ever be the same. This movie, like the first one but slightly more so, dives into a fantasy world with both feet and starts kicking and yelling.

As with the first film and *Starcrash,* writer-director Luigi Cozzi throws in every type of effect, including (in the space battle) *Tron*-esque neon outlines of people fighting. Cozzi has ambition. I don't know if he ever had the budget he needed to match that ambition. But throw caution to the wind and you'll have fun.

Lou is as fine as ever. They have him dubbed with one of the classic dubbing crew that did so many of these movies back in the day. The ladies who travel with Lou are gorgeous, so that's a plus. Lou takes on a stop-motion scorpion.

Is it as good as the first *Hercules*? I would say that it is the exact same quality as the first one. It's actually grander in scope than the first one and that's cool. I wouldn't be surprised to learn that the two films were made at more or less the same time. They have that feel to them. Like all of Cozzi's films, there is a tremendous amount of imagination on display. Some of it borders on the ludicrous but it's all fun. Watch it.

Inferno Thunderbolt

Director: Godfrey Ho

Screenplay: Stephen So, Godfrey Ho

Producers: Betty Chan, Joseph Lai

Cast: Richard Harrison (Richard), Fonda Lynn, Wang Tao, Pierre Trembley, Claire Angela, Rose Kuei, Donald Kong

There isn't a whole lot of action in *Inferno Thunderbolt,* ostensibly part of the Thunderbolt series. The movie makes up for it with a very long mud wrestling match. There's an also an old lady in a wheelchair who shoots arrows at people. She's crotchety and deadly.

A criminal gang, the Rockfords, kill a young woman. Her sister infiltrates the gang. Richard Harrison plays Richard, a cop. His wife is a reporter who gets too close to the Rockfords and starts to be threatened. Eventually, everyone is taking revenge on everyone. Richard gets angry a lot. His mustache rules.

There is action, finally, but it comes late in the film. By that time, so many people had taken so much revenge against everybody else that I got lost. Harrison does some great training in his backyard during one scene. There

is a huge Budweiser logo umbrella over a table, which I found pretty amusing. There's also some great karate moves from the man himself. Maybe not the most fluid movements but you can't have everything.

Every once in a while I will write about a movie and have lots to say. For this one, I've got Harrison, a wheelchair and a slo-mo fight with a strobing light going. Well, at least the final sequence with Harrison running through a house with a gun, hunting down the killer, is slapdash-wonderful.

King Solomon's Mines

Director: J. Lee Thompson
Screenplay: Gene Quintano, James Silke
Producers: Menahem Golan, Yoran Globus
Cast: Richard Chamberlain (Allan Quatermain), Sharon Stone (Jesse), Herbert Lom (Col. Bockner), John Rhys-Davies (Dogati), Kem Gampu (Umbopo)

The raucous Golan-Globus journey through the world of Indiana Jones begins! *King Solomon's Mines* is a non-stop push towards the mines with Nazis and crazy Arabs and train fights and airplane brawls and crazy traps and giant spiders. It's all under the guiding hand of J. Lee Thompson who knows how to direct action. Sometimes the action scenes happen too far away and the stunt people become a little obvious but it's still fun. Everyone is giving it their best. Sharon Stone, maybe, was giving a little too much of her best. However, as crazy as the film gets, by the end, it works. It's no *Raiders of the Lost Ark* but it is fun. Regardless of its shortcomings, of which there are many.

This film begins with Quatermain (Richard Chamberlain) trying to get Jesse (Stone) to the House of Isis. Her dad is there getting info on the Mines. But Dogati and Bockner get there first. Quatermain, Jesse and Umbopo set off to Africa in order to stop the Nazi and the Arab from reaching the Mines. The movie throws every action scene it can at the viewer, plus heroic Jerry Goldsmith music. Every time the Quatermain theme kicks in, it's huge and epic and makes everyone feel

good. But sometimes the film isn't actually at the point where that's justified.

The comedy quotient is a little high at times. Stone especially overdoes the comedy. Watch the scene in the runaway plane to gauge that. Some of her line deliveries make you cringe a bit. But the action keeps coming and the music keeps playing. Yes, some of the rear screen projection is awful and some of the undercranking is really a pain. There's a stunt sequence on a train ruined by speeding everything up.

Everyone seems to be putting their hearts into making this the Ultimate Indiana Jones rip-off. They may have succeeded. The problem is that they extend themselves beyond what Spielberg and Lucas knew could be done. So the convoy sequence in *Raiders* is perfect while the train sequence here goes off the rails (as it were) because they extend themselves too far.

The film dives right in and it's crazy and awesome. But the viewer has a tough time caring about Allan and Jesse. They are never properly introduced to us until the last 15 minutes. That's a bit of a liability because one wants to feel the goodness of the characters. Quatermain shoots a Nazi right in the balls in one scene and the music says it's heroic. Well, maybe it is. But, it also seems kind of weird. *King Solomon's Mines* is like that. Heroic and exciting … but kind of weird.

L.A. Streetfighters aka Ninja Turf

Director: Richard Park
Screenplay: Simon Blake Hong
Producer: Jun Chong
Cast: Jun Chong (Yong), Phillip Rhee (Tommy), Bill Wallace (Kruger), Rosanna King (Lily), James Lew (Chan)

L.A. Streetfighters is a film from the guys who brought the world *Miami Connection*. Is that a recommendation? You bet. This film brings back Jun Chong and his broken English. He kicks a ton of ass. He and his pals Tommy and Chan get in a bunch of fights with assorted groups and it's a joy to watch. *L.A. Streetfighters* is to *Hollywood Cop* as *Miami*

Connection is to *Samurai Cop*. Then enjoy your evening.

This fun movie is set in L.A.—in the high schools, on the streets. A place where everyone wants to fight everyone else. Yong and his friends are in the thick of things, kicking ass. One can only applaud the country-crossing of these films, from L.A. to Miami, and both fun. There is much talk of the American Dream. Yong's mom is kind of a jerk. There are nice girlfriends, drug runners, fights with a Mexican gang out in the desert, a ninja. The gang's all here.

It's like *Miami Connection*, but slightly more grounded. All the events fly at you in a slick miasma of strange dubbing, odd dialogue and fun fight scenes. The film doesn't have a real plotline running through it. It's

more a series of misadventures. An action film like this is a joy to watch. It stumbles (but never falls) from scene to scene and then there's a fight. The actors are awkward. It has the sort of almost personal feel that many low-budget direct-to-video horror films of the time have. It inhabits that same sort of wonderful, nebulous place where it is, clearly, set in our world but no one acts like someone from our world. Never fault a film for doing its own thing, especially when it's this damn entertaining.

Miami Connection is more fun. It has an extra level of craziness that is missing here. (Specifically, all those great band performances.) The print on the VHS of *L.A. Streetfighters* is atrociously dark with long scenes where the viewer strains to make out something … *anything*. Then the fights start. This film is highly recommended.

Light Blast

Director: Enzo G. Castellari

Screenplay: Enzo G. Castellari, Titus Carpenter

Producers: Galliano Juso, Paul J. Kelly, Achille Manzotti

Cast:. Erik Estrada (Ronn), Michael Pritchard (Swann), Peggy Rowe (Jacqueline), Bob Taylor, Thomas Moore (Dr. Yuri Soboda)

If you invented a death ray, would you just cause death with it? Why not a life ray? Is that so crazy? At least the death ray in *Light Blast* has some pretty cool (if familiar) effects on the human body.

Castellari strikes again! This time the writer-director brought Erik Estrada with him. Thank God for that because a mad scientist has built a death ray, and it will be turned upon San Francisco, destroying it, if $10 million

isn't coughed up. Call up Ronn the cop, played by Estrada. Ronn beats up and chases down a large number of people to find out what's happening.

It's good that he does because the two times we see the death ray being used, it's pretty horrific. It melts people *a la* the ending of *Raiders of the Lost Ark*. We know that Ronn is the right guy for the job because of the opening scene. Several jerks are holding people hostage in a downtown building. They ask for lunch but from an unarmed man. So Ronn arrives dressed only in his underwear, carrying a cooked turkey on a platter. But this turkey's got a gun in it. In a moment and a flash, the first of the crooks falls. This scene shows that Castellari is having fun with this film. There is a very entertaining car chase where Ronn drives what is more or less a go-cart the wrong way down a freeway. There is a scene at a mortuary where he gets in a brawl in a green-lit room with a nurse. Castellari plays with expectations beautifully in the opening scene. It involves a lover's tryst in a train yard and how it goes wrong. When Castellari is having fun, the viewer is having fun.

Estrada acquits himself well and looks great in his underpants holding a turkey. It looks like he's enjoying himself. But when you have to track down a crazy man with a death ray … what's not to enjoy?

Light Blast provides a good time via some great action scenes and some big, gory moments that are actually quite surprising.

Majestic Thunderbolt

Director: Godfrey Ho
Screenplay: Stephen Soul
Producer: Joseph Lai
Cast: Richard Harrison (Richard), Phillip Ko (Phillip), John Ladalski, Kuan Tai Chen, Kathy Evan

This is one of the first Ho-Lai cut-and-paste films. Richard Harrison stars as Richard, who has some diamonds stolen from him. Then the film moves on to a story about a fight between two families. One family is led by Chan, the other by Franco. Franco, an

Asian guy with a big black Afro, has his shirt unbuttoned halfway down his chest. He's awesome and he's nuts. In one scene, he and his boys enjoy watching ladies engaging in synchronized swimming. Love it!

Majestic Thunderbolt is crazy. The plot goes back and forth between these two families. There's retribution, torture, sex, an exploding toilet and a scene with a couple in bed and an awesome falling chandelier. Sometimes the "old footage" in these films simply isn't as good as the new ninja stuff that's been added, but here it's a tossup. The original film must be one of the craziest things ever. In one scene, a woman is tied up in the middle of a room and painted with Chinese characters before being killed; in another, a man in his underpants is tied to a crucifix and has a snake shoved in his mouth. Continue to love it!

Harrison is in the silliest scene. One of the bad guys is walking down a walkway with a bag of groceries. Suddenly Richard appears … on roller skates! With a baseball bat! Thank you, Ho and Lai, from the bottom of my heart.

Pink Floyd music is used, and I believe I heard some Edgar Winter in there. During the final fight scene between Franco's men and Chan's son Allan, "On the Run" from the album "The Dark Side of the Moon" cycles around a lot.

I think this one might be the most violent and sex-filled of all the Ho-Lai films I've watched. I wonder if Takashi Miike was involved because at times it feels like a completely goofball version of one of his films.

Mayhem

Director, Screenplay: Joseph Merhi
Producers: Rick Pepin, Joseph Merhi
Cast: Raymond Martino (Dino), Pamela Dixon (Misty), Robert Gallo (Ziggy), Wendy MacDonald (Rachel)

Dino and Ziggy, two small-time thugs, occasionally get involved with bigger fish. But mostly Ziggy talks about going to Alaska and Dino fantasizes about the assorted ways he will kill (or maybe has killed) his ex-wife. They take down some drug dealers, child molesters and pimps. The film's title indicates that there will be mayhem, but it comes in short bursts. It's more a lot of madness from Dino and slight indifference from Ziggy.

Mayhem has a proto-Tarantino feel. On at least two occasions, the movie is doin' its thing when something unexpected happens and the movie goes is in a completely different direction. In the hands of a master, this sort of "The narrative is making itself up as it goes along" feeling can be exhilarating. Look at *Pulp Fiction* and the three twists in its three main tales. Well, *Mayhem* doesn't quite do that because the twists aren't as thrilling.

The first big twist is when Ziggy's girlfriend gets pissed at Ziggy and runs away from his car. She ends up getting kidnapped by pimps. Ziggy enlists Dino to get her back. That comes out of nowhere! The second surprising twist not only shifts the story but the tone of the film.

Ambition, especially in this realm of filmmaking, is always welcome, narrative ambition doubly so. Rick Pepin and Joseph Merhi made loads of movies, many of them by-the-book action or otherwise. This film was made early in their careers, right at the start of their production company PM Entertainment, which would make a slew of low-budget action in the '80s and early '90s. *Mayhem* is ambitious because of the focus on character and the shifts in story. But the shifts don't lead to much. Mayhem is limited.

So what the viewer gets is the least-action action film in this book, but one which sets the precedent for future action films from PM Entertainment. Maybe this was Merhi's vanity project. Maybe they didn't have money for action. This was around the same time as their supernatural slasher *The Newlydeads*. Maybe they weren't settling in on action films just yet. Maybe stirring in Scorsese-styled drama was their thing at that moment.

All one can really say is that *Mayhem* is fascinating (but more interesting to think

First It Was
The Child Molesters
The Dope Pushers And the Pimps.

Now It's The Police.
Can He Survive?

CITY LIGHTS PRESENTS
A RICHARD PEPIN
JOSEPH MERHI PRODUCTION
MAYHEM
STARRING RAYMOND MARTINO PAMELA DIXON
ROBERT GALLO WENDY MacDONALD
WITH JEAN LEVINE SONIA KARA
EXECUTIVE PRODUCER RONALD L. GILCHRIST

about than watch) and slightly repetitive and dull. And it seems like an action film where they seem to have left out the action. Watching it might be a great evening. Dino and Ziggy are worth the time. It would have been great to see them kicking ass.

Miami Golem aka Miami Horror

Director: Martin Herbert
Screenplay: Frank Clark, Frank Wall
Producer: George Salvioni
Cast: David Warbeck (Craig), Laura Trotter (Joanna Fitzgerald), John Ireland (Mr. Anderson)

Craig works at a small Miami TV station. He's a matter-of-fact wiseacre enjoying his life. Some Atlanteans recruit him to collect an ancient group of cells found in a meteorite that can restore life to one of the most evil forces in the universe. Craig is confused, bemused and then up for anything. At long as it involves Joanna Fitzgerald and her unfortunate haircut, he's willing to try it. *Miami Golem* is a mix of sci-fi, horror and action where an evil John Ireland wants to rule the world. The theme music sounds almost exactly like the theme for *Beverly Hills Cop.*

This film rests right in that spot where the Italians moved themselves to Florida and began to shift from post-dubbed films to shooting on-set sound. *Miami Golem* is one of the last of the post-dubbed ones. From almost this point on, the Italian films with Florida exteriors would have live sound. They'd still feel weird but that dubbing group that we all know and love would be gone.

The concept of cells growing into a mutant fetus that has the psychic power to destroy the universe is either genius or crazy or both. And peppering the film with fistfights, gunfights and an air boat chase seems like the director is trying to fit in everything possible.

The film has at least one moment of everything that the average viewer might consider awesome, from horror to nudity to Craig shooting it out with a helicopter while taking cover in a random school bus driving through a place called "The Empty Field." David Warbeck handles it all like the pro he is.

The film seems like it might build to something apocalyptic but then takes time for an air boat chase. That's nothing to be ashamed of. I decided a long time ago that any film with an air boat chase is automatically an action film. The *Miami Horror* alternate title is clearly trying to rip off *Miami Vice* but why? This film is nothing like that show except for the fact that Craig doesn't shave much. When Italian horror and action collide, the universe is not safe.

Ninja in the U.S.A. aka U.S. Ninja

Director: Dennis Wu
Screenplay: Edmund Jones
Producer: Randol Ye
Cast: Alexander Lou (Jerry Wong), George Nicholas Albergo (Tyger McPherson), Tomas Yau (Luther), Alex Yip (Lt. Kwun), Rosaline Li (Penny)

Tyger, a bad guy selling lots of drugs in the U.S., has an army of ninjas. He gets on the wrong side of Jerry Wong by kidnapping his wife, a reporter with incriminating film of Tyger. Tyger can place as many ninjas as he wants between Jerry and his gal. But Jerry's pretty good. There might be problems.

Ninja in the U.S.A. has dubbing that borders on ludicrously funny. It has a semi-incoherent plotline. As long as one remembers who is good and who is bad, you can't go wrong. It has a lot of fighting. A *lot* of fighting. It ends so abruptly that it can cause Narrative Whiplash. It's also a film where one moment ninjas are fighting in a two-story office building. Then, 15 seconds later, it's a speedboat chase.

Like most of the Ho films, this one is a hell of a lot of fun. First, one can enjoy the fact that it is apparently set in the U.S. But it's really not quite any U.S. that I recognize. The U.S. in this movie is somewhere in Southeast Asia. Quite a few folks seem to be speaking English, but it's all dubbed.

There are hundreds of ninjas in the movie. Jerry may be a ninja but it's not like *American Ninja* where Michael Dudikoff is the ninja of choice in the film. And all the ninjas fight well. They have an awesome training camp where they not only perform ninja-style tricks and stunts but also defy gravity. On more than one occasion, the film is actually reversed to show ninjas going up onto balconies and such. You might consider something like that cheating in a regular ninja movie but this is *Ninja in the U.S.A.*.

The fights are plentiful. Lots of ninjas brawl with Jerry. Plus, there's a large number of shootouts between non-ninjas and Jerry. The finale is one big brawl in and around a waterfall, In perfect ninja fashion. Jerry wins. He kills Tyger in the water and THE END appears on the screen. Of course, Jerry hasn't actually been reunited with his lady but that's okay. The viewer knows what's up.

Ninja Warriors

Director: John Lloyd
Screenplay: Ken Watanabe

Cast: Ronald l. Marchini (Steve), Romano Kristoff (Tom), Paul Vance (Lt. Kevin Washington), Ken Watanabe (Kuroda), Mike Cohen (Dr. Anderson)

Steve is a very powerful name. What do you do when there's a problem? You call Steve. It's the only thing to do. The good guys in *Ninja Warriors* know what to do when ninjas steal a secret formula from a professor and plan to use it to take over the world. You might know too. Yes, call Steve.

Ninja Warriors is from the Philippines but it has the sort of verve that American action indies have. The willingness to do all sorts of nonsense if it will push the film forward. This film has hordes of ninjas and the goofiest-

looking bunch of bad guys, ever. It also has the kidnapped professor from *For Y'ur Height Only*. His voice is dubbed but one can't hide a bad actor under a dubbed voice. As always, he is a joy to watch.

Steve teams up with a cop to find the formula. The cop is annoying. At one point, he gets caught in the woods in one of those traps with the loop of rope on the ground that yanks you up so you're hanging upside down. As Steve fights a ninja, the cop keeps yelling, "Steve! Steve! Get me down!" It's incredibly annoying sound design. Steve gets the job done but he always looks like an uncle who just came back from jogging and now wants some beers.

Ninja Warriors is great fun. The dubbing is over-emphatic and silly as hell. How is the action, one might ask? It's classic ninja. They disappear. They throw shurikens. They leap out of the ground. It's all here. But in this film, the entertainment is in the incidentals. And, trust me, the incidentals are really screwy.

Operation NAM aka *Cobra Mission*

Director: Fabrizio De Angelis (as Larry Ludman)

Screenplay: V.J. Klemen, Fabrizio De Angelis (as Larry Ludman), Erwin C. Dietrich

Producer: Peter Baumgartner

Cast: Oliver Tobias (Richard Wagner), Christopher Connelly (Roger Carson), Manfred Lehmann (Mark Adams), John Steiner (James Walcott), Ethan Wayne (Mike), Donald Pleasence (Father Lenoir)

They can't all be fun. The Vietnam War was not a good time for America. But many of the Namsploitation films are a hoot. *Strike Commando* is a good, goofy time about a wound on the arm of American history. *Operation NAM* steps forward to reverse that. It's from Fabrizio De Angelis, who would make the football-players-save-women-from-terrorists movie *The Last Match* a few years later.

This movie is about four former POWs who decide to return to Vietnam, ten years after the war, and free some of the American prisoners from surviving camps. One guy is a working man. One is barely getting by. Another is married to a rich woman. Another is in a mental hospital. They head into the jungle to try and bring back as many boys as they can. But they discover that things aren't always what they seem. Frankly, it doesn't end well.

As *Operation NAM* starts, the four main guys are quickly sketched out. Maybe too quickly. Then they are in a bar as a World War II veteran berates them. That's fine. But, the World War II vet seems to be younger than at least one of the Vietnam vets. I don't know how that could happen but it's a good, strong scene anyway.

In Vietnam, they beat up a bunch of guys who run a "We'll find your POW" organization but really just rip people off. They get help from Father Lenoir who guides them to the camps. Then, the rescue begins. And the soldiers are wasted and tired. They reveal a bit of information that our heroes didn't know: The American government knows all about the POWs. They get released during bartering with the North Vietnamese. To justify why they are there so long, they have all been re-branded from military POWs to criminal prisoners of war. It's nasty.

The film sounds like it should be fun, but it's not. There is a scene where one of our heroes is about to sleep with a Vietnamese woman. When she takes off her top, we see that she is horribly scarred by napalm. She shoots him dead. It's going to be one of those movies where the hero team gets taken out one by one. The ending is particularly rough. I don't know if the film is being deliberately misanthropic and hopeless or if it's trying to make a point. Give it the benefit of the doubt and go with the latter.

Operation NAM is a pretty well done movie. The action is exciting but, because it's not a fun film, there's a kick to the violence that isn't there in the other films of this type. It takes all sorts to make a genre. This is a good addition to it.

Pray for Death

Director: Gordon Hessler

Screenplay: James Booth

Producer: Don Van Atta

Cast: Sho Kosugi (Akira), James Booth (Limehouse), Donna K. Benz (Aiko), Norman Burton (Lt. Anderson), Kane Kosugi (Takeshi), Shane Kosugi (Tomoya)

Akira and his family move from Japan to Los Angeles to open a Japanese restaurant. They get involved with crooked cops, mob guys and stolen necklaces. Akira's wife is killed and one of his sons is hit by a car, all because Akira and his family happened to be in the wrong place at the wrong time. Akira, a ninja who wears a metal mask, can take care of business because (this might come as a surprise) the cops are no help. Oh, and Akira and his family love watching ninjas on TV. (That is a fun self-referential bit that layers the film.)

In *Pray for Death,* Sho Kosugi kicks ass as a ninja. It features his two sons heavily. While the older one kicks ass as a budding ninja, the other one spends quite a bit of time glancing into the camera lens. Maybe that was meant to strike fear in the viewer's heart, but most of the time he just looks like a nervous kid. Sho is as stoic as ever until the ass-kicking breaks out.

Pray for Death goes through the exact motions that the viewer expects it to go though and doesn't hit any real heights. There's some fun fighting but the film gets lost in setting up all the stuff that Akira is going to avenge. Instead of being a series of exciting, ever-escalating fights, it has a few light skirmishes and then the big ending. At the end, after Akira has killed a passel of mobsters, he comes up against the slightly schlubby mob boss … who goes head to head with him for a few minutes!

I place the blame for this pretty bland ninja film at the feet of director Gordon Hessler, who made the great and mighty *KISS*

Meets the Phantom of the Park. It's very obvious that action scenes are not his thing. They should have brought in Firstenberg. He would have made this recycled material worth watching again.

Revolt

Director, Producer: J. Shaybany
Screenplay: Shield
Cast: Rand Martin, Fattaneh, Sepehernia, Jerry Luck, Lee Buck

Steve, a man with a beautiful mustache, is out to take down his town's #1 drug dealer, Mr. Macintosh. If Steve can't do it, no one can. *Revolt* knows what I like in an action film. Sometimes that's to just get down and dumb. This film is 72 minutes of fistfights, car chases, shootouts and the Iranian hostage crisis. Savor every moment.

Steve and his problem with the drugs exist in a hazy, post-dubbed world. A world where the thugs are everywhere. Where the biggest drug dealer in town is also the biggest philanthropist. A world where time seems to leap around. (More about that in a moment.) Some of the actors do a good job. Others seem to be screwing around. The synths and drum machines pump away.

Where did this movie come from? Who is J. Shaybany? Who on earth is Shield? Where was this made? Why is it so short? Why does it began with several minutes of earnest narration about drugs that wouldn't seem out of place in a classroom safety film? And where does the sudden introduction of the Iranian hostage crisis come from? The film has a 1985 copyright. The crisis was in 1979. For ten minutes, the film seems to fly back in time. Just long enough for jerks and prejudice to cause the death of Steve's son. Then the crisis is forgotten.

If a film begins with the sounds of synths, wailing guitar and the drum machine, I begin to feel very comfortable. The misty haziness of this film make my curiosity levels rise. Schizophrenic editing, jumping all around with little rhyme or reason, is enough seasoning on a movie that is already in Funky Town, U.S.A. Then the director adds a nice touch or two, such as the way Steve and his wife learn about their son's death. Then he throws in gratuitous sexual assault and a hilarious car explosion.

People shoot each other. Men trip over branches and logs. Car chases get a little bit sped up. Steve and his charming mustache remind us that Love is the Answer. Barring that, shoot some jerks and that will make things nicer for everyone else. There is much in what Steve says.

Scorpion Thunderbolt

Director: Godfrey Ho
Screenplay: Stephen So
Producers: Joseph Lai, Betty Chan
Cast: Richard Harrison, Juliet Chan, Bernard Tsui, Nancy Lim, Cynthia Ku, Maura Fong

It's tough to imagine a world without these offbeat films. It's also tough to believe that each of us is a part of the world where these films exist.

This Godfrey Ho-Joseph Lai concoction might actually be crazier than most of their others. *Scorpion Thunderbolt* is about a woman who turns into a giant snake monster, just like her mother. Richard Harrison wants to stop her. He's told that she is a "witch vampire." There's a lot of kung fu fighting (no real ninja action this time around) and a lot of footage of snakes and snake monsters mixed with gory stuff. There's a scene with a woman flashing her boobs on the side of the road to get a lift. (Claudette Colbert never thought of that one. *It Happened One Night* would have been a very different film.) She then dances nude in some sort of porno theater. And Harrison has sex with her. And…

This is a film made purely for commercial exploitation purposes. But, at the same time, it seems to have been made by people who had no concept of what might actually be commercial. Could you imagine showing this to a modern-day action film crowd? The concept that all they need to do is cram together two completely unrelated films and just dub in what they want is an amazing one.

Scorpion Thunderbolt dares the viewer to question its insanity. Dares the viewer to say, "Hey, this doesn't make a lick of sense" because the movie doesn't care that it makes no sense. There isn't a heck of a lot of action. It presents itself as an action film but it's really a horror film. What does one do when a movie like this is pretending to be action but isn't? Ho-Lai don't care. They wanted to make some cash. One wonders how much cash they actually made off of a film like this, shown somewhere on 42nd Street to a crowd who was probably too drunk to care.

Thunder Squad aka Wild Team

Director: Umberto Lenzi
Screenplay: Roberto Leoni
Producer: Maurizio Mattei
Cast: Antonio Sabato (Martin Cuomo), Ivan Rassimov (Fuego), Warner Pochath (Theo), Julia Furisch (Sybil), Sal Borgese (Paco), Dante Fioretti (Marius)

The Thunder Squad rules! They are sent deep into the jungles of Manioca to rescue the president's kidnapped son. The Squad is led by Martin. The other four use their fists, guns and bow and arrows. Sybil is a munitions expert. If anyone can head into the jungle and take on the evil General Gomez's army and get the boy back, it's them. Thunder Squad!

Thunder Squad is another in a series of entertaining films from Umberto Lenzi. This time he brings along several well-known Italian actors, like Antonio Sabato and Ivan Rassimov. The movie begins slow: setting up the world that the movie is set in, kidnapping the boy, introducing the Squad. A group of psychics is employed to find the boy with their minds. They are all hooked up to a computer. The psychic plotline is a brief one. But, it's fun.

Our Gang hits the jungle, coasting downstream with crocodiles. The shooting begins. Gomez is a real peckerhead. We see his men destroy a village full of innocent women and children. The ante is raised in the nasty department. The violence continues building and building—and they find the boy. Hooray! Then, the twists and betrayals begin. And the film keeps the surprises coming.

It's good stuff. When the action picks up, things get crazier. Then the Squad breaks out the hang gliders! They're awesome. If Ator can build a hang glider from his own imagination, the Squad can pack them in their bags. Where'd the metal frames come from? Stop asking questions and enjoy the good time.

Thunder Squad stands strong as a *Commando*-esque number from a great time for action films. It's a ragtag bunch of multi-dubbed accented characters who hire on to save a little boy who, by the way, seems to have a bit of mystical power, a cool addition to a film that could have been simply action. But, once you put Antonio Sabato in charge of the group, now you're in a different world.

Vigilante

Director: William Lustig
Screenplay: Richard Vetere
Producers: William Lustig, Andrew Garroni
Cast: Robert Forster (Eddie), Fred Williamson (Nick), Richard Bright (Burke), Rutanya Alda (Vickie), Dom Blakely (Prago), Willie Colon (Rico), Joe Spinell (Eisenberg), Carol Lynley (D.A. Fletcher)

In New York City, Vickie protects a gas station attendant from some thugs led by Rico and his pal Prago. So Rico and Prago kill Vickie's son and stab her. A lot. Her husband Eddie believes in the law until a crooked judge sets Rico free and Eddie ends up going to jail. Nick is a vigilante who has friends who are vigilantes. Good, old-fashioned street justice may prevail.

Vigilante is a *Death Wish*–type film by William Lustig, the man who gave us *Maniac*. Both films are good. *Maniac* exists in the slasher-psycho realm of the early 1980s while *Vigilante* emu-

lates the *Death Wish* films. But Mr. Lustig doesn't play fair. Many of the slashers (regardless of their actual subject matter) are fun to watch. *Maniac* is not fun at all. Many of the vigilante-type films are good fun too. In fact, *Death Wish 3* might be one of the goofiest films of the 1980s. But *Vigilante* is not fun. It never gives the viewer any sort of cathartic release. Its events happen and then it ends.

This makes it one of the most interesting of this genre of film. The gang members are ridiculously awful but always just on the side of reality. There's a possibility that Eddie being sent to prison is a bit too obvious of a plotline. But the rest of it has an inexorable movement towards the sequences of revenge. Although they are well shot, they're never fun.

Vigilante Nick is the one who says that people must take the law into their own hands. When Eddie asks how doing this

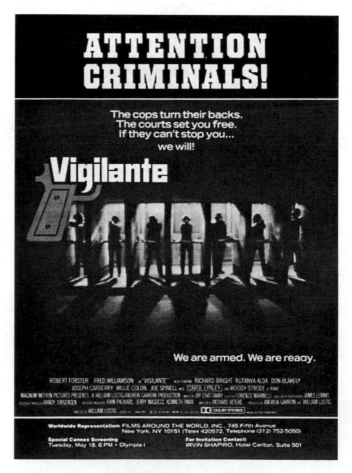

makes us better than the thugs, Nick says that's what each man has to face. That's what the movie presents to the viewer. It's tough to get a good feeling from any of this film. In that respect, it's quite a bit like *I Spit on Your Grave* in which a woman raped by four men takes her revenge. None of it is entertaining. She seemed alive at the beginning but has dead eyes at the end. And the men are terrible. Dramatically, it's wonderful to see them get their comeuppance but there's no joy there. *Vigilante* is like that.

If the acting in the film were bad or camp, it would fail. But everyone here is strong. And the film has that low-budget New York City vibe that gets into your soul. A few years later, *Street Trash* took the gritty and made it fun. But *Vigilante* is an almost tragic, Shakespearean journey as bad people do bad things and then good people do bad things to return the favor. No one comes out of this with their hands clean. So what is the solution? How do you get justice? There doesn't seem to be an answer.

War Bus

Director: Ted Kaplan
Screenplay: Ted Kaplan, John L. Fitzsimons
Producers: Francis F. Feels, Tony Miland
Cast: Daniel Stephen, Romano Kristoff, Urd Althaus, Gwendolyn Cook

Namsploitation seems like the strangest genre of cinema since the Spaghetti Western. For the Western, Italians appropriated iconic imagery from the Old West of America to make larger-than-life Westerns that became, in some ways, bigger and better than many of the films they were emulating. With the Vietnam War and American films about the war and the veterans, such as *The Deer Hunter* and *First Blood*, Italy did it again. They began to make action films based on the fighting in Vietnam, while sort of missing the emotion and the point.

What they did get, in spades, was the action. Lots and lots of Vietnamese characters being shot by Italians pretending to be Americans. *War Bus* is one of the best of these.

Christian missionaries are driving through the jungles of North Vietnam in a school bus, doing the things that missionaries do. Three tough-as-nails American Marines force them to turn the bus around and head to a supply base. It seemed to be the perfect set-up for a bunch of characters who no one cares about, shooting people we care about even less. It seemed like this was going to be a long 95 minutes.

Then the film does something unexpected. The characters began to develop. Not a lot, but some. They become likable. What seemed like a group of faceless missionaries and three fairly interchangeable soldiers becomes more interesting as they fight their way through the Vietcong. Romances develop. Connections between characters are revealed and new ones are created. By time they reach their final stand, in a small deserted village, I didn't want any of them to die.

There's a lot of well done action in this movie. The viewer can feel the grinding gears of this school bus as it goes along rocky terrain. The sweat on the actors almost jumps out of the screen. It may sound strange but, somehow, *War Bus* becomes an emotional, visceral experience and succeeds in being a good movie. By giving that much more energy to the relationships, this becomes a film worth watching.

Warrior of the Lost World

Director, Screenplay: David Worth
Producers: Robert Bessi, Frank E. Hildebrand
Cast: Robert Ginty, Persis Khambatta, Donald Pleasence, Fred Williamson, Harrison Muller

Almost non-stop shooting and car chases is the order of the day in writer-director David Worth's *Warrior of the Lost World*. Robert Ginty plays the mumbling Warrior, recruited to rescue an important man from the clutches of the Evil Prossor and his group of Omegas. They're planning to create a New World Order, and you know that stuff is never good. There is rescuing galore by the Warrior and the important man's daughter. When the daughter is left behind, they have to go back to get her. A bunch of gangs, *a la The Warriors*, are recruited to help fight the Omegas. There's a super truck called Megaweapon. Donald Pleasence is slimy. It's all here for the delectation of the viewer.

The mix of then-popular actors and lots of guys in jumpsuits getting shot makes this one of the most all-out entertaining post-apocalyptic films out there. There's very little actual unpleasantness like in, say, *2020: Texas Gladiators*. It's basically a loner with a talking motorcycle sent to rescue somebody and it's fun. I appreciate movies that are simply out to entertain. Some good guys, some bad guys. All varieties of shooting and car chases. Yes, the story isn't much. But it's post-apocalyptic Earth!

Warrior of the Lost World takes the fun chase bits of *The Road Warrior* and replays them over and over. Some viewers may have trouble getting around the Warrior's general mumbling man attitude. But, he's just following a template so the viewer can't really blame him. Life is too short to argue over whether a fun movie is worth watching. Watch this one. It's an action-filled, crazy experience that makes the post-apocalypse into a carnival for everyone involved.

Wheels of Fire

> *Director, Producer:* Cirio H. Santiago
> *Screenplay:* Ellen Collett, Fred Bailey
> *Cast:* Gary Watkins (Trace), Laura Banks (Stinger), Lynda Wiesmeier (Arlie), Linda Grovenor (Spike)

Producer-director Cirio H. Santiago gave Trace a flame thrower so there could be lots and lots of scenes of flame flying through the air and setting stuntmen alight. There are a few shots where flame just flies in from a corner of the frame and people catch on fire. It's fun. And it's post-apocalyptic. Here's what's memorable:

(1) The flame thrower
(2) A female character being topless for much of the movie
(3) White-haired dwarves called Sandmen

(4) A shot of men creeping along assorted levels of a mountain.

There's not much to the plot. Loner Trace tries to rescue his sister who was kidnapped by a gang led by a creepy guy named the Scourge. There are car chases, a mooning, dwarves speaking dubbed gibberish and lots of fighting. Sexual assault is thrown in because that's the sort of thing that these films do.

I can't say I'm a huge fan of Mr. Santiago's work. Some of it is nutty but a lot of times I have a tough time staying interested. *Wheels of Fire* is a post-apocalyptic thriller with even less backstory and shadings of characters and motivations than many of these types of films. It does have the action, though. Santiago does not short-change the viewer there.

But it's all been done before, and done better, elsewhere. Yes, the dwarves are great. (A Santiago specialty!) But getting excited about this is tough.

Wizards of the Lost Kingdom

> *Director:* Hector Olivera
> *Screenplay:* Tom Edwards
> *Producers:* Frank Isaac, Alex Sessa
> *Cast:* Bo Svenson (Kor), Vidal Peterson (Simon), Thom Christopher (Shurka), Barbara Stock (Udea), Maria Socas (Acrasia), Edward Murrow (Gulfax)

Simon, a young wizard's son, is sent away from his kingdom with a magic ring. A malefactor named Shurka takes over. The kid teams with Kor (Bo Svenson) and they have a series of adventures with dead warriors, monsters, midget wizards and one-eyed things. A large white Chewbacca-like sidekick, Gulfax, is with them. A good time is had by all. *Wizards of the Lost Kingdom* is only around 75 minutes, a good length for this sort of thing.

The movie does all the stuff that the sword-and-sorcery adventures of this time did. It is filled with awesome optical effects. Its plotline involves a magical ring and a magical sword. A loner warrior ends up helping the kid. It has the gloating bad guy and a mermaid with her top off. The latter was a bit surprising but then *Splash* had boobs in it and that was for the whole family.

The action is fine. The locations range from lots of woods to a beautiful system of waterfalls with a series of wooden fences around the edge of the cliffs to keep medieval warriors from falling in.

Bo Svenson is always fun. Gulfax is awesome. In effect he is Chewbacca, but in execution he's a bit closer to the polar bear from the North Pole sequence of *Santa Claus Conquers the Martians*. Regardless, Gulfax is a charmer.

Wizards of the Lost Kingdom has epic music, lots of extras and a whole slew of bad things to bedevil our heroes. In short, everything one needs from a film like this. If you like sword-and-sorcery films, this is one to try on a night when you just want to relax and Gulfax-out.

1986

Highest grossing films in the U.S.
1. *Top Gun*
2. *Crocodile Dundee*
3. *Platoon*
4. *The Karate Kid, Part II*
5. *Star Trek IV: The Voyage Home*

Highest rated TV shows in the U.S.
1. *The Cosby Show*
2. *Family Ties*
3. *Cheers*
4. *Murder, She Wrote*
5. *The Golden Girls*

Big historical events
Chernobyl
Challenger explodes
Halley's Comet
Iran-Contra scandal

Action movies
Top Gun, Platoon, The Karate Kid, Part II, Aliens, Cobra, Running Scared, Iron Eagle, F/X, Firewalker, Big Trouble in Little China, Highlander, No Retreat, No Surrender, P.O.W.—The Escape

Action U.S.A. aka *A Handful of Trouble*

Director: John Stewart
Screenplay: David Reskin
Producers: Alan Stewart, Susan Stewart
Cast: Gregory Alan Cummins (Osborne), William Hubbard Knight (Panama), Barri Murphy (Carmen), Ross Hagen (Drago), William Smith (Conover), Cameron Mitchell

A man with mob ties is killed. In his last moments, he gives his girlfriend Carmen some cryptic clues about diamonds hidden away somewhere. FBI agents Osborne and Panama put Carmen under protective custody. Drago, plus some other equally evil men, are all after Carmen because they're all after those diamonds. Action ensues. Friendships are forged. Wisecracks are delivered. Welcome to *Action U.S.A.*

The MacGuffin, a time-honored device in action films, is the thing that everyone in the film wants, whether it be microfilm, a painting, diamonds, whatever. Usually, the object is nothing but a plot device. *Action U.S.A.* has a great MacGuffin because the hunt for Carmen and the diamonds keeps the movie moving but never forces one to think too much about why everyone is doing what they're doing. (This sometimes happens with James Bond films.) All you have to remember is who is good and who is bad.

Once a MacGuffin is established, the rest of the film can be action. Stuntmen made this movie in Texas and did it beautifully. From the opening helicopter stunt scene to the finale on the bridge, it scorches along with strong action scenes and much excitement. It is helped greatly by the fact that the leads, Carmen, Osborne and Panama, are funny and charming and the viewer doesn't want them to be hurt. A problem with many action films is: who cares? The filmmakers can blow up whatever they want or have a car chase that goes on forever. But, if the characters are crap, then it's just images moving across a screen. To make it interesting, talent is required. Most of these films are not made by major talents.

Stunts, car chases, bar brawls, explosions, craziness. These are the words that make *Action U.S.A.* a real treat. It is a very entertaining and rather thrilling film that, even at its roughest moments, is still fun. It's almost in the same realm as Brian Trenchard-Smith's *Stunt Rock*, a movie about stunts and rock. It doesn't get more simple than that and it's all in the delivery. *Action U.S.A.* delivers. Its original title *A Handful of Trouble*, might be a better title. But the one they went with promises and then delivers.

America 3000

Director, Screenplay: David Englebach
Producers: Menahem Golan, Yoram Globus
Cast: Chuck Wagner (Korvis), Lauren Landon (Vena), William Wallace, Victoria Barrett (Lakella), Sue Giosa (Morha)

Some movies create beautiful, epic worlds that a viewer wants to become enveloped in, whether it be a recreated past, a future or a modern day reimagined in some fashion. But not all movies do it well. *America 3000* is post-apocalyptic, a man vs. woman thing. Kind of a comedy, it's around 90 minutes but feels much longer.

Women are in charge. They round up men. They force some of them to work and force others to breed. Gradually the men reawaken. It's also about learning what happened to our Earth. The whole thing is narrated by a guy named Korvis. In fact, he narrates so much that it smacks of post-production jiggery pokery. The narration confuses things.

The main problem with this action-comedy is that it creates a whole new language. The leader of the women is the Tiara. Men are prugols or something like that. There are a lot of made-up words. They're annoying and they show how silly made-up sci-fi words can be. Within the first two minutes, I'd written down half a dozen words, trying to match them to what they meant. Within the next two minutes, I said "To hell with it" and hoped I could get by okay without knowing these things. Most of the time it worked.

The action is decent. There are a whole bunch of fights and chaotic moments. There's a pretty good scene where the *1812 Overture* plays. So, as an action film, *America 3000* is okay. But story-wise it's not terribly interesting. Because the movie goes on and on, you get the feeling that those involved thought this was clever and groundbreaking when, really, it's kind of infuriating. At least, the women all have big hair. And why are the drums in this film so loud?

Assassin

Director, Screenplay: Sandor Stern
Producer: Neil T. Maffeo
Cast: Robert Conrad (Henry Stanton), Karen Austin (Mary Casallas), Richard Young (Robert Golem), Jonathan Banks (Earl Dickman), Robert Webber (Calvin Lantz)

A top secret government project robot breaks loose and goes on an assassination spree. Only one man can stop him: Robert Conrad as Henry Stanton. Since it's Robert Conrad, you know that he's gonna get 'er done. It'll be tricky, though, because the robot, named Robert Golem, is pretty much indestructible. It needs 20 minutes a day to recharge. If it's cornered and believes all hope is lost, it will self-destruct.

Assassin is a decent TV movie written and directed by the man who wrote the *Amityville Horror* screenplay. There are several excellent confrontations between the good guys and the bad guys. Mr. Golem leaps out of a lot of windows from great heights. It gets shot a lot. Yet it keeps going and going. Prof. DuBerry, who made Golem, made him well.

Conrad always seems a bit like he's going to punch someone anyways, so it's good to see him in a tough guy role where he should be punching people. They team him with the professor's co-worker (Karen Austin). Jonathan Banks, from *Breaking Bad*, plays a rather sleazy government agent.

Sandor does a fine job of directing. He keeps the action and suspense moving along. And, since the film is about a robot, rather than cyborg, there's no half-human fiddling around, no "issues." It's a straightforward "Find the Killer Robot" movie. It's like a *Westworld* robot had gotten out of the amusement park. But, it definitely feels more *Terminator* than *Westworld*.

A lot of the character development be-
tween Conrad and Karen Austin isn't terribly interesting. The focus on the robot hunt is more fun. *Assassin* is a good, entertaining *Terminator*-esque film, worth a viewing.

Avenging Force

Director: Sam Firstenberg
Screenplay: James Booth
Producers: Menahem Golan, Yoram Globus
Cast: Michael Dudikoff (Matt Hunter), Steve James (Larry Richards), James Booth (Admiral Brown), Bill Wallace (Delaney), John P. Ryan (Glastenbury)

The Pentangle is a group of elitist, conservative white guys in New Orleans. Not only do they hate everything that is not them, they amuse themselves by hunting people through the swamps, *a la The Most Dangerous Game.* They kill *Invasion U.S.A.'s* Matt Hunter's best friend (and his best friend's family) and they kidnap Matt's sister. You had better believe that the Hunters may become the Hunted.

Avenging Force isn't as much fun as *American Ninja 1* and *2* but it is very good with Golan & Globus watching over it all, Sam Firstenberg pulling out all the stops and Michael Dudikoff (with *American Ninja* pal Steve James) kicking, punching and winning. Chuck Norris is not here. but, Dudikoff is a worthy replacement. Dudikoff handles the action with his trademark aplomb and (small spoiler) he saves the day. There's the hint of a sequel that it never came.

If I know that Firstenberg, Dudikoff and swamp fighting are combined in one movie, there is nothing to do but watch and enjoy. The Pentangle are gross militants. They are good fighters. Out in the swamp, they kick ass. They even get dressed up in assorted outfits to make themselves scarier. Steve James is awesome as Larry. The scene where the Pentangle sets fire to his house is heartbreaking.

But it's Dudikoff's picture and he pulls off the Starring Role Win. After they kidnap his sister, he becomes a man possessed. He escapes with his sister (who is around 12) through the swamp, and the Pentangle come after him as if she's not there. The one with

"American Ninja"
MICHAEL DUDIKOFF

A killer cult just picked the wrong target.

AVENGING FORCE

6 PM TONIGHT (11) WPIX

the rifle shoots her in the shoulder. Those are some nasty jackasses. More nasty than the government agents who recruit Hunter to take the Pentangle down. They're basically just using Hunter to do their dirty work. The scene where Hunter enters the government office with his wounded sister is the movie's best moment ... maybe the most kick-ass moment of Dudikoff's career.

Avenging Force might not reach the stratosphere like *Invasion U.S.A.* but it's a really well-made film where everyone seems to be giving it their all. It's the flipside to the *American Ninja*s which are basically fun, slightly goofy, good times. This one is darker, a little more unpleasant but still top-notch action.

Behind Enemy Lines aka *Attack Force 'Nam*

Director: Gideon Amir

Screenplay: Malcolm Barbour, James Bruner, Avi Kleinberger, John Langley, Jeremy Lipp

Producer: Yoram Globus

Cast: David Carradine (Col. James Cooper), Charles R. Floyd (Sparks), Mako Iwamatsu (Capt. Vinh), Steve James (Johnston), Phil Brock (Adams)

Col. Cooper is sent into the heart of Vietnam to find POWs. The war is drawing to a close. Cooper is determined to find some boys in the camps or die trying. He even comes with his own credo. Carradine plays a tough colonel. When he says something, it is believed.

Behind Enemy Lines is a Cannon production. They had already had a hit with *Missing in Action* so it seemed logical to try again and bring on a Carradine. The movie ends up being a bit more of a serious film than was expected and, possibly, a little less fun. It's all in the structure.

The movie opens with Col. Cooper being sent to a prison camp to rescue POWs. He does ... but he doesn't make it out. And he spends quite some time being mistreated by Capt. Vinh. Eventually an escape plan is put together. There are traitors and heroes.

Behind Enemy Lines is okay for what it is: another movie about soldiers trying to get the POWs out of Vietnam. It gets better as it goes along. The camp sequences go on for a very long time and aren't all that interesting. The action, when it comes, is good. There's an excellent chase between two Jeeps at night on an old bridge. The final combat scenes are nicely done, with the soldiers rushing towards the helicopters to get out of there. There is a moment with a hand grenade that is painful and moving.

Behind Enemy Lines tells a story that you've probably seen before. But if you loved *Missing in Action*, try this one.

Bionic Ninja

Director, Screenplay: Godfrey Ho

Producer: Joseph Lai

Cast: Mike Abbott, Michael Cartwright, Peter Cressall, Marcus Egan, Morna Lee

When a roll of technical secret film is stolen by ninjas working for the KGB, CIA agent Tommy heads to the Far East to try to retrieve it. Along the way, there's a lot of sex, a lot of fighting, a lot of his cop friend Fatso and many of the glorious side trips that we expect from Ho-Lai productions. The side trips become so numerous that the viewer can forget what the movie is actually about.

It's about ninjas and that stolen film, which has some sort of secret something on it. Does it matter? It could be footage of Ernest Borgnine taking a bubble bath. It's not really important. All one needs to know is that Tommy wants it and the ninjas, led by the evil Number Zero, have it. Tommy does a lot of working out, running through parks and such in his kick-ass canary yellow workout outfit. He looks good.

Bionic Ninja doesn't have any bionic ninjas in it. Tommy is dubbed hilariously, as he should be. He looks kind of bizarre in that yellow work-

out suit. I recognized one of Jackie Chan's stuntmen, which told me that the fights were probably going to be pretty darn good. They are. There's quite a bit of sex in the film. Sometimes the quality of the film changes drastically from sex scene to sex scene, making me think that maybe they had spliced in bits from a porno film. They may have.

The ninjas are fantastic. They do work for the KGB, which explains why Japanese ninjas are in Hong Kong. The four main

FORCE 10 ENTERTAINMENT IN

BIONIC NINJA

THOUGHT, WORD, DEED AND ART OF KILLING. OF THE BIONIC WARRIOR IN THE WAYS OF THE NINJA

STARRING
KELLY STEVE • ALAN HEMMINGS • RICK WILSON
PETER CHAN • ANDY MAN • JACK YOUNG
PAULINE CHAO • ALEX BAKER

NINJA CHRONICLES VOL. 3   MADE IN U.S.A.

ninjas keep appearing in the best places. For example, several of the characters from the Hong Kong film will be talking. Then the film will cut to a car parked at the curb. Suddenly, a ninja head will appear around a corner. Then the other one right above that one. Then, the third above him and the fourth above him. And they don't lean into the shot, they *pop* into the shot. Sudden appearances! It is hilarious. If it just happened once, that would be funny. But, it happens several times and it is a laugh riot.

Bionic Ninja is right up there with *Ninja: Silent Assassin* as one of the nuttiest ones that Ho-Lai did. Partially because the action footage from the Hong Kong film is good. It's got that Hong Kong verve that all their films had around this time. Then, when it cuts to the ninjas, it is just one loopy adventure after another. The joy of these films is that there is so much weird stuff in them that you can't remembers it all. I'm thinking of about eight weird things right now that I'd love to mention … but I think you should discover it for yourself.

Catch the Heat

Director: Joel Silberg

Screenplay: Stirling Silliphant

Producer: Don Van Atta

Cast: Tiana Alexander (Checkers Goldberg), David Dukes (Waldo), Rod Steiger (Jason Hannibal)

This film was written by Academy Award winner Stirling Silliphant for his wife Tiana Alexander, who plays Checkers Goldberg, secret agent. It takes place mainly in Buenos Aires. There is a lot of great action, most of it involving Checkers kicking people's asses. The film is about heroin smuggling from Argentina to the United States.

From the lead's name

(Checkers) to the name she is given when she goes undercover (Cinderella Poo) to the fact that she can kick ass and is a very proficient action hero but seems to wind up in a lot of wacky situations, this film is out to entertain. Rod Steiger seems to know it. He gives one of those performances that involves him sometimes overacting, sometimes seeming completely detached from everything around him. A favor may have been called in from Silliphant's *In the Heat of the Night* days. But Steiger has nothing to worry about. This film is no embarrassment.

Checkers is fantastic. She's charming. She's tough. She's smart. She's got a good kung fu high kick that will take a man's face out. She's everything you could want from a female secret agent or, in fact, any sort of agent. She also does the tango. She pretends to play the submissive Asian female on occasion. But, this is usually followed by the aforementioned high kick to the head. Sometimes all a film

Feel The Suspense, Live The Action, Sense The Danger.

CATCH THE HEAT

needs is a charming lead (or leads) to elevate it. Ms. Alexander is a lot of fun in *Catch the Heat*. When she's onscreen, the film becomes even more entertaining.

This is one of those films that should simply be viewed. Sit down, watch, enjoy. There's not much to deconstruct here. This is an efficient, fun action film done well. There are days when that is all that the viewer needs.

Clash of the Ninjas

Director: Godfrey Ho
Screenplay: Kurt Spielberg
Producer: Tomas Tang
Cast: Louis Roth (Mr. Roy), Paul Torcha (Tony), Joe Redner (Mr. Foster), Eric Neff, Bernie Junkner, Stanley Tong

Clash of the Ninjas has as pointless a title as every other Ho-Tang ninja collaboration. You think it might be something mythological, *a la Clash of the Titans*. Nope. There is no ninja Medusa or giant ninja Kraken. The movie begins with illegal organ removal for fun and profit. A man is dragged down a hall, strapped onto a table and has bits removed (including his eyes). Several unwilling donors escape. Mr. Roy, who slings a hell of a bullwhip, sends ninjas (and himself) to recapture them. Tony from Interpol tries to protect them. It culminates in a glorious fight between Tony and Mr. Roy in full ninja regalia, Ho-style.

That synopsis implies more coherence than the film has. The whole organ donor thing seems to vanish away in the midst of multiplying characters and fights, some with ninjas, some without. Does coherence really matter in something like this? The organ removal scene adds a sleazy excitement and a nice touch of horror to the film. Frankly, I would have loved to have seen some more of it here.

Clash of the Ninjas benefits from all the usual Ho-Tang hallmarks: general incoherence, mismatching of footage, an offbeat concept of ninja dress sense, stolen music (this time from Pink Floyd's *Animals*), hilarious fighting in the "new" footage and pretty good fighting in the "old" footage. There's nothing to dislike about a film like this. It wants to be loved. Then it wants to take whatever money it can from you. But a movie that starts with

FILMARK INTERNATIONAL Presents
A TOMAS TANG Production
PAUL TORCHA · LOUIS ROTH · ERIC NEFF In
CLASH OF THE NINJAS
Starring BERNIE JUNKER · JOE REDNER · KLAUS MUTTER · EDDIE CHAN
MAX KWAN · TOM ALLEN And STANLEY TONG
Screenplay by KURT SPIELBERG Action Director TONG KONG
Special Effects By KELLY ADAMS Associate Producer DALLIE YEUNG
Produced By TOMAS TANG Directed By WALLACE CHAN
© FILMARK INTERNATIONAL LIMITED

a man having his eyeballs removed and ends with a ninja with a bullwhip fighting another ninja wearing a fashionable crimson head band thing has got to be good for something.

I don't know whether or not the Stanley Tong in the cast list is the man who directed *Rumble in the Bronx, Supercop* and *Mr. Magoo* (which is really quite a good movie). Any information would be greatly appreciated.

Diamond Ninja Force

Director, Screenplay: Godfrey Ho
Producers: Betty Chan, Joseph Lai
Cast: Richard Harrison (Gordon), Clifford Allan, Pierre Tembley, Andy Chrorowsky, Melvin Pitcher

This is another in the endless number of Ho-Lai ninja films that invaded home video in the second half of the 1980s. There's 10 or 15 minutes of new footage with ninjas talking about their burial sites and Gordon, the good ninja, fighting people. This is intercut with footage from an Asian supernatural film about a haunted house and the family trying to live there. It's got ghost rape, maggots coming out of taps, children being chased around by ghosts and a rather wacky sorcerer on the side of evil.

It's all a hell of a lot of fun. The supernatural bits are well done. Some of the scenes are too dark and the seduction scenes go on for a very long time. But it's actually rather creepy. It has a sort of "anything goes" quality which makes it entertaining. Now, the dubbing (which tries to mix the supernatural together with the ninja plotline) is as dumb as ever. A man named Firecracker gets the "really dumb dubbed guy" award for this film. But everyone, including the child named Bobo, gets in on the action.

Diamond Ninja Force takes disjointedness to whole new levels. Harrison's Gordon gets in some ninja fights. And there is the obligatory closing fight scene after all the supernatural shenanigans are wrapped up. Gordon and another ninja fight. Gordon wins. But the action is less important to this film than the other ones because the horror element actually works.

With *Diamond Ninja Force*, Ho-Lai got lucky: They ended up with a horror–kung fu cut-and-paste hybrid that stands on its own. Characters named Firecracker, Bobo and Fanny make it funny. I wonder who wrote the dubbed dialogue. If it was Godfrey Ho, he is a comic genius the likes of which we may never see again.

Eliminators

Director: Peter Mannogian
Screenplay: Paul De Meo, Danny Bilson
Producer: Charles Band
Cast: Andrew Prine (Henry Fontana), Denise Crosby (Col. Nora Hunter), Patrick Reynolds (Mandroid/John), Conan Lee (Kuji), Roy Dotrice (Abbott Reeves)

Somewhere deep in Mexico in a compound hidden by dense forests, a strange old man named Abbot Reeves creates a time machine and sends a mandroid, a half-robot/half-man (whose body was salvaged from a plane crash), to Ancient Rome on a test run. When the mandroid successfully returns, Reeves orders it destroyed. The mandroid, who retains some semblance of humanity, doesn't want to die, so it escapes from the compound. It goes to the U.S. and meets Col. Nora Hunter, who used to work with Reeves. Together with a grizzled riverboat captain and a ninja, they head into Mexico to stop Reeves from altering the entire history of humanity.

Yes, it sounds a bit crazy. However, if you skip *Eliminators*, you'll be skipping an excellent film. Director Peter Mannogian knows how to direct an action scene. The editing is crisp, the pace is on target, and the effects are plentiful and generally quite good.

Col. Hunter has a little robot named Search Patrol and Operation Tactician, SPOT for short. SPOT comes in very handy. Andrew Prine plays a great grizzled guy making a living by undercutting the other riverboat people. The ninja sorta appears out of nowhere. Of course, a movie can always benefit from a ninja. Denise Crosby, as Nora Hunter, has got a kind of wry smile that makes you want to help her stop a megalomaniac from changing the history of Earth. The mandroid is good.

Wooden but with that slight bit of humanity that makes him likable.

The film culminates in a huge attack on the compound. Plenty of thugs being shot at. Reeves wields some fantastic technology. There are a lot of great capture and escape sequences. Spolier: John the Mandroid is destroyed saving the other three. Then those three rush the time machine lab and save history, and the movie ends. There is never an appropriate sendoff for the mandroid. The ending is so joyous (they saved history) that our heroes forget the character who started everything. That seemed strange. It's different, certainly. Maybe that was the point. *Eliminators*, you are fun.

Equalizer 2000

Director, Producer: Cirio H. Santiago
Screenplay: Frederick Bailey
Cast: Richard Norton (Capt. Slade), Corrine Wahl (Karen), Henry Strzalkowski (Namo), Robert Patrick (Deke), Rex Cutter (Dixon)

Back to the Philippines … back to the post-apocalyptic wastelands … hunting for water and fuel. A bunch of jackasses wants Capt. Slade's gun. It shoots people in several different ways and it's really snazzy-looking. There is a woman named Karen, who's hot. Robert Patrick plays Deke; he's fine here, but he'd do better later. Cirio H. Santiago was in charge of this one. His fascination with the apocalypse and the society afterwards continues. His use of tiny people continues also.

The society isn't sketched out well. It looks more like a bunch of people hanging out in some desert area. The bad guys (the ones after the gun) look a lot more well-off than everyone else. Santiago's films are very hit-and-miss. Some of them work well and are grand exploitation fun. Others are very perfunctory, very matter-of-fact. Very blah. *Equalizer 2000* is in this category. It never takes off. The action is pretty constant but none of it has much style. The initial car chase with Karen is exciting.

Richard Norton is fine as Capt. Slade. He always looks good shooting, fighting or driving around. But when Karen takes him to meet "her people" and they look exactly like every one of the *Road Warrior*-type societies from every one of these films, my heart sank a little. The idea of meeting another group like this and being made to "befriend" another batch of people like this makes "Tired" the emotion of the moment. Not every one of Santiago's films can be a winner.

For folks who like this subgenre, *Equalizer 2000* will keep them interested. But it all seems a bit dull, a bit rehashed.

Final Score

Director: Arizal
Screenplay: Deddy Armand
Producer: Gopet Santani
Cast: Chris Mitchum (Richard Brown), Mike Abbott (Hawk), Ida Iasha (Julia), Dicky Zulkarneen (Maj. Handoya), August Melasz (Alex)

Sometimes you have to go way out of town to get a full-on fix of crazy-ass action. If one wants mindless and possibly endless carnage involving a wronged man shooting and chasing and blowing things up, get on board for *Final Score*. It is Indonesian or, as I think of it, Indo-Awesome. It stars Chris Mitchum, the man who lent his wonder to *The Executioner Part II*. When the evil Hawk kills your son and your wife (or was it his housekeeper?), all one can do is take revenge hard and swift.

Final Score includes blown-up buildings, shootouts and car chases. After a very lengthy car chase, Brown (Mitchum) is talking with a friend by some water about what had just happened. Then a speedboat goes by and starts shooting at him. This film is constant bloodshed.

The attack on Brown's loved ones is the catalyst for his journey of revenge. He goes after the four men Hawk sent after him. One by one, he kills them in assorted entertaining ways. Then he goes after everyone connected with Hawk. Mitchum keeps his game face on, which means he doesn't emote much. But it's okay. All you need to do is watch him and know that he is the good guy and the people he kills are the bad guys.

Final Score is brilliant. Best movie ever? Possibly. It starts off in high gear and stays there. The dialogue is hilarious, the chases are exciting and it's never-ending. The closing stunt involving a motorcycle, a helicopter and an exploding pagoda-type building is awkwardly filmed but nigh on hilarious. If one likes a film that requires brains to be checked at the door and shooting to become the tune of the day, this is it.

When Hawk and Brown match wits, it is exciting. It is hilarious. It is definitely worth watching. Twice. Maybe a third time.

Future Hunters

Director: Cirio H. Santiago
Screenplay: Anthony Maharaj, J. L. Thompson
Producer: Anthony Maharaj
Cast: Robert Patrick (Slade), Linda Carol (Michelle), Ed Crick (Fielding), Bruce Le (Liu), Richard Norton (Matthew), Bob Schott (Bauer)

One of Cirio H. Santiago's best films, *Future Hunters* has an epic *Road Warrior–Terminator–Indiana Jones and the Temple of Doom–Romancing the Stone* feel to it. It's more exciting than many of Santiago's films and the acting is a step above. Robert Patrick and Linda Carol as the leads really throw themselves into it. And, in true Santiago fashion, there's a scene with dwarves. There is also time travel and a quest to match up the blade and the shaft of the Spear of Longinus.

Longinus was the Roman who stabbed Jesus Christ in the side while Christ hung on the cross. Now, in 2045, five years after the apocalypse, it can be used to travel through time. A man named Matthew is sent back to 1986 to try and reunite the Spear, which will stop the future apocalypse. Or something like that. To be honest, I kind of lost track of the plotline. After the car chases and the fights with bikers and the Nazi attacks and the pygmies in the caves and the rockslides and the exploding helicopters, I could not remember what was up.

Future Hunters begins with Matthew and the head of the spear going back in time.

MAHARAJ/SANTIAGO PRODUCTIONS
PRESENTS
FUTURE HUNTERS
STARRING • ROBERT PATRICK • LINDA CAROL • ED CRICK • BOB SCHOTT
URSULA MARQUEZ • ELIZABETH OROPESA and RICHARD NORTON as "MATTHEW"
Story by ANTHONY MAHARAJ   Screenplay by J. L. THOMPSON
Produced by ANTHONY MAHARAJ   Directed by CIRIO H. SANTIAGO

AVID
Home Entertainment

Some bikers kill him. A couple of nice young people, Slade and Michelle, agree to complete his mission. That's when the crazy starts to happen. Everyone seems to know about the Spear and its power. In Hong Kong, Slade and Michelle meet up with Bruce Le, who is still doing his Bruce Lee shtick. Then a really ugly Aryan man arrives and the Nazis join the bunch.

There's something kind of free-for-all about this movie. After they get to the jungle, things start to go loopy. Robert Patrick, a few years before playing the T-1000, joins in the fun. Linda Carol is cute and handles herself well throughout. To be honest, seeing Bruce Le was the weird thing here. When he arrives, all I could think was, "Oh, it's one of those movies. Where's Dick Randall?" Le does pull off his shirt (awkwardly) before one fight but he doesn't really do that much.

Future Hunters stakes its claim to being one of Santiago's most ambitious with the century-spanning plotline, the globetrotting adventure and the epic musical score that sometimes gets a bit *too* epic. But it's exciting and something is always happening. That's good stuff. This might be my favorite Santiago.

Hands of Steel

Director: Sergio Martino (as Martin Dolman)

Screenplay: Elisabeth Paula, Sergio Martino (as Martin Dolman), Saul Saska, John Crowther

Producer: Luciano Martino

Cast: Daniel Greene (Paco Queruak), Janet Agren (Linda), Claudio Cassinelli (Peter Howell), George Eastman (Paul Morales)

Nowhere else in this book will you find a film that starts off as a political assassination thriller and then proceeds to take in *The Ter-*minator, *Blade Runner* and *Over the Top*. Most of *Hands of Steel* is set in the deserts of Arizona. Revel in the warm air and the hot sun. I'm not a big fan of the desert but I'll watch it in a movie. Especially if cyborg Paco Queruak is storming around shooting and breaking things with those hands of his.

Paco attempts to assassinate a political candidate. He goes on the run and winds up in the desert at a hotel run by lovely Linda. Several scientists are after Paco because Paco

is a cyborg. Everybody at the hotel loves arm wrestling. Bull Hurley from *Over the Top* shows up to have an arm wrestling match with Paco, Indian-style. That means there is a rattlesnake involved. Will Paco survive? Does he have any humanity left?

A hybrid movie to end all hybrid movies, *Hands of Steel* starts off a little boring, with the political stuff. And Paco does quite a bit of driving through the desert. Once Paco hits that desert hotel, though, things become pretty great. Slowly, the bad scientists and the authorities investigating the assassination attempt approach the hotel. And there's all that arm wrestling.

There are four screenwriters listed for this movie. One can only hope that each one of them brought a different element into it. One was bucking for *Terminator*-style cyborg stuff. One wanted to go more *Blade Runner*. One of them loved *Over the Top*. Then there's the political angle. The environment and acid rain comes up a lot.

Really, though, in true Italian '80s fashion, it's all about a lot of action. If you count arm wrestling as action, then this film is loaded with the good stuff. The action just keeps happening and happening. Paco is the strong center of it all. He's a big brick of a man who is either truly troubled by his half-humanity or thinking of something else most of the time. Regardless, viewers can put their own emotions on Paco and join the fray.

Hands of Steel is fine, furious desert action with arm wrestling and some sort of strange cyborg woman thrown in to confuse things.

The Intruder

> *Director:* Jopi Burnama
> *Screenplay:* Deddy Armand
> *Producers:* Dhamoo, Raann, Gobind Punjabi
> *Cast:* Peter O'Brian (Rambu),

Craig Gavin (John Smith), Lia Warokka (Angela), Dana Christina (Clara), Kaharuddin Syah (Andre)

The Indonesians made the wackiest action films of the 1980s. The jury was out for a while as the Italians churned out some pretty great stuff, but here it is, the deciding factor: From the makers of *The Stabilizer*, we have *The Intruder*. A title that makes very little sense for a movie made up of bits and pieces of other movies along with several wonderful moments of its own.

Peter O'Brian plays the great and mighty Rambu! Yes, Rambu. He helps the oppressed try and live a better life. He kicks ass whenever he sees injustice. Don't get on his

bad side because he will tear you up and then tear you back down. Rambu is one hell of a man. The cops are trying to recruit him and the evil Mr. Smith is trying to get him to turn to the dark side. None of it works because Rambu is all about working on his own and curing all the world's ills.

But Rambu is currently out of work. The movie doesn't say what sort of job he's waiting for. One would think that his great strength and sense of righteousness would be worth something cash-wise in Indonesia, but apparently not. If he stated what his profession was, I missed it. Much is made of the fact that he lives off of his girlfriend and he's not happy. Especially when she is sexually assaulted and killed. His love and his source of income, gone.

The film is filled with goofy things. Rambu complaining that he can't find work and he doesn't like living off a woman but all these places want to hire him to fight. And, randomly, when bad stuff happens, he appears and saves the day. Apparently, to be a super-hero, one truly does need to have some sort of outside income in order to make it. Rambu doesn't need cash for his fists but he does need to pay the rent.

The Intruder is awesome all the way around. This review has barely touched on the action because, like most Indonesian films, it's crazy and wonderful. Lots of shooting and fistfighting. There's even a fight in a field involving a fleet of small red golf cart–like vehicles. "Rambu! Rambu! That's I all hear about, is this Rambu!" says the bad guy, who is really unpleasant. At one point, he has potential sex slaves paraded before him and it's presented as if it's a runway model show. But the bad guy knows what the problem is: Rambu. The viewer knows what the awesome is: Rambu. *The Intruder* is a movie everyone should watch. Tonight.

Jake Speed

Director: Andrew Lane
Screenplay: Wayne Crawford, Andrew Lane
Producers: Andrew Lane, Wayne Crawford, William Fay

Cast: Wayne Crawford (Jake Speed), Dennis Christopher (Desmond Floyd), Karen Kopins (Margaret Winston), John Hurt (Sid), Leon Ames (Pop), Donna Pescow (Wendy)

In Paris, a young American woman is kidnapped by white slavers. Her family, back in Los Angeles, is distraught and the authorities seem helpless to find her. Grampa suggests hiring one of the great pulp adventure heroes, like Remo Williams or Mack Bolan or Jake Speed. At first, the family considers upping Grampa's daily meds. But, much to their surprise, Jake Speed turns out to be real. The Jake Speed series of books are based on an actual man's actual adventures. If you can contact his sidekick, Desmond, he will deliver you to Jake. Maggie, the kidnapped gal's sister, tracks down Desmond and earns an introduction to Jake. The next thing she knows, she and Jake are heading to an African country to save her sister. But is Jake for real? Or is he a con man? Or is he delusional?

The movie plays a constant "Is this guy a fake?" game with us. As the audience surrogate, Maggie remains unsure throughout. There are several moments where Jake makes meta references to the adventure including, at the very end, "We need a big finish." But, it never quite goes all the way with its conceit of the "Is He Real or Not?" It never seems to have the full courage of its postmodern convictions.

Karen Kopins as Maggie is a beguiling combination of Sherilynn Fenn and Linda Grey. One can sense her desperately wanting to believe in Jake but constantly disbelieving him too. Desmond writes about the adventure as the next book in the *Jake Speed* series.

When they meet up with nasty Sid the white slaver, one really hopes Jake can live up to his reputation because the viewer wants Maggie (and Jake) to get out of there. The books imply that he always does. But, what about reality? Are there times when Jake is the only one who makes it out and it's up to Desmond to supply the happy ending?

Jake Speed is, in the end, too self-conscious. It is less interested in action than in furthering the myth of Jake Speed. So, there aren't a lot of action sequences. The excitement is more of the adventure variety. Yes, in the last half hour there's lots of derring-do. Yes, in the end, it all makes sense. But up until the end, it all feels a little flat, a little less fun than we expected. But Jake, or the man playing Jake, is a hero. If you do get a little miffed at the lack of action, you can always enjoy watching him drive HARV, his armored vehicle, through an embassy building causing raucous amounts of destruction. That's fun.

The Lone Runner

Director: Ruggero Deodato
Screenplay: Steven Luotto, Chris Traimor
Producer: Ovidio G. Assonitis
Cast: Miles O'Keeffe (Garrett), Savina Gersak (Analisa Summerking), Donal Hodson (Mr. Summerking), Ronald Lacey (Misha), John Steiner (Skorm)

The Lone Runner (Miles O'Keeffe), aka Garrett, is a legendary gentleman who rights

wrongs out in the desert. He's hunky. He uses bows and arrows. He punches people. He saves young Analisa Summerking and her dad. Then she is kidnapped and he has to rescue her again. Desert landscapes, maniacal Arabs and constant O'Keeffe fights keep *The Lone Runner* moving.

Ruggero Deodato has made a lot of entertaining films. He's got sleazy down pat and he's pretty darn good with action films. *The New Barbarians*, anyone? So *The Lone Runner* stands up well as an entertaining mid–80s Italian action film. But I'm unsure which film Deodato was emulating when he made this one. *Lawrence of Arabia* with more fisticuffs and less splendor? When did *Ishtar* come out? The constant synths, which alternate between martial-style music and video poker triumphs, is a bit weird. This film could not have been made at any other time with that music. Could you imagine *Lawrence of Arabia* with music like that?

O'Keeffe is as fine as always. Wearing a neat hat and a cool outfit, he is a heroic legend here. Not a heroic legend that caught on like Ator did but how often does that happen? The rest of the cast is the mix of Italian actors who are always in these things and a lot of guys playing Arabs. The film keeps moving and it's not overlong. It's straightforward and has some good action.

If you like Deadato (and after *House at the Edge of Park* how could you not?), then you'll enjoy *The Lone Runner*.

Low Blow

Director: Frank Harris
Screenplay, Producer: Leo Fong
Cast: Leo Fong (Joe Wong), Cameron Mitchell (Yarakunda), Troy Donahue

(John Templeton), Akosua Busia (Karma), Diane Stevenett (Diane), Stack Pierce (Corky), Patti Bowling (Karen Templeton)

When the guitars start wailing and the *Invisible Touch*–style electronic percussion starts knocking you hard on the skull, it's Fong Time, baby! Leo Fong. He's back. This time he plays private detective Joe Wong. Troy Donahue plays a wealthy man named John Templeton. (With a name like that, he's got to be wealthy.) Troy's daughter has joined a cult run by Cameron Mitchell. Wearing a black hooded robe and dark sunglasses, Mitchell mumbles platitudes which his assistant repeats through a PA system.

Leo Fong, as always, is his ingratiating, ass-kicking self. He has a detective office with a sassy secretary. Joe Wong is sort of a Raymond Chandler but a little more amiable and with a black belt. He seems to constantly be stopping robberies or purse snatchings. He has a scene that I like to think of as "Classic Fong." Four guys in a car. Wong lifts the hood. Tears out the wires. Pounds the doors a lot. Takes a circular saw and cuts the roof off the car, making it a convertible. The bad guys run away. Classic Fong!

Fong is a fun presence. *Low Blow* is an entertaining film. The bad guys are clearly bad but it never becomes mean-spirited in the way that a lot of them do. Wong is having a good time solving cases. Plus, his car never starts! Joe Wong could have had his own detective TV show, although he probably wouldn't have been able to take out a cult every time.

Never Too Young to Die

Director: Gil Bettman
Screenplay: Steven Paul and Anton Fritz
Producer: Steven Paul

Cast: John Stamos (Lance Stargrove), Vanity (Danja Deeling), Gene Simmons (Velvet Von Ragnar), George Lazenby (Drew Stargrove), Peter Kuong (Cliff), Robert Englund (Riley)

This is a great film. A rollicking, silly, action-filled extravaganza featuring the star power of Stamos, Simmons and Vanity.

There is a disc with information about the Big City's water supply. Velvet Von Ragnar, transsexual rock star, wants it. Ragnar is going

to pump toxic waste into the water supply, ruining it forever, unless money is
sent tò him and his gang. A young man
stands in her way! Lance Stargrove!
Lance's dad is Drew, super-secret agent.
Drew sent Lance the disc right before
dying. Lance doesn't know he has it and
government agent Danja Deeling is
sent to help out. Danja Deeling is
played by Vanity at the height of her
drop dead gorgeous period. So any
good thing that is said about the film
here can be increased tenfold if you're
a fan.

Stamos, a solid action star, never
takes things too seriously but he kicks
ass. His character is a gymnast (shades
of *Gymkata*) and is able to move when
he needs to. The scene where he sends
a gang running and the final fight on
a dam are Key Stamos Moments. Simmons chews the scenery as only Gene
can. He also stays frightening, which
is a Key Simmons Thing. Vanity is,
well, a fine actress and pants-meltingly
hot.

Car chases, shootouts, fistfights,
acrobatic stunt sequences, all of it is
here. The movie never takes itself too
seriously, which makes it fun viewing. There
are moments that almost border on parody.
The tricked-out Stargrove house, for example,
is either the coolest house ever or a joke or
both.

Ninja Terminator

Director, Screenplay: Godfrey Ho
Producers: Joseph Lai, Betty Chan
Cast: Richard Harrison (Harry), Wong
Cheng Li (Tiger Chan), Jonathan Wattis
(Baron), Jack lan (Jaguar Wang), Maria
Francesca

The title *Ninja Terminator* is in the
World Book of Action Cinema as one of the
goofier entries in the Ho-Lai camp. That's saying something.

A ninja is given pieces of a small statuette
called the Golden Ninja Warrior. When they
are put together, the master becomes the
Supreme Ninja. Two disciples steal parts of
the statuette. Ninjas are sent to Hong King to
get them back. Random new scenes of Australian actors and "ninjas" are intercut with a
decent kung fu film. The old footage features
an all-time favorite character: Tiger Chan. The
Asian gentleman with the beautiful golden
hair is a hoot!

The differences between Godfrey Ho
films are a question of degrees and a question
of coherency. One of them might be a little
more coherent than another, and therefore a
little less crazy. The only thing all the films
have in common is (as far as I know): There
are no ninjas in the older footage. *Ninja Terminator* has a straightforward plot that goes
off on a dozen loopy tangents, including a lot
of time spent with that golden-haired gent
and a long sequences in a pawn shop. It also
has this exchange as a man is buying explo-

sives: "All I want to know is, will this blow the hell out of my enemies?" "I would say: sky high." The sky's the limit when it comes to crazy in the land of Ho.

Ninja the Protector

Director, Screenplay: Godfrey Ho
Producers: Betty Chan, Joseph Lai
Cast: Richard Harrison (Jason Hart), David Bowles (Bruce), Andy Chrowosky (Andy), Warren Chan (Warren), Vera Wang (Susan), Moran Lee (Hudy)

When a long sword is on a top of a short sword and covered with a red cloth, it's a ninja challenge. Jason Hart says that before donning his camouflage ninja gear in *Ninja the Protector*. And the fight in which Jason takes part actually involves motorcycles at first. They joust in a field somewhere and then the regular fighting begins.

Aren't ninjas great? They've got so many codes. They can do magic tricks. And they vanish! That's nutty. Never argue with a ninja. One of this movie's running plotlines is that Jason, a cop, keeps telling his fellow cops that ninjas don't exist. In the end, he proclaims that he's "the champion of the ninjas." And he looks good doing it.

This Godfrey Ho joint is not all that different from all the others. There are narcotics. There's an undercover guy who's pretending to be a model. It all makes sense in the world of Ho-Lai. Rape plays a bigger part here than in others, but I guess when one tries to exploit, one exploits wherever one can.

The ninja fights are as goofy as ever. Richard Harrison is costumed in camouflage, which seems odd for a ninja as they are supposed to blend in anyway. The "old" footage (the footage that Ho and Lai appropriated for their film) is okay. There's some good kung fu fighting going on it. There's a real jackass guy who mistreats a gal in

one scene that goes beyond narrative function and into "this feels like someone is living out some sort of unpleasant fantasy." But one of the joys of these films is they are some of the most unpredictable journeys in the history of cinema—where are we going here? Why are we going where we're going?

No Dead Heroes aka Commando Massacre

Director, Screenplay: J.C. Miller
Producer: Arthur N. Gelfield
Cast: Max Thayer (Ric Sanders), John Dresden (Harry Cotter), Toni Nero (Barbara Perez), Nick Nicholson (Ivan)

Commies everywhere! There's a super Russian guy named Ivan and another guy who looks like Fidel Castro. And music that

THE MISSION: TERMINATE THE KGB JUNGLE EXPERIMENTS. THE GOAL: DESTROY THE HUMAN KILLING MACHINES. THE ORDER: LEAVE NO ONE ALIVE!

NODEADHEROES

sounds like a progressive rock band noodling for ages without ever coming up with a melody or riff. The head Russian guy tortures people. He pulls out some fingernails and shoots people randomly. He captures two Americans, Sanders and Cotter. Sanders escapes. Cotter does not. In fact, Cotter is implanted with a microchip making him a super soldier who is going to kill the Pope!

No Dead Heroes is sleazy. It's a film that lodges in the mind and makes the viewer uncomfortable.

Cotter is a killing machine. There is a scene where he strolls in on a birthday party with his family and shoots everyone. The film has a proAmerican vibe. Ten years pass in the film. How can the viewer tell? Because all the actors now have white powder in their beards. That's aging!

This film might benefit from an HD transfer, one that really brings the images to life. That will probably never happen. As it stands, this is a grotty-looking number from the Philippines. It doesn't have much nudity but it does have some sodomy. That, mixed with the torture, makes the viewer feel like maybe he should turn off the TV and go volunteer his time at a church.

The film is violent. That is action. So it fulfills its role there. It also has a great shooting in a church where altar boys and bishops and churchgoers drop in the same way that everyone drops in these films when there is a spray from machine guns. Watch for some of the goofiest shoot-and-drop moments ever.

Commando Massacre is a sharp, dark, sleazy and kinda dumb adventure that mixes in mind control and some of the funniest Communists you'll ever see. Is it recommended? Yes. Emphatically? Well, let's not go crazy.

Quiet Cool

Director: Clay Borris
Screenplay: Clay Borris, Susan Vercellino
Producers: Robert Shaye, Gerald T. Olson
Cast: James Renar (Joe Dylanne), Daphne Ashbrook (Katy Greer), Adam Coleman Howard (Joshua Greer), Jared Martin (Mike Prior), Nick Cassavates (Valence), Fran Ryan (Ma)

Quiet Cool seems to have slipped through the cracks. It's a New Line Cinema production from around the time that the *Nightmare on Elm Street* series put them on the map. *Quiet Cool* is a tight (81 minutes), exciting, well-directed and well-acted film about a bunch of thugs growing pot in the

woods. They kill a group of people who stumble upon their pot farm. It's up to Joe, a cop on vacation, and Joshua, a relative of some of the victims, to stop the thugs.

This film provides an evening of good entertainment. The action scenes are well done. The climactic shootout is particularly good. The characters are nicely drawn. The actors are good, from Fran Ryan who used to call out the Gravy Train in commercials to Jared Martin who had recently finished a few seasons on *Dallas*. The script is sharp and taut, with no flab. It tells its story and then ends. The direction is strong. The editing is tight. And the woods are beautiful. But with all those thugs in them, they've become deadly.

The title *Quiet Cool* confused me until I realized that it referred to the film itself. In a world of loud, crass, overdone action films, this one succeeds on its own terms … and by being quiet cool.

Riot on 42nd Street

Director, Screenplay: Tim Kincaid

Producer: Cynthia DePaula

Cast: John Patrick Hayden (Glen Barnes), Kate Collins (Michelle Owens), Jeff Fahey (Frank Tackler), Michael Speero (Leonard Farrell), Frances Raines (Barbara), Carl Fury (Remy Wyler)

Riot on 42nd Street isn't always about the action. Long stretches of it are dramatic. This being a movie written and directed by Tim Kincaid, long stretches of it are sleazy. But in the end it comes back to the action: to the riot of the title. Rumor has it that this is Kincaid's least favorite film due to some sort of interference. To me, it's one of the best of his 1980s films and that includes *Breeders* and *Robot Holocaust*. It's

because of the characters, the locations and, when it starts, the constant fighting.

Glen Barnes is released from prison after accidentally killing a junkie in his father's theater. He returns to the theater, in a much sleazier 42nd Street that he remembers. The theater is in competition with Leonard Farrell's ultra-sleazy Love Connection. What starts as arguments becomes shoot-outs and then, in the end, a full-scale riot with Glen fighting with Remy Wyler, Farrell's buff goon.

In between all this, Glen reconnects with Michelle, a lost love. Glen tries to become pals with his brother. And there's drama and dancing women, sometimes naked. Plus a comedian who gets big laughs at a club, in disconnected cutaways.

Kincaid isn't the most dynamic of directors. But when the drama takes over this film, you begin to care about what's going on. The bad guys are bad, but the good guys are flawed fellows just trying to make a living in an area where a double feature of *Penitentiary III* and *Women's Prison Massacre* is normal. Although some of the threads of the drama are left dangling, it's interesting to watch.

The fighting and action are good. The riot at the end is intercut with Glen and some other folks trying to free Michelle from Farrell's clutches. So about 20 or 30 people from all walks of society fight in front of the Barnes establishment while Glen and friends shoot and fistfight with a pack of goons, including Remy. It culminates in a knock-down, drag-out fight between Remy and Glen where, at any point, one of them could overtake the other and kill. It's a good fight even though it isn't dynamically shot. Just two beefy guys fighting.

Then, at the final moments, *Riot on 42nd Street* does something really cool. The riot takes place in the middle of the night. It is violent and loud and raucous. When the cops show up and taking a deep breath is required, snow begins to fall. It's really quite a lovely moment. After all this violence and death, pure, white snow falls on 42nd Street. And suddenly everything seems calmer and fresher and more alive. It's an unexpected moment and it makes the film something interesting to watch.

Robot Holocaust

Director, Screenplay: Tim Kincaid
Producer: Cynthia DePaula
Cast: Nadine Hart, Joel Von Ornsteiner, Jennifer Delora, Andrew Howarth, Angelika Jager (Valeria)

Sometimes the post-apocalyptic fantasy is a big, globe-spanning epic. Sometimes it's limited to a few locations as individuals discuss their situation and their future. Then there are the movies that most resemble a bunch of kids goofing around, dressing some friends up in strange outfits and having them fight in a field or an abandoned warehouse.

One of those films is right here: *Robot Holocaust.*

Tim Kincaid is mainly known for doing quite a bit of gay porn. But in the 1980s, he made a group of exploitation films which always feel amateurish (even when there is some quality there) but are always very entertaining: *Mutant Hunt, Breeders, Riot on 42nd Street, Bad Girls Dormitory* and *Robot Holocaust.* The latter is probably the most ambitious of the lot. It takes place after the Robot Rebellion of '33.It feels, at times, like a mix of *Ator* and *Starcrash* ... but cheaper than both of them.

Basically, some guys fight Amazons. They fight robots. They fight worm monsters and giant spider legs. There's a Dark One with an assistant named Valeria who has a thick Eastern European accent and is given far too many lines to speak in English. There is a man who ends up looking like a giant avocado. There are stilted lines delivered in stilted fashion. There are post-apocalyptic clothes that look a little suspect. Everything about this film screams Amateur.

Or it screams stage production of some sort. Maybe at an off-off-off-Broadway theater? I like to imagine that *Robot Holocaust* was a play put on by a local high school, and that Kincaid adapted it into this low-budget film. A bit ponderous at times, the film cuts back and forth from the bland heroes with their goofy robots to Valeria saying things that border on incomprehensibility. But eventually, the film does get somewhere. Although it doesn't have the verve of *Mutant Hunt* or the elusive charms of *Riot on 42nd Street*, it has its great moments.

Scorpion

Director, Screenplay, Producer: William Riead

Cast: Tony Tulleners (Steve Woods), Don Murray (Gifford Leese),

Robert Logan (Gordon Thomas), Allen Williams (Phil Keller), Kathryn Daley (Jackie Wilemon)

Tony Tulleners was a black belt karate champ. Apparently, he beat Chuck Norris in a competition. William Riead fashioned this film about Steve Woods (Tulleners), who works for the government organization known as the D.I.A. Steve stops a terrorist hijack on a plane. But someone blew away a witness he's trying to protect. Luckily, Steve knows how to fight. Unluckily, William Riead either forgot about that or thought he was

working with Tony Tulleners, the guy who was big on forensics and proper police procedure.

They forget to have Tony fight a lot. Yes, he hangs out on his houseboat a lot. The star of *Malibu Express* does that too but he's not a black belt champion, and Steve *is*. As you watch Steve and a friend of his playing a recorder, you can see that, yes, there are quirks. The director is definitely up to something. But a lot of time is spent setting up the protection for Faud, the witness. Then a lot of time is spent in the police follow-up to all that. It's sort of like portions of *Police Story 2*, which hadn't come out yet. That film had long stretches of Jackie Chan and the cops engaging in non-action, procedural stuff. But, the way Jackie films it and edits it, it almost completely makes one forget that he's not fighting. *Scorpion* doesn't get that right.

The viewer never really sees Steve kick ass so there are no indications of what he can or can't do. Maybe Steve hurt his ankle. Maybe they were trying to do something different from a Chuck Norris–style film. Someone dropped the ball. Tony never got a chance to rectify the situation. Which, in a world where the McNamara boys made two films, seems a shame.

Silk

> *Director:* Cirio H. Santiago
> *Screenplay:* Fredrick Bailey
> *Producers:* Jose F. Buenaventura, Cirio H. Santiago
> *Cast:* Cec Verrell (Jenny), Bill McLaughlin (Tom Stevens), Joe Mari Avellana (Yashi), Fredrick Bailey (Brown), Nick Nicholson (Tyler)

In the opening scene, Silk, kick-ass one-woman cop army, rushes up to a structure to get to some terrorists. At the bottom of the girders, there is a sign that has written on it two words: "SLOW DOWN." Oh, I think we get what you're up to here, Mr. Santiago. Silk will not be slowing down. She's cut her hair short. She's slicked it back. She wears a big red coat. And she slays the bad guys.

Silk aka Jenny is one of the most well-respected cops on the Honolulu force. A group of men, led by a "Limey," are bringing Chinese mobsters to Honolulu, where they assume the identities of a citizen who has just dies. Pernicious evil of the most revolting kind! But, this is all a McGuffin right? This movie is about a series of breathtaking action scenes with Silk being cool like that opening scene. Right?

No. After that big opening, there is a lot—a lot—of time spent with the bad guys preparing the mobsters for sneaking over into the continental U.S. Santiago seems to forget that he has a kick-ass leading lady who stunts all over and thinks that the viewer is more interested in mobster protocol and cop-related nonsense. About 45 minutes in, I asked myself, "Where'd Silk go? She's here but why isn't she out there doing exciting things?" No answer was forthcoming. And then they bring in the cockfighting. Why? Why?

What starts of as one of Santiago's best films goes south fairly quickly. The ending kind of makes up for it. But Silk is captured by the baddies and held hostage as the ending draws close. So she isn't out there kicking ass. She's spitting bile while tied to a chair. There is the feeling of a missed opportunity here. A feeling that Santiago could have given us the most awesome female fighter of the 1980s, pre–Cynthia Rothrock.

In *Silk 2*, Monique Gabrielle plays Silk. Ms. Gabrielle is gorgeous and sexy as hell. But she's as much of an action film star as Selma Diamond.

Terror Force Commando aka Three Men on Fire

> *Director, Screenplay:* Richard Harrison
> *Producers:* Alphonse Beni, Richard Harrison
> *Cast:* Richard Harrison (Matthias), Alphonse Beni (Michael), Romano Kristoff, Ninette Assor, Lorenzo Piani, Maurizio Murano, Sebastian Harrison, Robert Harrison, Richard Harrison II, Jerry the American

In Cameroon, a group of terrorists, led by a crazy guy named Zero, kill several political figures. Guess who's coming to visit

Cameroon? The Pope. A cop named Michael (Alphonse Beni) goes to Rome to try and stop the Pope from visiting. He meets up with semi-rogue American agent Matthias (Richard Harrison), who is fanatical about getting to Zero. Will the Pope be safe? *Terror Force Commando* will answer that question.

Richard Harrison plays a slightly goofy, rather tough cop throughout. Alphonse Beni (who was in many Ho-Lai action films) plays it straight, except when he gets hooked up with a boxer named Killer Milani. Whoever dubbed Killer's voice was having a laugh. Harrison should have kept a tighter rein on the dubbing artists. (Or not.) Zero and his gang are sort of vague political people who want to change the world through killing random people.

Terror Force Commando is as unencumbered by logic as any of the ninja films these guys were involved in. But it's all-new footage. It goes from Rome to Cameroon so there must have been a bit of money involved. There's something about Michael and Matthias going up against this semi-incompetent gang that brings good things to life. It's a sound action film with enough weirdness to make it a great evening's entertainment. *Terror Force Commando* teeters on the verge of insanity, inanity and being The Best.

Thunder Run

Director: Gary Hudson
Screenplay: Charles Davis, Carol Heyer
Producers: Carol Lynn, Cliff Wenger
Cast: Forrest Tucker (Charlie Morrison), John Ireland (George Adams), John Shepherd (Chris), Jill Whitlow (Kim), Wallace Langham (Paul)

Charlie is an old trucker. A pal in the government, George Adams, offers him $250,000 to haul some plutonium. But there are terrorists who will come after Charlie. So he and his grandson Chris soup up a big rig and set out. It's a heck of a good time. Lots of explosions and endless car chasing, including a quite incredible leap of the 18-wheeler over a stalled train.

It's a lot of fun to see a veteran like Forrest Tucker appear in the cab of a truck in an action movie like this, which clearly owes a bit to *The Road Warrior*. The long haul surrounded by the terrorists is very exciting, made more so by the souped up rig. A motorcycle pulls up alongside the rig and the rider starts shooting. In the cab, we see a metal plate with buttons on it. Chris presses a button and

Could anyone survive...

THUNDER RUN

FORREST TUCKER • JOHN IRELAND • JOHN SHEPHERD

Executive Producer - PETER E. STRAUSS   Producer - CAROL LYNN   Co-Producer - LAWRENCE APPELBAUM
Directed by - GARY HUDSON

fire shoots out of the side of the rig. It's like the buttons on the *Speed Racer* car. Every time Charlie asks for a button to be pressed, it's a thrill. There are lasers in one scene!

The film has one foot firmly in the action films of the 1980s but one in a different time, I would say the 1970s. The film begins quickly with some folks being attacked by the terrorists. Then there is a meeting with government brass, including George. They hire Charlie in the next scene. Then the movie spends 20, 25 minutes on Charlie's life: his lady friend, his grandson, the mine he owns. Then he gets the truck. About 45 minutes in, you've forgotten that this is an action film. It feels like the story of an old trucker living his life and preparing for one final run. (The original *Gone in 60 Seconds* goes on for about 55 minutes before the huge car chase begins.)

Then the long haul begins. For about 35 minutes, it is almost one long chase. The action is very good. The action has the feel of people showing off, like in *Gone in 60 Seconds, Stunt Rock* and *Action U.S.A.* That's not a bad thing. *Thunder Run* may be of two parts but the second part is immediately awesome.

The Ultimate Ninja

> *Director, Screenplay*: Godfrey Ho
> *Producer*: Joseph Lai
> *Cast*: Stuart Smith, Bruce Baron, Sorapong Cahtree, Anne Aswatep, Pedro Massobrio

In *The Ultimate Ninja*, one ninja kills another and steals a small Black Ninja Warrior figurine. A guy named Charles will avenge himself on the evil ninja. But first, there'll be lots of fighting, some of it involving a big bald fighter and a woman named Sarah who kicks ass. And then there is an awesome Australian Rules Ninja fight in a gazebo-filled public park area. All the hands flying around, flipping and disappearing make it a surreal masterpiece or nightmare.

The Ultimate Ninja is, kind of, the Ultimate Nothing. But there are some laughs in it, unintentional or not … I can't tell any more. Ho and Lai had something here. What it was? We'll probably never know. But I can't stop watching these damn things. And I can no longer imagine my world without them.

Unmasking the Idol

> *Director*: Worth Keeter
> *Screenplay*: Phil Behrens

Producer: Robert Eaton

Cast: Ian Hunter (Jax), C.K. Bibby (Stan), William Hicks (Whale), Boon the Baboon

Damn, I love ninjas. I also love coming upon franchises (even if they are only composed of two films) within genres that I love. *Unmasking the Idol* is the first in the Duncan Jax series. Jax is a super suave secret agent with a British accent and Boon the Baboon as his assistant. Jax is also a ninja. He wears one of those metal-type mask things and kicks the ass of evil everywhere he goes. In the first scene, he beats up a bunch of guys and then leaps from the tenth floor of a building into a swimming pool. (His body does seem to become a bit dummy-like on the way down to the pool but that is simply a ninja skill.) Jax is sent on a secret mission involving a deep-voiced villain, more ninjas, a hidden idol and the man who played the fat Sheriff in *House of Death*. Well, that should be all any viewer needs. Go out and enjoy!

This film was made in the vicinity of North Carolina, near the great and fabled Earl Owensby studios that gave us *Wolfman, Rottweiler, Final Exam, House of Death* and many others. The studio was also used in the James Cameron film *The Abyss,* because it had the largest water tank in the U.S. at that time. *Unmasking the Idol* is a semi-serious "James Bond with a touch of Indiana Jones" number. It never takes itself too seriously. There are Jeeps attached to hot air balloons, ninjas flying out of the woodwork and people laughing endlessly at Boon the Baboon.

There's absolutely no reason why any viewer should come away empty handed from *Unmasking the Idol.* At its heart, it is simply fun. So many of the films in this book are not really fun. Action should be exhilarating and a thrill. But a lot of times, in following the blockbusters of the day, rip-off artists end up taking their own films too seriously and not seeing the fun they could have. *Unmasking the Idol* is a joyous time. Film is there for fun. The sequel *Order of the Black Eagle* ups the ante. It even brings back the sheriff in a completely different role: crazy Nazi anyone? Watch them both for a great evening.

Vampire Raiders vs. the Ninja Queen

Director: Godfrey Ho
Screenplay: Antonio Gassner
Producer: Tomas Tang
Cast: Martin Bukes, Walter Jackson, Agnes Chan, Chris Peterson, Deborah Tao, Ruby Cohn

The Red Ninja Queen has to fight the Vampire Raiders to the death or they will engage in nefarious corporate duplicity. She is being helped by a bunch of hotel switchboard gals and their friend Fatty. Kung fu fighting abounds. Zombies on a boat. Hopping vampires. Someone throws a big pig off a building, a scene that's some sort of classic.

This film is kind of nuts. This reviewer says that about a lot of films with *Ninja* in the title but this Godfrey Ho creation is legitimately nuts. This time Ho is working with Tomas Tang, not Joseph Lai, and apparently Tang let things get crazier than Lai did, impossible as that sounds. The head lady ninja is awesome and very Australian, and very sexy, even though she sometimes looks a bit like a man.

In one scene, the queen reclines on her beach towel and is attacked by hopping vampires who grab her from under the sand. Their fight is silly. At the end, she has a fantastic knock-down drag-out fight with the vampires. Her portion of the film is solid.

The "old" footage, from a Hong Kong supernatural comedy, is fun too. It's one step away from being an anime about three giggly young women fighting zombies. Vampires are mentioned in the dubbing but they're clearly fighting zombies. The switchboard gals overhear someone talking about vampires and start hunting down clues. One gal gets scared and is told to read a Bible. She reads some of Exodus, which mentioned Yahweh requesting that Moses get a pen to write down the Ten Commandments.

The closing sequence in the "old" footage, which takes place on a boat filled with zombies, has the same sort of verve as *Mr. Vampire* and *Encounters of the Spooky Kind*. Even if the dubbing is hilariously nonsensical. The sequence where they make one of the guys fill a bucket with his urine (because he's a virgin) brings me joy. It's goofy, scary and never too serious.

Which is perfect because over in Ninja Town, things are mega-serious. The Ninja Queen is always ready to kick some ass. Even though the ninja scenes are clearly much sillier than anything else, the characters' po-faced looks makes the contrast between the sections of the film a joy.

The Vindicator

Director: Jean-Claude Lord
Screenplay: Edith Rey, David Preston
Producer: Don Carmody
Cast: David McIlwraith (Carl Lehman), Teri Austin (Lauren Lehman), Richard Cox (Alex Whyte), Maury Chaykin (Burt), Pam Grier (Hunter)

In Canada, scientist Carl Lehman works hard on some sort of experiment with monkeys. One night, he is caught in a lab explosion. His body is reconstructed into a sort of robotic Frankenstein-Robocop-type fellow. He is sent out to wreak havoc as a "special weapon." When he rebels, Pam Grier is called in to catch him. Maury Chaykin is there too but he's not quite as fun as when he was Nero Wolfe but he's still very good. The question becomes: Is *The Vindicator* vindicated? Does it make the grade?

Its heart is in the right place. Sometimes it's tough to tell if its head is. There are a lot of references to Frankenstein (an alternate title was *Frankenstein 1988*). I'm not sure that they are pertinent apart from the fact that the guy is brought back to life. The Monster was assembled from assorted human parts and Frankenstein was trying to do something good. The Vindicator (not actually sure if he's called that) is created by people who want to use him as a weapon, like RoboCop. Of course, Robocop *was* a cop, and this guy was a scientist, so the people who brought him back to life were jerks. That's probably why the Vindicator revolts so quickly. That's why I would.

The monster suit is fun. The monster shows off his power in a great moment when he leaps from a choir loft and smashes through church floorboards. But the suit may have been better kept in the shadows more. It covers up almost all of the actor's face, so there's a lack of emotion. After a time, it makes his talking as boring as the Civil War spirits in *Night of Horror*.

Pam Grier is awesome. She shows up, kicks ass and takes over her scenes in the movie. But her character does feel kind of shoehorned in. She shows up several times to cause some trouble for the Vindicator and that's about it. It is a step above the sort of cameos that Cameron Mitchell did.

Maury Chaykin is great as Burt, who at first seems like a real good guy. The amiable lab tech helping out, showing sympathy, helping the girlfriend of the man who just became a cyborg. But—Spolier!—when he goes bad, he is skeevy and gross. One wants to run a long mile from him. Thank Heaven there is a cyborg around.

The Vindicator is really not all that special. The director made the early 1980s slasher *Visiting Hours*. While that didn't have more energy, it had more suspense and sleaze to it. *The Vindicator* is nothing too fantastic. But worth it if you, like me, need to see everything.

Wired to Kill

Director, Screenplay: Franky Schaeffer
Producer: Jim Buchfuehrer
Cast: Emily Longstreet (Rebecca), Devin Hoelscher (Steve), Merritt Buttrick (Reegus), Kim Milford (Rooster), Tommy Lister, Jr. (Sleet), Frank Collison (Sly)

In the then-future year of 1992, the T.A.P.E.X. virus threatens the world. There are quarantines and martial law. By 1998, the plague is over but there's still martial law. There are numerous scuzzy Road Warrior–esque gangs out there hurting people ... until Rebecca and Steve fight back with a lot of gumption and a little robot guy that tools around and shoots people.

This is not a post-apocalyptic film, as I was expecting. It's more a dystopian kind of film. The area where Steve lives with his

SCHAEFFER BUCHFUEHRER PRODUCTIONS Presents A FRANKY SCHAEFFER Film
WIRED TO KILL
Starring EMILY LONGSTRETH • DEVIN HOELSCHER • MERRITT BUTRICK • KRISTINA DAVID
DOROTHY PATTERSON • TOM (TINY) LISTER, JR. • FRANK COLLISON
Music Composed and Performed by RUSSELL FERRANTE with THE YELLOW JACKETS
Co-Producer PETER CHESNEY Editor DANIEL AGULIAN Director of Photography TOM FRASER
Executive Producer PAUL McGUIRE Produced by JIM BUCHFUEHRER
Written and Directed by FRANKY SCHAEFFER
from American Distribution Group · DOLBY STEREO

The rest of the gang are just drug addict creeps. The opening scroll implies that everyone knows about these violent gangs. But the cops don't actually seem to do anything about them until the end, when they show up to examine the wreckage. Does the phrase "too little, too late" ring a bell?

Steve and Rebecca are nice enough. After Steve is crippled, he takes on a sadistic streak when it comes to the crazy gang members. Mainly he spikes drugs with caustic content. Rebecca seems to be slightly disconnected from all of this. In fact, when called upon to really emote, the actress isn't quite up to it. So, although it's nice to see them give the gang their comeuppance, it isn't as exciting as it could be. It's a little dull with flashes of cool stuff.

The grandmother and mother identify the two head crooks as the guys who invaded their home and crippled Steve. Then a lawyer shows up and says that the crooks must be set loose. And the cops do. Why? There is no mention of bail just … "Let them loose." I know this society is screwy but if everyone knows about these awful gangs, isn't this a terrible idea?

The answer is: yes, it is a terrible idea. The gang kill Grandma and break Mom's back and the cops do nothing. Presumably, if they did, the lawyer would just get the guys free again. Stuff like this might (might) work in a film like *Dirty Harry* but here it's weird. Because after a plague and martial law, shouldn't gangs who spend all day invading homes be imprisoned after they're identified? Maybe T.A.P.E.X. was a crazier plague than I imagine. Justice has gone stupid here.

mother and grandmother looks like a bad suburban neighborhood. Sort of like the alternate 1985 of *Back to the Future Part II*. The gang breaks into their house one night and breaks Steve's legs. Steve rigs that robot and keeps sending Rebecca right into the heart of everything.

The gang is sufficiently scuzzy. Its leader, Reegus, is a soft-spoken, handkerchief-wielding fellow who hides great deviancy inside him.

1987

Highest grossing films in the U.S.
1. *Three Men and a Baby*
2. *Fatal Attraction*
3. *Beverly Hills Cop II*
4. *Good Morning, Vietnam*
5. *Moonstruck*

Highest rated TV shows in the U.S.
1. *The Cosby Show*
2. *A Different World*
3. *Cheers*
4. *The Golden Girls*
5. *Growing Pains*

Big historical events
"Black Monday"
Klaus Barbie sentenced
DNA used to convict criminals

Action movies
Beverly Hills Cop II, The Untouchables, Stakeout, Lethal Weapon, Predator, Robocop, The Living Daylights, Full Metal Jacket, Jaws IV, Superman IV, Over the Top, Death Wish 4

Allan Quatermain and the Lost City of Gold

Director: Gary Nelson
Screenplay: Gene Quintano
Producers: Menahem Golan, Yoram Globus
Cast: Richard Chamberlain (Allan Quatermain), Sharon Stone (Jesse Huston), James Earl Jones (Umslopogaas), Robert Donner (Swarma), Henry Silva (Agon), Cassandra Peterson (Queen Sorais)

The sequel to Cannon Films' *King Solomon's Mines* (and actually made at the same time), *Allan Quatermain and the Lost City of Gold* is another Indiana Jones–type film. It channels more of the style of 1930s cliffhanger serials and films like *Gunga Din* but with a lot more wackiness, a truly annoying "religious" guy named Swarma, and Henry Silva in the best-worst wig ever made.

Allan and Jesse are preparing to leave Africa for America where they are to be married. A man appears; a friend of Quatermain and his brother, he tells the story of tribesmen who live in a city of gold. Quatermain decides he needs to find this city and make sure his brother is okay. Jesse joins him. They team up with a warrior named Umslopogaas (James Earl Jones) and Swarma and head into the African wilds. They get involved in many adventures along the way, including a mad ride through a cave, meetings with random tribes, a stretch of ground that opens up beneath them and crazy-looking bats.

The moment the viewer sees writer Gene Quintano's name in the credits, they should know what to expect: fun adventure, some good jokes, some overdone bits, some bad jokes and a sense that he didn't quite get the script to go where he wanted it to. Watch *Treasure of the Four Crowns* or *Police Academy 4: Citizens on Patrol*. None of them ever quite does what it promises.

As Quatermain and friends approach the city, the film remains raucous fun. It clearly has a decent budget. This film and *King Solomon's Mines*) might be the most expensive films in this book. But it's never quite as exciting as it should be. The ground-opening-up sequence is cool. The final fight, which involves falling molten gold, is quite good. But, overall, the film is never great. Everyone is trying hard but, like the first film, it doesn't quite make it.

On many occasions, Cannon movies "don't quite make it." *Superman IV: The Quest for Peace* feels underdone. *River of Death* doesn't work. A lot of their films are like this. They knew to include lots of good stuff. They knew how to package them. But, in the end, the films aren't completely satisfying. It doesn't matter how many heroic musical cues *Allan Quatermain and the City of Lost Gold* has, something is lacking.

American Ninja 2

Director: Sam Firstenberg
Screenplay: Gary Conway
Producers: Menahem Golan, Yoram Globus
Cast: Michael Dudikoff (Joe), Steve James (Jackson), Larry Poindexter (Charlie), Gary Conway (The Lion), Michelle Boles (Alicia)

The boys are back! Joe and Jackson, the charming, ass-kicking heroes of *American Ninja,* are now Army Rangers, sent to St. Simon, which seems to be in the Caribbean, to discover why Marines are going missing. It has something to do with drugs and, yes, it has something to do with ninjas. There seems to be no reason for ninjas to be here, at least for a while. The fact that Joe and Jackson are already known to viewers means that this film leaps right into the action, with no need to stop for character development.

I missed the romantic subplot of the first film. In some respects, that made the first one seem like a bigger movie. *II* doesn't bother with it. Jackson does most of the talking. Joe does most of the ass-kicking. Ninjas pour out of buildings and off of rooftops. And, as with everything else from Mr. Firstenberg, the fights are well-done and exciting.

There is a huge ninja stronghold on an island, with a bad man named "The Lion" running things. The film is peppered with fights that get more and more elaborate. The first super-fight in this one is the fight in the bar, a big brawling number with Joe, Jackson and some Marines beating the crap out of, pretty much everyone in St. Simon. When Jackson fights a crowd of ninjas in the end and reveals his knives and swords, they are hilarious. The film doesn't take itself terribly seriously, like the first one … until it needs to take itself seriously. Then it is deadly, ninja-style serious.

American Ninja and *American Ninja 2* are super examples of high-energy, fun American low-budget action from the 1980s. They should be watched immediately.

Angel of Death aka *Commando Mengele*

Director: A. Frank Drew White
Screenplay: Gregory Freed, A.L. Mariaux, D. Khunn
Producer: Daniel Lesoeur
Cast: Howard Vernon (Mengele), Fernando Rey (Ohmei Felsberg), Jack Taylor (Aaron Horner), Chris Mitchum (Wolfgang von Backey), J.C. Lerner, Shirley Knight

I did not think I'd get a Eurocine film in here. But, check it out: *Angel of Death,* a strange film about Josef Mengele living in the Paraguayan jungles and continuing to carry out his awful experiments with a huge crowd of guards, including Chris Mitchum. A group of folks stumble upon the compound and return with a squad of soldiers to take Mengele down once and for all.

In typical Eurocine fashion, when one links up Howard Vernon and Jack Taylor, things get sleepy. This is meant to be a tense action thriller about ridding the world of Mengele! But it all kind of meanders along for quite some time. Fernando Rey shows up briefly and doesn't accomplish too much.

Angel of Death should be exciting. Instead, it's a bit dull, rather incoherent and very Eurocine. The same bit of synth music plays over and over. People talk and talk. It doesn't seem like we ever move closer to getting where we need to be. And then, suddenly, we're there. Howard Vernon is Mengele and we see that his experiments are still going on. The film makes itself rather unpleasant but forgets to make itself fun. As always, Chris Mitchum is a bit goofy. He does some odd kung fu and seems to be the main man in charge of training all the guards. It's weird to have him show up in a movie like this. Did his plane break down on the way back from Indonesia?

Angel of Death is an action fan's confused evening. Because, as things move towards the end, there is action. A bunch of people attack the compound. A lot of shooting happens and it picks up a bit. But it never picks up that much.

The history of Eurocine is probably ut-terly fascinating. And why they decided to make this film, when their focus was horror and softcore films, eludes me. But they did make it, and it features a cast of folks known mainly from '70s and early '80s horror films … and Chris Mitchum. That's where the world goes crazy.

Mengele as a character in a cheap, low-budget seems a little bit weird.

Ator 3: *Iron Warrior*

Director: Alfonso Brescia
Screenplay: Steven Luotto, Alfonso Brescia
Producers: Ovidio G. Assonitis, Maurizio Maggi
Cast: Miles O'Keeffe (Ator), Savina Gersak (Janna), Elisabeth Deeva (Phoedra), Iris Peynado (Deena), Tim Lane (King)

Joe D'Amato decided not to make a third Ator film, and the very idiosyncratic Alfonso Brescia took over. He's probably best known for making a series of very cheap *Star Wars* rip-offs in the late '70s. *Star Odyssey* is one of the strangest films any viewer might encounter. What Brescia did to the Ator films is a wonder to behold. Whether it's good or not, may be beside the point.

In wherever this movie takes place, an evil woman named Phoedra kidnaps Ator's brother. She is placed into a Phantom Zone-esque world and has her power to kill taken from her. Princess Janna is run out of her palace by Phoedra. Janna joins forces with Ator. There's a silver-skulled warrior in a red cape. There is a golden chest on an island. Three Muse-like women speak in whispers and echoes. There's a lot of multi-colored lights and hair being blown around. It all comes across as madness. (*Star Odyssey* does the same thing.) Apparently, the producers didn't keep much of an eye on Brescia.

Ator fans might get a little cheesed off by this film. The Ator of the first two movies is nowhere in sight. This one is still strong and kicks ass in a mighty way, but the science is gone. Thong is gone. The big hair is replaced by dark hair slicked into a ponytail. And Ator barely speaks. One wouldn't think the sketchy character of Ator was open to this much interpretation but apparently Brescia does what Brescia wants.

The film is an amalgam of several films. Obviously there's some *Conan* here, and also some *Superman*. The music keeps alternating between sounding like the "signal for a gory moment" music from *Horrible* and the *Star Trek: The Next Generation* main theme. And there was actually on-set sound for portions of the film. This is getting later in the 1980s and some Italian films (this one is Italian, filmed in Malta) were beginning to use sync sound. It adds another layer of difference from the first two.

Iron Warrior is a weird film in a genre populated with weird films. Its closest cousin is probably Fulci's *Conquest*. But, whereas *Conquest* is stand-alone insanity, this is the third film in a series. Trying to figure out everything that Brescia was up to in this twisted fairy tale might take a lifetime.

The Barbarians

Director: Ruggero Deadato
Screenplay: James R. Silke
Producers: Menahem Golan, Yoram Globus
Cast: Peter Paul (Kutchek), David Paul (Gore), Richard Lynch (Kadar), Eva la Rue (Ismene), Virginia Bryant (Canary)

Cannon Films is at it again! This time, they brought along the director of *Cannibal Holocaust* and they gave Richard Lynch a long flowing blond wig. He looks good.

The Barbarians stars two really big guys, the Paul Brothers, billed as "The Barbarian Brothers." Oiled chests and loincloths are the big thing in this film. Kutchek and Gore are twins raised by the evil Kadar. But the boys come of age and break away, trying to save a kingdom and assorted people from Kadar. There are dragons and all sorts of warriors. There is a hot rocking soundtrack. There are long arguments between the brothers, who aren't the most articulate guys. A group of travelling entertainers called the Randicks (?) appear to have escaped from the outtakes of a forgotten Fellini film.

This is a rousing, action-filled, silly and somewhat adult film starring two big lunkheads who start off annoying but grow on you as things progress. By the time we get near the end and they are arguing about a missing ruby, I was laughing out loud. The way they talked, alongside the music, give this film a nice anachronistic feel that one might almost say is meant to evoke the fairy tale feel of *The Princess Bride*. In fact, I *will* say it: the tone, the fact that the brothers sound a bit like Andre the Giant and the opening narration that sets up the fairy tale world make this *Conan the Barbarian* via *The Princess Bride*. The film doesn't take itself too seriously, even when big George Eastman shows up for a scene involving some ass-kicking. The Paul boys aren't great actors but they are buff, and when they break hangmen's nooses by flexing their neck muscles, the viewer believes it.

Black Cobra

Director: Stelvio Massi
Screenplay: Danilo Massi
Producer: Luciano Appignani
Cast: Fred Williamson (Detective Malone), Eva Grimaldi (Elys Trumbo), Karl Landgren (Bandit Leader), Maurice Poli (Chief Walker), Vassili Karis (Malone's Partner)

Black Cobra. I thought titles like *Blacula*, *Blackenstein* and such had ended in the 1970s, and it never occurred to me that this movie is the "black" version of *Cobra*. It sure is. Fred Williamson has more heart than Cobra Cobretti but this is still *Cobra*. A New York City fashion photographer sees some mean bikers kill someone. They come after her. Detective Malone is put in charge of protecting her. Do I need to mention that Malone breaks all the rules? That he'll do whatever it takes to keep the scum off the streets? (The lead gang member has a tattoo of a black cobra, so maybe this *isn't* a *Cobra* rip-off although it does use the *Cobra* template.)

Malone punches and shoots and takes no prisoners. In the opening sequence, he takes care of a hostage situation by shooting all the bad guys. That's how he rolls. And he's on top of protecting the photographer from the bikers. He shoots the door of an apartment about 20 times in one scene. That's a lot of shooting.

This Italian film has that post-dubbed, disconnected-from-reality feel to it. The biker gang is fun. They're clearly meant to be tough bastards. They kind of are but they also look a bit like they're goofing. It's all the sexual assault that makes them unpleasant. Malone is put up against them and Fred Williamson seems to be into it. As the sequels go along, there's more goofiness (possibly unintentional) but this first film keeps it tough.

Cobra was severely cut (from almost 120 minutes to 85) upon its release. Sylvester Stallone removed most of the plot and character scenes. The film is already very violent (cut from an X) and wonderfully gross and sadistic. That fun, sleazy film rode the blockbuster-exploitation wave. *Black Cobra* is nowhere near as sleazy or crazy, and nowhere near as incoherent. *Black Cobra* is just an entertaining movie. Possibly that's why I never associated it with the Stallone film. It definitely takes the plot but the rest of it is almost PG fun compared to the original.

Cross Mission

> *Director:* Alfonso Brescia
> *Screenplay:* Donald Russo
> *Producer:* Ettore Spagnuolo
> *Cast:* Maurice Poli (Gen. Romero), Richard Randall (William Corbett), Brigitte Porsh (Helen), Peter Hintz (David), Nelson de la Rosa (Astaroth)

In Latin America, Gen. Romero is working with the U.N. and destroying drug crops. He's a hero. So why is Helen, a reporter, so interested in finding out more about him? And who is that William Corbett guy she's hanging around with? What's with Romero's ability to conjure up Astaroth? Astaroth is played by the 2'4" Dominican Republican actor Nelson de la Rosa. And what's with those strange blue rays that Romero and Astaroth shoot at people?

It's all down to the wacky mixed-up mind of the great and mighty Alfonso Brescia. He's the man who made the four craziest *Star Wars* rip-offs of the late 1970s and the "unofficial" Ator movie. His films are illogical, crazy, jaw-droppingly silly and sometimes very slow all at the same time. Going through his films can be a bit of a chore because there never seems to be any pacing to them. But treasures await. *Star Odyssey* is my favorite but *Cross Mission* is a close second.

The film would be a very standard action film if it wasn't for Astaroth. Well, as standard a film as Brescia could make. The plotting is a little loopy. Romero burns dope crops and declares himself a Great Guy. Helen tries to infiltrate Romero's world. There's a kung fu fight. A tiny man appears and shoots blue rays from his hands. Sandinista-style rebels lurk in the woods, one of whom sings for no discernible reason. There is a final attack on Romero's fortress that seems like it should be full of excitement but, apart from one surprising moment, it's just people running and firing guns.

Cross Mission is an illogical, loopy film that adds a small dose of supernatural to the regular action. Little traces of insanity make the Brescia filmography one of the most fascinating ever. He made a film whose title, translated to English, is *Naked Woman Killed in the Park*. The guy knew exactly what he was doing.

Day of the Panther

Director: Brian Trenchard-Smith
Screenplay: Peter West
Producer: Damien Parer
Cast: Edward John Stazak (Jason Blade), Jim Richards (Jim Baxter), Michael Carman (Damien Zukor), Paris Jefferson (Gemma), John Stanton (William Anderson)

A very dumb film made by a very smart guy can be very entertaining. *Day of the Panther* is in this category. The acting isn't so hot, the storytelling won no prize. But the movie moves at a great pace and there are brilliant action scenes, many of them kung fu–related. There is also a great aerobics-related seduction scene which should get the average pair of jeans excited. Even though it's about a guy avenging his partner, it has a feeling of "This is fun. This is goofiness." That's good.

Brian Trenchard-Smith, the man behind this Australian feature, has been making movies for decades. He made one of my all-time favorite films, *Stunt Rock*. Then there's his *Death Cheaters*, *The Man from Hong Kong* and *BMX Bandits*. The man knows how to make a good film. Specifically, for our purposes here, he knows how to direct a good action sequence.

Jason Blade and his partner get inducted into a Panther-related martial arts society by William Anderson. Things go south. Blade's partner is killed. Blade goes undercover to find the killer. There is fighting and interpretive dance. Edward John Stazak is not what one would call a good actor. When Jason Blade gets the phone call telling him that his partner is dead, it's almost impossible to figure out what emotion he is feeling. But that's okay because Stazak is a kick-ass fighter. When he starts brawling, all is forgiven.

This is a fun film. The fight scene with Blade's partner in a warehouse goes on for a very long time, but it's a *good* very long time. It's the sort of fight scene that goes on and on and the suspense builds as the partner just can't get away from the jackasses who are trying to kill her.

Dead Man Walking

Director, Producer: Gregory Brown
Screenplay: John Weidner, Rick Marx
Cast: Wings Hauser (John Luger), Jeffrey Combs (Chaz), Brion James (Decker), Pamela Ludwig (Leila), Leland Crooke (Nomad Farmer), Sy Richardson (Snake)

Some time after 1997 and the devastation of the Black plague, the world is divided into three groups, the infected, the non-infected and the Zero Ones. The last group are noncontagious Black plague sufferers who get a little erratic. (So says the film's opening scroll.) The Zero Ones do stuff like play Russian roulette with chainsaws. Brion James plays an infected man who kidnaps a wealthy man's daughter. Chaz, who is the wealthy man's chauffeur, and John Luger go into the infected areas to get her back.

Dead Man Walking paints a picture of the future where many people are infected and the government is always verging on the edge of finding a cure. As Luger and Chaz explore the infected zones, the movie cuts to footage of newscasters delivering news of the day, much of which involves the president doing awesome things in a horrible way.

The film is not as action-packed as it seemed like it might be at the start. The opening scene with the Chainsaw Russian Roulette is pretty tense and exciting, and a bit gory. Then Decker and his gang ratchet the action up. But after the kidnapping, things die down, almost making this movie outside of the realm of the book. But it has Wings Hauser and Brion James in it! How can it not be an action film? As it goes along, and the pursued draw closer to the pursuers, the action does pick up.

There is a crazy nightclub which has a deranged, plague-ridden *Cabaret* feel to it. A lot of the film is filtered through the mind of Chaz, who has not seen the world in this fashion. Luger is always a bit cynical but he joins in the journey for his own undisclosed reasons. Then there is a strange sequence with Decker and Leila making out. That's a creepy scene as Leila does not seem to have a problem with it. (She once argued with her dad about how the plague victims are treated.) This obviously leaves her infected at the end of the day.

Death Code Ninja

Director, Screenplay: Godfrey Ho
Producer: Joseph Lai
Cast: Mike Abbott, Judy Barnes, Edgar Fox, Peter Sung, John Wilford

How does *Death Code Ninja* stack up to the regular Ho-Lai films? It's about the same. It starts up with Mike Abbott (maybe the most entertaining of the ninjas) and some maps. After some ninja fighting, which is pretty much the same as all the other ninja fighting, the movie becomes about a woman seeking revenge for the death of her husband.

The ninja stuff is goofy. That's a given. Mike Abbott was funnier in … well, everything. But here he has a mustache, so now he looks like somebody's drunk uncle. He's got some good kung fu moves but looks silly with the mustache and the ninja garb. There's a hilarious fight on a cliff road. We learn that ninjas can snap their fingers and their clothes change, and that they can strip down to their boxer shorts in a moment's notice. Ninjas rule.

The old footage in the film spends a lot of time setting up the revenge portion of things. Sometimes the pace goes slow as molasses, sometimes it is lightning-paced. The death of the woman's son is cursorily referred to in dialogue. In fact, one is never quite sure when the son is actually dead and what the mom knows. A little vagueness keeps us all on our toes.

The fight scenes within the old footage are okay. The revenge plotline

In the future, life is a disease…death is a relief… and danger is the ultimate passion.

DEAD MAN WALKING

REPUBLIC PICTURES HOME VIDEO

Only one man (Mike Abbott) can prevent the destruction of the entire world when the United States and the Soviet Union battle an infamous Ninja warlord (John Wilford) for possession of a strategic war map which could mean the start of World War III!

0576
Color/90 Min.

PREBOOK DATE: SEPTEMBER 30
ON SALE DATE: OCTOBER 14

WATCH FOR
TRANS WORLD ENTERTAINMENTS
"TRIPLE D" offer!
Dynamite Discount Deal.
12 TWE titles for ONLY $18.95 each
and every tape includes
200 valuable BONUS BUCK POINTS
ALL OFFERS VOID IN CANADA

becomes such a big part of the film that all the opening with ninjas is kind of forgotten. At the very end, ninja fighting begins again.

Deathstalker 2: Duel of the Titans

Director: Jim Wynorski
Screenplay: Neil Ruttenberg
Producer: Frank K. Isaac
Cast: John Terlesky (Deathstalker), Monique Gabrielle (Reena/Princess Evie), John Lazar (Jarek the Sorcerer), Toni Naples (Sultana), Maria Socas (Amazon Queen)

Deathstalker is back! He has a rousing synth theme that gets played a lot, even by a midget with a lute. He's as roguish as he was in the original film but he's far less willing to engage in random sexual assault. He's traveling the countryside, enjoying life, when he meets Reena the Seer. She enlists him to go the land of Jzafir to stop the evil Jarek and Sultana. It seems they have deposed the rightful princess and replaced her with a blood-sucking clone. The odds are vastly against 'Stalker (as Evie calls him) and the Seer: hordes of warriors, soldiers, sorcery, zombies, everything but the kitchen sink. (Although, one can see a Volvo in the corner of one shot.) *Deathstalker 2* has it all and takes none of it seriously.

'Stalker is a wiseacre in this one, constantly sassing off. He also knows all the tricks in the book. At one point he mentions the old "Moving Wall" routine. The movie is filled with a lot of silliness. Reena, played by Monique Gabrielle, spends most of the movie going over the top. In fact, when the sexy clone appears, it's a little tough to tell that she's the same woman because there's such a difference. The film always seems to be enjoying itself. It's sort of the anti–*Conan*. Nothing is sacred. It's all about the fun.

Director Jim Wynorski is having fun and he loves women with large breasts. It's a living. Some of the humor is definitely on the forced side. Not all of 'Stalker's one-liners are funny. He's no comic guru. But he's got a lot of charm. Less than 80 minutes, the movie doesn't wear out its welcome.

The film was one of Roger Corman's made-in-Argentina numbers. Like many of the others, it has an air of chintziness to it. The opening sequence where 'Stalker steals a jewel and gets attacked by soldiers takes place in the cheapest-looking faux–*Raiders* treasure room ever. In fact, during the fight with the soldiers, 'Stalker bumps a wall-mounted stone dragon head and it bounces up and down. There is a pendulum sequence (an homage to Mr. Corman?). Throughout, 'Stalker goofs and that music pounds away, keeping the pace and drive of the movie going. Everyone seems to be enjoying themselves, especially during the scene where 'Stalker has to wrestle a gigantic woman named Queen Kong. One doesn't see stuff like that every day.

Devil's Dynamite

Director: Godfrey Ho (as Joe Livingstone)

Screenplay: William Palmer

Producer: Tomas Tang

Cast: Mick Stuart, Walter Bond, Richard Phillips, Ted Wald, Eddie Leo, Mark Coston

Devil's Dynamite is one in a series of movies (well, two or three) about hopping

FOR THE SHADOW WARRIOR - NO ENEMY IS TOO DEADLY

Chinese vampires versus some sort of robotic guy. This Godfrey Ho picture isn't as nutty as *RoboVampire*, which mixes in some newly shot footage (including a fantastic fight on the beach) with the movie it's stealing from. *Devil's Dynamite* looks like it might be something Ho shot all by himself. That's surprising. And probably wrong.

Hopping vampires are killing people and causing problems. The police are pretty powerless. One of them is marrying a woman named Mary. Mary, it turns out, is controlling the vampires. Enter the RoboVampire, who takes the hopping vampires on in several fights. A couple of little kids, one of whom wears kabuki-style makeup, keep encountering the vampires. They are annoying. The kids, not the vampires.

Devil's Dynamite doesn't have as much robo-adventure as the other film. In fact, the robo-guy (I don't know what to call him) looks more like the Prince of Space from the movie of the same name. In fact, he doesn't look robotic at all. Maybe he's not actually meant to be robotic, maybe he just gets in the outfit—which doesn't even look like a robotic suit. It looks like a jumpsuit.

Devil's Dynamite just wants you to watch a bunch of fighting with hopping vampires. There's also a lot of chicanery involving Mary, the wedding, etc. Maybe we should stick with *RoboVampire*. *Devil's Dynamite* is not one of the best although that robo-guy, or whatever, does look a bit funny fighting. That might be worth your time.

Double Target

Director: Bruno Mattei

Screenplay: Claudio Fragasso, Vincent Dawn

Producer: Franco Gaudenzi

Cast: Miles O'Keeffe (Robert Ross), Donald Pleasence (Senator Blaster), Bo Svenson (Col. Galckin),

Kristine Erlandson (Mary McDouglas), Richard Raymond (Toro)

Bruno Mattei films always feel like they're trying. But one does not always know *what* they're trying. They start off seeming like they might make sense and then go off on tangents or introduce elements of strange humor or just get weirder as they go. It's his thing and the filmgoers of the world enjoyed it for several decades. I generally have a good time.

Double Target starts with several folks, in Hong Kong and Southeast Asia, on suicide missions. The U.S. government is worried so they send Robert Ross, ex-commando, into the jungles to find out what's going on. Ross is also looking for his son who is somewhere in those jungles. There's a lot of shooting and 1001 beautiful explosions of the sort that Mattei is always so good at. This film is squarely in the area of *Strike Commando*. Miles O'Keeffe is a fun hero. He doesn't have the shriek of Reb Brown but he has his own stoic charms. Donald Pleasence plays an unpleasant Senator who complains a lot.

The subplot of the son is interesting. After the war, Mom was put into a Vietnamese re-education camp, where she died. The son grew up there, never meeting his father, so he's bristles when he meets Robert for the first time. But he changes his mind pretty quickly and gets on the side of his dad. That interesting plot thread is sewed up shut with little to no regard for drama so the film can get to more shooting and explosions. Of which there are many.

My favorite sequence comes after the son is rescued. Robert, his son *et al.* are at some sort of beachside hangout. There's a roofed area where a bunch of guys sit, drink and eat. Robert walks away from the area as a man machetes a piece of the fruit. There's a bomb inside! A huge shootout ensues, capped off with about ten explosions. No one can argue with the pyrotechnics in a Mattei film.

Double Target is entertaining but a little too long. One wishes that Mattei had the brevity of an Arizal. Plus, it alternates between Sense and No Sense, the way many Mattei films do. In Mattei fashion, the song over the closing credits seems to come out of nowhere and is hilarious.

Hammer aka *Hammerhead*

Director, Screenplay: Enzo G. Castellari
Producer: Giorgio Salvioni
Cast: Daniel Greene (Hammer), Melonee Rodgers, Jorge Gil, Frank Zagarino, Donna Rosae, Deanna Lund (DD)

Hammer's pal Greg calls him and says he's in trouble. Hammer says, "Let's just kick some ass." Yes, another Enzo G. Castellari film begins. *Hammer* kicks off in Miami with Greg being crushed by one of those huge storage containers by the docks. Within a half hour, everyone is in Jamaica and there's a jet ski chase going on. If you believe that *Police Academy 3: Back in Training* has the ultimate in jet ski chases, *Hammer* may change your mind. Castellari keeps it moving and keeps it brutal, and yet kind of fun at the same time.

It's the mid–1980s and the world wants the new Stallone, the new Schwarzenegger. Daniel Green was so good in *Atomic Cyborg*, why not him? Well, he didn't become that next big thing but his straightforward "just want to kick some ass" attitude shines through in this Italian action film, lensed mainly in Jamaica. There are drugs involved. A goofy guy named Jose. A really hot writer who does a striptease that may ignite men's drawers through the screen. Hammer falls in love and may or not have a daughter. It's all good stuff, *Hammer*-style.

This is the sort of film that Castellari was perfect for. The plot is slick and swift. Very little time is wasted getting Hammer from Miami to Jamaica. He is placed in the thick of things again and again. After a while, one starts to think that by now, Hammer must have punched or shot at every person in Jamaica.

Then these buoyant, semi-rough, all-in-fun good times culminate with a shootout and a series of fistfights at a sugar factory. Castellari keeps the surprises and the shocks coming. Out of all the several big climactic moments, which was your favorite? The man getting buried under a ton of raw sugar? The kick-ass fight sequence around the circular saw? No moderation is the best moderation.

Hammer goes in, kills who he needs to, punches others and the day is saved. The final twist, a really good one, makes you rethink everything you just saw. Hint: It won't make you rethink whether or not Hammer is cool. He's still cool.

Hands of Death

Director: Godfrey Ho
Screenplay: Stephen Soul
Producers: Joseph Lai, Betty Chan
Cast: Richard Harrison (The Colonel), Mike Abbott (Baron), Stefan Brendhart, Phil Parker, Simon Heagan, Lars Anderson

I would like to state right here: Mike Abbott is my all-time favorite ninja ever. He has an awesome mullet and a rough-and-tumble acting style which some might call "not so good" but I call "oh so great." If Mike Abbott comes to your town, you're going to have a great night.

There is treasure in a cave and some ninjas and a bunch of ladies and some generic kung fu guys go looking for it. An old woman has been in the cave for 30 years. And when a lady mentions treasure to her, the old woman declares that those rumors are "Bullshit!" Thanks, old lady in the cave. You are the best.

Godfrey Ho and Joseph Lai strike again with one of their patched-together "ninja" movies. As always, it is made up of a lot of footage from an Asian action film of some variety (most of the cave stuff). This footage is mixed together with newly shot footage of Richard Harrison, Mike Abbott and others dressed in lovely pink and gray outfits with headbands that say "Ninja." This stuff is a hoot. These films almost always entertain and this one is no different.

A lot of *Hands of Death* seems to involve a group of women running around and screaming, sometimes near streams. Trying to guess what the original film was like can drive a viewer mad. In one of my favorite scenes, Baron is talking to a guy about creating an alliance to find the treasure. The guy is in the old footage, sitting in medium shot in a living room area. Baron is in a head-and-shoulders closeup standing in front of a wall. They try to get the dubbed voice on the old footage to match Mike Abbott's volume and tenor. It has to be seen to be truly enjoyed.

The fighting is as awesome as always. Within the older footage, it's good stuff. The new ninja footage is all very silly. The final fight between the colonel and Baron involves a lot of flipping and spinning around, swords thrown and that kind of thing. But there doesn't seem to be a whole lot of fighting. Just many closeups and a lot of sneering.

An enormous book needs to be put together on the cinema of Godfrey Ho. How they acquired the old movies. How they wrote the scripts. It's some sort of achievement to put together a film like this. The fact that the films within the films can be random genres makes it more delicious.

Hard Ticket to Hawaii

Director, Screenplay: Andy Sidaris
Producer: Arlene Sidaris
Cast: Ronn Moss (Rowdy Abilene), Dona Speir (Donna), Hope Marie Carlton (Taryn), Harold Diamond (Jade), Rodrigo Obregon (Seth Romero), Cynthia Brimhall (Edy)

Donna and Taryn are kick-ass undercover agents in Hawaii. Donna is no-nonsense. Taryn is more of a goof. She likes James Bond films and looks forward to being a part of one. There are some very bad men smuggling diamonds. The gals get involved. Rowdy Abilene is the cousin of Cody from *Malibu Express*. Like Cody, he's hunky and can't shoot straight. But in this film, he's got it covered. There is also a giant poisonous snake slithering around the island, appearing randomly and killing.

Writer-director Sidaris abandoned the murder mystery–style plotting of *Malibu Express* and went for all-out action good times with boobs. There are many shootouts, chase scenes and monstrous snake attacks. Buff people throw each other around and shoot one another. Taryn has a poster of *Malibu Express* above her bed.

The complete random plotting of *Malibu Express* is a little bit more interesting than this film's secret agent shenanigans. Both are extremely entertaining. In this Sidaris film, and some of his others, there are so many characters spread all over the place that one can lose track of what's going on. "Why are they here exactly?" "Was that a good guy or a bad guy?" It's in no way a bad thing. And if everything turns out to not quite make sense, it probably doesn't actually matter.

Ronn Moss (formerly Ridge Forrester of *The Bold and the Beautiful*) is top-billed so one would assume that he plays the lead guy. But he doesn't really have much to do in the first hour or so. (Granted, it does take a lot of time to bring James Bond into *Thunderball*.) When he does arrive, he uses a bazooka. And it's pretty funny.

The characters go through hell for the U.S. government and then can laugh in hearty unison before the credits roll. Andy Sidaris sifted through the elements of his first action film, refined things and gave the world *Hard Ticket to Hawaii*. Nothing to complain about.

Hitman the Cobra

Director: Godfrey Ho
Screenplay: Stephen Soul
Producer: Joseph Lai
Cast: Richard Harrison (Phillip), Mike Abbott (Mike), Philip Parker, Nathan Chukeke, David Selvik, Robert Muller

This Ho-Lai non-ninja film starts off as a World War II film with a guy named Max who saves a lot of people from the Japanese forces. Then it hops to the 1970s. There are mobsters and cops and sleazy clubs. Throughout it all, Richard Harrison and Mike Abbott (along with some other goofy commando guys) are spliced in to try to bring some semblance of

non-craziness to the proceedings. Nice try. It doesn't work.

From the opening sequence involving a guy speaking to a crowd about getting rid of the Japanese to a quick cut to Harrison chasing a man, the movie doesn't rest. In fact, the opening credits play as the speech is given and then continue through the start of the foot chase. There's so much happening that credits just don't have time! Phillip ends up killing this guy, and then his brother, Mike, comes after him. Mixed in with all that is Max and the jump in, maybe, 30 years. Of course, Phillip and Mike have not aged a day.

The craziness begins with the title.

Cobra, got it. Stallone. What does that have to do with the movie? Zero. *Hitman the*? You got me there. That makes no sense. Many of the Ho-Lai films don't seem to have much sense in the title department (or anywhere else) but this one takes the cake.

These films are known for snatching music from wherever. The *Miami Vice* theme plays. I think I heard the *Magnum P.I.* theme. As rebels are being handed guns, the opening minute of the Genesis song "Mama" plays. That familiar drum machine with those creepy synths. During a sneaking-around-the-woods sequence, the familiar electronic drum opening of the Genesis Top 5 hit "Tonight, Tonight, Tonight" starts playing. Except it's slowed down and it goes on for a couple minutes and there are no vocals. Where did this version come from? Is it from a demo? I want to call Ho-Lai up and get more info.

Hitman the Cobra is as action-packed and idiot-packed as every one of their movies. The World War II portion is over 25 minutes of the film. One can spend that time trying to figure out if Ho-Lai pilfered one movie for this or if they actually used two movies (along with their new footage) that had the same cast members to make this one.

Best credit? "Direct or editing— Vincent Leung." It's your choice, Vincent.

Hollywood Cop

Director, Screenplay: Amir Shervani

Producers: Moshe Bibiyan, Simon Bibiyan

Cast: Jim Mitchum (Feliciano), Cameron Mitchell (Capt. Bonano), David Goss (Turk), Julie Schoen (Rebecca), Lincoln Kilpatrick (Jaguar), Troy Donahue (Lt. Maxwell), Aldo Ray (Mr. Fong)

Hollywood Cop has the standard done-on-a-synthesizer '80s low-budget action score. It keeps the pulse pound-

ing, keeps the heart racing, keeps a drum machine going in the heart of the viewer.

Hollywood Cop has the crazy one-damn-thing-after-another style of plotting that writer-director Shervani's similar film *Samurai Cop* has. The cast of characters includes Turk, a good-looking guy with an African-American partner, Jaguar. A man named Joe Fresno once did some work with a gangster. They stole some money. Fresno skipped out with the

cash. So the gangster has Fresno's son Steve kidnapped. Steve's mom Rebecca goes to the police and hooks up with Turk and Jaguar! And they are off into the seedy parts of Hollywood to find the boy or Joe Fresno or somebody.

Turk is first seen stumbling upon a "rape robbery" and saves the day. He and Jaguar argue endlessly with an Asian desk clerk at a hotel. The scene starts off annoying and then becomes funny. Then, there's kung fu and naked women in spas. Steve spends a very long time trying to get a dog to help free him from the kidnapper's clutches. The kidnappers are tough guys who are almost all incompetent. Joe Fresno shows up. The ladies love him! And he's still got the money.

Cameron Mitchell yells! Troy Donahue is a bit of a simp! Aldo Ray's voice is less raspy here than it was ten years before. He plays Mr. Fong(!). There are appearances by character actors everyone will recognize and they bring a verve to the proceedings. Mr. Shervani may not shoot the best action scenes but there's always something happening, always another bit of action-adventure right around the bend. This is not the all-around crazy classic that is *Samurai Cop* but it's close. *Hollywood Cop* looks a lot more normal but it's got a driving craziness that makes it a good time.

Interzone

Director: Deran Sarafian

Screenplay: Claudio Fragasso, Deran Sarafian

Cast: Bruce Abbot (Swan), Beatrice Ring (Tera), Tegan Clive (Mantis), Jon Armstead (Balzakan), Kiro Wehara (Panasonic)

Filmirage, welcome back into the life of all good film-watchers. The wonderful majesty of Filmirage and their weird way of making films is all over *Interzone*. The strange characterization, offbeat plotting and weird-looking people. A book on Filmirage should be in the works. If it isn't, I'll make it.

Swan is the Max of this *Mad Max*–type film. There are different gangs. There's an ancient relic being guarded by some monks in a cave. There's a very beefy female bodybuilder who can do a very entertaining dance. To all this insanity—which also includes car chases, shootouts and kung fu fights—Bruce Abbot brings a fun swagger.

Unlike Max and unlike all the Max wannabes, Swan is having a good time. The post-apocalyptic world is not a hoot, but Swan is not as moody and unpleasant as a lot of the others of his sort. The Interzone may not be the cleanest place but Swan is making the best of it. Swan has charisma.

There are several moments of silliness. Sometimes it's tough to figure out what the hell Filmirage is up to. Sort of a Eurocine but without the touch of class that even the craziest Eurocine free-for-all had. To me, the oddest moment is the behind-the-shade nude dance by Mantis. She was in *Sinbad of the Seven Seas* and she's just as beefy there. Here she does a dance for Swan and it is from another movie altogether. However, the actress gets into it. She gives it her all, and, I'll be damned, it works. That's a fun scene and it makes her character (who, up until that point, was a little bland) more entertaining.

Interzone has a good pace and some silly moments that actually work. One can't say that about a lot of these movies.

Jack Tillman: The Survivalist

Director: Sig Shore
Screenplay: John V. Kent
Producers: Steven Shore, David Greene
Cast: Steve Railsback (Jack Tillman), Marjoe Gortner (Lt. Youngman), Cliff De Young (Dr. Vincent Ryan), Susan Blakely (Linda), David Wayne (Dub Daniels)

The Cold War had people pretty desperate. Well, most people. I don't remember my family being too worried about it. But then, 1987 was when I entered high school. That was tough enough. *Jack Tillman: The Survivalist* is a pretty well-done glimpse at what martial law and lawlessness would do to America. As it goes along, it loses some of that tension and becomes more of a straight-on action film.

Sig Shore directed *Super Fly*. That movie is a cool period piece but it's not that well-directed. The acting gets pretty ripe. Shots aren't in focus. But that could have been part of the verisimilitude that Shore was going after. There's certainly nothing like that here. The film is a little too mid–80s bright to get properly gritty. Shore pulls off the action here, especially during the closing sequences.

The story: An American nuke goes off in Siberia. Martial law is enforced in America in expectation of retaliation. Jack's (Steve Railsback) wife and daughter are killed by looters. All bank accounts are frozen, so Jack breaks into a bank to get his dough. This puts Lt. Youngman on his trail. Jack and two friends head out into the desert to get his son out of a summer camp. Jack is a survivalist at heart. But by the end, he's being chased by Youngman and his troops *and* a biker gang. Will he survive?

There is a lot of violence in the film, much of it unpleasant. Jack's group meets up with Dub (David Wayne), an old grizzled guy. They spend some quality time with him in a lovely scene. Jack tells Dub that "they'll" be coming this way soon, meaning that Dub will probably lose what little he has.

Jack Tillman: The Survivalist is a silly title. The video box simply lists it as *The Survivalist* and that works better. Everyone here does a good job. Railsback is a convincing Texas survivalist. Marjoe Gortner is always Marjoe Gortner. You either love him or hate him. Or both. He seems lovable, even when he's being a jerk, which he is in this film. This

one's worth watching. It's the violent side of a movie like, say, *Shame* and all the better for it.

The Karate Warrior

Director: Fabrizio De Angelis

Screenplay: David Parker, Jr., Fabrizio De Angelis (as Larry Ludman)

Producer: Fulvia International Films

Cast: Kim Stuart (Anthony), Ken Watanabe (Master Kimura), Janelle Darretto (Maria), Jared Martin (Anthony's Father)

There was bound to be a *Karate Kid* rip-off from Italy at some point. It's surprising that this isn't more well-known amongst fans of Italian rip-offs of American action movies. There are *six Karate Warrior* movies. *Six!* There were only two *Strike Commandos*. There were only two *Bronx Warrior* films. How on Earth did they make six of these? Apparently these films were big hits somewhere.

The Karate Kid is quintessential 1980s teen "coming of age," with action and drama, too long but definitely charming. Ralph Macchio and Pat Morita make a great team. The fight choreography is excellent. There is an brilliant rock tune to get every viewer up and yelling. There's that fun Halloween sequence. A cute gal, mean guys. It's a good time. Its rip-off *Karate Warrior* tells the story of Anthony Scott going to meet his dad in Manila. Kind of a jerk, he gets beat up a lot. He is found by Master Kimura in the jungle. Anthony is trained for a big tournament. Will Anthony have to use the "Dragon Blow" move, which involves not touching your opponent but releasing a cloud of blue optical effects? Possibly.

Karate Warrior pretty much gets everything wrong. Anthony is kind of a prick, unlikable, so when he gets beat up, it's okay. So much of it is set in the jungle that it all be-

comes disconnected. One can understand the filmmakers trying to create their own kick-ass move for the end of the final fight, but the "Dragon Blow" is a special effect, not a kung fu move. It's as if they tried combining what they thought were the winning elements of the first two *Karate Kids* but they chose all the wrong elements. The training sequence is nonsensical and Master Kimura is no Mr. Miyagi. And the final fight is over very quickly. There's almost no suspense at all.

IMPERIAL ENTERTAINMENT CORP. presents A LARRY LUDMAN film "KARATE WARRIOR" Starring JARED MARTIN • JANET AGREN • KIM STUART and KEN WATANABE Music by SIMON BOSWELL Produced by FULVIA INTERNATIONAL FILMS Directed by LARRY LUDMAN

Yet, in getting everything wrong, *Karate Warrior* seemed to strike some kind of chord. Six movies is not a series, it's a franchise. I'd be interested to know why this series was so well received. Frankly, the film is entertaining but kind of dumb.

Mankillers

Director, Screenplay: David A. Prior
Producer: Peter Yuval
Cast: Edd Byrnes (Jack Marra), Gail Fisher (Joan Hanson), Edy Williams (Sgt. Roberts), Lynda Aldon (Rachael McKenna), William Zipp (John Mickland), Christine Lunde (Maria Rosetti)

A gang of tough broads are sent to stop a bad man involved in sex slavery and drug

running and responsible for the death of several undercover FBI agents. One broad, assigned to line up yet more tough broads, goes to a prison for recruits. They are sent deep into the woods to stop this guy and all of his men. It's women vs. men in this Action International Pictures extravaganza, made by David A. Prior.

Mankillers is exactly what one thinks it's going to be, except with very little nudity. Mostly gals in short shorts with guns. It's not particularly titillating, if that's what you're after. It's also not incredibly exciting. In fact, it's quite boring during the rather interminable training sequences where the women bond. The scenes with the psychopath are far more interesting. He really is nuts, and considers himself invulnerable. He uses a chainsaw to torture people. Left to his mercies, this reviewer would probably turn chicken fairly quickly.

The women get trained and they go to fight. In one tense scene, a man tracks down one of the women and kills her violently. But, apart from that, it's mostly long shots and medium shots of people firing guns at each other with occasional bouts of fisticuffs.

The difference between a great action director and an average action director is probably in the way they photograph their gunfights. A great action director puts the viewer into the fight, swooping in, keeping the suspense high and making it clear where everyone is in relation to each other. An average action director just has people shooting. The viewer never grasps where anyone is in relation to anyone else. No suspense. Just noise and fury. David A. Prior might be in the latter category.

Masters of the Universe

Director: Gary Goddard
Screenplay: David Odell
Producers: Menahem Golan, Yoram Globus

TBS AWARD THEATER

MASTERS OF THE UNIVERSE

TODAY 10:35 AM

TBS

Cast: Dolph Lundgren (He-Man), Frank Langella (Skeletor), Courteney Cox (Julie Winston), James Tolkan (Detective Lubic), Christina Pickles (Sorceress), Meg Foster (Evil-Lyn), Chelsea Field (Teela), Jon Cypher (Man-at-Arms), Billy Barty (Gwildor), Robert Duncan McNeill (Kevin Corrigan)

The reputation of Cannon Films' *Masters of the Universe* is not great. Dolph Lundgren's rather wooden performance as He-Man; the relocation of much of the action to modern-day Earth; some effects and masks that are on the chintzy side; they didn't take full advantage of the mythos that the Filmation animated series had created. Yes, these are all problems. And yet the film is pretty darn en-

tertaining. It verges on cheap and camp—how could it not?—but the Earth segments and the Earth characters, and their responses to the people from Eternia, make it fun.

In the land of Eternia, there's the evil of Skeletor and his minions and the good of He-Man and the Sorceress and their pals. Skeletor is after a "key" that will allow him to access the power of Castle Greyskull and become a god. But the "key" is in the possession of He-Man, Teela, Man-at-Arms and the dwarfish Gwildor. They wind up on Earth in 1987. Skeletor sends his forces after them, including Beastman and Evil-Lyn. The gang from Eternia teams up with some folks from Earth, including Julie, her boyfriend Kevin and the always bewildered cop Lubic. The fight for Eternia has begun!

The movie starts off in Eternia and is a trifle Cannon-style chintzy. Lundgren doesn't quite register as He-Man but everyone else is trying. Then it goes to 1987 and for 15 or 20 minutes, I was lost. But it got better and bigger and funny and fun. An hour into it, I was hooked. I think the film has a bit of a structural problem because when Skeletor and his army appear on Earth and battles begin … that's clearly the climax. But there's another 20 minutes after it, including the big battle between He-Man and Skeletor. The film feels like it should be at the big climax when Skeletor arrives but it's not quite. The film didn't lose me there but maybe that should have concluded it. (Or the battle could have stretched into Eternia.)

Miami Connection

Director: Richard Park
Screenplay: Joseph Diamond, Richard Park; Story: Richard Park, Y.K. Kim
Producer: Y.K. Kim

Cast: Y.K. Kim (Mark), Vincent Hirsch (John), Maurice Smith (Jim), Siyung Jo (Yashito), Kathy Collier (Jane), Joseph Diamond (Jack)

Somewhere in Miami, there's drug-dealing, shootouts, guys fighting, bikers and some kung fu. Everyone is out trying to make their connection—their *Miami Connection.* Who will succeed and who will fail? And who will remember their lines? The man who gave us the wonderful off-kilter and almost completely screwball *LA Streetfighters* has another film, one that will Light Up Your Life. Although that might just be the cocaine talking.

A great sign of insanity is how many different elements a film can include. For *Miami Connection* see the list above. Insanity also shows up in the way that actors react to having something violent happen to them. One man has his arm cut off. We see it hit the ground. Then, it cuts to the guy who gives a sort of yell that isn't convincing and provokes mirth. Oh, it's going to be *that* kind of movie.

At a big club in Orlando, the kick-ass pop band Dragon Sound has a theme song that's all about them being friends forever. The guys in the band are all orphans and they are all black belts in taekwondo. One of the band guys is going out with a band gal; her brother wants to beat them up. The brother is also deep into drugs and all sorts of mischief. It's going to culminate in one big-ass fight with a lot of people who look like the director's buds that showed up on set one day.

"You cannot escape the Miami Ninja!" And there is no reason to want to escape from this film. It's full-on action with a touch of silliness to it. It ends piously with a caption stating that violence must be eliminated in order to achieve peace. I have no argument with that, but the end of a full-on action film is an odd place for that sentiment.

There are films that you don't want to see end, films that (as far as you're concerned) could go on forever. For me, *Rushmore* and Ingmar Bergman's *The Magic Flute* fit that description. *Miami Connection* does, too. There's a joyous, off-center loopiness to all of it. Drug dealers, ninjas, jerks … but they all

end up looking inferior to the Dragon Sound guys. And in classic exploitation film fashion, the band is sort of forgotten as new plotlines appear, including one of the orphans discovering his dad. Life is good when one watches this movie because it is fun and it is positive even when people are being decapitated and ninjas are going mad.

Mutant Hunt

Director, Screenplay: Tim Kincaid
Producer: Cynthia DePaula
Cast: Rick Gianasi, Mary Fahey, Ron Reynolds, Taunie Vernon

Inteltrax has accidentally created a group of psychosexual killer mutant cyborgs. They are loose on the streets of a future New York City, like all the garbage, graffiti and general filth wasn't bad enough. Luckily, there's a beefy guy named Matt Riker whose friends are trained Federation Operatives. They'll kick ass. Even in their tight white underpants. Thank you, Tim Kincaid, for doing it again. *Mutant Hunt* is entertaining, positing this slightly futuristic world where cyborgs are normal and everyone seems a little depressed. It's sort of *Blade Runner*–esque but on a much smaller budget. It's one of those films that has to "tell, not show." That's part of the fun.

The film says it is in the future and that psychosexual killer mutant cyborgs are on the loose. That's awesome. But, really, it's hunky guys and hot women fighting big, beefy guys on dirty streets or in bedrooms that look like fallout shelters. The incongruity of the fight for humanity that we're told about and the one guy with the big porno mustache and Rick Gianasi in his underpants and the redhead with big hair and the short skirt all kicking around guys is something that could really goof up the viewer's mind.

It's called cognitive dissonance. It's when there is an obvious detachment between what you are seeing (or being told you're seeing) and what your mind actually takes in. *Mutant Hunt* could almost be a school play about a group of folks hunting these mutants. Most of the time the camerawork places us some distance from what's going on. The action scenes are not shot in high-intensity style with lots of camera movement and editing. It is just a camera set down and people punching each other with the edits occurring, probably, at the points when the actors ran out of choreography or when someone made a mistake.

None of this is a bad thing. Everyone's doing their best to make the film be what it says it is. Does it look funny when our hero fights mutants in his underpants? Sure does. When the main music kicks in, is it from another movie? (Or vice versa.) Sure is. It's from *Dreamaniac.* One of them stole from the other or it was written for both. Who knows? But, it's great music regardless.

Mutant War

> *Director, Screenplay:* Brett Piper
> *Producers:* Charles H. Baldwin, Arthur Schwitzer
> *Cast:* Matt Mitler (Harry Trent), Kristine Waterman (Spider), Deborah Quayle (Beth), Cameron Mitchell (Reinhart Rex), Steve Balyga (Punk Leader)

Mutant War doesn't take itself too seriously but it takes itself seriously enough so that the sense of menace remains. This makes it more fun to watch than if it had a stronger camp flavor. It's a fine line and whenever the film brings out Cameron Mitchell, it steps over that line. But the star and his traveling sidekick make this post-apocalyptic weasel of a film entertaining.

There's a lot of narration from our main character Harry Trent. Here's how the story goes: Aliens (Iuzags?) came to Earth. A group of men, including Trent, retaliated with neutron 90, which killed the aliens but left mutant cannibals and giant stop-motion animals behind. The Earth is no longer a nice place. Trent teams with a gal named Spider and they take on Reinhart Rex (Mitchell), who is banding the mutants into a fighting force and trying to get them to mate with the remaining women. Fighting ensues.

The leads have some charm and wit. That's what sold the film for me. Trent travels around in his car, cracking wise and trying to get out of trouble. He's not generally laugh-out-loud funny but the more he does, the more evil he fights, the more we like him. Spider is a sweet kid, sort of the post-apocalyptic version of the young gal from *Neon Maniacs.* I liked her almost instantly. She's a little on the foolhardy side but brave. Cameron Mitchell brings a lot of ham to his role. He seems to be acting in something far more campy than *Mutant War* is. But he's not in it much and he's got a fun helmet. The mutants and stop-motion monsters aren't nice.

Like many movies of this type, it's low-budget and a little rough around the edges. (The mutant masks made me wonder if the mutants were wearing masks or whether those were supposed to be their faces.) But *Mutant War* wins by being serious alongside not-so-serious but never in a way that saps the suspense. Recommended for a rainy afternoon.

Ninja Avengers

> *Director:* Joseph Lai
> *Screenplay:* Stephen Soul
> *Producers:* Joseph Lai, Betty Chan
> *Cast:* Richard Harrison (Gordon), Stuart Smith (Ringo), Stefan Bernhardt, Frederick Sutbjerg, Patrick Kelly

Ringo is let out of prison. He believes he has been betrayed by Gordon's brother. So Ringo sends a group of ninjas off into the wild to find the brother. The brother carries around a big cross at all times. He meets a man named Dragon, and then they hook up with a woman. It also involves some sort of sacred statue that was stolen by the Japanese. Every once in a while, a ninja shows up and Gordon fights him in completely unrelated scenes.

In this Ho-Lai hodgepodge, the brother and Dragon wander along and get in fights. Sometimes there's a lady there. I don't want to spoil any surprises by mentioning the purpose of the cross but let's just say: I never thought I'd see *Django* coming up in one of these films. There's barely any ninja footage in this one.

This film has the most ridiculously straightforward plot in the Ho-Lai canon. Ninjas are trying to kill the brother. Gordon stops them. The brother and his friends are wandering the countryside. It's almost poetically simple. But, as with many of these films, the secondary plotline overtakes the ninja plotline.

Apparently Godfrey Ho is alive and well and teaching film in Hong Kong. What in the world would he be teaching students? Does he ever show them any of his own films? Do people take his course because they think they'll watch a lot of ninja films? Is the course he teaches on the history of ninja films?

It's tough to dislike a film like this. It's dumb but it knows that it's dumb. Gordon just wants to protect his brother. And his brother, most of the time, doesn't seem to realize that he actually is Gordon's brother. How could he forget that?

Ninja Commandments

> *Director:* Joseph Lai (with Godfrey Ho)
> *Screenplay:* Stephen Soul
> *Producers:* Joseph Lai, Betty Chan
> *Cast:* Richard Harrison (Gordon), Dave Wheeler, Peter Kjaer, Adam Frank

This is probably the strangest Ho-Lai cut-and-paste ninja film I have encountered:

(1) There is the least amount of connection between the "ninja" footage and the "old" footage of any of them.

(2) During long sequences, the "old" drama is interconnected with a ninja reciting the Ninja Commandments. And it makes less sense than things normally make in these movies.

(3) The "old" footage is actually from a drama about a broken family and the time they spend broken. The ninja footage seems to take place over a much shorter period of time.

(4) The ending of the "old" footage is a big tragic moment. This immediately cuts to a ridiculous fight between Gordon and this movie's bad guy.

(5) The "old" footage has moments of decent drama that are goofed by the dubbing.

Basically, the ninjas have lost their master and Gordon goes after him. Somehow

that is linked to the "old" footage, which is about a couple. She is pregnant. He leaves. The mom rescues her baby from fire but is horribly burned. The child is told that his parents are dead and that the disfigured woman raising him is his aunt. The boy goes out to find his parents, with tragic results. Intercut with this drama, every ten minutes or so, is Gordon fighting another ninja. The link between the new ninja footage and the "old" footage is pretty much non-existent. They are two separate threads.

The drama in the "old" footage is almost affecting. The story of the burned woman raising her child and being mistreated by everyone would have brought a tear to my eye except for the dubbing and the distracting burn makeup, which looks like someone melted marzipan or milk chocolate over one side of her face.

If the dangers of cut-and-paste filmmaking had a poster child, it would be *Ninja Commandments*. The "old" footage tells a good story. The ninja footage doesn't actually get near it. The "old" footage simply isn't an action film and no amount of intercut ninja fighting will change that. An odd experience awaits anyone who wanders into the world of this movie.

Ninja Phantom Heroes aka
Ninja Empire

> *Director:* Godfrey Ho
> *Screenplay:* Duncean Bauer
> *Producer:* Tomas Tang

Godfrey Ho is a master of a certain kind of ninja movie. The man made over 100 movies, the majority of them in the 1980s. If I had the stamina, I would write a book called *Ninja Godfrey Ho* that would cover each and every one of Ho's ninja films from the 1980s in detail. Critical discussion and actual differentiation of each and every one. It needs to be done.

Ho would take an unreleased or simply unknown Asian action film (gangster films, war films, horror films, etc.). Then, he would shoot sequences with ninjas. Sometimes these ninjas wore headbands that said "Ninja" on them. The new footage would be edited into the older film. A whole new soundtrack would be dubbed in that would bend the film to fit the story Ho had created. As one might imagine, this is a nutty way to make films. These films are some of the oddest films that the 1980s have to offer. My favorite is *Ninja: Silent Assassin*, which uses the *Miami Vice* theme and has good kung fu fighting (non-ninja related) within the butchered film.

In *Ninja Phantom Heroes,* three guys constantly run around acting goofy. One is called "Fatty." They threaten to take over a film that has already gone off in eight different directions. There are a ton of brawls but not a lot of ninja action. Somewhere along the line, this film was retitled *Ninja Empire.* But Ho had already made a film called *Ninja Empire* so if you discuss that title with someone, be sure to differentiate between the two.

Ninja: Silent Assassin

Director: Godfrey Ho
Screenplay: Stephen Soul
Producers: Joseph Lai, Betty Chan
Cast: Richard Harrison, Alphonse Beni, Stuart Smith, Grant Temple

Of all the Ho-Lai films that I've seen, *Ninja: Silent Assassin* has the most new "ninja" footage alongside of the best action footage from the original Hong Kong(?) source. There is plenty of goofy ninja fighting mixed with some fantastic Jackie Chan–style fighting by the leading man in the "old" footage. *Ninja: Silent Assassin* should be at the top of anyone's list when it comes to cut-and-paste ninja–kung fu films.

A drug dealer kills Gordon's wife. Gordon goes to Hong Kong with Richard Harrison to get the dealer. This storyline gets mixed up with something about drug- dealing at the Kowloon docks and a bad guy named Tiger. A tough good guy fighter joins the fray when his dad is killed by thugs at the docks. The hilarious ninja sequences, which seemed to have been shot and edited by seven-year-olds, are intercut with some good action scenes.

The scenes within the "old footage" are dubbed hilariously. One goofy-looking lanky guy is given a slightly high-pitched voice which is pretty funny. The hero has a tendency to lift up guys' shirts to look for tattoos. So he says "Take your clothes off" a lot and lifts up the shirt of a young woman. He then apologizes: "I did not know you were a girl." All great.

The film is elevated by the almost constant string of great kung fu fights. The hero does a lot of flipping and using props. He also does some great stunts, including jumping through the back window of a moving bus and landing on the pavement in one take. There are more people leaping over speeding cars than in any other movie I've seen. *Ninja: Silent Assassin* is one of the few cut-and-paste ninja films where you look forward to the old footage, because the fighting is good.

If you're going to see only one of the Ho-Lai ninja numbers, *Ninja: Silent Assassin* should be it. The new footage hits bold heights of hilarity with acting, costumes and fighting while the old footage is packed with worthwhile action.

No Retreat, No Surrender 2: Raging Thunder

Director: Corey Yuen
Screenplay: Roy Horan, Keith W. Strandberg, Maria Elena Cellino
Producer: Roy Horan
Cast: Cynthia Rothrock (Terry), Loren Avedon (Scott Wylde), Max Thayer (Mac Jarvis), Patra Wanthivanond (Sulin Nguyen), Matthias Hues (Yuri, "The Russian")

Corey Yuen and Cynthia Rothrock should be enough to get anyone into this film. Corey directed the first film in this series, the one that set Jean Claude Van Damme up as an A-1 Asskicker. He also directed the extremely entertaining *Dragons Forever* and my favorite Rothrock film, the rough-and-tumble, stunt-filled *Righting Wrongs. No Retreat, No Surrender 2* isn't as much fun as those but it is good stuff. It is top-loaded with kick-ass fight scenes. It also starts calm-ish and then gets crazier and crazier.

Cynthia had yet to whomp the bad guys in the China O'Brien series. But she had been in *Righting Wrongs* where she kicked ass, and had a great charm that she brought to her high kicks. Once one sees her name in the credits, it should be cause for a thrill. She's great in this, with several wonderful fight scenes.

Scott Wylde goes to Bangkok to visit his Thai fiancée. She is kidnapped and her family is killed. Scott is framed and sent to Singapore. He ends up in Cambodia with his mentor Mac and Terry, a kickboxing pilot, attempting to rescue Sulin from a camp filled with Vietnamese and Russian jerks. The camp is run by a big Russian known as Yuri. He's a

variation of Drago from *Rocky IV* except it's all about the karate and kickboxing.

The movie is a little long. The theatrical cut is about seven minutes shorter than the version currently available for home video and that version is the recommended one. The film could be a bit tighter but it has more than enough action it. At first, it seems like it might be a *Rocky*-style film set in kickboxing rings. But it breaks out of that very quickly and becomes life-or-death fighting out in the wilds of Southeast Asia. And it's good stuff. None of the actors (apart from the bad guys) seem to be taking it too seriously. The main guys are a bit dull. Cynthia is cool even though her hairdresser didn't do her any favors.

No Retreat, No Surrender 2: Raging Thunder has an unwieldy title but it's a good action film. It has just enough of that Hong Kong inventiveness, mixed with the American action style which, frankly, could be a bit of a drag. I enjoyed it more than the first one in the series. When you see Rothrock spinning flipping and kicking, it's killer.

It's not a rematch ... IT'S WAR.

No Retreat No Surrender 2 — Raging Thunder

Order of the Black Eagle

Director: Worth Keeter III
Screenplay: Phil Behrens
Producers: Robert P. Eaton, Betty J. Stephens

Cast: Ian Hunter (Duncan Jax), William T. Hicks (Von Tepisch), Chuck Bibby (Star), Jill Donnellan (Tiffany Youngblood), Anna Maria Rapagna (Maxie Ryder), Joe Coltrane (Hammer)

Jax Is Bax! is what the ads for this 1987 good time action comedy did not proclaim. That sums up *Order of the Black Eagle*. Who would have ever thought that the cool secret agent Duncan Jax, star of *Unmasking the Idol*, would get a second film? Probably no one. But here it is and Boon is back. Boon the baboon, that is.

This time around, Jax is sent to the jungles of South America to stop a neo–Nazi uprising, led by the vicious (and large) Baron von Tepisch. (Von Tepisch is played by the fat sheriff from *House of Death* and the world is a better place because of it.) Jax and Boon recruit a bunch of scuzzy mercenaries with names like Hammer to help them out. Bigger that anyone has realized, the neo–Nazi plan involves blowing up large numbers of communication satellites with lasers as well as...

Spoiler: This group has Hitler's body cryogenically frozen underground. With the help of a kidnapped scientist, they will bring Der Fuehrer back to life. Jax and Boon *must* win. For the Free World!

The first Jax film had a very big Indiana Jones vibe. This one is more of a James Bond sort of thing, with Jax getting his team together and heading deep into the jungles—and making a quick stop at an Old West town on the way. (There must have been an Old West street at Earl Owensby's studios.) Jax flies in on a hang glider. There is a daring kidnap involving a hot air balloon. The movie has everything.

Good production design prevents the movie from looking cheap. Occasionally moments betray them. A few of the sets, when lingered on for too long, don't look terribly sturdy. But everyone is working hard and I had a good time watching. Jax still has that vague accent, which sounds like it might be British. It also might be Swiss. It might be Dutch for all I know.

Order of the Black Eagle is just as much fun as *Unmasking the Idol*. The films were made in quick succession and there's a *joie de vivre* that flows through them that is quite enchanting. Jax is Bax. Let's all be there.

Overkill

Director, Producer: Ulli Lommel
Screenplay: Ulli Lommel, David Scott Kroes
Cast: Steve Rally (Mickey Delano), John Nishio (Akschi), Laura Burkett (Jamie), Allen Wisch (Collins), Antonio Caprio (Chief of Police)

Mickey Delano and his good cop pal Collins want to take down the Yakuza (Japanese Mafia), which is spreading violence and fear across downtown Los Angeles. But the Yakuza doesn't play fair and things will get a lot worse before they get better.

Ulli Lommel strikes like the cobra in this urban action thriller. Big hair, pounding synths and drum machines. Men being men. Women enjoying the company of men. A twisty-turny plot with double crosses and corrupt people all over the place. And Yakuza members shooting the hell out of innocent Japanese citizens. Would that Delano and Collins could be in every place at once!

Overkill looks like all the other low-budget direct-to-video action films of this time—lack of depth and multi-colored lighting. Horror films can pull it off because they usually get up to weird things. But an action film like this one, rooted in reality, needs to be grittier. This one almost looks like an episode of Alan Spencer's satire TV show *Sledge Hammer!*

Maybe that's what makes it fun. *Overkill* never hits the stratosphere of great action films but it's mostly entertaining. Collins loves sex. Delano wants to take down the Yakuza. They team with a guy named Akschi. A young man is shot and put in a wheelchair. Pathos, action, some boobs, violence—in short, *Overkill*. There's a beheading in the film, and it's kind of fun. Quick cuts and a little bit of blood. If you're familiar with the Lommel oeuvre, you know he doesn't shy away from blood.

Might this all be a parody of the action film as the cinema knew it at this time? Calling your film *Overkill* and then getting nowhere near that title implies a fun perversity in the same way that the overuse of flashbacks and the weird storyline of Lommel's *Boogeyman II* did. Maybe Lommel is goofing around and this is his very sharp satire. So sharp that it looks exactly like what it's satirizing. It's been done before (*Don't Go in the Woods*). Lommel is a smart man who has made a lot of movies.

The Power of Ninjitsu

Director: Joseph Lai
Screenplay: Stephen Soul
Producers: Joseph Lai, Betty Chan
Cast: Richard Harrison, Grant Temple, Mater Lee, Geoffrey Ziebart, Adam Frank, Peter Ujaer, Rita Bachmann, Joe Render, Jenny Park

The opening credits roll as awesome guitar-synth power music makes your want to jump around your living room and rock out. As the music plays and the regular Joseph Lai cast member names flash across the screen, Richard Harrison works out with a sharp sword. Every once in a while the sword is very close to the camera, prompting the thought, "Oh My Goodness! 3-D ninjas with Lai and Ho!" Sadly, Ho isn't listed as director here, although there's actually no discernible difference in the direction of *The Power of Ninjitsu* from any of their other films. It's just as nutty as anything they've ever made. Oddly enough, the only difference may be a significant one: there is no "Ninja" in the title.

In an Asian city Richard Harrison's yellow-suited ninja kills a man. We cut to a building that features, in huge lettering, "KOITO" on its side. On the rooftop of the "KOITO" building, some great kung fu fighting takes place. During the rooftop brawl, a strange man tells a very well-dressed man, Jackson, that he must die for not cooperating with them and that his son will be attacked next. Suddenly, they're all fighting in a field, where Jackson is shot dead.

Some Australian bad guys in an office say that only Black Dragon remains. But, it's all right because the lead baddie, Paolo, has sent Phoenix to take care of Black Dragon. However, Raymond, Jackson's son, might show up for revenge so everyone has to be on the lookout for him. Plus, Paolo has decided that they will no longer work for the Organization, run by his uncle. They will work on their own. The other men seem worried about this announcement. Paolo assures them that that once Black Dragon and The Scorpion are taken care of everything will be all right. (Of course, this is the first time they've mentioned The Scorpion.) Raymond shows up and serves as his father's proxy.

As the film goes along and the plot becomes tougher to follow (due to Lai's unwavering ability to remain completely vague), one must focus on the power of the Ninja. Plus, one can look forward to those great moments with those goofy Australian actors in their office debating whatever it is they're talking about re: The Organization. And, there is just enough of Richard Harrison in this film to make it feel like it might be normal. (Brother, it ain't.)

What's it all about? Who knows? I like to think that it never occurred to Lai to actually nail anything down. Or maybe he thought he had but hadn't really. I am confused. You are confused. Trust me, *Power of Ninjitsu* will do that to you.

Quest for the Lost City aka The Final Sacrifice

Director, Screenplay, Producer: Tjardus Greidanus
Cast: Christian Malcolm (Troy), Bruce J. Mitchell (Zap Rowsdower), Shane Marceau (Satoris), Ron Anderson (Pipper), Bharaba Egan (Aunt Betty)

Director Tjardus Greidanus made *Quest for the Lost City* for a class at an Alberta film school. It's a high-energy, slightly amateurish, lots-of-fun action film about a kid named Troy teaming with a grizzled Canadian named Zap Rowsdower. They are hunting for the Lost City of Ziox, which Troy's dad was also seeking with an even more grizzled guy named Pipper. An evil man named Satoris, who has his own cult, is also after the lost city. It's a race against time!

This film is great because its ambitions constantly outstrip its resources. There are underground caves that look like they were constructed from cardboard. There is a scene where Troy is chased by a truck. Troy is on a bike. There's no way Troy could outrun the truck. But, the truck keeps at a steady pace and Troy wins this one. When the lost city is revealed in the end, it is gloriously chintzy in the most charming way. And, always a sign of student films, there are lots of people running around doing slightly crazy stuff (Satoris's cult members, all in dark tank tops and ski masks). A student filmmaker can always get friends to do stupid stuff for movies. I speak from experience.

Greidanus has constructed a good movie. If his ambitions get left behind by his budget at times, that is not really a problem because no one was expecting *Terminator 2.* When a viewer turns to a film like this, he's hoping to have some fun. The keyword here is excitement: Does watching the film provide a fun, exciting time? I have to say yes. The acting is fine, the action is well shot. The film moves at a good pace. Those are the plusses that make it worth your time. It was famously riffed on *Mystery Science Theater 3000* under the title *The Final Sacrifice.*

The Retaliator aka *Programmed to Kill*

Director: Allan Holzman
Screenplay: Robert Short
Producers: Don Stern, Allan Holzman
Cast: Robert Ginty (Eric), Sandahl Bergman (Samira), Alex Courtney (Blake), Paul Walker (Jason), Louise Caire Clark (Sharon), Peter Bromilow (Donovan), James Booth (Brock)

In this fun action film, Robert Ginty's CIA contingent of mercenaries go after a group of terrorists in Greece led by Sandahl Bergman. There is a lot of shooting and a lot of good times in the action realm. That's all that is needed. The first half involves a standard black ops team sent to stop terrorists. But then it becomes a sort of *Silent Rage* or *Terminator* number, with Bergman's Samira kicking ass.

What happens next is that Eric and his team take out the terrorists. Samira is brought into a hospital; she's brain-dead but her body still lives. Scientists make her into a fairly unstoppable cyborg. To get her to obey commands (or something), they leave a bit of her own memory in so she isn't completely robot. And she goes rogue. She begins killing every-

one who took out her pals. Eric is last on the list.

Bergman makes a fun Terminator. Ginty is a good hero. The moment when she begins slo-mo-flipping towards him and he lets out a quiet mutter of "Shit" is quite funny. And the final confrontation is suitably filled with explosions and excitement.

Return of the Kickfighter aka Mission: Terminate

Director, Producer: Anthony Maharaj
Screenplay: Joe Mari Avellana
Cast: Richard Norton (Brad Cooper), Dick Wei (Bad Brother), Franco Guerrero (Capt. Anan), Rex Cutter (Col. Ted Ryan), Bruce Le (Quan Nhien)

Gold! Soldiers! Asia! Fighting! Lots of shooting in the second half! Richard Norton being more of a commando than a kung fu guy. Dick Wei doing a lot of kung fu. *Return of the Kickfighter* is an action film all right. No one would ever put down its pedigree. It's also a generic action film. Very generic.

When a film is this generic, what is there to say about it? Norton was in a film called *Kick Fighter.* This one is a sequel. The first one was more straightforward martial arts. This is army stuff and soldiers all the way, except when an occasional kung fu fight breaks out. The fighting is not all that memorable.

In Vietnam, American soldiers raid a village and steal some gold. Now a Vietnamese gentleman is killing the soldiers and trying to get the gold. Cooper is sent to find out what's going on. It culminates in some kung fu fighting but mostly a decently put-together, very long shootout between two opposing forces.

Norton is a little leaden but okay. The movie is saved by the appearance of Bruce Le aka the Man Who Is Not Bruce Lee. A very good fighter, he could bring out the excitement in a fight scene. He has some moves here that give this the feel of one of the films Jackie Chan made in the U.S. in the 1980s, like *The Big Brawl* or even a much later film like *Rush Hour.* (Watching Le fight here is like the *Rush Hour* pool hall scene where Jackie fights a bunch of guys. Clearly, everyone here is giving it their all, from Jackie to the stuntmen to the fight director. However, the camera is too damn close to everything and there's too much editing. A major fight scene is diminished.)

If a *Return of the Kickfighter* viewer wants action, congratulations, here it is. But it's all so blah. None of it truly reaches out and just takes hold. Which is too bad but it happens.

Run Coyote Run

Director: James Bryan
Screenplay, Producer: Renee Harmon
Cast: Renee Harmon (Ann Wilmington), Frank Neuhaus (Father), Timothy De Haas (Josh), William A. Luce (Commissioner), Mike Allen (Bill Whitmire)

Ann Wilmington, played by the great Renee Harmon, flies into Los Angeles to find out why her sister Linda Allen was killed. Ann is a psychic Interpol agent who is not welcomed into the realm of Los Angeles by the Feds. Her psychic abilities are derided and her abilities are considered suspect. But, Ann doesn't care. She will do whatever it takes to find out what happened to her sister.

In the *Maximum Underdrive #3* supplement to the VHS release of this movie, James Bryan says that Renee Harmon came to him with tapes of all their movies and wanted him to edit together a new movie they could sell. They would shoot a minimum amount of new footage on VHS that would tell the new story. Then, they would include footage from the other films every chance they could. It was an audacious, but not uncommon, plan from the video crazy second half of the 1980s.

The new footage with Ann Wilmington all has a bad, hissy camcorder sound. The movie features quite a few of the actors from previous Bryan/ Harmon films. The new footage overlays other movies including *Lady Streetfighter*, *Frozen Scream*, *Hell Riders* and *The Executioner Part II*. The footage from *Lady Streetfighter* is used the most and *Run Coyote Run* can be viewed as a semi-sequel. Sometimes the original footage is used to portray Ann's psychic vision of her sister's ill-fated exploits.

The action from *Lady Streetfighter* is entertaining. The new video footage doesn't add much action. There are a couple of lazy to fist-fights and car chases, most of which are intercut with footage from the previous movies. Limited to her psychic visions, Ann doesn't actually fight like Linda did, but then again, she doesn't end up like Linda did, either.

Or does she? Ann goes to Los Angeles to find out who killed her sister Linda. At the start of *Lady Streetfighter* a woman is shown being tortured and killed. Then, Linda arrives in Burbank. The woman who was killed was her sister. Linda is there to find out who killed her sister and why. Try working that out.

SFX Retaliator

Director: John Gale
Screenplay: Timothy Jorge, Paul Van
Producer: Silver Star Film Company
Cast: Chris Mitchum (Steve Baker), Linda Blair (Doris), Gordon Mitchell (Morgan), David Light (Mancini), Christine Dawson (Kate)

In *SFX Retaliator*, Chris Mitchum star as Steve Baker, FX expert for the movies. He gets involved in a very entertaining "if it ain't one damn thing it's another" variation on the 1986 movie *F/X*.

Two gangsters, Morgan and Mancini, don't like each other. Doris steals one million dollars from Morgan for Mancini. Her car breaks down as she's fleeing. Steve (just passing by) helps her out. At that point, high-speed shenanigans begin. Steve's wife is kidnapped and he has to get Doris. Then he gets Doris to Morgan but she doesn't have the money. So he has to get the money and things just keep happening. In one wonderful moment, when Steve's wife Kate is in the hospital, Morgan shows up to kill her. Steve says to him that it's all over, Doris is dead. Steve doesn't know where the money is and he had nothing to do with it anyways. Morgan doesn't care. It's fun to see a movie hero look at the villain and just say, it's over, man. Knock it off.

Of course, it isn't over until it's over. Steve has to protect himself and Kate using all the tricks in his FX playbook. And, they are pretty entertaining. Steve pulls out all the stops and, eventually, he pulls out a tank. Yes, a tank.

SFX Retaliator is a wonderfully awful title for a very enjoyable film. Steve keeps fighting the good fight. I don't think I've ever seen a film where a person who accidentally stumbled into chaos was forced to go back and forth between the bad guys so much. It certainly seems funny, which gives this film a bit of an advantage over other films of its sort.

Strike Commando

Director: Vincent Dawn

Screenplay: Clyde Anderson, Vincent Dawn

Producer: Oscar Faradyne

Cast: Reb Brown (Mike Ransome), Chris Connelly (Radak), Loes Kamma (Olga), Alan Collins (La Due), Alex Vitale (Jakoda)

Mike Ransome (Reb Brown) is part of the Strike Commando squad. They are wiped out except for Mike. He winds up in a Vietnamese village full of people who need to be rescued. Double-crossing American commanders get in his way. A huge Russian named Jacoda leads a group of Commies and Vietcong out in the jungle. They're kidnapping America soldiers and spreading propaganda.

Brown shoots the hell out of anyone who gets in his way. If he can't shoot them, he yells at them. Loud. "Jacoda!" and "Radak!" are two names that get yelled a lot. He starts off calmly leading the group of Vietnamese to safety. Then he begins having to kill again and again. He leaps from places. He was probably trained by John Rambo. And the world is the better for it.

Ransome goes through an intense torture session. Then, when you think he's down and out, he beats the crap out of everybody, with yells and then bullets. This is the best kind of hero because he's doing it for us. The

Vietcong line up in a row of five. It's very easy to shoot them all down. When he has a rocket launcher or some grenades, exploding bodies are everywhere. The cheering you hear is from the assembled forces of the free world.

Strike Commando is an exploding hoot. It is non-stop action, sometimes bordering on cartoon, extravaganza, held up on the strong shoulders of Reb Brown. He can be tender when he needs to be. A sequence when he talks with a young Vietnamese boy about Disneyland is the Other Side of Ransome. When

STRIKE COMMANDO

A ONE MAN WAR MACHINE!

STARRING REB BROWN • CHRISTOPHER CONNELLY
LOCS KAMME • ALAN COLLINS
DIRECTED BY VINCENT DAWN

NOT SUITABLE FOR AUDIENCES UNDER 17 YEARS OF AGE

A.V.I.D.
Home Entertainment

he finds the villagers slaughtered, he cries. Each tear that hits the ground will equal 100 bullets that will soon find their way into the Commie camp nearby.

Survivor

> *Director:* Michael Shackelton
> *Screenplay:* Bima Stragg, Martin Wragge
> *Producer:* Martin Wragge
> *Cast:* Chip Mayer (Survivor), Richard Moll (Kragg), Sue Kiel (The Woman)

Some action films hold off on the action and get more philosophical then one would expect. Maybe more philosophical than they should. *Survivor* is one of those.

Survivor is a guy who was in space when the apocalypse hit. He now spends his days wandering the Earth, looking for people. Whenever he does they want to fight. Eventually he meets the Woman, who has her own boat. A group of bad guys want to rewrite evolution and do all sorts of crazy things with the help of Survivor, who has not been damaged in any way because he was above the world. The main bad guy is Kragg, played by Richard Moll. There is a lot of internal dialogue in the film, most of it from Survivor, some from the Woman.

There is some great stuff in a large factory, which was clearly influenced by the Thunder Dome in *Mad Max Beyond Thunderdome*. People hang from chains and swing out across the factory floor, several stories below them. Survivor gets in a big tussle with a bunch of guys on the chains. It's not as exciting as the Thunderdome scenes but it's high off the floor so that adds an element of tension. Then there's a big drag-out fight between Survivor and Kragg in the end, as there should be. But more of the film is spent with philosophy than action.

Which brings up the question: Is this an action film? How many action sequences does a film need to have, to qualify as an action film? *Survivor* seems like it wants to be an action film, and then it wants to be more than an action film. If you can get into the wandering and talking, then the action is a fun surprise. If the wandering and talking puts you to sleep, then maybe *Survivor* is not for you. I enjoyed it more than I thought I would. I'd be interested in watching it again now that all pre-conceived notions have gone out the window.

They Still Call Me Bruce

Directors, Producers: James Orr, Johnny Yune

Screenplay: Paul Ross, Johnny Yune, James Orr

Cast: Johnny Yune (Bruce), Bethany Wright (Polly), David Mendenhal (Billy White), Pat Paulson (Psychiatrist), Joey Travolta (Ronnie)

In this sequel to 1982's *They Call Me Bruce*, Bruce is in Houston looking for Ernie Jones, a man who saved his life in Korea. Bruce says the reason he came to America was to give Jones a gift. Bruce gets involved with gangsters and fixed fights and martial arts schools and an orphan boy and a lovely blond. Where did the dirtiness from the first film go? And is this Bruce the same Bruce from the first movie?

They Call Me Bruce was an almost parodic road trip with lots of kung fu talk, silly fights, dirty jokes and brief nudity. *They Still Call Me Bruce* has a few dirty jokes. But when Billy White shows up and reveals that he's an orphan, the viewer waits for the joke. But there's no joke here. There really is an orphan boy who needs a home, and he does get beat up by gangsters, and he does break out of his hospital room to inspire Bruce at the concluding fight.

Where did the parody go? The first film got trimmed for a DVD release so it would get a PG. This film feels very different, from the orphan plotline to the beautiful woman actually in love with Bruce to the music, which is full-on mid–1980s Inspire Rock. There is goofing around in the film but it feels so different. The first film was kind of cheap and rough but fun; this film is a noble attempt but ends up being kind of blah.

The first film is based on Bruce being the one Asian who can't do kung fu. But in the sequel, during the final fight, he becomes a kung fu master. How did that happen? It means that the ending makes zero sense. Sorry, Bruce. Or the guy they call Bruce.

Thunder Warrior 2 aka Thunder 2

Director, Producer: Fabrizio De Angelis
Screenplay: Fabrizio De Angels, Dardano Sacchetti
Cast: Mark Gregory (Thunder), Raymond Harmstorf (Rusty), Karen Reel (Sheila), Bo Svenson (Sherriff), William Rice (Thomas)

The second installment in the *Thunder*

Warrior trilogy is more or less like the first one. Treated unpleasantly by people, Thunder goes on a rampage while invoking his Native American heritage. Unlike the first movie, this one doesn't have any characterization; things just sort of happen because they happen. Whatever needs to occur to move us towards the big rampage, happens. (There isn't anything as cool here as the bulldozer craziness in the first one.)

When I noticed something in the credits, it all becomes clear: Dardano Sacchetti. Sacchetti co-wrote the *Thunder Warrior* films. Around my house, that name comes up in reference to the horror films *The Gates of Hell* and *Demons*. Sacchetti's work has a surreal element to it. These Thunder movies are what you get when that type of storytelling is brought to an action film series. And it's insane. I believes that it's Dardano style of story that makes these films so odd.

Another source of confusion: Thunder is now a police officer. Yes, the man who led the police force on a merry chase in the Arizona desert in the first movie is now a police officer—in fact, he's on the force that just chased him. And the main jackass in that force, Rusty (the man who got the arrows in his arms), is still there. Rusty frames Thunder and he's sent to an awful prison. Then he breaks out and now there's no stopping him. In a helicopter, Rusty attacks Thunder and his group, which leads to the best scene. Thunder wraps a cable around the helicopter landing skids and is taken for a flight through the canyons of Arizona. It's beautiful, breathtaking and pretty exciting.

The first *Thunder* film was an entertaining *First Blood* variation with Native Americans. This film is more of the same, except for that element about Thunder being a cop. It's never explained why he's a cop now. He just is one. Mark Gregory finally debuts another expression: He smiles when he's with his wife and looking over their new house. I was surprised. He looks a bit uncomfortable smiling but it is definitely smiling.

The Time Guardian

Director: Brian Hannant
Screenplay: Brian Hannant, John Baxter
Producers: Robert Lagettie, Norman Wilkinson, Harley Manners
Cast: Tom Burlinson (Ballard), Nikki Coghill (Annie), Dean Stockwell (Boss), Carrie Fisher (Petra), Pete Merrill (Zuryk)

In 4039, a race of cyborgs called the Jen-Diki are swarming the Earth, intent upon killing all humanity. There seems to be no way for the dwindling numbers of humans to survive this relentless onslaught, until humanity discovers time travel. They send a man named Ballard and a woman named Petra back to the

1980s. Their mission: to find a safe place for the remaining humans to relocate. They end up in the Australian Outback. Unfortunately, some of the Jen-Diki have followed them with murder on their minds. You can bet your life that when one of the cyborgs refers to Ballard as "The time agent who has run out of time" … all hell is going to break loose. Ballard and Petra, along with a lovely lady named Annie, now have to save 1980s humanity from the Jen-Diki in order to allow the last of humanity from 4039 to come back and settle peacefully.

The Time Guardian has good action, good acting, good music and, near the end,

an awesomely huge gun being wielded by our hero, Ballard.

Urban Warriors

Director: Giuseppe Vari (as Joseph Warren)
Screenplay: Piero Regnoli
Producer: Pino Buricchi
Cast: Karl Landgren (Brad), Alex Vitale, Bjorn Hammer (Marty), Maurice Poli, Rosenda Schaschmidt (Julia), Malisa Lang (Angela), Tiziana Altieri

Brad, Marty and another guy are in an underground bunker doing something or other when the apocalypse hits. They wander up to the surface and find that an entire post-apocalyptic system is in place, involving lots of crazy people, called Headhunters, who must ingest the "spinal marrow" of others. Marty and the other guy get killed. Brad fools around with some ladies. There are chases and a few fights. The whole time, the viewer can't help thinking "How did this world spring up so fast?" On the other hand, one might also think, "Aren't those flashbacks scenes from *The Final Executioner*?" Yes, they are scenes from *The Final Executioner*. A character named Angela tells Brad her pre-apocalypse story and she's not in it. Aristocratic jerks shoot at a hill full of people trying to get away. It's chilling and goofy all at once.

As for the question of how the Head-hunters took over in such a short period of time, the answer may have to do with screen-writer Piero Regnoli's style. Back in the 1950s, he scripted *I Vampiri* and around 1980, he wrote *The Nights of Terror aka Burial Ground*. The latter is an extremely entertaining, gory, bordering-on-silly zombie film. Part of the joy of this movie is the lack of story logic and human-style charac-terization. In *Urban Warriors*, Reg-noli takes that same logic-challenged approach to the post-apocalyptic genre.

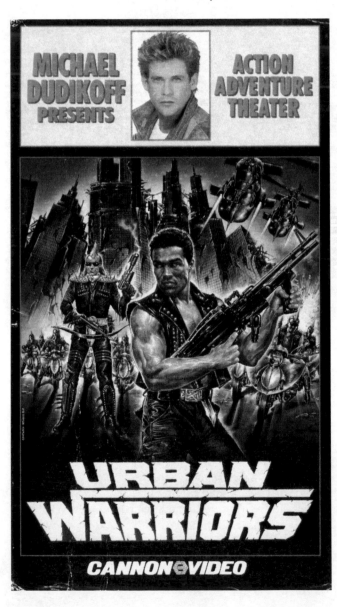

Not a lot of questions get an-swered in *Urban Warriors* but there is some action (much of it from an-other movie), a couple hunky guys and good-looking gals and quite a bit of silliness. I kind of hope the post-apocalyptic Earth is like this, apart from the "spinal marrow" thing.

La Venganza de los Punks aka *Intrepidos Punks 2*

Director: Damian Acosta
Producer: Ulises P. Aguirre
Cast: El Fantasma (Tarzan), Olga Rios, Bruno Rey, Luz Maitito Guillen, Anais de Melo

The Intrepidos Punks are back! Tarzan is still in charge, although he's lost the lovely mask he used to wear. Now he wears a large wizard's hat that covers his face. He's still tough as hell. The punks are still crazy. They have an orgy. They worship Satan and they continue causing problems.

La Venganza de los Punks picks up some time after the first film. Thunder and another woman free Tarzan from prison. They take shel-ter in a bombed-out old building in the countryside. They vow revenge on Marco, the cop who led the squad that arrested them in the first movie. They invade Marco's home during his daughter's Quinceañera party. Sexual assault and murder ensue, as one imagined they would. The Intrepidos Punks have not mellowed with age. And Marco has gone rogue in a strange, unpleasant way.

This sequel begins a lot like the first film with the punks causing all sorts of trouble. It's a little less fun than in the first one. No one dresses up as a nun, for example. But one can imagine that they've got vengeance on their minds. By the second half, Marco has taken up a new position: exterminator of the Intrepidos Punks, and he's not family-friendly.

Marco begins to off the punks one by one: snakes, spiders, acid, spike in the head and so forth. Thunder is kidnapped and tied to a bed where she is whipped a lot. Things start going very badly for Tarzan and his group. In fact, after a time, the viewer almost begins to feel kind of bad for the bikers. Marco really is going over the top, especially when he starts torturing via flame thrower. Don't get me wrong, the punks are still jerks. It's just strange to see the movie shift as it does.

A lot of the punks declare their allegiance to all things good as they are being tortured or about to die. Only a few of the gang, including Tarzan, stay true to themselves. Many declare that they never wanted anything bad to happen but that's a little tough to take seriously. Marco is now a manically laughing crazy man who is out to destroy the entire gang.

La Venganza de los Punks is as entertaining as the first film, just in a different way, which is good. It keeps the over-the-top craziness of its predecessor but adds odd scenes with Marco torturing or killing the bikers. This unexpected turn of events and makes the film more gripping as it goes along. The bikers really do seem to just want to have fun and don't seem to have realized what they were doing. But, then the ending comes and it's up to the viewer to decide whether to throw something at the screen or not.

1988

Highest grossing films in the U.S.
1. *Rain Man*
2. *Who Framed Roger Rabbit*
3. *Coming to America*
4. *Big*
5. *Twins*

Highest rated TV shows in the U.S.
1. *The Cosby Show*
2. *Rosanne*
3. *A Different World*
4. *Cheers*
5. *The Golden Girls*

Big historical events
Pan Am Flight 103 bombed over Lockerbie
Goodbye Reagan, hello Bush

Action movies
Die Hard, Rambo III, Action Jackson, Above the Law, Bloodsport, Iron Eagle 2, Mission in Action II, The Hero and the Terror

Alien Private Eye

Director, Screenplay, Producer: Viktor
Cast: Nikki Fastinetti (Lemro), Cliff Aduddell (Kilgore), John Alexander (Scama), Robert Axelrod (Scunge), Judith Burke (Suzy)

Soma, an addictive alien drug, is being used by Kilgore, a very bad man with a little skull jewel thing on one of his front teeth. There is a lovely young woman, Suzy, whose brother is forced into addiction. Suzy has half of some sort of alien artifact that Kilgore wants. Lemro is the good guy. He's an alien with big hair that covers his pointy ears. He wears cool hats and cool clothes and dances like Michael Jackson. He's also trained in the art of Alien Ass Kick.

Alien Private Eye is one of Raedon Home Video's more professional-looking releases. It was shot on film. Everything can be seen and heard. It stars actors who are generally okay, or at least doing their best. Nikki Fastinetti was the star of the amateurish movie *Games of Survival*. However, *Games of Survival* is much shorter and much more fun. *Alien Private Eye* is sort of like *Alien Nation*. The big distinguishing alien factor here is that they have pointy Spock ears. One of them constantly does a bad Peter Lorre impersonation.

Things to remember: Kilgore is a rough guy. Too many doses of Soma will kill. Lemro is mainly interested in saving Suzy from Kilgore's clutches. There are shootouts, kung fu fights in discos, car chases and, in the end, laser fights. The film keeps thing moving at a fairly decent pace. It's just that the film could have dumped a few of the exposition scenes, or at least sped them up a bit.

The scenes with Kilgore always feel like they're getting close to something huge. But whenever they cut to Lemro in his private detective office or that freaking Peter Lorre imitator, things slow right down. The plot is straightforward. However, it's as if the explanation gets lost in some sort of metaphorical plot molasses. The movie feels like it should be much faster and leaner. The action scenes certainly cruise along but the rest of *Alien Private Eye* is almost daring the viewer to focus. Yes, Lemro is fun when he dances like Michael Jackson, but you can't build an entire action movie around that.

American Force 2: The Untouchable Glory

Director: Philip Ko
Screenplay: Benny Ho
Producer: Joseph Lai
Cast: Pierre Kirby (Brian O'Reily), Patrick Frzebar (Gen.

Karpov), Rafael Martinee, Timothy McDonell, Renato Sala, John Whitney

When you find out that a bunch of Commies, led by the oddly voiced General Karpov, wants to build a missile base in the middle of your Indonesian village, what do you do? Start a commando force called the Untouchables to slow down the base construction. Then call in Brian O'Reily … part of the American Force! Although he sounds Australian. O'Reily brings with him a group of awesome guys with names like Samson and the White Tiger. They will defeat Karpov and associated Communist plans for a rebel base.

The Joseph Lai–produced series of random cut-and-paste action films continues. *The*

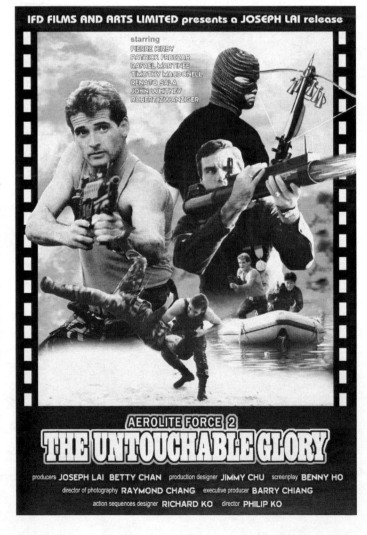

IFD FILMS AND ARTS LIMITED presents a JOSEPH LAI release

starring
PIERRE KIRBY
PATRICK FRBEZAR
RAFAEL MARTINEE
TIMOTHY MACDONELL
RENATO SALA
JOHN WHITNEY
ROBERT ZWANZIGER

AEROLITE FORCE 2
THE UNTOUCHABLE GLORY

producers JOSEPH LAI BETTY CHAN   production designer JIMMY CHU   screenplay BENNY HO
director of photography RAYMOND CHANG   executive producer BARRY CHIANG
action sequences designer RICHARD KO   director PHILIP KO

Untouchable Glory has more mismatched footage than any of its predecessors. Brian O'Reily isn't anywhere near the proceedings with the villagers. Unfortunately for this film, whatever that Hong Kong–Indonesian film is that features the villagers, it's kind of Dullsville. One wants Brian O'Reily and the quite amusing Gen. Karpov to take over that movie.

If the filmmakers had any sort of integrity, they would have given us more of these great silly characters. When O'Reily shows up, he automatically gets in a fight with a guy. He ends up kicking the guy so hard that the guy flies over the edge of a hill, to which O'Reily says "What a useless guy." O'Reily truly is a match for Karpov.

As mentioned, the footage from the cut-in film isn't much. It's a ragtag batch of fighters shooting at superior forces. It's the plotline around all of that acquired footage that brings it to life. Possibly there is just enough O'Reily and Karpov to lift it out of the rut. As always, the folks at Lai's production company do beautiful work with dubbing. No one says sillier stuff than the people in these movies.

Although the films themselves are, technically, rather awful cut-rate adventures that rip off audiences, the sheer audacity alongside the actual work that went into the making of this piecemeal stuff, means something. Someone with a sense of humor must have been involved. The dialogue is so silly for such an extended period of time. That's not done by someone who doesn't know what he's up to.

American Force 2: The Untouchable Glory is one heck of a title for any movie. The fact that very little of that title actually has anything to do with the movie is what makes it all awesome.

Battle for the Treasure

Director: Burt Peterson
Screenplay: Derek Law
Producer: Tomas Tang
Cast: Bert Brooks, Pat Carver, Randy Donner, Stephene Mitchell, Ted Evans, Tom Richards.

Battle for the Treasure takes the cake for being a completely generic Tomas Tang–Fil-mark production that keeps doing really odd things. It is cut-and-paste like almost all of the films from this realm. It starts off with white guy Marine mercenaries in Vietnam, more specifically Kampuchea, where there is a civil war going on. A gemstone goes missing. A princess is kidnapped. A gang of mercenaries are sent to rescue and reclaim the stone. There is a lot of talk about the Vietcong. As the Vietcong were the names given to South Vietnamese people who fought for the North Vietnamese, that's a distracting thing to call these people as Kampuchea is supposed to be involved in a civil war. But, really, all of these films are confusing anyways so why let something like that get in the way?

To get involved, focus on who the "good guys" are and who are the bad. There is a good guy named Fatty. He's fun. There is another one with a really goofy dubbed voice. (This film has quite a few of the goofiest dubbed voices around.) A kick-ass gal, a member of the Red Cross, kills it on more than one occasion. There's the evil general. He has a ton of troops and they never stop shooting. Then, there's that shiny gemstone. It's featured in the opening segment with the white guys. It spins through the air and glows with an optical effect. It is referred to throughout the movie but, honestly, it looks like a tacked-on section to a Vietnam War–related movie.

There are some excellent shootouts in the film. There is an absolutely fantastic shot where three of our heroes back into a brawl with the bad guys in a small room. The shot is in slo-mo. It's very nicely done. The Red Cross gal kicks a guy so hard that he flies out through a window. During the final fight scene, one of our heroes straps on a jet pack *a la* the one James Bond wears at the beginning of *Thunderball* and begins flying around.

Battle for the Treasure has good fighting throughout. When that damn jet pack guy takes off, it's hilarious. In fact, the jet pack saves the day in the end.

Battle Rats

Director: Briggs Benjamin, Sr.
Producer: Ben Yalung

Cast: Bruce Burns (Jack Gilbert), Corwyn Sperry (Paul), Mylene Nocum, Parul John, Louie Katana

Battle Rats is one of those rare Namsploitation films that stays in Vietnam during the actual war. A squadron of men are sent into the Vietcong underground tunnels to flush out a bad man and his squadron. There seems to be a neverending supply of Vietnamese in this film. American soldiers fall in love with Vietnamese girls. Get shot, shoot back. The captain has his eyes gouged out and lives. And *Battle Rats* makes the Tunnel Vietcong scary. They're constantly dropping from the ceiling or popping out of water. The main bad guy seems nigh on indestructible. It makes the whole Vietnam War thing seem even more futile than it actually was.

There are quite a few fantastic underground action sequences. There is a suspenseful opening sequence with a child and a hand grenade. And the climactic action is excellent. But this is a military film with quite a few tactical meetings and quite a few scenes of soldiers talking with one another. These scenes go on for some time. And quite a few of the soldiers have very silly voices.

The scenes with one of the soldiers falling in love with an enemy gal are nicely done. Granted, they may go on a little too long. But bigger budgeted films of this nature tended to have romantic interludes so *Battle Rats* can't be blamed for continuing that tradition. In fact, the romance pays off in the end because the viewer doesn't want to see the gal side with the nasty man in the underground caves.

When the Vietcong leader jabs out the eyes of the captain, it's pretty gross. After the eyes are out, the scene cuts away. Well, imagine the viewer's surprise when, much later in the film, the main guy and his gal friend find the captain, still alive, chained to a wall, with his eyes hanging out. The captain yells for the private to kill him as his eyes dangle out of their sockets. Can he still see? He's acting like he's blind. One can understand that they were trying to show off the terror of torture but this almost seems a little silly. *Battle*

Rats adds that to its catalogue of intriguing or interesting incidents. It's worth watching.

Commander

Director: Paul D. Robinson
Screenplay: Paul D. Robinson, Larry D. Jonathan
Producer: Regal Films
Cast: Craig Alan (Commander), David Light, Max Laurel, Larry Brand, Tania Gomez, Mike Monty, Ken Watanabe

Commander begins with a Rambo-esque guy named Commander and two buddies freeing a bunch of Asian prisoners from some Asian jerks in the middle of a jungle. There's a slight feeling of disorientation because the movie doesn't explain what's happening. For all we know, the prisoners could be terrible people and Commander is making a mistake. One hopes that is not the case, although a twist like that would be something. While you wait to learn what's up, enjoy the awesome synth score.

The Cambodians and the Soviets are hanging out together. They are getting laid waste by Commander and his group of commandos. The movie begins quickly with the bad guys almost immediately finding Commander's base, a village where his pregnant wife and her family live. Chaos reigns supreme! Commander goes to his military bosses and says, "One more mission." He and his guys are sent to steal some Soviet electronic equipment. Things don't go as well as Commander might have hoped.

Commander has been in the jungles fighting the Vietcong so long that he's sick of it, and he looks like he's sick of it. Craig Alan plays Commander with a sort of vagueness on his face that says, "I'm a battle-weary veteran but I'm also semi-constipated." His hair is a little too bouffant for the look they're trying to achieve. He doesn't look Rambu-goofy. But he doesn't look completely convincing until after the bad guys have killed his wife and start to torture him.

At that point, he had me convinced. He gets very angry when the Soviet-Cambodian baddies kill his wife, the best moment being when the Soviet leader says that he wants Commander alive. So Commander beats up about 15 guys before falling. Then they torture him by wrapping a plastic bag around his head and filling it with water. It doesn't look pleasant.

Commander plays by the Action Movie Manual. One last mission. There are going to be problems. Eventually, the hero will take revenge on the crazy jerks who ruined his life. The action scenes are fine. The film is 110 minutes long, one of the longest films in this book, 15 minutes longer than *Rambo: First Blood Part 2*. Is that a problem? Not really. As it goes along, Commander becomes more likable. There is a scene where he is on the shore of a river where all the bodies of people that the bad guys killed wash up. He finds his wife. He builds her a funeral pyre. That is intercut with him preparing for the final battle ... and it feels like it's going to be good. And it is. Don't hurt yourself rushing to see *Commander* but, if you get a chance, give it a watch.

Cop Game

> *Director:* Bruno Mattei
> *Screenplay:* Rossella Drudi
> *Producer:* Franco Gaudenzi
> *Cast:* Brent Huff (Morgan), Max Laurel (Hawk), Romano Puppo (Skipper), Candice Daly (Annie), Werner Pochath (Kasler)

A bunch of jerks in full military fatigues shoot the hell out of two American soldiers fighting in Vietnam. The movie is set at the end of the war but the viewer may have a tough time remembering when it's supposed to be. Most of the folks look like they're hanging out in Vietnam in the late 1980s. There are several scenes in a club where women dance to 1980s synths. But forget all that.

The Army has called in Morgan and Skipper to find the culprits. Morgan and Skipper swear a lot.

They are also kind of mean, prone to breaking people's fingers and punching. In the end, it does get the job done. This is the point in the Vietnam War where the U.S. guys know they've lost and they're trying to engage in some sort of dignified retreat. In fact, there is one soldier in particular who they pin their heroic hopes on. It turns out he's the link to the reason for the killing. It gets complicated and a little nasty. But our cops ferret everything out, with the help of a lovely lady informant.

Director Bruno Mattei does it again. He makes a semi-incoherent, completely odd film

that has characters acting weird and situations that seem like they're either borrowed wholesale from other films or should be. A favorite moment is an MP getting yelled at by a Vietnamese cop. The MP says, "This war sucks more and more every day." Here, here, soldier. In Mattei's previous films, Vietnam was a heroic loss that American soldiers always got involved in to save innocents. (*Strike Commando* is the grandest example.) But, here Mattei seems to be channeling films like *Full Metal Jacket*, *Gardens of Stone* and *Casualties of War*.

He's not actually ripping those off. Just the attitude. There's nothing heroic or good about this war. It was a waste of time. The Americans might have been dumb for getting involved. However, in true Italian fashion, it seems like all this is being used as window dressing to drum up emotions. When, really, this is all about the shooting.

Brent Huff acts a lot rougher here than he did in *Strike Commando 2*. He's prone to more Reb Brown–style yells and being a badass. But that's the sort of film this is.

Dead End City

Director, Producer: Peter Yuval

Screenplay: Peter Yuval, Michael Bogert

Cast: Dennis Cole (Chief Felker), Greg Cummins (Jack Murphy), Christine Lunde (Opal Brand), Robert Z'Dar (Maximum), Durrell Nelson (Brett), Aleana Downs (Nancy)

The cities of the U.S. are being rezoned. A gang called the Rats (led by Robert Z'Dar as Maximum) swarm in and kill everybody willy-nilly. Jack Murphy, plus a bunch of pals, stand up to the thugs. *Dead End City* is a movie about this group holed up in a warehouse trying to protect themselves from

gangs who are being employed by the local government. Being a hero can be a real bitch.

As this film starts off, the Rats, on cycles, roam the streets. A woman steps out of a doorway asking for a light. They shoot her dead. It escalates from there. Even though a lot of people are killed, the film has a wicked streak of humor running through it. It doesn't take itself completely seriously. From shootouts where the people are firing automatic weapons at each other from about 15 feet away to one guy getting beat up with his face on a photocopier, to the fact that Maximum never seems to be taking anything too seriously, it's a fun film. And that's surprising as most AIP attempts at comedy don't work out so well.

If you like action, there's a lot of it. Many shootouts litter the film. There's also some swell fistfights mixed in. The action is never through-the-roof-exciting but it is good and

it is loud, which sometimes is really what you want. The fact that the film shifts from the Rats shooting random people to the warehouse siege keeps it tense throughout. The pace never wavers, even when it's spending quite a bit of time explaining what's going on.

There are no bad performances here. Well, maybe Christine Lunde isn't the best. Her character Opal Brand is a local TV reporter who appears at the warehouse. At first, she's extremely unpleasant, taking advantage of the situation for her own gain. But then becomes part of the team. Lunde, a very lovely gal, has a bit of a dazed look in her eyes; she acts her heart out but her eyes are up to something different. Most of her scenes are with Murphy and he does good work. And I think Robert Z'Dar gives one of his best performances.

Dead End City sneaks up on you. At first it seems like a fairly standard AIP film but it's a little bit more exciting, a little bit more self-aware and a lot less clunky than many of the roster. It moves at a good clip and it presents a world that seems like it might not be too implausible even if it has Robert Z'Dar in it, leading a gang of goofs called the Rats.

Death Run

Director, Screenplay, Producer: Michael J. Murphy

Cast: Rob Bartlett (Paul), Debbi Stevens (Barbara), Wendy Parsons (Jenny), Eddie Kirby (Hero), Patrick Oliver (Messiah), Kay Lowery (Eileen Saunders), Steven Longhurst (Spike)

Death Run is very post-apocalyptic. It's also very British. It takes place 25 years after the Nuclear War. A scientist has put her son and his girlfriend in suspended animation. They awaken in time to find mutants, cannibals and a group of people worshipping a jerk named the Messiah. After numerous encounters (deadly or otherwise), the young man is put through the Death Run. This is probably the biggest film, and yet still rather charmingly small, from Michael J. Murphy, a wonderful, weird, idiosyncratic British director making cheap films across the British countryside throughout the 1980s and beyond.

Murphy made several horror films in the 1980s, including the short films *Invitation to Hell* and *The Last Night*. They're great little films with a wicked streak in them. *The Last Night* is interesting because it was shot at a speed that was too fast so the whole film runs a little slow but it's dubbed at normal speed. He also made the chamber drama *The Hereafter* and the odd horror show *Bloodstream*. *Death Run* has a bigger cast, more action and movement. It has songs, by a band. It feels bigger. But, again, not too big.

Revived after suspended animation, the couple learns what happened and where they are. Then a gang of the Messiah's jerks chase them around and catch them. The Messiah mistreats large groups of people, especially women. The young man, his girlfriend and two others from that time, try to bring him down. Along the way the girlfriend gets eaten by cannibals and a lot of people are killed. And then there's the Death Run.

I was impressed by the idea behind the Death Run: Paul is handcuffed to a cable that has been stretched along a field and through the woods. Traps have been set along the run. Lots of jerks with spears and knives are there too. Paul has to run from one end to the other. The idea is great and so simple. The scene where Paul runs is exciting. Plus, it's near the end of the film so several other tensions are mounting as we go along.

The tech credits of the film are semi-shaky, like on the other Murphy films. The sound can be a little off. Occasionally the image goes out of focus. Paul and Jenny are walking through woods and then another image begins to appear way too early (Paul and Jenny on a bridge). And some of the action is awkwardly shot. But, all in all, Murphy does a good job in *Death Run*. It might go on a little too long, and at 69 minutes, that's saying something. However, it's worth a viewing to see some folks on the very low-budget end of filmmaking make an entertaining trip through the post-apocalyptic world.

Deathstalker III: The Warriors from Hell

Director: Alfonso Corona
Screenplay: Howard R. Cohen
Producer: Robert North
Cast: John Allen Nelson (Deathstalker), Carla Herd (Carissa/Elizena), Thom Christopher (Troxartas), Terri Treas (Camisarde), Aaron Hernan (Nicias)

Deathstalker has returned! And he's involved in more non-specific fantasy-related shenanigans. This sequel is not as exciting as the first film nor as funny as the second. It's definitely a movie. A fantasy one at that. There's not much more to be said for it. The sword-and-sorcery–fantasy genre seems to have run out of steam right within this film. Everyone tries and a world is sort of semi-created but it comes out kind of disappointing.

There are two stones. They must be united in order to reveal the majesty of the lost city Arandor. The evil Troxartas, with an army of dead warriors, wants the stones. There's a princess, with a twin sister, who may or may not have the second stone. Deathstalker hangs out with a wizard named Nicias, being heroic and somewhat snide. He's not such a charmer in this one as he was in the second. He seems to be channeling sort of a Steve Guttenberg type of thing. One must decide on their own whether this makes for a good sword-and-sorcery hero.

The film almost has that "we shot it on video and transferred it to film" look but it is film. It's just missing any grit and all the wit. In fact, it reminds me of the 1983 TV show

Wizards and Warriors with Jeff Conaway and Julia Duffy. Except the TV show is far more charming and has some actual laughs in it. *Deathstalker III* seems like an episode of that show if it had gone completely off the rails. Maybe writer Howard R. Cohen was completely out of ideas. It's too bad they tried to continue the concept that they had worn out.

It's not all bad. Some of the acting is over the top in a funny way. The strange mother-and-daughter team who live in a valley eating potatoes have their charms. And the concept of the dead army is a fun one. Troxartas

keeps their souls hidden away in jars. But, in general, the series has run out of steam. And yet, there was a *Deathstalker IV*.

Delta Force Commando

Director: Pierluigi Ciriaci

Screenplay: David Parker, Jr.

Cast: Brett Clark (Lt. Turner), Fred Williamson (Capt. Beck), Mark Gregory, Bo Svenson (Col. Keitel), Divana Maria Brandao (Maria)

Mark Gregory without his long beautiful locks is kind of frightening. After being used to him as Thunder or Trash or Adam in *Adam and Eve Versus the Cannibals*, to see him with short hair took me aback. It didn't look like him. He looked like a larger Antonio Sabato but without the ability to break into the big Doblone laugh. He's a very convincing villain in the rather silly *Delta Force Commando*

In Puerto Rico, terrorists break into a U.S. Army base and steal a nuclear bomb. They also kill Lt. Turner's pregnant wife. Now they've got Turner (Brett Clark) following them to the ends of the Earth. Or into the South American jungles. Turner commandeers Capt. Beck (Fred Williamson) and a lot of shooting and killing ensues. Eventually, Turner and Beck become buddies.

A strange miasma of a film, *Delta Force Commando* follows our heroes as they head out to get the nuke back and shoot the hell out of the terrorists. There is a lot of shooting and a lot of fighting. The director seems to love the concept of having a lot of action in a scene but the camera isn't always in the optimum position. Some movies, like many by David A. Prior, simply point the camera at people shooting or punching. That can be effective. It can also

be dull. Directors like Sam Firstenberg seem to always get the camera in the right spot.

There is a very funny scene where Williamson walks along an open stretch of field as people rush up to him with swords, shrieking. But Fred has a gun and just shoots them down. The look on his face as he does this is awesome. So casual and cool. The camera moves along, following him as he shoots. But sometimes the camera's too far away. And several of the sword guys are positioned so that they block or almost block Fred as he raises his gun to shoot them. That's not the way to do it. Much of the action in this film

has a "So the camera's pointing in the wrong direction— who cares?" attitude.

This feels inconsequential even by Italian rip-offs of things. But Williamson is great. Mark Gregory is scary. And Brett Clark is so wooden that he's almost funny. Actually, at times, he's really funny. Maybe watch it for those three elements.

Desert Warrior

> *Director:* Jim Goldman
> *Screenplay:* Bob Davies, Carl Kuntze
> *Producer:* Silver Star Film Company
> *Cast:* Lou Ferrigno (Zerak), Shari Shattuck (Racela), Kenneth Peer (Baktar), Mike Monty (Dr. Creo), Anthony East (Cortez)

THE GREATEST, THE MIGHTIEST WARRIOR IN THE ARENA BATTLES THE FORCES OF EVIL! LOU FERRIGNO as DESERT WARRIOR starring SHARI SHATTUCK TONY EAST · KENNETH PEER · MIKE MONTY CHRISTINE LANDSON · JAMES McKENZIE · JERRY BAYRON · MIKE COHEN in "DESERT WARRIOR" Screenplay by Carl Kuntze · Story by BOB DAVIES Director of Photography Fred Conrad · Directed by JIM GOLDMAN

Desert Warrior is as close to genius as a movie made by insane people could probably ever reach. Well, maybe the horror genre has a few close examples but none with Lou Ferrigno in his best role since *Sinbad of the Seven Seas*. And his best acting since he won the *Battle of the Network Stars* tug of war.

The combined forces of Lou, Jim Goldman and characters with names like Baktar prompt me to nominate *Desert Warrior* as the silliest film in this book. It's post-apocalyptic. It's got a bunch of underground dwellers led by a very amusing fat guy. It's got an evil scientist. It has the silliest music around, filled with lots of synth "doo doo doo"–type noises that seek to rouse the viewer into excitement but ends up making one feel as silly as the movie. It ends with a big shootout between white-clothed people and black-clothed people with Lou taking command. Silly and lovable, that's *Desert Warrior.*

The film has something to do with infertile people after the apocalypse. Lou is Zerak, the great hunter, sent out to find a fertile woman. That's Racela. She's a member of that underground race of goofballs. There's a bunch of fighting. Zerak betrays his gladiator pals. It's all worth the time. It's all good stuff.

The bad guys are out in the desert and some of them are in this strange city. Dr. Creo is a real creep. The bad guys end up tying beautiful blondes to giant X-shaped crosses on hills. Lou goes through it all with his shirt off, a big smile on his face and an eyepatch. He's dubbed well throughout the movie. Great action, silly bad guys, goofy names, the occasional boob and Lou with an eyepatch. Why is this movie not shown in every film class in the world?

It has a hilariously goofy plot that doesn't always make sense. It has fight scenes that range from good to jaw-droppingly silly (the escape from the underground city). It keeps moving along and, no matter how silly things get, there's always another silly thing right around the corner.

Empire of Ash aka Empire of Ash II

Directors: Michael Mazo, Lloyd A. Simandl

Screenplay: Saul Urboans, Michael Mazo

Producers: Lloyd A. Simandl, John A. Curtis

Cast: Melanie Kilgour (Danielle), Thom Schioler (Orion), Frank Wilson (Shepherd), James Stevens (Iodine), Sandy Mackenzie (Chuck)

The setting is post-apocalyptic. There are jerks driving around killing people. They have a man with them who is constantly spouting pseudo-religious jargon. People run from them. Two wacky guys talk a lot and get hung upside down. For a film titled *Empire of Ash,* it doesn't have a lot of ash in it. It has a lot of driving. It has a lot of shooting. There are some funny-looking guys wearing surgical masks. And that preacher guy talks for 1000 hours. Maybe this was originally a four-hour miniseries cut down or a serial abbreviated into feature form. It goes on and on, getting nowhere fast.

Empire of Ash is almost a dare. It dares the viewer to spend 90 minutes with it. Events occur but the energy is low. It was released as *Empire of Ash*, then appeared on video under the title *Empire of Ash II*. Yes, this movie and its "sequel" are the exact same movie. How many people, do you think, remembered it being the same movie? For every person that did, I bet someone else just thought "This is a lot like the first one." The audacity of this is astound-ing and far exceeds the imagination of the film itself.

The Firing Line

Director: Jun Gallardo
Screenplay: Jun Gallardo, Sonny Sanders
Producer: Silver Screen International
Cast: Reb Brown (Mark Hardin), Shannon Tweed (Sandra Spencer), Kahlena Marie (Laura Gomez), Melvin Davidson (Milton Green), Carl Terry (Julio Monteiro)

Mark Hardin, a U.S. Army officer in a South American country, gets mixed up with the local corrupt government. He joins a group of rebels who live in the jungle. He brings San-

dra Spencer, an innocent American, with him. Much shooting occurs. Mixed in are rebels distrusting each other and a white guy golfing.

The Firing Line has charming stars to recommend it. But it's tough to get worked up over it. One gets the feeling that the sequences where Mark has to bring Sandra along into the jungle are sort of an action movie type of meet-cute but it all feels a little stilted, possibly because they're preceded by a scene where Hardin is tortured. The scenes with them going deep into the jungle might be meant to have some sort of *Romancing the Stone*-type kick.

It's also one of those weird movies where, somewhere along the way, it just becomes a lot of shooting. The rebels argue a lot but it's not interesting. The last 15 minutes is just shooting, to the point that I completely forgot who was shooting who and why. I lost focus and suddenly ... they were in a cave! Where'd the cave come from? What's happening? Why are they blowing up a bridge? There comes a point where the mind shuts off. It happens, for example, in horror films. Specifically slasher films. There are a few, like *The Prowler* or *Friday the 13th: The Final Chapter* where the Final Girl spends so much time creeping around that everything becomes a haze. Time means nothing any more.

The Firing Line is for the undiscriminating action fan. Reb Brown is great in it, though.

Fists of Blood aka Strike of the Panther

> *Director:* Brian Trenchard-Smith
> *Screenplay:* Peter West
> *Producer:* Damien Parer
> *Cast:* Edward John Stazak (Jason Blade), John Stanton (William Anderson), Fiona

Gauntlett (Julia Sommers), Paris Jefferson (Gemma), Jim Richards (Jim Baxter)

Everyone is back for this hot sequel to *Day of the Panther*! I don't know how soon after the first film this was made but it feels like an immediate continuation. All the characters are back (except the dead ones) and the ante is upped a bit in the action and stunt department. Edward John Stazak is a better actor here.

The plot continues from the end, more or less, of the first one. In fact, this film begins with a lengthy recap of the first movie. While it's fun to see those scenes again, maybe it's too lengthy. The new story starts with Jason Blade being recruited to rescue an important man's daughter from a brothel. He does so, with punches and kicking. Then, Baxter, Blade's nemesis from the first movie, gets out of jail and kidnaps Blade's main squeeze Gemma. Agents are called in. There are chases. It all ends up inside a big factory, with Gemma tied up in her leotard and Blade fighting for his life.

Even more so than the first one, this film seems to be having a lot of goofy fun. There is another leotard dancing scene. It's as awesome as the first one. There's something about Gemma … once she gets in a leotard, she has to dance for Jason Blade. It simply happens. Gemma's dad is beaten up. Again Blade takes it personally. And the movie goes from there.

The action is as strong as before. A highlight is a crazy chase between Blade and one of Baxter's henchmen. It culminates with the two men scaling the side of an apartment building—pulling themselves up balcony by balcony until they get to the top. It is well shot and exciting. Great stunt work. The closing sequence is a big kick-ass fight in that factory with agents swarming in to help, especially Julia Sommers, a lady who is working closely with Blade. She is very Australian. She kicks a lot of ass, even after being wounded.

I wish there had been more films in this series because, although Stazak is not the best actor, he's great with action. The two films are so straightforward and no-nonsense that they are a delight. Double feature evenings ahoy!

Full Metal Ninja

Director: Godfrey Ho (as Charles Lee)

Producer: Joseph Lai

Screenplay: Benny Ho

Cast: Pierre Kirby (Leon), Jean Paul (Boris), Sean Odell, Renato Sala (Eagle), Sam Kind

Leon is a ninja. He's after Boris. Eagle is a warrior. He's after a warlord who killed his family. The warlord is doing bad stuff with Boris. No one is going to be happy until they end up killing someone else. Families get involved. Wives are kidnapped. And those damn ninjas go spinning through the air (in the woods) at all hours of the day and night. Welcome to another Ho-Lai hasty assemblage of an action film. This one featuring Pierre Kirby, who not only has a sword but packs an old pistol too.

Full Metal Ninja's base film is a period piece. It features Eagle and the Warlord. The

ninja stuff with Leon and Boris is, presumably, set in the same time period. But, there's something about all that purple and yellow in their ninja outfits, and their hairstyles, that says "This is 1988." Consequently, we end up with one of the most schizophrenic of the ninja numbers. The obvious clash between the period piece and the slightly slicker "ninja" stuff is something to behold, especially when Leon pulls out that awesome old pistol.

There are the usually synths, sometimes moody but much of the time hilariously inappropriate. In *Full Metal Ninja* (which, by the way, is one of their wackiest titles ever), the soundtrack is packed with Bach and Holst and other bits of classical music, all just as inappropriate as using the *Miami Vice* music and cues that sound like they come from *Star Wars*. But, possibly, a little more appropriate here because it is trying to match a different time period. The music is incredibly wrong for the Asian places it's in. I believe some Pink Floyd may have popped up on here too.

The end fight scene between Dragon and the warlord, taking place in the large central area of the warlord's pagoda, is a good one. It even has a moment of poignancy right at the end: As Dragon is set to kill the man who killed his family, the warlord's daughter runs out and asks for leniency. Dragon is conflicted. It's actually a moment of emotion in the land of these weird films. And it's completely taken from the base film. It's nothing to do with the ninja headband–wearing goofballs who can't stop flipping through the air in the woods.

Have the production companies actually done anything in these films that was ever kind of appropriate? Stolen footage, reused footage, stolen music, completely misleading titles, hilarious weird costume ideas ... they all conspire to make Ho-Lai ninja films some of the oddest cinema of the 1980s.

Games of Survival

    Director: Armand Gazarian

    Screenplay: Lindsay Norgard, Armand Gazarian

Producer: Lindsay Norgard

Cast: Nikki Hill (Zane), Cindy Coatman (Cindy), Roosevelt Miller, Jr. (Skull Blaster), Steve Dalton (Gothic)

On another world, in another galaxy, a strange dictator plays a game with some of his most hardened criminals: a fight to the death for a spiked orb. Whoever holds this orb, at a predetermined time, will be given their freedom. But, in this current game, there is a hero involved, a man named Zane. There is a familiar planet involved: Earth. The band of *Road Warrior*–esque fighters are sent to Los Angeles to find the orb. Will the City of Angels ever be the same? Or will no one really notice?

The correct answer is the latter. Los Angelinos are really blasé towards the contestants. But the viewer shouldn't be. This is a fast, fun, fight-filled film with the star of the offbeat *Alien Private Eye*. It is all post-dubbed, which ups the ante on the alien feel of the thing. The music is usually inappropriately distracting from the action.

The action is well done and there's plenty of it. One guy finds the orb. He fights another guy. That second guy gets the orb. A dwarf rolls out from under a pool table and hits the second guy over the head. The dwarf takes the orb and is thrown around by another guy. Etc., etc. Zane occasionally gets the orb but never possesses it for a long amount of time, just at the right times. This movie sets things up quickly on an alien planet with weird-looking people and vehicles, then jumps right into the excitement. Zane almost starts up a romance with a young woman named Cindy, who helps him out. It's implied that the romance will continue after the movie is over. Not much gets in the way of action. Cheap action, done well, is still great action.

Zane is told by a cop not to sleep on a park bench. Guys in alleys keep trying to sell things to the fighters. Cindy makes Zane a Celeste Pizza for One and he gobbles it up. Best of all, the orb has been hidden in the snack aisle of a Skid Row convenience store. This clash of the bizarre with the banal is fun to watch.

Games of Survival is a low-budget romp that has some pretention to social change (with Zane going into a tirade against the dictator) and even social mores (the assorted people who meet our fighters, including a character called "Gay Driver"). But it really is an entertaining action film that feels like it was made by energetic 11-year-olds with access to Dad's credit card—a card with a low limit on it.

Hell on the Battleground

Director, Screenplay: David A. Prior
Producer: Fritz Matthews
Cast: Ted Prior (Lance), Fritz Matthews (Casey), Chet Hood (Hayes), David Campbell (Kelly), Johnnie Johnson (Johnson), William Smith (Corp. Meredith)

In the Prior Brothers' war film *Hell on the Battleground*, William Smith, star of many a biker film and here playing Corporal Meredith, recites a poem. It is a voiceover as the viewer watches the soldiers getting ready to go on a mission to kill some Russians. The poem begins. The viewer watches the two main guys, Lance and Casey, with their big beautiful blond hair, climb into choppers and take off. The thought of a poem being recited in a David A. Prior film is akin to seeing a Three Stooges short where the boys don't hit anybody. One doesn't expect it. One is not sure what to do with it.

But somehow, the poem works. The first half-hour of the film has been shooting and soldiers talking. Then they fool around with their gals. But there is a melancholy to it all. This is not like *Deadly Prey* where the cry that goes out is "Hang on! This is going to be a hoot!" This film is filled with action, most of it up to the usual Prior levels, which means it kicks ass but it's nothing revelatory. As the soldiers leave for this rendezvous with the enemy, the poem adds a touch of class and a lot of sadness to the next hour of the film. Referring to Lance and Casey, the poem says that one will lie and the other will die, which adds gravitas to the proceedings. Normally, one wouldn't get something like this in an action film. Shit happens. People die. But, in a war film, saying that one of our leading men will die makes the viewer sit up a bit. And then Prior has fun with it, flirting with our expectations of who will die and who won't almost to the very end.

Much of *Hell on the Battleground* looks like standard macho guys arguing and then shooting. I never knew where or when it was set or why they were engaging in combat with Russians. But it didn't matter. This film works best with a generic template. It can build its world from there. These young men dying in dirt is no way to resolve a problem. All those futures cut off in a moment.

It didn't seem possible but, much like *War Bus*, *Hell on the Battleground* becomes a rather touching film about soldiers just trying to survive in a war they didn't begin but they are desperately trying to end. The acting is a bit overwrought but the concept is there. And the film transcends any feeling of giving us this message of how terrible war is while titillating us with action and violence. Yes, it's exciting. But it's neverending and it's not fun. Well done, Dave and Ted.

Jungle Assault

Director, Screenplay: David A. Prior

Producer: Fritz Matthews

Cast: William Smith (Gen. Mitchell), William Zipp (Kelly), Ted Prior (Becker), Maria Rosado (Rosa), David Marriott (McClosky)

Jungle Assault takes us into the heart of the South American jungles for kick-ass, roughshod action guaranteed to turn a boy into a man. Gen. Mitchell's daughter has gone there to join a rebel guerrilla group. Mitchell sends two of his best (retired) soldiers, Kelly and Becker, to bring her back. They go into hos-

tile territory to shoot some guerrilla rebels and bring back the clueless young lady.

Another AIP adventure. Another trip into the woods of Mobile, Alabama, which really don't look like the jungle at all, to fight bad guys. Screenwriter David A. Prior's dialogue seems to be the same from film to film, just shifted from character to character. William Zipp is fine, as always. Ted Prior kicks ass, as always. The bad guys are vicious. They kill everyone they can and, yes, there is a quota of sexual assaults scenes met. The final 20 minutes consist of running through the woods and a lot of shooting. Some of it is fun. But, as with most AIP Prior pictures, some of it is simply running around.

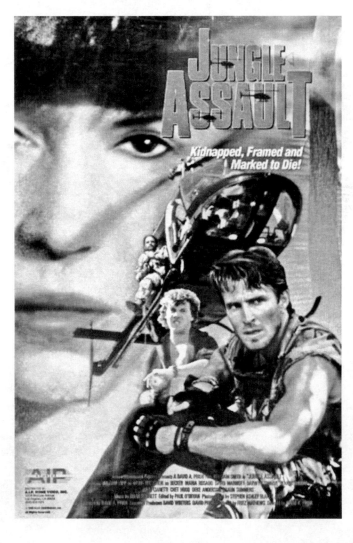

All of the AIP films that I've seen have action in them: shooting, fighting, explosions. But just having these things happen isn't really enough. There's no real excitement in much of the running around. Action is more than having violent things occur in front of the camera. The direction and the editing must be a part of it. The stunts mixed with the action and the technical aspects make for great action.

Jungle Assault definitely has the quantity. It's not so hot on the quality. There is a fight scene in a bar that illustrates this. While Kelly and Becker are in a bar, bikers show up with a woman they've kidnapped. They prepare to rape her. Kelly and Becker proceed to beat the crap out of the bikers. In Jackie Chan films, the camera can sit and watch as Jackie and the stuntmen spin and flip and kick. Here, not so much. When a crazy female biker jumps on Becker's back, the camera just looks at the scene. Apart from the head butt to the biker's face, it's a little dull. It's lacking in vitality.

Later in the scene, Becker fights in the foreground of a shot while Kelly is in the background. And Becker looks like he's fighting his heart out while Kelly seems to be goofing in the background. For one confusing moment, it looks like a free-for-all instead of two guys against a gang. That's the thing with action. Things need to make sense. This person needs to be punching this person. This movement needs to match with this other movement. In *Jungle Assault*, there are moments of confusion.

It can be fun to just point the camera and have people shoot and blow things up. But, after several movies, a certain

flair needs to be added. *Jungle Assault* is okay but it's missing that flair.

Kick Fighter aka *The Fighter*

Director, Producer: Anthony Maharaj
Screenplay: Noah Blough
Cast: Richard Norton (Ryan Travers), Erica Van Wagener (Katie), Angel Conifado (Quan), Benny Urquidez (Jet), Ramon D'Salva (Mr. Pina)

Benny the Jet fights in this film. In fact, he gets a special credit saying that he's an undefeated kickboxing champion and really very

cool. Well, he is very cool. But the other films he's in are more fun than *Kick Fighter*. In fact, the *Wheels on Meals* climactic fight he has with Jackie Chan is stellar. His *Force Five* appearance is more fun. Benny shows up at the end of *Kick Fighter* to get in a big-ass plastic hassle with the star of this movie, Richard Norton. And they have a good time. It's too bad the movie is a little too clichéd and a touch ponderous, even when it kicks ass.

We are in Bangkok and Manila throughout most of this film. Ryan Travers is a real rascal. He's a grownup Artful Dodger who will beat the snot out of anyone who gets in the way of his stealing from people out on the streets. He's arrested and put away for three years. Right when he gets out, a gangster blows up Ryan's parents' store (with parents inside), and Ryan's sister Katie becomes very ill. Ryan must street fight for money to help his sister and to find out who blew up his parents.

Kick Fighter has some great kick fighting (street and ring). There are some scenes of Richard Norton stunting around with cars. But there's also a whole lot of nothing-in-particular happening. Katie gets sick and she's in bed a lot. She goes out to party. Ryan brings her home. The gangsters arrange the big Travers-Benny fight. Then when the movie seems to be proceeding towards its climax, there is a training sequence.

I wonder what the first film with a training sequence might have been. From a long time ago, no doubt. But apart from a few training sequences (several of the *Rocky* films and *The Karate Kid*), most of them are kind of dull. Sometimes they're actively silly. (Hello, *Karate Warrior*.) In *Kick Fighter's* training sequence, Richard Norton has to pretend he doesn't know how to kick everyone's ass. It's not terribly convincing. And it slows down a film that could have used a trim of five or ten minutes.

Kick Fighter has very good fighting in it. Everyone is giving it their all. The final fight in the ring has a couple of brutal moments although the camera is sometimes a little too far away from everything, almost as if the filmmakers couldn't get proper access to their own fight. The movie itself is very clichéd. But, if the viewer is a fan of Norton and/or Benny the Jet, it's worth a viewing. Just don't expect anything as entertaining as, say, *Dragons Forever*.

Lady Terminator

> *Director:* H. Tjut Djalil
> *Screenplay:* Karr Kruinowz
> *Producer:* Ram Soraya
> *Cast:* Barbara Anna Constable (Tania), Christopher J. Hart (Max), Claudia Angelique Rademaker (Erica), Joseph P. McGlynn, Adam Stardust

Long ago, in Indonesia, the South Sea Witch inhabited the body of a young woman. The Witch became an eel. Then it journeyed into the woman's vagina. And the woman was able to castrate men from within herself, as it were. A guy pulls the eel out and a curse is placed on his family. In modern times, a female anthropologist is possessed by the eel and goes after the great-granddaughter of that guy. Mayhem ensues.

This is an action film? It sounds like a strange mystical fantasy or horror film. For the first 40 minutes of the film, up until the moment when the possessed woman (Erica) finds Tania. Then the film becomes *The Terminator*, including rip-off action scenes and lines ("Come with me if you want to live!"). There is a ton of shooting and car chases and an epic battle on a runway in the end. Yes, the "Lady Terminator" comes back from the dead, and she removes an eye in a scene that may not make much sense.

The film is crazy. Nudity, gory castrations, lots of shootouts and action and goofy dubbed dialogue. (My favorite characters are the mulleted cop and the two guys who stumble upon the nude anthropologist when she comes out of the water.) In true Indonesian fashion, the film has glimpses of what look like reality. Christopher J. Hart would be one of these things. But most of it is just weird and so skewed and so beautifully brilliant. One wants to say that this film is fun for the whole family, but it would have to be a grown-up family.

The most interesting aspect of this *Terminator* rip-off is that it crosses a genre. *The Terminator* is pure time travel sci-fi. In its transfer over to Indonesia, somehow it became a fantasy film that shouldn't have any elements of sci-fi in it. But it sticks so close to its source that it becomes a strange not sci-fi but "kinda sci-fi" film. The removal of the eye, for example, makes no sense in this film. Arnold Schwarzenegger was a cyborg. Eye replacements are standard. The archeologist is not. How is she removing an eye and putting in another one? Because, presumably, if someone removed the eel from her vagina, she'd go back to normal. Her invulnerability and ability to return from the dead could be a zombie side effect of being possessed by the South Sea Witch. But if it is, it's nothing anyone told viewers about.

Lady Terminator is an illogical action-filled hoot that will hold your attention from the moment the eel is pulled out of the woman's vagina until the terminator rises from the ashes of an explosion still ticking. Indonesian action films do it again.

Lethal Hunter

Director: Arizal
Screenplay: Deddy Armand
Producer: Gope T. Samtori
Cast: Chris Mitchum (Jake Carver), Mike Abbott (Frank Gordon), Peter O'Brian (Tom Selleck), Ida Iasha (Janet), Ray Marten (Roy), Bill "Superfoot" Wallace (Adam)

Missing microfilm might have been the best MacGuffin back in the day. It's something small enough to be easily filched. It's always loaded with all kinds of covert information. *Lethal Hunter* knows the power of microfilm. Secret agent Jake Carver and villain Frank Gordonare are both after this microfilm. There will be a lot of car chases, shootouts, kung fu fights and torture before things are resolved. A man with a falcon on his shoulder is called in to try and stop the power of Carver.

Arizal may be my new favorite action director. He is like Cirio H. Santiago but at Mega-Santiago levels. Things start crazy and

stay crazy. *Lethal Hunter* is in the same pocket as *The Stabilizer* and *Final Score* and even features Chris Mitchum and Peter O'Brian from those two films. And the mighty Mike Abbott, who spent half his time in Indonesia and the other half in Hong Kong with Godfrey Ho. Arizal and Deddy Armand made cool action films.

This one begins several stories up in a building. Then a Jeep bursts through the window. They are several stories up. Of course, chaos ensues. A guy begins shooting everything up to get to the microfilm but no dice. Then there is a great shootout on the side of a building. That involves Jack Carver falling through several stories of scaffolding. Then Chris Mitchum shows off his kung fu skills, which never quite look right, especially when he's surrounded by people who do have kung fu skills. During the final fight with Adam (Bill "Superfoot" Wallace), Mitchum's Jake Carver looks like a slightly touched kung fu fighter.

But it's all great stuff. There's something about these Indonesian action films. There's a kinetic energy to a film like this. The acting is always just to the left of being good. But everyone gives so much of themselves when the action kicks in. it's almost some sort of madness.

Notice how many buildings they seem to demolish or burn down, and all the public places that they litter with broken and burning cars. I picture Indonesia as littered with nothing but the remains of kick-ass action films. Somewhere, high on a hill, there is a bronze statue of Chris Mitchum. Everyone worships it. They have to. If they don't, Carver will kick their butts.

Maniac Cop

Director: Bill Lustig
Screenplay, Producer: Larry Cohen
Cast: Tom Atkins (Frank McCrae), Bruce Campbell (Jack Forrest), Laurene Landon (Theresa Mallory), Richard Roundtree (Commissioner Pike), William Smith (Capt. Ripley), Robert Z'Dar (Matt Cordell), Sheree North (Sally Noland)

A horror-action hybrid, *Maniac Cop* is about a crazy cop who was put away for something he didn't do. He gets mutilated in prison. He is declared dead. But he lives and he kills … everyone. People are afraid of cops. One scared woman shoots an innocent cop. Jack Forrest, an innocent man, is arrested for the killings. It sounds like more of a horror film than an action film. But not with Bill Lustig in charge. This movie is one of the best films in this book.

The closing chase sequence is almost on par with *The French Connection*. The final chase has stunts galore and moments that reminded me of one of my all-time favorite films, the original *Gone in 60 Seconds*. The ending takes a slasher film vibe and goes freaking crazy with the action and stunts. There can't be too many films that nail the vibe like this.

Bill Lustig made *Maniac*, one of the most reviled slasher films of the early 1980s. But it's a good movie in its own way. And Lustig just got better and better. And then we have Larry Cohen, who's a brilliant writer. His scripts always have something happening that surprises you and most of the time it's awesome.

The action is so good here. Add the slasher element and it's a movie you want to watch over and over. The initial killing is unexpected and not unexpected at the same time. And that's good filmmaking. *Maniac Cop* has a great cast. Robert Z'Dar is as strange and wonderful as ever. And *Maniac Cop 2* is actually much better than this film. And this film is good!

Mannigan's Force

Director: John R'yan Grace
Screenplay: Joseph Le Carre, James Gaines, John R'yan Grace
Executive Producers: Delza V. Lazatin, Rose Loanzon Flaminiano
Cast: George Nicholas (Mannigan), Eric Hahn (Roberto Arand), Mel Davidson (Tim Ross), Tsing Tong Tsai (Hang Sang Kook), Khorshied Machalle (Lucrecia)

In Central America, Mannigan leads a group of commandos engaging in all sorts of assaults. After he retires, he is asked to take on one more mission: to go back into Central America and rescue some Americans from an awful prison fortress. He accepts after being offered a million dollars. He reassembles his force and the mission begins. But all is not what it seems.

Mannigan's Force is a pretty entertaining action film from the Philippines. It's filled with shootouts and lots of violence, and the violence is not pretty here. Luckily, many viewers are after this in an action film and Mannigan and his boys deliver. Most of the actors are solid. The film is also paced quite nicely.

The only element that I found distracting was George Nicholas as Mannigan. He's not very good. He always feels like he's acting. The other actors work hard around him and do a fine job. Nicholas always seems like he just missed the final part of the acting class that showed him how to deliver a line. Of course, I buy him as Mannigan. Just not as an actor. For all I know, Mannigan acts just like this.

Mannigan's Force has great action and the ending has a twist that's pretty obvious. The film, luckily, keeps it moving. The opening, a 1984 attack on a military base, is filled with a lot of great killing, including a lot of women and children dying. Sometimes the movie seems to be making a point about something but I'm not sure what exactly. Is the filmmaker trying to show that violence is not for fun? Then why the heck did you make a film called *Mannigan's Force*? That sounds like high action-adventure to me. Of course, I never really felt too bad about the action. As long as Mannigan kept acting the way he acts, I was amused.

This is a solid action film. Mannigan and his boys are ready to kick ass in the name of saving lives. No arguments here.

The Master Demon

Director, Screenplay: Samuel Oldham
Producers: Eric Lee, Art Comacho
Cast: Eric Lee (Lee/The White Warrior), Gerald Okamura (Qua Chang/Master Demon), Kay Baxter Young (Medusa), Steve Nave

(Cameron Massey), Sid Campbell (Wayne Berserker)

The Master Demon is a phantasmagorical journey through low-budget martial arts, female bodybuilders, severed hands and ancient curses. It's really quite madcap and wonderful, in its own way. The White Warrior cuts off the Master Demon's hand. As long as the hand is kept from the Master Demon, the Demon cannot return to the world. In the present day, some bad folks are trying to reattach the hand. Lee and Wayne and Cameron stand in their way.

When Qua Chang teams with bodybuilder Medusa, and they assemble a gang of kung fu thugs with painted faces, one can feel the world of the cinema buckle as it tries to hold in all this craziness. Along comes Cameron Massey, private eye. Lee and Berserker are cops. Everyone is trying to stop the Master Demon from returning to life. Much of the story involves the lead characters engaging in a lot of jokey dialogue. Massey has most of this dialogue. He's a bit of a wiseacre. He has a great secretary who also does kung fu. Lee speaks much mystical dialogue. But the Master Demon don't take no sass. Neither does Medusa. *The Master Demon* also involves a lot of kung fu fighting. Some is quite good, some looks awkward. Every fight veers between exciting and goofy. Actually, more goofy that anything, to be honest.

This very cheap film seems to have been a one-man creation. Samuel Oldham gave his all so that the world would enjoy another kung fu film. But is it worth a viewing when the action can be lame and the story is goofy (especially when the dismembered hand goofballery begins) and the acting is pretty ripe? Of course it's worth a viewing. The White Warrior would demand the attention. I will not argue with the White Warrior, especially with his beautiful White Warrior wig.

Mercenary Fighters

Director: Riki Shelach Nissimoff
Screenplay: Bud Schaetzle, Dean Tschetter, Andrew Deutsch

Producers: Menahem Golan, Yoran Globus
Cast: Reb Brown (T.J. Christian), Peter Fonda (Virelli), Ron O'Neal (Cliff Taylor), Joanna Weinberg (Nurse Ruth Warwick), Robert DoQui (Col. Kyemba)

An African dam is going to be built even though several villages will be flooded. A man named Kuruba is leading a pack of rebels within the villages. The president sends a group of mercenaries to destroy the villages. Among the mercenaries led by Virelli is a man named T.J. Christian. As the villages are wiped out, the loyalties (or non-loyalties) of some of the mercenaries (mainly T.J.) begin to change.

Mercenary Fighters is a swift-moving, intelligent (for this sort of movie) and exciting film that keeps the viewer always on the verge of cheering and yelling on the action scenes. There are a lot of great explosions in this movie, all shot at the perfect distance. They are large and powerful. Almost as large and powerful as Mr. Reb Brown.

Reb has one strange acting thing he does whenever he has to yell or get angry. Actually, angry is not the problem. It's his yelling. I imagine that everyone's yell is different, kind of like everyone's laugh. But Reb really lets loose with it. I wish I could include some sort of sound file with this book, so you could push a button and hear Reb shout. The shouting sometimes leaves me on the verge of giggles. This film has several shouty moments. But in the rest of the movie, he is at his best. He's a pretty convincing actor. The constant cuts to his face as atrocities are being committed make the viewer know that he's going to do something. Unfortunately, the final big fight is not as good as the penultimate big fight.

I would imagine that this is one of the higher budgeted films in this book. The production values are high. *Mercenary Fighters* only lets us down with the score. Strange synths trying to be orchestral. Wah-wah guitar moments that don't quite work. During the final fight scene, we hear what seems to be library music. Perhaps the owners of a 1970s blaxploitation film sold off some of their music to *Mercenary Fighters*. It's unfortunate that the score couldn't have been given the same touches of love as the rest of the movie.

Nightmare at Noon

> *Director, Producer:* Nico Mastorakis
> *Screenplay:* Nico Mastorakis, Kirk Ellis
> *Cast:* Wings Hauser (Ken Griffiths), Bo Hopkins (Reilly), George Kennedy (Sheriff Hanks), Kimberly Beck (Cheri Griffiths), Brion James (The Albino), Kimberly Ross (Julia), Neal Wheeler (Charley)

Nightmare at Noon is a sort of Western variation of *The Crazies*. The Albino (Brion James), probably with the CIA, contaminates the water of Canyonland, a small desert town near Moab, Utah. People begin to go crazy. The sheriff, his daughter, an attorney, his wife and a drifter (Bo Hopkins) need to figure out what's going on and stop the craziness. Warning! There will be shooting and people growling a lot.

This one isn't long on explanations. The Albino has a bunch of computer screens constantly printing things but nothing is fully explained. The thought is that the CIA is testing some sort of drug on this desolate town. And then, when their tests are done, they will torch the place. The Albino guy is kind of weird. He could be from *Buckaroo Banzai* for all I knows. It's one of Brion James' oddest roles. Wings Hauser brings a slightly off-kilter tough guy quality to this one. Kimberly Beck does some excellent growling. George Kennedy gets a kick-ass death scene with lots of guns and fire. The mighty Bo Hopkins is mysterious and constantly yells "Shit!" when one of the infected people gets the best of him.

EN **NICO MASTORAKIS** FILM
NIGHTMARE AT NOON
Med: Wings Hauser, Bo Hopkins, Kimberly Beck og George Kennedy som sheriff Hanks.
© Copyright Omega Entertainment

The film is loaded with action: car chases, horse chases, helicopter chases, everything. It has a slowly escalating, fly-by-the-seat-of-your-pants feel, for the first hour as the infected people attack and then goons with their flame throwers show up. Then, everything switches to the desert and it just becomes a bunch of shootouts as there are no more zombies there. But, really, who wants to complain? The viewer gets fast-paced, exciting, well-acted scenes that have Brion James looking really weird and lots of Hans Zimmer music. That was a surprise. Early Zimmer is as much fun as prime period Zimmer.

Ninja Force of Assassins

> *Director, Screenplay:* Godfrey Ho

Producers: Joseph Lai, Betty Chan

Cast: Mark Tyler, Chester Howe, Michel Stevens, Edgar Fox, Jim Davis

There are gangsters, Interpol and ninjas in this one. The "old" footage, wherever it's from, is actually quite good, sort of like *Ninja: Silent Assassin.* The "new" footage with all the white guy ninjas is as dippy as ever. The Ho-Lai team dress them up, put them in fields and have them fight and fight. *Ninja Force of Assassins* isn't a bad film, as far as these films go.

Boss Cole, the head gangster, has an enemy who is a White Ninja. Also, there is this guy from Interpol and a gang of ninjas and something called the Ghost Shadow Squad. The "old" film with the Interpol agent and ladies is dubbed "brilliantly" to bring it in line with whatever it is that is going on in the ninja footage. I wish I could have figured it out. They keep talking about an "organization," which I took to be the mob guy's thing. Of course, that's bad. And there's a final shootout fight in a warehouse that is pretty awesome.

There are huge puffs of blue smoke thrown by ninjas. The black ninjas, when they die, disappear in a huge puff of mystical smoke. Thank goodness that everyone went out there and emoted their behinds off. But it's all about the ninja work. All about the silly fighting. In the case of the "old" footage, the actual good fighting. Ninjas are fun.

Ninja, Demon's Massacre

Director: Tommy Cheng

Producer: Tomas Tang

Screenplay: Harold Owen

Cast: Ted Brooke, James Lear, Edmund Morris, Ken Ashley, Chris Cole, Molly Maxwell, Fanny Bower, Arthur Young

The big mystery with this film is: Who is Tommy Cheng? It's not a misprint of Tommy Chong, I don't think. There isn't a single pot gag in the movie. Is he Godfrey Ho under a pseudonym? Maybe. Is it Tomas Tang himself? I bet it is a man named Tommy Cheng even though his style of directing is absolutely no different from Ho's, except he uses more colored smoke when the ninjas fight. The main thing that makes me feel that this is not Ho is that this is the least interesting of the ninja films I've seen from this company. And, one thing they are not, generally, is uninteresting.

Ninja, Demon's Massacre has the most ridiculous title of the series. There are some ninja fights but there is no Demon Massacre. Most of the film is about a bunch of really boring people who hang out in a bar and some fields. The good guy's main fight tactic is acting like he's dead and then shooting or knifing his opponent. There are some bad guys who have rotten mustaches and all seem to be in their late 40s with beer guts. And there are a bunch of women who are almost continually getting sexually assaulted.

The ninja fights aren't as well integrated into the story as they are in the other movies. Maybe Tommy Cheng wasn't as great at this as Tong thought. I wonder what Godfrey Ho was up to at this time. He was probably in a park somewhere with Richard Harrison making eight other films.

I spent about 80 minutes waiting for a demon massacre. Some of the these films actually feature supernatural elements. Then the golden ninja shows up and there's a cool fight on the beach. The scenes with the ninjas are fun but really don't go anywhere. Life is strange wherever it is this movie is set. Demon's Massacre my Aunt Fanny. Where did Ho go? Bring him back.

Operation Warzone

Director: David Prior
Screenplay: Ted Prior, David Prior
Producer: Fritz Matthews
Cast: Joe Spinnell (Delevane), Fritz Matthews (Holt), Bill Zipp (Butler), John Cianetti (Hawkins), David Marriott (Smitty), Sean Holton (Adams)

Another AIP–David A. Prior, *Operation Warzone* takes us into Vietnam. Undercover agents are out to stop a man called the General who is running guns and training soldiers. These agents meet up with a group of regular soldiers and they go head to head with, apparently, everyone in Southeast Asia. Joe Spinnell plays a government higher-up who spends the whole movie sitting at a long table. The movie alternates Spinnell and his table with the soldiers out in the woods shooting people. And that's the movie.

David A. Prior and his brother Ted must have felt like kids out there shooting these movies. I used to make lots of short films,

ACTION INTERNATIONAL PICTURES presents
a DAVID A. PRIOR film OPERATION WARZONE starring JOE SPINELL as General Delevane
FRITZ MATTHEWS, WILLIAM ZIPP, JOHN CIANETTI, DAVID MARRIOTT, SEAN HOLTON
Director of Photography ANDREW PARKE Edited by TODD FELKER Music by TIM JAMES
STEVE McCLINTOCK, CARM BEALL Executive Producers DAVID WINTERS, MARC WINTERS
Produced by FRITZ MATTHEWS Story by TED PRIOR Written and Directed by DAVID A. PRIOR

They Told 'Em War Was Hell... They Were Right!

mainly on video, when I was a kid, and you always cut to the chase, went right to the excitement and the fun parts. That's what *Operation Warzone* does. And whether or not one gets a lot of enjoyment out of the film simply comes down to how much constant shooting of faceless characters one can take.

This issue has come up before within this book. Yes, lots of people shooting at other people in the jungles or just in general is action. Someone like John Woo can make it into an art form. Other people just point their cameras at people firing guns and that's that. Prior is in the second category. Watch the first five minutes of this film. Rather humorless and faceless American soldiers fire at a group of Asian guys, who may or may not be soldiers, in some woods. There are lots of gun barrels flashing, lots of sounds of gunshots and many explosions. But is it exciting?

I think there's a definite thrill to it. One can appreciate that effort has gone into it. One can also have trouble differentiating who is who. One can also wonder why it isn't more exciting. Gunfights can be thrilling excitement; take the last 30 or 40 minutes of *Hard Boiled*, for example. So, why are the *Operation Warzone* gunfights unexciting? Again, it's sort of like what we used to do when we were making films as kids. Until we saw films like *Die Hard* and *Raiders of the Lost Ark* and started to see some style and craft and how things could be done differently.

Almost all the AIP films that I watched for this book, feel like this. It's a bunch of guys doing something or other (it's pretty interchangeable). They get macho at each other for periods of time. Then there's shooting. The music gets so odd that one can't help but giggle. On two occasions (the more memorable being as the soldiers are escaping from a prison camp

type set-up), the music kicks in really loud and it's so 1980s big synths and drum machines Good Time Music that one expects them to be in Saigon at the Mall of Vietnam.

Order of the Eagle

Director: Thomas Baldwin
Screenplay, Producer: William Zipp
Cast: William Zipp (John Billings), Casey Hirsch (Scout Greg), Frank Stallone (Mr. Quill), Perry Hill (Freddie), Jill Foor (Monica)

In the woods, Greg, a Boy Scout, stumbles upon the wreckage of a plane with a dead body and a briefcase filled with top secret information linked to Mr. Quill (Frank Stallone). Soon Greg and a man named Billings are under attack from a squad of jerks working for Quill. Fight to the death!

Order of the Eagle is fast-moving. It's set in good locations, deep in the woods and, overall, it's well-made. It's only a little bit goofy. It's mostly exciting. In fact, the goofy keeps the movie moving along during the slow spots.

Order of the Eagle is a strong entry in the AIP catalogue. It is very straightforward. Bad guys go to the woods to retrieve some floppy disks. They encounter this Boy Scout, then Billings and his pals. Action all over the place. My favorite moment is the joke about why the guy got thrown out of the Boy Scouts. I almost got thrown out of the Boy Scouts for a similar reason. And it would have been worth it.

Outlaw Force

Director, Screenplay: David Heavener
Producers: Ronnie Hadar, David Heavener
Cast: Paul Smith (Inspector Wainright), David Heavener (Billy Ray Dalton), Frank Stallone (Grady), Robert Bjorkland (Washington), Stephanie Cicero (Holly Dalton)

My VHS copy of *Outlaw Force* begins with an ad for the soundtrack for *Outlaw Force.* The songs are sung by the star of the film, David Heavener. I called the number on the ad but have been unable to get a copy, although they did say that they had eight-tracks in stock. And that ad sums up the glory of this movie. It's a one-man show: David Heavener putting himself forward as a redneck Clint Eastwood, singing, loving and shooting a lot.

Billy Ray Dalton's (Heavener) wife is killed by a bunch of Los Angeles thugs and his daughter is kidnapped. Billy Ray must get her back. The cops, led by Paul Smith and Frank Stallone, don't care as much as they should. However, in the end, everyone gets involved.

Outlaw Force recycles the sort of vigilante justice thing that you have seen many times. Billy Ray is impossibly wonderful. When he needs to kick ass, whether it's fighting in an alley or shooting people in an old theater, he does it well. The cops are fairly useless although not completely so. The punks are sleazy and don't care about human life. Except for the fe-male punks; *they* care. And then there's the nice punk gal who befriends Billy Ray.

Outlaw Force doesn't do anything new apart from all those songs sung by the leading man. Is it worth seeing? I would say yes. There isn't much action in the first half, but once Billy Ray ends up in that alley fighting thugs, things take off. David Heavener is not averse to David Heavener doing some stunts, including climbing down a wall. He wields a mean gun in his long trench coat and cowboy hat.

The ending is exciting but, at least on the VHS, too dark. The music drones and drones, sometimes in a good way. Billy Ray sneaks through a theater looking for his daughter. The neverending punks come at him. Smith appears to help him out. The creeping around and droning music is punctuated by gunshots. It all culminates on the roof of a building. Does Billy Ray save the day?

Phantom Raiders

Director: Sonny Sanders
Screenplay: Timothy Jorge, Sonny Sanders
Producer: Silver Screen International
Cast: Miles O'Keeffe (Python Lang), Don Holtz, Mike Monty (Col. Marshall), Kenneth Peerless, Anthony East, Jim Moss

Phantom Raiders literally begins with shooting, a three-minute firefight in a field between a bunch of guys in green and a bunch of guys in black. The guys in green are good guys, the guys in black are part of a Communist training camp run by American traitor Col. Marshall. The credits appear over the fighting.

Phantom Raiders does have a lot of action. It's made for it. The plot cries out, There Will Be Shootouts! Imagine a film with guys running through the woods or fields and people come out of patches of trees or run around corners ... and the heroes mow them down. Now amp that up by about 10 notches and include quite a few shots in which the camera follows the good guys as people run out of areas and fall down ... that's *Phantom Raiders.* It's as exciting and silly as it sounds.

Col. Marshall has opened a training ground for Communist terrorists in the Viet-

fall, coupled with the number of things that get blown up, adds up to a hell of a lot. But is it interesting? Is it actually exciting? I think so, but with a caveat: It is fun watching the endless shooting and the bodies falling. It is also exhausting. But, if one can watch it for what it is, then this is a fun 84 minutes. If you want something more than that, *Phantom Raiders* isn't for you.

Phantom Soldiers

Director: Teddy Page (as Irvin Johnson)

Screenplay: Rod Davies, Jim Gaines

Producer: Joy Tunners

Cast: Max Thayer (Daniel Custer), Jack Yates (Col. Hammer), Corwyn Sperry (Michael Custer), Jim Gaines (Red Legs), Richard King (KY), David Light (Hammer's Aide), Mike Monty (Col. Barker)

Phantom Soldiers begins with a very strong action scene. A group called the Phantom Soldiers attacks a defenseless Vietnamese village. Dressed all in black with gas masks, they cannot be taken down with bullets. They just keep coming and shooting and killing. After they've devastated the village, they take the survivors to the beach. There, they release poisonous gas and stand impassively as the villagers die.

This powerful, almost surreal scene sets the tone for the movie; most of the rest of it matches up to the quality of that scene. Michael Custer is fighting in Vietnam. He becomes a POW. His brother Daniel, a Korean War vet and currently a Texas Ranger, goes after him. Daniel finds that his brother had discovered these phantom commandos had killed before. So the hunt is on.

Director Teddy Page comes through with awesome action in *Phantom Soldiers*. As mentioned, the images of those invulnerable soldiers flooding in with their gas masks is eerie.

nam jungles. A man named Python (Miles O'Keeffe) is told to create a team of Phantom Raiders, go into the jungle and destroy it. There is a long training sequence, which is distinguishable from the regular action scenes because there aren't tons of people being shot. Then the action beings. The compound is stormed and many men in black outfits with red berets are shot and fall in jerky fashion. One of the Raiders is the son of Col. Marshall.

Can you have too much endless shooting of people? The director does keep things moving. The camera Steadicams along while members of the Raiders shoot the Communists. The number of people who get shot and

The action comes at us hot and fast. Plenty of explosions and shootouts. The movie also has nice character touches, which one doesn't expect in a film like this. Daniel and Michael's relationship is handled well. They are close. They look out for one another. Daniel heads into the jungle with a Vietcong helper to sort out what is going on. In action film fashion, things are all a little screwy out there, but Daniel is a tough guy. He acquitted himself well in Korea. It should be fairly obvious who might be involved when the government won't help him find his brother.

Phantom Soldiers has all the action that one wants from a film like this. And it's well done. This is a fun one. One of the things about the Namsploitation films is that they are generally fun. That opening scene, however, is almost too much. It lingers in the mind long after the film is done. Those soldiers are scary guys. And that scene (along with some of the moments of character development) set this film apart.

Picasso Trigger

Director, Screenplay: Andy Sidaris
Producer: Arlene Sidaris
Cast: Steve Bond (Travis Abilene), Dona Speir (Donna), Hope Marie Carlton (Taryn), Harold Diamond (Jade), John Aprea (Salazar), Roberta Vasquez (Pantera), Cynthia Brimhall (Edy)

The third Andy Sidaris softcore action film marks the return of Donna and Taryn from *Hard Ticket to Hawaii*. There is another Abilene relative. With this one, Andy is finally able to create an international espionage–filled action film, like a James Bond epic or a more coherent version of *Rescue Force*. All the elements from his other films are here. He's just upped the ante on global locations, There are no giant snakes or crazy mystery plots, but there is a lot of fun to be had.

We start off hopping from Paris to Dallas to Los Angeles to Las Vegas to Hawaii. It all makes some sort of sense. An agent is killed. A criminal named Ortiz is responsible. An agent in Dallas recruits another in the Abilene clan (Travis), who is relaxing on the Malibu

Express. In Hawaii, Edy is still running her restaurant, this time in a lime-green mini-dress.

Donna and Taryn hook up with almost all of the gang from *Hard Ticket*. Ortiz tries to kill them. The girls travel from one part of Molokai to the other on a very tiny train. Travis falls in love with an agent called Pantera but she is "practically immune to emotion." Pantera and Travis go dancing to country music. This must have been right before line dancing appeared because it's a crowd of very awkward white people dancing. The innuendos keeps flowing. Sidaris must have some sort of "Naughty Encyclopedia" for these things because they never stop being great.

This one has something nutty or sexy or violent or all three going on in every scene. A man called the Professor designs Q-style gadgets. Sidaris also adds intertitles cluing us into what day it is. (I actually forgot the purpose of these but it sure upped the ante.) He handles the multiple plotlines better in this one. There is one about cowgirls dancing in Vegas that left me semi-confused but everything else seems to come together. A bunch of good guys in assorted locations around the globe are out to stop a bunch of bad guys. It doesn't get much simpler than that. Luckily, almost everyone is distinguishable from everyone else. In the final reel, events occur that make everything feel as if it all made sense even if it actually didn't. Plus, the ending has a great action moment that is mighty clever. There's a touch of intelligence in each of these films that elevates them to a whole new level of awesome.

These are the films that home video was made for back in this time period. Mixing Playboy Playmates and hunky guys with tons of action seems like something that a thousand people would have thought of. Fittingly, it was the man who pioneered the "Honey Shot" that came up with it. The "Honey Shot" is that moment in a sporting event when the camera zooms in on the cheerleaders or a pretty girl in the stands. Sidaris knows what he likes. Who can argue?

Plus, the synth score of this film is what I hear in my head whenever I'm walking around my neighborhood.

Platoon Leader

Director: Aaron Norris

Screenplay: Harry Alan Towers, David L. Walker, Andrew Deutsch, Rick Mult

Producer: Harry Alan Towers

Cast: Michael Dudikoff (Lt. Jeffrey Knight), Robert F. Lyons (Sgt. Michael McNamara), Michael DeLorenzo (Pvt. Raymond Bacera), Jesse Dabson (Pvt. Joshua Parker), Rick Fitts (Sgt. Robert Hayes)

Cannon Films makes their *Platoon.* Michael Dudikoff plays Lt. Knight, a soldier fresh out of West Point. Initially he does not have the respect of his men. He fouls up a few times, and that doesn't help, but eventually he wins them over. The men's mettle is tested in the final fight with the Vietcong to protect a village.

The thought of Cannon taking a well-respected drama like *Platoon* and making it their own almost makes the viewer reject *Platoon Leader* right off the bat. Shouldn't a company like Cannon be sticking to more obvious crowd pleasers? Make another *First Blood Part II*? The good thing is that Dudikoff pulls off the action scenes effortlessly, as always. He isn't able to engage in kung fu kick-assery but one can't have everything. His voice is again a bit too high. There may be a reason why the soldiers don't respect him. His voice is a moment away from sounding like helium is in it. But he does shoot a gun well, when he's not bumbling over land mines.

The plot is pretty much a series of vignettes. Commanding officer William Smith sends Knight to the jungle. Knight arrives with his platoon. There are attacks. Scenes with soldiers being killed. New recruits arriving. One of the boys is a junkie. People are injured. Helicopters fly in. All the classic Vietnam War film drama.

The actions scenes are exciting. The drama works, for the most part. A few of the actors are a bit weak and there is that weird feeling of Namsploitation about the film. The Italian rip-offs that were actually set in Vietnam always end up feeling weird but have the cultural disconnect that one can find in, say, Spaghetti Westerns. They go so over the top that whatever they were originally about goes

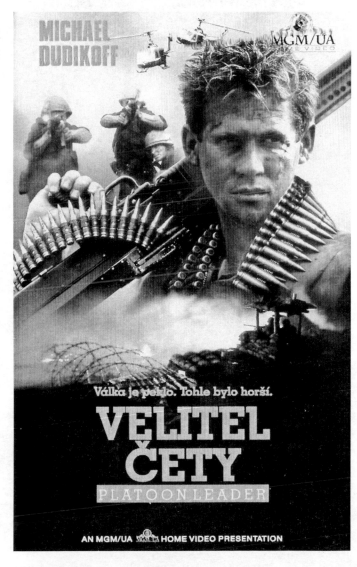

out the door and is replaced with mock hero-ics, strange dubbing and action.

However, an American film taking on *Platoon* feels different. The action scenes in *Platoon* are part of the movie. They may occasionally get flashy but they're part of the film's tapestry. By the very nature of Cannon Films and Dudikoff, the action scenes in *Platoon Leader* would be better suited to a POW film or something different. But this film makes its points simplistically and gives us action. The social and political ramifications are a whole different thing here.

Platoon the Warriors

Director: Phillip Ko
Screenplay: Godfrey Ho (as Benny Ho)
Producer: Tomas Tang
Cast: Mark Watson (Bill), Mike Abbott (Rex), James Miller, Dick Crown, Alex Sylvian

Rex and Bill are drug dealers. A big deal goes south. Everyone gets shot. Rex sets out after Bill. Meanwhile, a guy named Michael (in the "other" footage from this cut-and-paste adventure) is killed. Michael's brother vows revenge against the thugs. From that point on, the film is a lot of thugs acting cruel, sexual assault, the obligatory scene in a club—all intercut with a bunch of white guys in the woods fighting, somewhere. Occasionally someone is in a military outfit.

The white guy fighting is as gloriously silly as ever. Things are undercranked. Overcranked. Cranked all over the place. And the fighting scenes occur randomly with no rhyme or reason. The other movie is a bit of a dour affair. It's just a nasty bunch of people messing with this family for what seems like a series of co-incidences. The dubbing isn't up to snuff except possibly during

the scene when the father of the family dies. He's in a hospital bed fading fast and Mom just keeps yelling "No! No!" as if that will reverse the dying process. It doesn't.

Platoon the Warriors, one would think, might have something to do with a platoon of something-or-other. It doesn't. Mike Abbott, as Rex, brings his great Australian accent and his odd look. Any film that he's in, I will go for. The cast of the "interior" film are fine. There's a fun scene in a massage parlor where baby powder is used to blind a thug.

I wish that this film was a bit more fun. The "interior" film seems like a rather dull revenge film that spends too much time lingering on the sexual assault. In the movie's defense, it has a great opening musical theme. Some great bouncy synths. And several scenes mix the old footage with the new footage. There's something about the audacity of that that I always like.

R.O.T.O.R.

Director: Cullen Blaine
Screenplay: Budd Lewis
Producers: Cullen Blaine, Budd Lewis, Richard Gesswein
Cast: Richard Gesswein (Capt. Coldyron), Margaret Trigg (Sonya), Jayne Smith, James Cole, Clark Moore

There are movies that make political statements. Others that comment profoundly on the human condition. There are movies that unite audiences across the world through laughter. Then, there's *R.O.T.O.R.* That stands for Robotic Officer Tactical Operation Research. This film is a *RoboCop* homage straight out of Texas. Rarely does a viewer come across a film where it feels so much like a bunch of folks with a camera out having a good time, regardless of whether or not they know what they're doing.

Coldyron, the captain in charge of the Dallas Police Department's robotic division, is working on the ultimate in technology: a robot cop dressed from head to toe in black leather, wearing a motorcycle helmet and sporting a mustache. A cop with super powers, full knowledge of the law and something called "Sensor Recall." (R.O.T.O.R. can see events from the past even though he wasn't there.) R.O.T.O.R. is activated and sort of goes on a rampage. Coldyron and a cop named Steele must destroy the rogue robot.

Every scene in this movie is awkward in some way. Some actors' voices are dubbed but others aren't. In a meeting, Coldyron and some scientists make Beach Boys references in dialogue which gives Ed Wood a run for his money. There are inept action scenes and Steele's hilarious skunk mullet. This film oozes a feeling of "It doesn't matter that we don't know what we're doing. We're doing it."

Everything is in focus and visible. That's a plus. But every scene has dialogue that would defeat the strongest actor. However, everyone charges in and speaks one strange sentence after another. Nothing fazes them. Everything is fun to watch. During the aforementioned Beach Boys scene and another with a scientist and a robot, the jargon is so nonsensical that Cyber-Lewis Carroll seems to be lurking right around the corner. Ed Wood had passed on by this time but his memory survives here.

R.O.T.O.R. surprises the viewer in different ways until it ends. One must go out and watch it. Experience it. There are two versions: the VHS and the Blu-ray-DVD. The latter version has extra scenes including one with a scientist doing a Columbo impersonation.

Rage of a Ninja

Director: Godfrey Ho
Screenplay: Benny Ho
Producer: Joseph Lai
Cast: Marko Ritchie, Mike Abbott, Morna Lee, Peter Cressall, Knaap Paul, Nina Pachy

Mike Abbott is back! And he's after the manual. There isn't much known about the manual. Mainly that Mike doesn't have it and he wants it. A guy named Steve has it! Steve is assaulted from every which way as Mike tries to become the Main Ninja in his beautiful yellow robes with the Ninja headband. But Steve's not so easy to pin down, especially when one of Mike's thugs ends up sleeping with Steve's wife. Steve runs from the law and hides out in the house of a beautiful young woman. After beating her up a bit, they fall in love. There is some sexual assault. Lots of fighting. And more ninjas using semi-automatic weapons than I would have expected. It all culminates in the final fight between Mike and a guy who I'd forgotten about (because Steve is not actually in the footage with Mike). This fight brings out the true *Rage of a Ninja*.

The movie starts off strong with talk about the manual. Then there's a ninja fight and a shootout. Discussions between guys who sell insurance. Then Steve. Then, this woman gets undressed and rubs lotion on her legs for what seemed like about 21 minutes. Then there's fighting. And … it's a whirlwind. Setting that aside, is *Rage of a Ninja* an entertaining ninja film? Sure. Who knows? Who cares? Ho and Lai probably didn't care. Mike Abbott continues to be one of the goofiest looking guys who ever did martial arts. The non-ninja footage (whatever the film with Steve in it is) is fine. All requirements for Ho and Lai fun are met.

Ragin' Cajun

Director, Screenplay: William Bryon Hillman

Producers: William Byron Hillman, Michelle Marshall

Cast: David Heavener (Cage), Charlene Tilton (Ali Webster), Samantha Eggar (Dr. May), Allan Rich (Regetti), Sam Bottoms (Legs), Hector Elias (Pedro), Benny "The Jet" Urquidez (Fighter), Jesse Borja (Dr. Death)

Cage, a kickboxer, is having lots of Vietnam flashbacks, which get in the way of his fighting and his budding relationship with country singer Ali Webster. Ali is kidnapped. Cage is forced to fight. What will happen? And is any of it as important as the songs and all the singing?

Of all the David Heavener films I've seen, this is the closest to being a musical. Some of his films have been almost more about him singing than fighting or action-ing it up. *Outlaw Force* has a commercial for the soundtrack on the VHS. But this one is the ultimate in music-filled movies. Songs such as "I L.U.V. Y.O.U.," "The Heart of You," "I Slipped on My Best Friend," "Makin' Love to the Beat" and "We Can Make it" fill out the film. And generally not on the soundtrack but with people on-camera singing the songs. It almost becomes Heavener's *Nashville*. Except for the kickboxing.

Ragin' Cajun comes to us courtesy of William Bryon Hillman who seems to have gone into this with the focus on giving David as much time for his songs as possible. A variety of people sing the songs in the film. One

guy has a good country voice. Stella Parton sings a song! She sounds like Dolly and looks quite a bit like her too. But the big surprise is Charlene Tilton. Not only is she super-mega-hot in this film but she sings quite a few of the songs. She's got a real sweet voice, heartfelt and honest.

Tilton was on *Dallas* from its start in early 1978 until the end of the eighth Season in 1985. *Ragin' Cajun* is copyright 1988 so it's safe to assume that this was made before she returned to *Dallas* around 1988 for the twelfth Season. When *Dallas* began, she was 17 and was America's favorite Lolita. But by 1985, the soap operas' reign was fading and Lucy Ewing's character had run out of steam. So Lucy left and Charlene went out into the world. When she returned to *Dallas*, she was older, leaner and hot as hell. This is in that period. She's charming and beautiful and she has a sweet voice and when she's kidnapped, one wants to punch through the TV.

Ragin' Cajun is a bit shameless in the tugging-the-heartstrings department. That probably is because of all those songs. It's included in this book because Heavener can kick butt when needed. Consider this the *Heart of Dragon* of low-budget American action films of the 1980s.

Raiders of the Magic Ivory

Director: Anthony Richmond
Screenplay: David Parker, Jr.
Producer: Camillo Teti
Cast: James Mitchum, Cris Ahrens

Two American ex-vet mercenaries are sent by an old Asian gentleman into the jungles to find an ivory tablet with a series of mystical incantations that do strange things, like make people disappear. The vets are joined by one of the Asian gent's helpers. They spend the movie driving through the jungle in a Jeep, shooting Vietcong and fighting natives as they try to claim the tablet. One of the vets is hilariously foul-mouthed. His use of "peckerhead" was prime and right on target. The chunky guy leading the gang is an entertaining addition to the film.

This movie is an Italian *Raiders of the Lost*

Vampire is startlingly stupid in ways that are astounding. The title should probably clue you in. And the title is perfectly correct. The movie is filled with hopping Chinese vampires. At one point, a dead police officer is transformed into a robotic cop. The cop fights all sorts of jerks out in the jungle and on the beach. And then he fights hopping vampires.

This one begins with a bunch of soldiers being attacked by a hopping vampire with a cannibalistic streak. A cop is killed. Another cop says something along the lines of "I'd like to take that dead cop's body and make it into a robot." The reaction is: "Okay. You have permission." It's that easy. The robotic cop is sort of like RoboCop except he's less metallic and more silver jumpsuit-pajamas. Every time he moves, there is a metallic noise on the soundtrack. And

Ark rip-off with a touch of *Rambo* thrown in. The odds seem stacked in the viewer's favor. Lots of jungle footage, mainly three guys talking and shooting and fighting. A mystical glowing ivory tablet waits at the end of it. The film has a lot more aimless driving than any film needs, but the constant flood of Vietcong soldiers and those natives makes it fun.

Robo Vampire

Director: Godfrey Ho (as Joe Livingstone)

Screenplay: William Palmer

Producer: Tomas Tang

Cast: Robin Mackay, Nian Watts, Harry Myles, Joe Browne, Nick Norman, George Tipps

This is the dumbest movie in this book. (I may have said that before and I may say it again. I mean it every time I say it.) *Robo*

whenever the hopping vampires hop, there is an almost metallic sound on the soundtrack. It all gets very confusing, especially if one's mind wanders.

The cyborg cop hunts down a plague of hopping vampires. It culminates in a sequence on the beach. First, the bad soldiers try to kill the RoboCop guy, and they fail. Then a series of hopping vampires appear. A man in silver pajamas fights a bunch of guys dressed as vampires that hop around. That four minutes of cinema might be the most entertaining ever. One musical theme so greatly resembles the Ian Anderson song "Fly by Night" that I had to put on the album when I was done with the movie.

Hopping vampires are always weird. They can be scary when handled well (*Mr. Vampire*, for instance). But, when handled wrong, they are goofball creations. Mix in a

RoboCop rip-off and the world is no longer normal. I just wish there'd been a sequel.

Robowar

Director: Bruno Mattei (as Vincent Dawn)
Screenplay: Claudio Fragasso, Rossella Drudi
Producer: Flora Film
Cast: Reb Brown (Black), Catherine Hickland (Virgin), Alex McBride (Guarino), Romano Puppo (Corey)

Robowar sounds like it's going to be a *RoboCop* rip-off. It is but it isn't. A group of Marines called the BAM (Bad Asses Motherfuckers) are sent to the jungle to stop the Omega-1 from wreaking havoc. It's an advanced technological something-or-other. The BAMs are straight out of *Predator*. Arnold Schwarzenegger isn't here but the always shrieking Reb Brown is along for the ride and we see thermal imaging POV shots. Elaborate traps are set and *Predator* is brought to mind.

It turns out that Omega-1 is a *Terminator-RoboCop* kind of guy and the movie be-comes more like those movies but still in a jungle. But now they've got a female missionary helping them out; her name is Virginia but the credits call her Virgin. There are exploding things and waterfalls and plenty of scenes of Reb Brown shrieking. About 19 minutes in, the BAMs are heading downriver looking for Omega-1 and over-rousing pop music (with pounding drum machines) start up. All of this goes on for a very long time. It happens again around 33 minutes in.

Robowar picks and chooses from recent sci-fi–action blockbusters and hits all the big action moments. It even throws in those Marines (who could also be from *Aliens*). If you haven't seen much action-adventure from this time period, maybe one viewing of *Robowar* could teach all you need to know.

As always Bruno Mattei does a decent job with the action and adventure. He's no master but the camera is always in the right place. His sheer audacity, ripping off the blockbusters so exactly, is fun.

Silent Assassins

Directors: Scott Thomas, Lee Doo Yong
Screenplay: Will Gates, Ada Lim
Producers: Jun Chong, Phillip Rhee
Cast: Sam Jones (Sam Kettle), Linda Blair (Sara), Jun Chung (Jun Kim), Phillip Rhee (Bernard), Bill Erwin (Dr. London)

Early in the movie, a family gets off an elevator and is attacked by ninjas. An old man and his granddaughter are kidnapped. Everyone else is killed. Ninjas are basically hired assassins, so one imagines that "Kill a family coming out of an elevator" is a logical assignment if the price is right. It seems like overkill to me.

A creepy guy and his hot partner are trying to work up some sort of biological warfare something-or-other. In order to do this, they force the old guy to do all sorts of computer things, circa 1988, that will help them out. The creepy guy has a vague German accent. His partner is a beautiful woman who first appears in a short skirt with a gun, shooting cops. They even torture the old guy to get him to keep working. On the other side of the fence, the good side, Sam and Jun Kim are tough guys who are going to kick the behinds of every bad guy from here to Cleveland and back. Sam is engaged to Linda Blair. She's sweet and understanding.

This movie's pretty darn good. It feels a bit like a *Running Scared* or *Stakeout* kind of film with two mismatched folks joined up and getting involved in action. The film goes a little heavy on the "torturing old guys" and "little girl in terror" angles. Presumably the moviemakers wanted to make the bad guys so bad that the good guys kicking their collective asses will be justified. But sometimes it can be overdone. Mainly in foreign films (Italy!) where there seems to be a different set of morals.

Silent Assassins is an entertaining action film, filled with ninjas, that doesn't take itself seriously. And it has Sam Jones and Linda Blair so that is worth something.

Space Mutiny

Director, Producer: David Winters
Screenplay: Maria Dante
Cast: Reb Brown (Dave Ryder), John Phillip Law (Elijah Kalgan), James Ryan (MacPhearson), Cameron Mitchell (Alex Jansen), Cissy Cameron (Lean Jansen)

The spaceship *Southern Star*, filled with generations of humans, has been traveling for so long that people no longer remember what it was like to step outside of it. The evil Kalgan, who commands an army of genetically modified soldiers called Enforcers, try to take over. Luckily, Dave Ryder is on hand. He's big and beefy and he's been put in charge by the man who runs the ship, Alex Jansen. Dave is also wooing Jansen's daughter Lena. Everything is very smooth and sexy during this *Space Mutiny.*

David Winters takes us into the realm of space opera with this one. But, as it is an Action International Picture, there is plenty of action. Lots of ray gun shooting and speeding around in carts that don't go very fast. Much of the movie takes place in factory-like areas on the spaceship. There is plenty of time (if one has the inclination) to fall from a railing. It's action in space.

Reb Brown still retains that strange habit of yelling too loud and hoarsely when action is going on. *Space Mutiny* has the ultimate version of that. His cart is headed for a cart that is on fire. Ryder lets out a huge, harsh shriek. And then stops shrieking on a dime. And leaps out of the cart. Possibly there should have been a cut there as it's a very strange moment.

Space Mutiny is dippy fun that uses a lot of space footage from *Battlestar Galactica.* The *Southern Star* is the *Galactica* and all the outer space dogfights (done with models) are scenes from the show. Where did they get this footage from? Did they break into Glen A. Larson's garage? I imagine it saved a ton of money but still—it's not like *Battlestar Galactica* was an obscure TV show no one had ever seen. The fans who may have checked out *Space Mutiny* in 1988 were probably very familiar with that show.

But *Galactica* did not have Reb Brown or Cameron Mitchell or John Phillip Law. David Winters' action-filled space opera has enough exciting moments to draw attention and keep one watching.

Strike Commando 2

Director: Bruno Mattei (as Vincent Dawn)
Screenplay: Claudio Fragasso
Producer: Franco Gaudenzi
Cast: Brent Huff (Mike Ransome), Mary Stavin (Rosanna), Richard Harris (Vic Jenkins), Richard Raymond (Jimmy)

Mike Ransome is back! So, are Mattei and Fragasso! *Strike Commando 2* is an all-out, out-loud, loud-shooting action film.

At the end of *Strike Commando*, the film was in "Present Day." So either Part 2 was going to go back into Vietnam or tell a different story. Namsploitation is left behind. Ransome winds up mixed in a sort of James Bond-Indiana Jones-*Romancing the Stone* kind of thing with Richard Harris as Vic Jenkins, his former commanding officer, now a CIA agent.

Like the first one, many shots are fired.

Jenkins is kidnapped. Ransome meets Rosanna near the Burmese Plain. There is shooting. Double crossing. Ransome and Rosanna flirt a lot. Then something blows up and the movie ends. Unlike the first one, there is sync sound. (Many of these Italian films shifted to sync sound in the second half of the '80s.)

This sequel succeeds in being just as much fun as the first *Strike Commando* while actually being a completely goofy rip-off of more lighthearted 1980s action films. A lot of the banter between the leads seemed smuggled in from *Romancing the Stone* or *High Road to China* or *Jake Speed*. The viewer knows they'll end up together the question is: Will there be as much wonderful, senseless violence as in the first film? The answer: almost.

The film starts in James Bond territory. Then there is a drinking contest in a bar owned by a wisecracking dame. The *Raiders* lightbulb flashes on. Except instead of the contest involving drinking someone under the table, the loser is whoever belches first. Nuttiness reigns supreme here. For 15 or 20 minutes, the film is in *Raiders* land. Then the couple head out into the jungle and it's *Romancing the Stone* or, in this case, stones. Several big diamonds. Then the film becomes an all-out melee.

There's nothing like a good melee to keep a film going. *Strike Commando 2*, once it runs out of plot, survives on good old-fashioned melee. Ransome shooting over here. Rosanna shrieking over there. Pure sweet chaos. That's what makes this film worth a viewing. It keeps ripping off various films until it slides hard into an overwhelming mass of dead bodies and bullets. Even the closing freeze frame, with our heroes arm in arm walking off into the sunset, features a dead body.

Striker

Director: Enzo G. Castellari (as Stephen M. Andrews)

Screenplay: Umberto Lenzi, Tito Carpi

Producer: Giorgio Salvioni

Cast: Frank Zagarino (John Slade), Melonee Rodgers (Marta), John Phillip Law (Morris), Werner Pochath (Houtman)

It turns out John Rambo wasn't an isolated incident. There are a lot of guys like Rambo in this world. Most of them are American and incredibly buff, but have a gentler side. Most of them keep getting sent into jungle-type regions to kick ass and shoot crowds of jerks with guns. John Slade is one of these gentlemen. He's just trying to live his life in Florida. He's been in the Armed Forces. Now he wants to rest. But he keeps getting pulled back in. Shooting ensues.

Another Italian *Rambo: First Blood Part 2* rip-off, this one finds the large John Slade being sent to Nicaragua to rescue a journalist named Morris from Sandinistas. Russians are involved. A woman named Marta is going to help Slade. She may or may not be on his side. Slade goes in. Rescues Morris. Betrayal occurs. Shooting follows. In the end, Slade is back in the U.S. enjoying life.

Is it exciting? Yes. It's directed by Enzo G. Castellari, who always does a great job. *The Bronx Warriors* indicated that he was an expert at shooting down large groups of people. *Striker* is no different. Some character development is thrown in but it doesn't go above and beyond the very basic amount needed to keep things moving when the action has paused or to get Slade really whipped up into a frenzy. There is also some brief political debate but it feels like a trope is being repeated, not because the filmmakers seem to have any stake in that. They are simply doing what the film that made all the money did.

The opening scene takes place in a sweaty arena with large groups of people cheering and cheering as a cockfight begins. The enjoyment of watching two enraged roosters ripping each other apart while people scream themselves into a frenzy escapes me. But the people here seem to love it. There are many cockfighting scenes in Italian films. It makes one wonder if these cultures really engage in this much cockfighting. Or did the Italians think that this was what these cultures did. There's no reason to show them engaged in philosophical debate. Bring out the cocks and have them fight.

Striker has shooting, fistfighting, torture, betrayal, evil Commies and cockfights. If you put that on a pizza, all those toppings might be too much. But, with brain on or brain off, this film definitely does exactly what it says, and exactly what action films should do: It gives us action, plenty of it. It's all shot well and the

film doesn't overstay its welcome. And, in the end, Slade says, "I hate violence."

The Sword of Bushido

Director: Adrian Carr
Screenplay: James Wulf Simmons
Producer: John Lamond
Cast: Richard Norton (Zac Connors), Judy Green (Billie), Rochelle Ashana (Suay), Kovit Wattanatoon (Chal)

The Sword of Bushido is one of the few films I've encountered that mixes World War II with Vietnam. Zac Connor is a Vietnam vet and overall great guy whose grandfather fought in World War II. Grandfather was killed in the jungles of Thailand by the Japanese. When Zac flies there to find his body, he also finds a katana sword called "Hand of the Goddess of Mercy." He decides to return it to Japan. But first he has to fight a whole slew of guys and gals who want the sword for their own.

Richard Norton is one hell of a martial arts guy. He carries the fight scenes throughout *The Sword of Bushido* well. There are also several wonderful non-martial arts action scenes in which he takes part. A chase scene in which Zac takes a go-kart and races after a car in the streets is very entertaining. The stunts are quite thrilling. One can see how Norton ended up in Hong Kong films as they were the only ones that had action and stunt sequences quite like this.

The movie moves at a nice pace from San Diego to the jungles of Thailand to Japan. Zac takes time out to fool around with army personnel (i.e., a hot lady) over a copier. Then he meets a jungle commando named Suay and he fools around with her a bit in Japan. Interspersed with these dalliances, there is good action. Zac wields a hell of a katana when he needs to. There are swordfights, gunfights and kung fu brawls.

As an actor, Norton has sort of an Australian Dean Martin quality. He's not a great actor but he has charm. He occasionally feels like maybe he's coasting on the acting side of things. But definitely not in the action. He's not as wooden as, say, Edward John Stazak but he's no Gregory Peck. He simply kicks ass.

There is something interesting about a film that begins with a black-and-white flashback to World War II and then has as its hero a Vietnam vet. Two very different wars. It was the World War II vet who committed a theft (Grandpa stole the sword) and the Vietnam vet who has to go back into the jungle to find out what happened and get the sword out. Sort of like a *Missing in Action* but with a dead grandpa and an ancient katana sword.

Ten Zan: The Ultimate Mission

Directors: Ferdinando Baldi, Pak Jong-Ju

Screenplay: Yane Sempleton
Producers: Seino Glam, Massimo Vigliar
Cast: Mark Gregory (Jason), Frank Zagarino (Lou), Romano Kristoff (Ricky), Sabrina Siani (Glenda)

Evil scientists are up to no good (it has something to do with injections and super soldiers). Several American soldiers, played by Italian actors, are sent to stop them. Mark Gregory, from the *Bronx Warrior* films, plays a tough guy with a short haircut. There is a lot of shooting, some car chases and some widespread destruction.

According to Wikipedia and the IMDb, the film was made in North Korea. One doesn't see a lot of action films coming out of there. The North Koreans must have loved the action films that the Italians were making so they hired Ferdinando Baldi to visit their country and make *Ten Zan*. I am a big fan of Baldi's work, especially *War Bus,* so I would probably hire him too. Apparently, there was some fiddling around and some addition of propaganda to make North Korea seem more advanced.

There were so many low-budget Italian films in every genre at that time. To think that North Korea hired Italians to make a film. Then the film was shown at festivals as an example of North Korean cinema. That seems to be the strangest moment. That would be like China hiring Ted V. Mikels to make a film for them and then showing it as a cultural exchange. Why go to the Italian cinema? Why an action film? Maybe it was an attempt to show themselves as being "with it"?

There are better films to watch than *Ten Zan* if one wants to see Italian action-exploitation at its best. But there is only one example of North Korea using Italian filmmakers to try to show them at their best. It's a very strange bit of filmmaking. I wish it was more exciting.

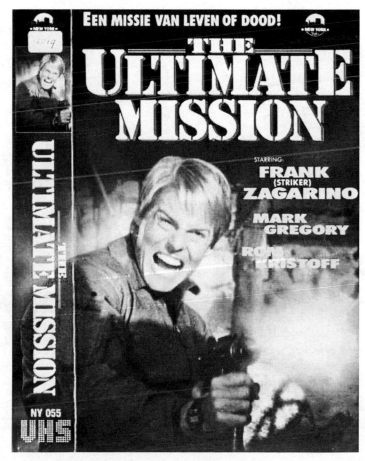

Thunder Warrior 3

Director, Producer: Fabrizio De Angelis
Screenplay: Fabrizio De Angelis, Dardano Sacchetti
Cast: Mark Gregory (Thunder), John Phillip Law (Sheriff Jeff), Horst Schon (Bill), Werner Pochath (Colonel Magnum), Ingrid Lawrence (Sheena)

The Thunder Warrior saga ends in a strange, slightly inconclusive way that doesn't actually follow on from the previous adventures. Thunder protects an Indian reservation from a bunch of white guys who have formed a paramilitary survivalist organization and go crazy killing Native Americans. Thunder enters the town. John Phillip Law is the sheriff and the white guys "who run the county" are killing. The movie is as much fun as the others but feels as disconnected.

The characters from the first two films are gone. Rusty the Deputy is gone. Bo Svenson's sheriff is gone. Sheila is gone. Thunder may be the same guy but he's slightly different now. He has a more financial agenda, which seems a little out of character. But with Fabrizio De Angelis and Dardano Sacchetti in charge, I'm surprised a gate of Hell wasn't opened.

Thunder Warrior III continues chronicling the really weird world of Thunder, the Navajo warrior who lives in the Arizona desert right near the town in the U.S. with the largest concentration of racists since the big Southern cities broke up after the Civil War. Thunder is first seen hunting with a bow and arrow alongside a Native American child. Then we see a group of white guys storming onto the reservation and blowing up mobile homes filled with innocent Native Americans. Thunder heads into town to speak with the sheriff and demand financial retribution.

The Billy Jack of Italian cinema is as goofy as one might imagine him to be. Mark Gregory does come up with another facial expression in this film. The white guys pepper his home with bullets and he shows fear. It

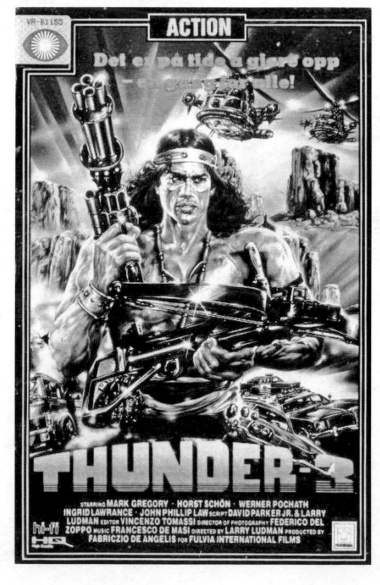

is as odd as one might imagine. It seems strangely inappropriate for the scene as he's come up against much worse. But it *is* another face.

Traxx

Director: Jerome Gary
Screenplay: Gary DeVore
Producer: Gary DeVore, Richard McWhorter
Cast: Shadoe Stevens (Traxx), Priscilla Barnes (Mayor Cray), Willard E. Pugh (Deeter), Robert Davi (Aldo Palucci)

Traxx fought in several wars. A no-nonsense tough guy, he lives in a Texas town with a lot of crime but he has decided to give it all up and bake his own brand of delicious cookies. One cannot fault a man for following a dream. When Traxx discovers that he needs more capital to produce his scrumptious delights, he gets himself hired on as the man who will clean up his town. And then, he'll retire and make those cookies.

Shadoe Stevens heads up *Traxx* with his awesome hair, his big smile and that great voice. He has no problem sitting on the hood of his Jeep with a submachine gun and shooting the thugs who line the streets. He has no problem telling "scum" in a bar to have a nice night and if they come back they're dead. He has a bit of Sledge Hammer's attitude towards crime but he's a bit more genial. He smiles more. And he doesn't sleep with his gun.

This movie is a parody of action films of the time (specifically films like *Cobra, Raw Deal* and *Sudden Impact*): films whose lead character is a cop or peace officer working outside of the law to do what no one else will. Like Sledge Hammer, Traxx is that character taken to the extreme, although, technically, if you've seen *Cobra*, you might think they could have been more extreme. *Traxx* has a real glorious bonhomie to it. It's sort of a par-

ody but not quite. If one was unskilled in the ways of 1980s action films, one might be tempted to take this seriously.

The film glorifies the violence it presents but in a funny way. As mentioned, a smiling Traxx sitting on the hood of his car shooting a gun could be misconstrued by someone with no sense of humor. The follow-up scene where the viewer sees all the dead bodies hanging by their feet with labels on them, marking their crimes, is even funnier. There is a scene in a bar where Traxx separates the "good" from the "scum." He lets the "good" go. And then he admonishes the "scum."

"You've got three choices. You can be good, gone or dead." The "scum" leaves in a line. And Traxx shakes each of their hands and says, "Have a nice night. Don't come back or I'll kill you." "Nice to meet you. Come back and die at my hands." "Goodnight and be-gone." It's a very funny scene.

One wonders why this film wasn't a huge hit. It perfectly nails the action hero of the time, as *Sledge Hammer!* did at its best. Possibly too many people were upset by the cartoon violence? It's been known to happen. In 1983, I watched *Airplane!* with someone who sat stone silent the whole time and then let out a shout of "Come on! That couldn't happen!" *Traxx* somehow got lost in the mix of 1980s excitement. Watch it today. At least to hear Mr. Stevens' awesome voice.

Troma's War

Directors: Samuel Weil, Michael Herz
Screenplay: Mitchell Dana, Lloyd Kaufman. Eric Harttler, Thomas Martinek
Producers: Lloyd Kaufman, Michael Herz
Cast: Carolyn Beauchamp (Lydia), Sean Bowen (Taylor), Michael Ryder (Parker), Jessica Dubin (Dottie), Steven Crossley (Marshall)

Troma's War is a gloriously epic battle set on an island full of revolutionaries, commandos and survivors from a plane crash. In Troma fashion, much of the film is played for maximum gross-out, maximum offense-giving and absolute insanity. And it works. It also has slightly sharper satire than usual and characters who you get to like amidst all the shooting and insanity.

This film was meant to be Troma's Big One. Their film *The Toxic Avenger* got some good word of mouth going, and then *Class of Nuke 'Em High* made the rounds. They had been acquiring quite a few films to bolster up their backlog, often retitling them to make them sound crazier than they were. *Curse of the Screaming Dead* became *Curse of the Cannibal Confederates.* *In Deadly Heat* became

Stuff Stephanie in the Incinerator. With *Troma's War,* the guys at Troma were poised to make the big step.

In the mid–80s they were at the same level as New Line Cinema. Then New Line released *A Nightmare on Elm Street* (1985) and their fortunes were about to change. Troma put all their eggs in the very expensive basket of *Troma's War.* Then they proceeded to spend several years going back and forth with the MPAA, having the hell cut out of it. It turned into an incoherent, neutered mess. Troma never became one of the majors. But they certainly are one of the Funsters.

Troma's War is now available in its complete form, and it rocks. It begins a lot like *Lost:* the aftermath of a plane crash and the survivors trying to figure out where they are. They meet the revolutionaries, led by a very Aryan gentlemen, and they learn that group's plan (a plan that the MPAA hated): It involves AIDS and it is offensively strange almost to the point of comedy but not quite. The survivors must stop these nuts, and that involves a lot of training, a montage with people being shot out of trees in slow motion and—this is the kicker—several shootout action scenes that are so kinetic and so crazy that they are all almost overwhelming. That's a compliment.

It's too bad Troma got screwed because *Troma's War* is an excellent addition to their catalogue. There are actual moments of character development and, surprise surprise, several characters that the viewer doesn't want to see die. When did that happen before or since in a Troma film? It showed that when they really tried, they could make a film that was 100 percent Troma but also a little more classy, a little more powerful, than their regular output. With of course lots and lots of violence, dumb jokes, great offensive moments and some boobs.

White Ghost

Director: BJ Davis
Screenplay: Gary Thompson
Producers: Jay Davidson, William Fay
Cast: William Katt (Steve Shepard), Ros-

alind Chao (Thi Hau), Martin Hewitt (Wacko), Wayne Crawford (Walker), Reb Brown (Major Cross)

Fifteen years after the end of the Vietnam War, Steve Shepard decides it's time to leave the jungles of Vietnam with his girlfriend Thi Hau. The Vietnamese soldiers know him as the White Ghost. He's a stealthy monster living in a big thatched treehouse. And he has been collecting information about dead soldiers in the jungle. Shepard contacts the U.S. government to have someone bring him back. The government sends a Special Force led by the crazy Walker, who has a score to settle with Shepard. Has this group been sent to rescue or kill the White Ghost? How many Vietnamese soldiers will get gunned down?

Well, a *lot* of soldiers get shot down. As in many of these Namsploitation film, the heroes shoot down a dozen of them. Suddenly, a dozen more run up. One can only imagine what the extra casting call was like. "Seeking Vietnamese men willing to wave guns and get shot down a lot. May play multiple roles." Someone with more time on their hands can tally up the body count.

It seems as if the government would send someone to rescue Shepard. But, they send in this group led by a guy who wants revenge on Shepard. So it becomes more of a "dead or alive" thing with Walker's group attacking Shepard and Thi Hau, while the Vietnamese attack everyone. As this goes on, Shepard is trying to get himself and Thi Hau to the spot where the chopper will pick them up.

William Katt turns out to be a pretty great action hero, a human guy who has become one with the jungle. Rosalind Chao spends a lot of time being tortured and she's

good at it. Walker's group is a mix of crazy guys (one named Wacko) and guys who don't think this mission is a good one. The Vietnamese commander is an asshole.

White Ghost starts as a standard bit of Namsploitation and gets better as it goes. The last half-hour is particularly exciting. There could be a little more clarification regarding what Walker is supposed to be doing. Was he sent to kill Shepard? Or is this his own deci-

Starring WILLIAM KATT, ROSALIND CHAO, MARTIN HEWITT, WAYNE CRAWFORD, and REB BROWN
Executive Producer JOEL LEVINE   Written By GARY THOMPSON
Produced By JAY DAVIDSON and WILLIAM FAY
Directed By B.J. DAVIS

sion? The viewer is a little unsure as to what exactly is going on throughout. Reb Brown is in this as the officer who learns about Shepard. Brown doesn't arrive in the jungle until the very end. He's saved like a really good dessert or a nice cup of cappuccino. He leaps out of the helicopter, guns blazing and shrieking. Suddenly, all seems right with the world.

World Gone Wild

> *Director:* Lee H. Katzin
> *Screenplay:* Jorge Zamicona
> *Producer:* Robert L. Rosen
> *Cast:* Richard Israel (Lance), Bruce Dern (Ethan), Adam Ant (Derek), Michael Pare (George), Catherine Mary Stewart (Angie)

World Gone Wild is set in 2087, long after the apocalypse. Long after all the water in the world has dried up. But a small community in the desert has some water. A crazy man, Derek (Adam Ant), has a group of white-suited zealots following him. Derek wants control of the town. Actually, he's mainly a jerk who likes hurting people who aren't his white-suited pals. Along comes Ethan (Bruce Dern), who may have magic powers. He will help protect the people in the desert. Dern spends most of the movie acting like he's in another movie. He listens to his Walkman and smokes some doobies out in the desert. There are some scenes where one might think that they were formed around whatever it was Bruce Dern was doing at that time.

World Gone Wild is an post-apocalyptic adventure made past the prime of the post-apocalyptic films but still carrying on some of the traditions. Ethan is a hippy. There's a biker guy, a cowboy guy and a guy in a purple leotard. Actually, it all sounds like post-apocalyptic Village People but it's not. There are good actors having a good time with a script that might be on the parodic side. But it's tough to tell. Like the slasher parodies of the early 1980s, the closer they get to perfectly parodying the films, the more they look exactly like the kind of films they are parodying.

Let's call it a serious post-apocalyptic film with touches of humor in it. There's some great action and a fine sense of scope when the people of this small town surround it with a wall of wrecked cars. There's a sense of community with children being schooled in a school bus. Derek and his gang are frightening. One of the gang members, Lance, is played by Richard Israel of *Police Academy 7: Mission to Moscow* and he does a good job of bringing the loner-being-brainwashed feel of things to life. Bravo!

World Gone Wild is well-made and exciting. Now, at the same time, it does wander through the exact same tropes we'd been deep in for most of the decade. And it presents all these ideas (water shortages, for example) as if they were brand new. But there is enough brio in this film to recommend it.

1989

Highest grossing films in the U.S.
1. *Batman*
2. *Indiana Jones and the Last Crusade*
3. *Lethal Weapon 2*
4. *Look Who's Talking*
5. *Honey, I Shrunk the Kids*

Highest rated TV shows in the U.S.
1. *The Cosby Show*
2. *Roseanne*
3. *Cheers*
4. *A Different World*
5. *America's Funniest Home Videos*

Big historical events
Berlin Wall falls
The Simpsons premieres
Exxon Valdez spills oil
Tiananmen Square
World Wide Web is born

Action movies

Batman, Indiana Jones and the Last Crusade, Lethal Weapon 2, Tango and Cash, The Karate Kid, Part III, Licence to Kill, Road House, No Holds Barred, Kickboxer, Cyborg, Red Scorpion

Aftershock

Director: Frank Harris
Screenplay: Michael Standing
Producer: Roy McAree
Cast: John Saxon (Capt. Quinn), Richard Lynch (Commander Eastern), Elizabeth Kaitan (Sabina), Jay Roberts, Jr. (Willie), Chuck Jeffries (Danny Girard), Russ Tamblyn (Hank Franklin), Chris Mitchum (Col. Slater)

What a cast! Look at those names. Add Michael Barryman as a very strange fellow out in the wilderness and the excitement ratchets up a little bit higher. And Chris Mitchum! What? This would seem to be the post-apocalyptic action thriller to end all post-apocalyptic action thrillers. But it's not. *Aftershock* evokes a shrug. It feels like it should be better.

A series of big earthquakes rocks the world, reducing the population. Everyone is registered with bar codes on their arms. A young woman named Sabina appears without a bar code. Who is she? Why are Capt. Quinn and Commander Eastern after her? Can the loner rebel Willie save her from them? Is Russ Tamblyn in the same film as everyone else?

There's a feeling of everyone trying in this movie but its ideas have cropped up so many times before that the general level of energy is low. The action scenes are okay. The actors are fine. The mystery of Sabina is interesting but isn't developed. After a time, I got a bit exhausted from all the chasing around and shooting. And all those characters!

This American film seems more lackadaisical than, say, the Italian post-apocalyptic films. There's less verve. *Aftershock* is okay … about as okay as Santiago's *Equalizer 2000*. Neither of these films have too much verve. Each of them are sort of as bland and safe as a crazy post-apocalyptic adventure can be.

Having said that, I really liked Chuck Jeffries in this film. Chuck is doing his best Eddie Murphy impersonation and it's pretty darn good. Chuck makes one think, on more than one occasion, that Eddie has joined the party. He brings life to his scenes, making them fun and enjoyable, more so than a lot of the other actors. Elizabeth Kaitan spends most of her time wide-eyed and clueless. That's her character, unfortunately. She's more fun in, say, *Hellroller*.

Aftershock is the post-apocalyptic film one might show their Grandma if she liked this kind of movie and didn't want to watch anything too wild and crazy.

American Force 3: High Sky Mission

Director: Philip Ko
Screenplay: Benny Cho
Producers: Betty Chan, Joseph Lai
Cast: Mike Abbott, Arthur Garrett, Gregory Rivers, Peter Bosch, Patrick Helman, Alan English

This Joseph Lai film intercuts footage of American troops trying to protect the Philippines from the Japanese with footage from a film with Filipinos attacking the Japanese. All of it dubbed in an amusing manner. In response to someone asking what he thinks about going after the enemy, the commander says, "I'll tell you what I think. Let's fuck them up!"

The sign of a truly strange movie is this: You watch the movie and write down the names of the actors in the opening credits. Then you go online to get their character names. And the online lists of the actors are different from the names you wrote down from the credits. How does that happen? What movie are we all watching? That's just plain goofy.

No, that's The Power of Lai.

The third entry in the *American Force* series is as screwy and filled with shooting as the previous ones. After the bombing of Pearl Harbor, the Philippines are being swarmed by Japanese. A crack team of American Marines, led by Cobra, enters the jungle. Their mission:

stop the Japanese. The Japanese army guys are wacky because they are so damn honorable. The Filipinos swear a lot, which is great. And the Americans ... well, if you've ever seen Mr. Abbott in any of the Ho/Lai ninja films, you know that the Americans are in super-competent, yet slightly goofy, hands.

There are very long scenes of darkness. Epic battles are fought but it's impossible to see a damn thing. The groups of guerrillas argue with each other, the shooting begins, and it's impossible to see what's going on for minutes on end. In fact, it looks a bit like those dark scenes could be made up of one long shot. For long stretches, it doesn't look like the slivers of light that *are* visible move at all.

American Force 3 is dumb fun with action that runs contrary to the way many humans act.

American Ninja 3: Blood Hunt

Director, Screenplay: Cedric Sundstrom
Producer: Harry Alan Towers
Cast: Steve James (Jackson), David Bradley (Sean), Michele Chan (Chan Lee), Marjoe Gortner (The Cobra)

It's *American Ninja 3* and Michael Dudikoff is gone. His replacement is a karate champ (also a ninja) named Sean. Second, Sam Firstenberg is gone, and Cedric Sundstrom is in charge of the action. Third, Golan & Globus are no longer the producers (although Cannon did release the film). Harry Alan Towers produced this one. He was an exploitation producer of the highest order and his films always had a sort of sleazy cheapness to them unlike, say, Cannon Films at their best. *American Ninja 3* feels like Towers all the way.

There are several good comparisons to moving from Golan & Globus to Harry Alan Towers. Imagine the Doors continuing after Jim Morrison died. Imagine the TV series *Community* continuing for a season after its creator-creative force had been fired. The first two *American Ninja* films feel like high-class low-budget action of the 1980s. *Blood Hunt* feels, and looks, kind of cheap. It has several scenes that appear to be post-dubbed. The ac-

tion isn't shot as well as in the first two. In several fight scenes, the camera is too far away. And in true exploitation style, plotlines start and then fade away. The first two movies balanced on a razor's edge of comedy and action without getting too ridiculous, *3* piles on the silliness.

Sean never fully takes control of the film. He doesn't have much presence and is rather nondescript. Jackson is still large and in charge but even he feels slightly restrained. More time is spent with Marjoe Gortner as the evil Cobra (who even gets his own closing credits song) and Chan Lee the Asian Ninja who helps the guys. Chan Lee actually fights more in the last half-hour than Sean does due to some plot developments with a terrorist general and a wicked virus that doesn't really seem that bad.

The film is a jumble of action scenes, some decent, others just okay. Gortner delivers speech after speech about something or other. And the heroes creep around right before and after fight scenes. The film starts off seeming like it's going to focus on a world-wide karate championship at Port San Luco. But the karate championship fades away after a bit. Sean's ninja master is kidnapped.

The ninjas here are supernatural. Chan Lee is a master of disguise, *a la* Scooby Doo villains. Sean is able to reject the ravages of a deadly disease simply by thinking hard and having a bright red light flashed on him. And a series of men in their underpants become fully clothed ninjas with a flask of smoke and an explosion.

If this review sounds negative, it's not. *American Ninja 3* is foolishness. It seems as if the filmmakers watched the first two and didn't quite understand. Everything about *3* is slightly off. That makes for a great evening of entertainment! It's not lovable like the first two but it's screwball. Thank you, Harry Alan Towers.

The Black Cobra 2

Director, Screenplay: Edoardo Margheriti (as Dan Edwards)
Producer: Luciano Appignani

Cast: Fred Williamson (Lt. Malone), Nicholas Hammond (Lt. McCall), Emma Hoagland (Peggy Mallory), Majib Jadali (Asad Cabuli), Ned Hourani (Mustapha)

Lt. Malone is back! And he's in Chicago. But unorthodox police procedures somehow get him sent to the Philippines where he becomes involved with terrorists and crazy people. He is teamed with Lt. McCall, a real no-nonsense cop. This film seems to have less of an involvement with any sort of *Cobra* rip-off than the first film did. In fact, this film has a slight touch of whimsy mixed in with the action.

When Malone is told he's being reassigned, he says "Paris?" His captain says, "Manila." That's a bit of a heart-sinker because that means this is another cheap Italian action film shot in the Philippines—and with no Weng Weng, But there are a few moments of fun here. The closing sequence with Malone and McCall invading an office building to stop terrorists is great. Until they actually have to stop the terrorists, and then it goes a bit flat.

Black Cobra 2 reminds me of *Karate Warrior II*. The first *Karate Warrior* was a straightforward *Karate Kid* rip-off, as serious as that movie with occasional lighter moments. But the second one was set in Florida and was kind of goofy. They get the main character wrong and make him unlikable and the whole thing never gets too serious. *Black Cobra 2* is like that. Putting Malone in the Philippines is a bit too exotic for this cop. If the movie did a fish-out-of-water sort of thing (and it does briefly), it may have gone somewhere. But after a time, the location becomes generic and one has to focus on Fred and the leading lady.

At the end of the day, *Black Cobra 2* is fine. What it has to do with the first film is a question that may never be answered. And it makes the mistake of putting the most exciting chase at the start of the movie (Malone chases a motorcycle rider through a series of streets and parking garages). Williamson is agile but there are several moments where he loses his balance. And he's presented as out-of-breath near the end but he still keeps coming, which is cool. Plus, the way he takes out the biker is awesome and gross. Fred Williamson is always cool. He gets in there. He kick ass. His mustache takes names. He does that in this film, as always. But there are better places to go to check out his true-to-form cool-ass action hero style.

Born to Fight

Director: Bruno Mattei
Screenplay: Claudio Fragasso
Producer: Franco Gaudenzi
Cast: Brent Huff (Sam Wood), Mary Stavin (Maryline Kane), Werner Pochath (Duan Loc), Romano Puppo (Alex Bross), John van Dreelen (General Weber)

Brent Huff was in Bruno Mattei's *Cop Game* and *Strike Commando*. In *Born to Fight*, he plays Sam Wood, emotionally scarred but cool, like Michael Douglas in *Romancing the Stone*. Sam, a POW in Vietnam, lost several friends in the prison camp. Maryline, a reporter, wants to do a story on the prison camp and hires Sam to return to Nam and find it. But everything is not what it seems.

For a Mattei-Fragasso joint, this film is actually fairly normal. Usually their films go off the rails and become crazy and memorable. *Born to Fight* is pretty straightforward. There's our good guy, Sam, who dresses like Indiana Jones but fires a lot of submachine guns. There's the attractive lady who kind of vanishes from the film for a long time. Then there are the bad guys. It might be Mattei's least crazy film (that I have seen).

The film has solid action scenes. Maybe Sam with his submachine gun firing in slo-mo is a bit over-the-top but why would you be reading this if you didn't enjoy over-the-top action? Sam even has his own Al Festa–composed theme, a rousing synth tune that mixes John Williams and something from a 1980s video game. It usually plays when he is doing something heroic.

There's a scene where he's hiding out, slowly approaching the prison camp, and we see several guards with guns strolling around on watch. And that music is playing. One would expect something to happen right there but it doesn't. It does later but not there. Maybe it's a clever Al Festa ploy to throw expectations off.

The film does have a slightly overcomplicated plot. With POWs, two bad guys, Maryline's story, Sam trying to rescue his buddies, flashbacks … there's a lot going on. It also has a suspenseful, nicely done scene where a POW is made to swim across a booby-trapped river. Later on, Sam has to

recreate that swim. That time it isn't quite as suspenseful, especially because they keep cutting to Huff treading water with his head sticking out of the water staring daggers up at the prison camp commander. After the second time, it becomes a little funny. But the first time it was done, it was good.

A Bruno Mattei film that works. One doesn't quite know what to say

The Cage

Director, Producer: Lang Elliott

Screenplay: Hugh Kelley

Cast: Lou Ferrigno (Billy), Reb Brown (Scott), Michael Dante (Tony Baccola), Mike Moroff (Mario), Marilyn Tokuda (Morgan), Al Leong (Tiger Joe), James Shigeta (Tin Lum Yin)

The Cage begins strong with best buddies Billy and Scott saving each other's lives out in the field in Vietnam. While hanging onto Scott, who is dangling from a helicopter, Billy is shot in the head. Years later, the two run a bar together. Billy is now a gentle giant with the brains of a seven-year-old. Scott takes care of him. They have a good time together.

The film starts off being about the two pals, one brain-damaged, and gradually it becomes about Chinese and Italian gangsters arranging underground cage fights, many of which end in death. Billy and Scott get mixed up with them, along with a Mexican gang, some low-rent hoods, a reporter and an undercover police officer. Billy is kidnapped and must fight in the cage.

There is action. Some good fighting in the cage (if that's your type of thing). Some drama. Scott and Billy make a good team. But the film separates them too soon and doesn't reunite them until late in the game. They would have been more entertaining together than apart. Lou Ferrigno is big and charming as ever, and Reb Brown lets out some awesome shrieks during the fighting. *The Cage* would have been a more interesting film if it had stuck to the stars rather than getting lost in its secondary characters.

City Cops

Director: Chia Yung Liu
Screenplay: Barry Wong
Producer: King-Fai Siu
Cast: Cynthia Rothrock (Inspector Cindy), Kiu Wai Miu (Ching Shing), Ken Tong (Kent Tong), Suki Kwan (May Tong)

There's a reason why I left proper Hong Kong action films out of this book: They really kick ass. They're astounding. Hong Kong went into crazy realms that no one would have anticipated. From the crazy stunt action of Jackie Chan's films, such as *Project A* and *Police Story,* to Sammo Hung's more straightforward action films like the wonderful *Eastern Condors* ... this world was incredible. It deserves its own comprehensive book (and several have gotten close). So I kept away from those films for this book. (Yes, a few Ho-Lai films have shown up.) However, Cynthia Rothrock is awesome. I felt I needed to do at least one from her Hong Kong world. I chose *City Cops.*

It's pure Hong Kong, with action scenes that are exciting and surprising mixed with comedy scenes that seem ridiculously out of place but somehow seem to be perfect. Jackie Chan used to do that a lot. *Police Story* and the Lucky Star films are loaded with that. It's sort of the same way that Indian films have all those musical numbers (even during intense horror films). It's a cultural thing that is really freaking wonderful. Never argue with awesome. *City Cops* is awesome.

Everyone is after a diamond smuggler, including a woman from the FBI (Cynthia). It leads to a lot of fighting. Cynthia really goes to town and the fight scene are great: flipping, spinning, kicking. If you have watched one of her American films and thought that she was too slow or awkward, watch this. The scenes

are sped up, but only slightly. The stunts are the stunts. You can't fake when she does the running up the wall and flipping thing. Hong Kong films from this period continually impress.

The dubbing is silly. There's probably a subtitled version out there somewhere. This is a good Hong Kong action film. This was a time period where you'd be hard pressed to find a bad one.

Cy Warrior: Special Combat Unit

Director: Giannetto De Rossi
Screenplay: Giannetto De Rossi, David Parker, Jr.
Producer: Fabrizio De Angelis
Cast: Frank Zagarino, Henry Silva, Sherri Rose, Brandon Hammond, James Summers

Cy Warrior sounds like the story of an old Jewish warrior who is making one last stand before closing down his deli forever. But it is in fact an Italian take on a sort of *Terminator*-type thing with a touch of *Terminator 2* (even though *2* was still in the future). On top of that, the film gives us Henry Silva playing to his "I'm yelling at everybody" perfection.

The government is working on an experimental cyborg warrior. Cy is accidentally sent out into the world. Silva and a team of men are assigned to destroy it before it goes on some sort of rampage. Cy befriends a kid and his older sister and learns a bit about humanity. There are a lot of shootouts, many of them involving Silva's soldiers shooting up public places. It culminates in a fight in the woods.

Cy Warrior is kind of dumb. It starts very matter-of-factly with the warrior being accidentally released and the soldiers going after him. Cy himself isn't all that cyborg. When he turns his head, they dub in a whirring sound but it ends up looking silly after a while. The kid and his sister are about as clichéd as one might imagine. The kid is all "Gosh! Wow! A cyborg!" The sister wants to teach the cyborg how to be more human. Cy is on the dull side.

Luckily, Silva is there at his angriest to get in some real good yelling. He's pretty much hilarious in this one. Clint Eastwood in *Heartbreak Ridge* didn't yell at his soldiers this much. In fact, after some of the semi-bland, semi-silly sequences with Cy and the siblings, Silva's constant profanity and belittling is a breath of fresh air.

The action scenes are mainly lots of people shooting at Cy, and Cy not falling down. It's all pretty straightforward. There's something about Fabrizio De Angelis–related films that makes everything so strange. They seem removed from the world that any human being might live in. Cy is actually a less convincing robotic guy than R.O.T.O.R. That's saying something!

Cy Warrior has one sequence that really sells it. The closing sequence does something that one rarely sees in films like this. It actually became poignant and sweet for a few moments. All I will say is that the boy is wounded, he's getting operated on and it's very serious—and Cy saves the day. (That's not much of a spoiler.) But the overwrought music, hectic editing and stoic skills of Frank Zagarino combine to make the closing minutes quite something. I watched those closing minutes three times in a row.

Deadly Breed

Director, Screenplay: Charles T. Kanganis

Producers: Richard Pepin, Joseph Merhi

Cast: Blake Bahner (Jake), William Smith (Captain), Addison Randall (Kilpatrick), Mitchell Berger (Lana), Rhonda Grey (Alex), Joe Vance (Vincent)

Pepin and Merhi's PM Entertainment presented *Deadly Breed* as full-on action, the video box featuring the star shrouded in darkness with a huge gun and draped in bullets. There is a naked woman behind him and an exploding car flying through the air at the bottom.

Not all of these things will happen in the film. And the title doesn't quite make sense, as the film is about a crooked cop named Kilpatrick starting a white supremacist militant group. Social worker Jake tries to help nonwhites out. There are murders and corruption and William Smith playing a jerk. The film feels like it is building to big action, maybe even *Final Score*–style revenge. But even though there is some sexual assault and some violence, the whole thing ends in a quote from Leviticus about welcoming strangers. So this film's head may be in a different realm.

Corrupt cops. Good guy shaken down, arrested. His wife is killed. His best friend turns against him. It feels like a build towards an epic battle against Kilpatrick and his men. But by the time the film gets to this point, it's almost over. The director puts all the elements in place for a barn-burner of an action film but forgot to do the action part. It's like watching an elaborate heist film where the planning takes four-fifths of the film and the actual heist is over in a few moments.

From PM Entertainment, this is weird. One expects hyperbole on horror or sci-fi

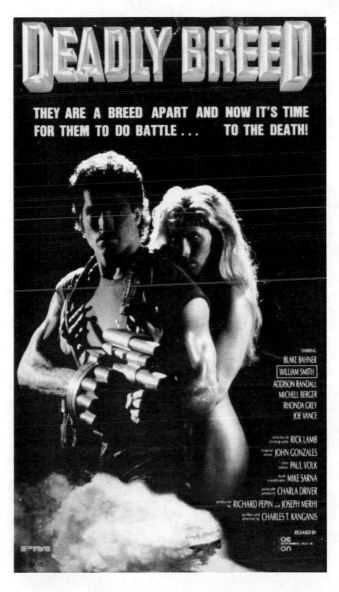

video boxes. That's the name of the game. Look at the packaging and one has no idea what to expect from the movie itself. That works with those genres because what can scare someone or what the future might be are nebulous things. But action is pretty simple. It's movement. It's excitement. It's adrenaline. The *Deadly Breed* video box promises much and doesn't deliver. Maybe that Bible quote is a sign. Maybe this is meant to be a different sort of action film.

However, the final shootout has a lot of violence. And the sexual assault and killing of Lana, Jake's wife, is dwelt on. So is the Bible quote disingenuous? Possibly. The video box certainly is. PM Entertainment, you got me once with *Mayhem* but I let it slide. You got me twice now. Shame on me.

Dragon Hunt

Director: Charles Wiener

Screenplay, Producer: Michael McNamara

Cast: Martin McNamara (Martin), Michael McNamara (Mic), B. Bob (Jake), Heidi Romano (Marla), Sheryl Foster (Nicole)

The McNamara Brothers are back, along with their silver-mohawked nemesis Jake. Jake now has a metal hand to reflect what the Brothers did to him in the previous film. Jake assembles a huge number of mercenaries, ranging from ninjas to paramilitary to just plain rednecks, on one of the Thousand Islands. The purpose? Get the Brothers there and kill them. Will they succeed?

This is hilarious excitement of the highest order. This film, made in an area of the Thousand Islands, is my favorite crazy-ass Canadian film, alongside *Science Crazed* and *Fireballs*. The plot of *Dragon Hunt* involves a series of separate groups going out into the woods and attacking the Brothers. Literally. First it's some guys with a dog. Then some ninjas. Paramilitary folks. Jake acts weirder and weirder and repeats himself a lot.

The Brothers have great mustaches but limited charisma. Their van advertises their martial arts school and they do have kick-ass haircuts. But they don't speak much in the film. The action scenes aren't as exciting as they should be, but they're frequent. And, just as frequently, they are overlaid with a kick-ass power ballad. The main one, written by Billy Butt, about survival and survivors, is appropriate to what's happening.

Dragon Hunt is a very silly movie, from the bad guys who call themselves the People's Private Army to all the slow motion during the final battle scene to the fact that one of the brothers is shot in the leg right before the final fight scene … but in the final fight scene, his leg is fine. This movie may be the best movie ever made.

I don't like to let loose with the hyperbole too often but *Dragon Hunt* is a joyous film that may not be the ad for themselves that the McNamara boys wanted but it is fun to watch. Never take that away from a film. This film is a freaking hoot!

Fist Fighter

Director: Frank Zuniga
Screenplay: Max Bloom
Producer: Carlos Vasallo
Cast: Jorge Rivero (C.J. Thunderbolt), Edward Albert (Punchy), Brenda Bakke (Ellen), Mike Connors (Billy)

C.J. Thunderbolt heads down to the South American town of Rosario to avenge the death of his brother, something he'll do even if it means getting involved with shady characters like Edward Albert as Punchy. Family is everything.

The soundtrack is filled with lots of synths, sometimes leaving the realm of action film and veering into music that might be used to score a video game or maybe home videos of go-kart racing.

A film can shoot itself in the foot when it is, frankly, kind of dull but features a lead character with such a great name. C.J. has a great mullet. He's a little older but still tough as nails. The man was born to fight and, as an added bonus, he was born to avenge his brother's death. C.J. gets an annoying agent to represent him in the fight world and he builds himself up until he gets to the final match.

Fortress of Amerikkka: The Mercenaries

Director, Screenplay: Eric Louzil

Producers: Lloyd Kaufman, Michael Herz

Cast: Gene Lebrok (John Whitecloud), David Crane (Sheriff), Kellee Bradley (Jennifer), William J. Kulzer (Commander Denton), Kascha (Elizabeth)

Action and big boobs do go hand in hand. This was what I learned from *Fortress of Amerikkka,* one of the oddest Troma films I've seen. It begins with a very portentous narrator talking about freedom and America and a lot of '80s-style jingoistic stuff, which might be meant as a joke. The narrator tells us of the problems of the beautiful town known as Troma City, California. It has a corrupt sheriff and police department. And in the woods, mercenaries are up to something. But mainly they party with each other, kill each other when they "disobey" and hunt down people who get too close to them. Then there's John Whitecloud, half-breed, a guy the sheriff hates.

At times, it feels like there are two films going on, one with Whitecloud and the rednecks in the town and one with the mercenaries. Occasionally they meet. Three people go camping in the woods. Two are kidnapped by the mercenaries. The other encounters Whitecloud on the road. It seems like the two threads in the film might never actually come together.

The Whitecloud plotline is a standard racist-cop-gives-someone-who-is-not-white-a-hard-time. The mercenary plot thread has a lot of violence and actresses who are porn stars. There's a liability there. One of the kidnapped campers is played by a porn star named Kascha, a lovely woman with big boobs. But her acting is not so great. The scene where Kascha talks to her friend in a tent probably has the worst acting I've ever seen in a Troma film. I literally had to look away.

The film is maybe a little too long and some of the scenes of the partying mercenaries might have been trimmed. Or some of the more obvious scenes with the racist sheriff could have hit the road. But once the sheriff and some fat vigilantes storm the mercenaries and all hell breaks loose, it become worthwhile. Then the narration returns and one cannot figure out what the hell Troma is up to. But it's nice that they tried it. Whatever it is.

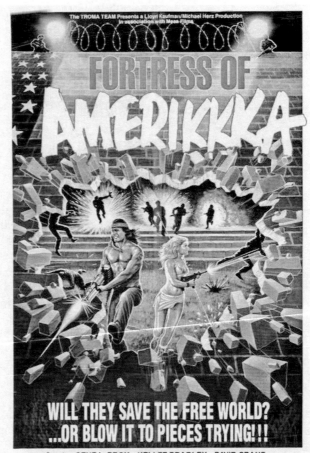

Future Force

Director, Screenplay: David A. Prior
Producer: Kimberley Casey
Cast: David Carradine (Tucker), Robert Tessier (Becker), Anna Rapagna (Marion), William Zipp (Adams), Dawn Wildsmith (Rosanne)

Future Force is my favorite David A. Prior action film. In the future, C.O.P.S. is the name of the main private enterprise company that runs the Los Angeles police department. Tucker is a bounty hunter-police officer. There is a constant scrolling readout that lists fugitives and the dollar amount on their heads. It is pretty dog eat dog. One particular dog, Adams (played by the mighty William Zipp), wants control of everything. He rigs the computer to declare an innocent reporter guilty of treason. Marion, the reporter, hooks up with Tucker and they go on the run. Adams will do whatever it takes to kill this duo.

Tucker has a robotic fitting that goes over his right arm. Invented by a super-nerdy scientist, it's super strong and shoots lasers. The portentous opening narration makes one think this will be like *RoboCop*. David Carradine seems to be having fun shooting a lot of people (with bullets and lasers) and getting in car chases. Marion holds her own. She's played by Anna Rapagna, who was in *Order of the Black Eagle*. She's smoking hot there and does not disappoint here. Zipp overacts with some great slicked-back hair.

Prior's finest action hour-and-a-half is a rip-off but one with clever moments, including nice use of the Fugitive computer on both sides. At the end, there's a twist that actually pays off. The characters work. The film never gets too nasty. Adams has a kick-ass sidekick played by Robert Tessier (*Starcrash*). He's big, bald and scary, but with a sense of fun to him.

This isn't *RoboCop*. The budget is low and sometimes it shows. But, generally, Prior is able to work around and within the confines of his budget. Tucker is a cool anti-hero. Marion is a lovely sidekick. Maybe it was the slight future setting that made this film more fun than the average Prior film. However, just to remind the viewers that this is Prior Town, there are several scenes set in a bar that's also a strip joint. *Future Force* knows where its bread is buttered.

The Hard Way

Director, Screenplay: Michael E. Lemick
Producer: Orlando Corradi
Cast: Miles O'Keeffe (Bull), Milton Morris (Karl), Chuck Biskel (Paolo), Philip Wagner (Pinero), Sarah Sharman (Joanna), Henry Silva (Capt. Wesson)

United States and Colombian relations are at an all-time low. A cocaine drug lord in Colombia won't let anything pass that will not help his Land of Drugs. But, the U.S. government have got a plan. Someone has infiltrated the drug lord's ranks. He will bring out the drug lord and a special group of three commandos will assassinate him. That group is led by Bull, played by Miles O'Keeffe, who speaks with his own voice here. But Bull and his friends are set up. A chase through Colombia begins, with Bull and his gang running from Henry Silva's evil Capt. Wesson.

The Hard Way is Italian all the (hard) way. Like a lot of Italian action films (or Italian exploitation films in general), there isn't much logical set-up. The world is put in place immediately and, suddenly, Bull and his group are in the jungles fighting for their lives and encountering piranhas. The film is mainly a very long chase that sometimes is mighty exciting, sometimes not so much. A lot of helicopters fly around and shoot and people shoot back. Helicopters, in theory, are rather thrilling, but it takes more than pointing a camera at one to make it interesting.

The film really is a long series of tussles between Bull and his guys and Capt. Wesson and his hundreds of men. It's all pretty standard. *The Hard Way* gets out of the gates so quickly that I thought it might be fantastic. It almost is. It could be O'Keeffe's best acting job.

A lot of jungle. A lot of clichéd situations. Henry Silva gives it his all, as always. And it doesn't quite gel into much excitement. Occasionally it's a little tough to figure out who is who. Some of the fights go on past the point where they're worth much. And yet, this isn't a stinker. It's decently put together. The obviousness of the plot is very charming in its own way.

Karate Warrior 2

Director: Fabrizio De Angelis

Screenplay: David Parker, Jr., Fabrizio De Angelis (as Larry Ludman)

Producer: Fulvia International Films

Cast: Kim Stuart (Anthony), Ken Watanabe (Master Kimura), Amy Baxter, Christopher Alan

Anthony has made it back to America. Somewhere around Miami. The music pounds away rather gratingly and a little too upbeat, especially when it plays during the fight scenes. (In the scene where Anthony and his friend are getting their asses handed to them, the music would be more appropriate for a scene in which Valley Girls prance.) Anthony gets mixed up with some guys who know karate. One of them tangled with Anthony's dad back in the day. Fighting ensues. Kimura returns and the Throat of the Dragon is used!

Hello, *Karate Warrior 2*. Anthony is dubbed by the guy who does all of David Warbeck's voices. The fight choreography is better than in the first one. And there is much more fighting and some car action. Plus, the viewer gets to meet Anthony's grandparents. That's something to look forward to.

Anthony is not such a great guy. He has a friend in this movie who is fairly whiny. There is an amusing moment where Anthony's friend enjoys the broadcast of the final fight in the hospital, lets out a "Woo hoo!" and bounces on the bed in his hospital gown. But the film is so perfunctory. The fights just sort of start between Anthony and the bad guys and they escalate until the final fight with Mark Sanders.

Mark Sanders is probably the one weird element of the film. These are college kids fighting. But when Mark Sanders shows up, things gets nasty. The bad kids were part of Sanders' school. They call Sanders back in when Anthony whoops the students' butts. Mark Sanders is kind of a nasty customer. He threatens to break a neck. He clearly wants to kill Anthony. He kind of comes out of nowhere and makes the movie feel quite Italian.

The fact that the filmmakers went backwards in the world of the *Karate Kid* movies

THE ONLY WAY TO SAVE HIS LIFE WAS WIN

FABRIZIO DE ANGELIS presents

KARATE WARRIOR 2

with KIM STUART · KEN WATANABE

directed by LARRY LUDMAN

FOREIGN SALES

V.I.P. INTERNATIONAL FILM srl. Via Caravetti St–Rome–Phone 06-8100521/8100528 Fax 06-8104172

means that when Anthony meets the bad kids here he's already a super karate guy. Yet he keeps getting his ass whooped throughout the film. He even calls Kimura back in. It feels strange because he shouldn't have to reaffirm all of his karate skills. The shifting of the films has made much of what goes on here feel weird. And yet, there are still four more *Karate Warrior* films to come. What's that all about?

Ministry of Vengeance

Director: Peter Maris

Screenplay: Mervyn Emrys, Brian D. Jeffries, Ann Narus

Producers: Brad Krevoy, Steven Stabler

Cast: John Schneider (Reverend David Miller), James Tolkan (Col. Freeman), Ned Beatty (Reverend Bloor), Apollonia (Zarah), Robert Miano (Ali Aboud), Yaphet Kotto (John Whiteside), George Kennedy (Reverend Hughes)

John Schneider has a mustache as the Reverend Miller and he no longer looks like one of them Duke Boys (unless John Holmes was one of the Duke Boys we never saw). Miller is a Vietnam vet. When his wife and daughter are killed by terrorists in an airport attack in Rome, the reverend heads to Lebanon to kill the man who killed his family. James Tolkan shows up and kicks some ass. Ned Beatty plays a rather obsequious priest. George Kennedy is as awesome as always. Yaphet Kotto appears for a few scenes.

That's a lot of professionalism before the camera. And behind the camera, everyone seems to be on their game. The action is exciting. The pace is nice. There might be a bit too much torture and lag time lead-

ing up to the final shootout but, in the end, it's not a problem. Overall, this is a strong action film with the exception of one small mistake that the script makes at the start: The film begins with around ten minutes of Vietnam stuff. Then Miller wakes up from dreaming of Nam in an airport in Rome. He's a reverend. He has a wife and a daughter. Within five minutes, his family is dead and he's back at the U.S. at their funeral. He soon begins to lose his faith and starts his crusade to find the

MINISTRY OF VENGEANCE

Starring JOHN SCHNEIDER, NED BEATTY, JAMES TOLKAN, APOLLONIA, GEORGE KENNEDY, YAPHET KOTTO

They killed his family.
They killed his faith.
Now, they haven't got a prayer.

MEDIA.

terrorist. That is quick-fast plotting. Guaranteed to get the viewer from point A to Point B. Except that the main thrust of the film is about losing faith, believing in something and evaluating whether vengeance is right. But the film doesn't actually show the Reverend Miller being a reverend until after the killing and when the revenge has already set in. In the end, it doesn't really matter. But this isn't a completely brainless action film. It's trying to advance thoughts on the aforementioned subjects. It just doesn't show us that Miller has faith before he loses it.

Ministry of Vengeance isn't tripped up by this issue. It's still a good action film. Recommended. Just an extra scene with him in the pulpit before the killing would have improved things. Plus, after his final speech as he leaves the church to applause, they could have left the saxophone off the soundtrack.

Ninja Academy

Director, Producer: Nico Mastorakis
Screenplay: Jonathan Gift
Cast: Will Egan (Josh), Gerald Okamura (Chiba), Kelly Randall (Gayle), Michael David (Philip), Jeff Robinson (The Mime), Kathleen Stevens (Suzy), Lisa Montgomery (Lynn)

At a ninja academy, a group of wacky misfits, including a mime, prepare to become ninjas. There is a rival academy of ninjas and our group may have to meet them in combat. But first, there's time for zaniness. A lot of falling down and yelling. There will be cleavage. There will be some full frontal nudity. That's all part of the rich tapestry of this Nico Mastorakis production.

Mastorakis was the maker of such films as *Island of Death, Bloodtide, The Zero Boys* and *Blind Date* with Kirstie Alley. The viewer might ask himself: Is he the right man to make a wacky comedy in the style of *Police Academy*? Certainly someone like, say, Jerry Paris was well qualified to direct *Police Academy 2* and *3* after directing over 200 episodes of *Happy Days*. But what about Mastorakis whose film *Island of Death* ends with a man being thrown onto a pile of dry lye followed by a man peeing on him and the lye so he

burns alive? Was this man the new comedy king?

No. he wasn't. He wasn't supposed to direct the film and only got involved at the last minute. He really has no flair for comedy. There's no finesse here, and not a whole lot of laughs. But it's not terrible. The gags come quick and fast. Eventually, the film has a bit of charm that wins the viewer over.

Ninja Academy falls down when it comes to what I call the movie's "Mahoney character." In the first four *Police Academy* films, Steve Guttenberg was Mahoney, the charming wiseacre who always saved the day. He was a great character because he's almost not a misfit at all. Presumably, he is making a decent living working at the parking lot. He just doesn't like authority. In *Ninja Academy*, "the Mahoney character," Josh, is awful. He's a spoiled rich boy whose dad is cutting off his grown-man allowance unless he goes to the academy. Josh is unfunny and totally devoid of charm. That leaves a big hole in the film. *Ninja Academy* needed some sort of strong central comedy force. It doesn't have one.

But it does have the mime who becomes a ninja. And some lovely ladies showing off cleavage. And a strange scene involving a nudist camp and a lot of full frontal nudity. That scene makes it an R-rated film.

Prime Target

Director, Screenplay, Producer: David Heavener
Cast: David Heavener (John Bloodstone), Isaac Hayes (Capt. Thompkins), Tony Curtis (Marrietta Coppella), Robert Reed (Agent Harrington), Jenilee Harrison (Kathy Bloodstone), Andrew Robinson (Commissioner Garth)

Prime Target is the most entertaining of the David Heavener films reviewed in this book. This is Heavener's answer to *Midnight Run*. It is less heavy on the songs than previous films, although "I'm a Honkey Tonk Man" is a fun credits song. It features one of the most eclectic casts he's had in any of his films: Isaac Hayes, Robert Reed, Tony Curtis, Andrew Robinson and Jenilee Harrison.

John Bloodstone (Heavener) is an unorthodox cowboy cop about to lose his job, his house and his wife in quick succession. He is put on a case by the FBI and a slightly crooked commissioner: His job is to transport mob guy Marrietta Coppella from one spot to another. Secretly, no one wants Coppella to make it because he *knows* too much. But Bloodstone doesn't know that. He and Coppella head across the landscape, piling up the bodies as they go.

This one is a bit more of a comedy than the other Heavener films. David seems more suited to do this than his normal Vietnam-flashback-racked heroes. He seems to be having fun in this film, especially during his scenes with Tony Curtis. They turn out to be a good team, arguing with each other like a veteran comedy duo. The film spends its first half hour or so setting up the world of Bloodstone. His answer to a group of kidnappers holding hostages in a warehouse is to grab a flame thrower and set them on fire.

The moment Robert Reed shows up as a tough FBI guy, all rules go out the window. Does Carol know Mike is doing this? She thought he was an architect and he's doing stuff like this? Mike, come on.

Prime Target is a little too slow and then it's a little too fast. Some of the plotting is sent home with a sledgehammer. But Heavener's films always have integrity and some charm, this one most of all.

Provoked

Director: Rick Pamplin

Screenplay: Steve Pake, Tara Untied, Rick Pamplin

Producers: Anthony Bozanich, Rick Pamplin

Cast: Cindy Maranne (Casey Kennedy), McKeiver Jones III (Capt. Rader), Harold Wayne Jones (Mad Dog), Sharon Blair (Eve Carpenter), Phyllis Purante (Big Mama)

In the pleasant town of Sundale, a group of thugs, led by Mad Dog and Big Mama, break into a payroll company to steal their money. At the same time, Casey Kennedy has just gotten married and has to stop back in her payroll company office to grab plane tickets. Casey's husband is taken hostage by the thugs. Casey contacts the police. It turns out that there is no money at the office but the thugs won't go unless they get something. (One of them asks the value of a stapler.) A hostage situation is created and the authorities will do nothing. Casey becomes *Provoked*!

Is *Provoked* a serious film dealing with problems in our so-

ciety, like coddling criminals and allowing innocent people to die while the crooks are given all their rights? Or is *Provoked* one of the goofier action films anyone will ever see? With its overwrought actors who seem to be improvising quite a bit (i.e., yelling over one another) and its strange concept of how bureaucracy works (the head officer at the site keeps calling the mayor to find out what to do), this film seems to be making a point but is doing so in ways that are so obvious and so silly that one can't help but love it. The way one loves a wounded animal or a comedian who desperately wants to make everyone laugh but just can't get a funny joke out.

Mad Dog and Big Mama will steal your heart. They are the most dimwitted loonies ever to be allowed to purchase a gun. They spent the movie in a small office yelling at the hostages and each other. Their assistant thugs (including Mama's rapist son) yell a lot too. They demand things from the police. They kill a TV reporter on live TV. And they never think to double check if the money they were after was in the building. Glorious!

The authorities are not much help either. They constantly manhandle Casey. They wait and wait while crowds chant "Kill them!" Concerned only with his reputation, the mayor is so vague about what should be done that he just keeps having the same conversation with Capt. Rader. The TV reporter is out for herself and has an interview with the most hilariously inept excuse for a psychologist ever.

Casey is the only sane one here and she's overwrought too. However, she meets up with a man named Machine Gun Joe and they save the day ... after viewers endure lots of scenes that keep putting off the action. At one point Casey says, "Why don't you do something real? Take action. Physical action!" *Provoked* is an action film that thrives on strange human behavior as it holds off on the action.

The VHS box says that the ending of this is like Peckinpah. Were there two Peckinpahs who made movies? Gomer Peckinpah, perhaps?

Rapid Fire

Director: David A. Prior
Screenplay: William Zipp, David A. Prior.
Producer: David Marriott
Cast: Joe Spinell (Hanson), Ron Waldron (Mike Thompson), Michael Wayne (Eddy Williams), Dawn Tanner (Corrie), Doug Harter (Pappy)

Joe Spinell's last movie. The appearance of the grandly bearded Doug Harter as Pappy. A special gun that fires all different types of ammunition. David Prior, with no Ted in sight. Music that uses every single key and setting on the latest in 1989 synth technology (and electric guitar). A whorehouse called the Banana offering 23 different flavors of women. *Rapid Fire* is in your living room. The boys at AIP are back.

It's too bad that the film itself is kind of bland because it certainly seems to have all the elements it needs. Yes, Pappy does appear in this one. He is some sort of vague government guy with a huge beer gut, big bald head and a long, scraggly beard. Pappy likes two things: beers and ladies. (Yes, he is 100 percent awesome.) He helps our hero throughout. But, his best scene doesn't involve saving the day. It takes place as he's lounging by a pool with a bunch of gals and his wife shows up with a shotgun.

High hilarity? You bet. But the rest of it just seems to be going through the motions.

Eddy Williams (Michael Wayne, son of John) is a mercenary who frees a prisoner named Mustapha from a naval vessel. Thompson is sent to get Mustapha back and take down Williams. Thompson and Williams were in combat together. Thompson was left for dead by Williams. There may be some clichés involved here. Yes, there is a lot of shooting, but it isn't that thrilling. A lot of it is the "long shot of someone standing with a gun and firing off to one side" variety. There's no verve to the action. Eventually the two guys going at each other for revenge or whatever becomes a little played out.

No one in *Rapid Fire* seems too interested. Yes, some of the actors are acting their hearts out. Yes, they assembled a lot of lovely ladies for the Banana scene. Yes, they have a big Navy boat in the opening sequence. But Joe Spinell doesn't look well. His scenes are tough to watch. And Michael Wayne is just not so great.

The action is just not exciting here. It has that sort of chintzy feel that a lot of AIP action has but chintzy doesn't necessarily mean bad

or bland. A director can have $150 million and have no idea how to shoot action. Many an exciting action video was shot for zero dollars. It's the angles, the editing and the conviction of the actors. *Rapid Fire* definitely has the conviction. Only Pappy seems like he's goofing off. But it doesn't have the angles or the editing. For some reason, one would think end of the '80s Prior would be stronger than earlier in the '80s Prior. That's not really the case here.

Rescue Force

Director, Screenplay, Producer: Charles. L. Nizet

Cast: Lenny Boivin (Yoseph), Kelly Bowen (Kelly), Keiri Smith (Kiki), Cynthia Thompson (Angel), Pierre Agostino (Bandana), Michael St. Charles (F.M.D.), Bo Gritz (Lt. Col. Steel)

This is Charles L. Nizet's masterpiece. He made several other films, including the wonderfully titled *Slaves of Love* (1969), the bland *Commando Squad* (1968) and the strange horror film *Help! I'm Possessed* (1976). But *Rescue Force* is the all-out, kinetic, balls-to-the-wall (with ladies participating) action extravaganza. It was made in Sandy Valley, Nevada, and released on Raedon Home Video at the end of the 1980s. It features a lot of shooting in the deserts around Las Vegas. These stand in for several Middle Eastern locations. There is also some random footage from European locations that could have been shot at any time and for any movie. Whiskey Pete's Casino in Primm, Nevada, features heavily. As do a lot of rooms. Rooms with phones and men on those phones. One of these men, a CIA boss, commands a female operative named Angel to come back to work or risk receiving a "hot fudge enema."

© Raedon Home Video
All rights reserved.

bassador in retaliation for a CIA attack. The Rescue Force is assembled! Operatives around the world are called in. Any time you are planning on assembling an international rescue squad, you know that two things are going to be needed: maximum courage and a series of open phone lines. Planning is everything, and there's a lot of planning going on here. *The Great Escape* doesn't have this much planning and it's twice as long.

Phone calls are made all around the world. Onscreen captions tell us so. We go to Syria, France, Washington, D.C., and Las Vegas and yet it feels like the Force rarely left the general confines of the desert outside of Vegas. That's how intimate *and* international this film is. Eventually they do assemble the group and there is a planning meeting that seems to go on for quite some time. But, luckily for those people less interested in Robert's Rules of Order and more interested in shooting, explosions and gunplay, action completely takes over the last half-hour of the film.

Some films have very precise action scenes. Scenes where the viewer always knows where everyone is in relation to everyone else. James Cameron does action scenes

The average viewer may have never had a boss threaten them with a confectionery enema of any kind. But most people never worked for the CIA. They were never a woman named Angel who spends her vacation hanging out by the pool at Whiskey Pete's and they're not being sent to the Middle East with an elite squad of people that have names like Kiki and Striker.

This is action cinema at its most wild and semi-coherent. It tells the over-complicated story of terrorists who kidnap an Israeli am-

like that. Jackie Chan fight sequences are like that. Then there are the action scenes that seem to be randomly edited montages of people firing guns, explosions going off and people falling down. Hello, *Rescue Force*. Members of the Force shoots randomly at everybody in the desert landscape who isn't them. It is exhilarating.

People hang up very quickly after important phone calls. This is a high-intensity mission that requires razor-sharp precision but would it kill you to say "Goodbye"? What if you never talk to that person again? Aren't you going to feel rotten having left the conversation like that?

Rescue Force is a disjointed, violent mess covered with absolutely awe-inspiring library music from the Riviera Library that will make the average viewer want to climb up onto the nearest roof and leap down on an unsuspecting neighbor. Phone conversations send us around the world in whiplash fashion. One must simply hold on and trust that when the dust has cleared and the calls have ended we will have all the members of the force we need and that they will all be in the same spot. The film is filled with strange experts like the middle-aged Striker and gals with big hair like Kiki and Angel. Generals chomp on cigars. Good wins in the end and everyone winds up in a hot tub at Whiskey Pete's, warm, nude and contented.

Rising Storm

  Director: Francis Schaeffer
  Screenplay: Gary Rosen, William Fay
  Producers: Jay Davidson, James Buchfuehrer
  Cast: Zach Galligan (Artie Gage), Wayne Crawford (Joe Gage), June Chadwick (Mila Hart), Elizabeth Keifer (Blaize Hart), John Rhys-Davies (Donwaldo)

  The Reverend Jimmy Joe II runs America in the year 2099. He uses a mix of 1980s style tele-evangelism mixed with guys and gals wielding huge guns to keep everyone under control. People live in large rooms as refugees. The reverend's propaganda plays at them constantly. When *Rising Storm* begins, Artie Gage is getting his brother Joe out of prison. The duo meets up with the Hart sisters and head into the desert. They are trying to find some way to overthrow the power of the Reverend Jimmy Joe II.

  Rising Storm is a pretty wonderful satire of tele-evangelists finally getting what they want mixed with the "We all love guns and violence" of Rappin' Ronnie's 1980s. The reverend talks and talks in that low, simpering way of evangelists, which lulls everyone into a false state of security at the same time as all their rights are removed. His squad of guards are constantly blessing people as they shoot them to death or haul them away. The Gage brothers and the Hart sisters are all that stand between freedom and dull, totalitarian rule.

  The whole adventure is pretty amusing. One of the tricky things about satires or parodies is that the filmmakers can't use people who aren't good at this kind of thing. They need good actors to pull off comedy. And everyone in this film is up to it. It's always nice to see John Rhys-Davies having a good time.

  The action scenes are great. High adventure car chases through the desert. Shootouts in the reverend's compound and a particularly wonderful scene where our heroes (after finding the evidence that will get Jimmy Joe tossed out of power) have to fight their way out of a shantytown compound filled with bad guys. That scene, set to the William Tell Overture, is fantastic. Huge explosions. Well-shot action and a sense of brio that is missing in a lot of films like this. And this film is a satire.

  One doesn't come across a lot of films that could be called "smart" when journeying through the 1980s action catalogue. Most of the time one settles for "not that dumb" or "completely dumb." So it comes as a bit of surprise when a satire arrives that is funny and very entertaining. Occasional moments go on a bit longer than they maybe should, but one is going to have an occasional misstep in a film like this. Enjoy it for some sharp action and the very funny scene where the brothers are digging and Wayne Crawford's character can't stop complaining.

River of Death

  Director: Steve Carver
  Screenplay: Andrew Deutsch, Edwards Simpson
  Producers: Avi Lerner, Harry Alan Towers
  Cast: Michael Dudikoff (John Hamilton), Robert Vaughn (Dr. Wolfgang Manteuffel), Donald Pleasence (Heinrich Spaatz), Herbert Lom (Col. Diaz), L.Q. Jones (Hiller)

  An adventurer named Hamilton (Michael Dudikoff) heads into the South American jungles with a motley group of goofballs (some Nazis). There are missing women, lost tribes, hidden treasures and a retreat full of some very evil men. *River of Death* is based on Alistair MacLean's same-name novel, which has giant spiders in it. The movie does not have giant spiders but it does have Dudikoff narration. His voice seems higher in this film than it did in the *American Ninja* films.

All manner of older actors having a good time show up, from Vaughn to Pleasence to Lom to the always welcome L.Q. Jones. They add some ham to the table. Even some of the extras playing members of assorted lost tribes bring some goofiness to it. Apparently, Christopher Walken was supposed to be involved in this. The mind boggles at what that version of the film would have been like.

The film has a lushness to it, especially in the opening sequences in Germany and the jungle scenes. There are some nice action scenes throughout. They have definitely cut down on the perils of the jungle. In the book, they are myriad. (Those darn spiders.) In the movie, it's mainly angry natives throwing spears. That leaves us more time to focus on the characters and what they're up to.

The ending feels like a novel ending. I won't give it away. But on paper, this ending was a strong, powerful confrontation that tied everything together. Here, the viewer has spent too much time with these characters bickering and not enough adventure. (Plus, Hamilton, nominally the hero, doesn't do much in the end.) So the ending is the ultimate in anti-climaxes. It's basically a big revenge moment. This ends like an episode of an adventure TV show like *Tales of the Gold Monkey*. A show working under the theory that one can't give everything away in a single episode or there'd be nothing to do next week. Here, there was no next week, so the ending should have been bigger.

Riverbend

Director: Sam Firstenberg
Screenplay, Producer: Sam Vance
Cast: Steve James (Maj. Samuel Quentin),

Margaret Avery (Bell Coleman), Tony Frank (Sheriff Jake), Julius Tennon (Sgt. Tony Marx), Alex Morris (Lt. Turner), Vanessa Tate (Pauline)

Riverbend, Georgia, 1966. The town is mixed, black and white, but the sheriff is all-white. Pure redneck racist. And a crook. Meanwhile, three African-American Vietnam vets are being taken to a court martial. They escape from the MPs and end up at the home of Bell Coleman, whose husband has just been killed by the sheriff. Maj. Quentin trains the blacks in the community to fight. One night, they take a whole lot of white hostages…

Riverbend is about race relations in the South. It has a bit of the late '60s sort of *The Black Angels* or *The Brotherhood of Death* feel to it with African-Americans rising up against the whites oppressing them. It pairs Steve James, who normally kicks ass in a ninja-related capacity, and Margaret Avery, who a few years before had been nominated for an Academy Award playing Shug in *The Color Purple*.

This is not quite an action film. It's really a drama. But there are several action signposts. Steve James. Sam Firstenberg. The way the fighting and shooting are shot. The music gives the game away. The film is set in 1966 but the music is late-1980s drum machine-synth-wailing electric guitar, the sort of music that appeared in many action films of the day. Every time James gets in a fight, the cutting starts and the camera starts sliding back and forth, action film-style. The film has its heart in the right place. But Firstenberg's direction really only seems to come alive during those fight moments.

Riverbend works in shades of gray. Only Quentin and the sheriff are absolutely sure of themselves. Quentin knows that the blacks have to take the town by force. The sheriff knows that he's a horrible racist. All the other characters have shading to them. Which means the film can't truly become the action film it seems to want to be. Imagine a film about three Marines going into a Vietcong prison camp with evil people in charge. Our good guys storm in. They shoot the shit out of everybody and they save who they need to save. That can be fun. An action film like that keeps the issues black and white so we know who to cheer. *Riverbend* bends its rules a bit. So while we know the sheriff is in the wrong, part of us is convinced that there must be another way. When the action comes, it ends up feeling weird because the two sides need to work in peace but the racist cop has taken it to the point where that is no longer an option.

How much does Firstenberg seem to want to do more action here? During the final scene, the town's whites and the town's blacks approach each other on the street. Two large crowds. The camera moves around them. Cuts around them and then hovers overhead. And for one moment, it feels like a huge street brawl is going to break out ... but it doesn't. Almost action. *Riverbend* is fascinating because of what it actually is and what it almost seems to be.

Robot Jox

Director: Stuart Gordon
Screenplay: Joe Haldeman
Producer: Charles Band
Cast: Gary Graham (Achilles), Anne-Marie Johnson (Athena), Paul Koslo (Alexander), Robert Sampson (Commissioner Jameson), Danny Kamekona (Dr. Matsumoto)

Throughout the 1980s, Empire Pictures, run by the Band family, produced quite a few low-budget pictures (such as *Dreamaniac*) and also distributed a few films on Wizard Video (like *Headless Eyes*). They also made some more well-respected pictures, such as Stuart Gordon's *Re-Animator*. As the 1980s went along, the company grew larger until at the end of the decade, they began work on *Robot Jox*, an epic sci-fi film about giant robots fighting one another. It bankrupted

the company. (Similar to what happened to Troma after *Troma's War*.) It was later finished by another production company and is currently distributed by MGM. Charles Band went on to form Full Moon Pictures and really go crazy with his main love: tiny things attacking people.

Fifty years after the nuclear holocaust, all war has been outlawed. Any big dispute is handled by specially trained fighters climbing inside giant robots and fighting. There is a dispute over Alaska. Achilles and Alexander are the fighters. They fight twice in the movie. In between, there is a lot of drama. Too much drama. In fact, one might not be wrong in

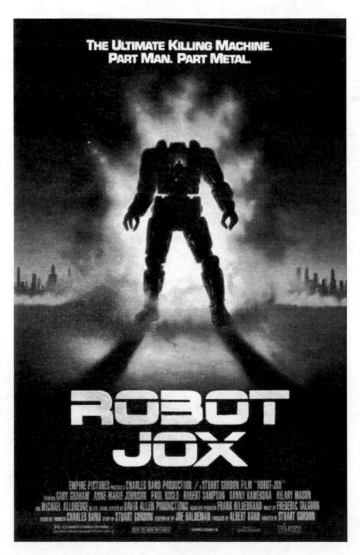

thinking that the budget meant that there was only enough cash for two big robot fights.

It's a shame *Robot Jox* isn't very good. The robot fights look pretty darn good. David Allen's stop-motion animation brings it all to life. Some of the rear-screen projection looks a little obvious but the actual fighting works. It's all that in-between nonsense that drags things down. Back and forth political squabbling. Achilles filled with angst due to the accidental killing of spectators at the first robot fight. A fighter named Athena keeps trying to draw Achilles back out, to make him a fighter again.

Dammit, there should be more robot fighting in this film. That's fun. The rest is subpar *Rocky* material that the audience has seen a thousand times. Frankly, I lost interest in all the assorted machinations. Athena is dull. Achilles is made into a guilt-ridden hero before the viewer really knows who he is. Alexander is kind of ridiculous.

Robot Jox goes for the gold with its big robot scenes. But, it needed to take a page from the Japanese TV series *Super Robot Red Baron*. That show is about a hero robot and a bad guy with a neverending supply of bad robots. There is a fantastic robot fight in every 25-minute episode. And the episodes build to that fight (sometimes there is more than one) and they're men in robot suits but they're entertaining. The human drama is breezed past us. This movie should have taken a page from that show. It's good when robots fight. When people talk, it's a snoozer.

The Russian Ninja

Directors: Mats Helge, Anders Nilsson
Screenplay: Mats Helge
Producer: Mats Helge, Roger Lundgren
Cast: Frederick Offrein (Mark Robinson), Helle Michalesen (Eve Garland), Mats Hydden (Sherman), Timothy Earle (Eve's Dad)

"What are we going to do now?"

"Let's kick some asses."

The Russian Ninja is awesome. An old guy is hired to find a woman or her father or something. There's a couple of guys who look very similar. There's several blond women who look very similar. The women are on either sides of the fence. The guys eventually team up to kick ass. Whose ass? Well, there is a ninja and he is Russian. Plus, there are a whole slew of other characters. There is a lot of shooting. And there is the same sort of slightly insane feel that *The Ninja Mission* has. The ninjas are part of the film and they are in the title but the film itself is more straightforward action. And it's from the director of the horror film *Blood Tracks* so that should be enough to make the day of any viewer.

Possibly teaming this film up with *The Ninja Mission* would create a beautiful double feature. *The Russian Ninja* isn't as good as *Mission* but almost. That old guy who is called out of retirement is great. He looks a little too old be the trained government agent–assassin guy that he's declared to be. He does get his ass whooped but he makes it to the end. That character reminded me of the ex–KGB assassin from the *X-Files* episodes "Tunguska-Terma." That guy looks way too old but the episodes presents him as a crack assassin. Every once in a while it works but sometimes it looks like Grandpa with a deadly weapon. Something like that might have entertained Grandma but it can be a little rough for the grandkids.

The actors aren't the best. But then, English is not their first language, so they awkwardly deliver lines that were probably written by people who didn't have English as *their* first language. But they know action. Lots of running through halls, firing weapons, fighting. This film's list of awesome things is endless.

The title: *The Russian Ninja*. What? Come on, Sweden, hit us with some more of this kick-ass action. Was there a *Ninja Mission 2*? Possibly. But, that's for another book.

Samurai Cop

Director, Screenplay: Amir Shervan
Producers: Amir Shervan, Orlando Corradi
Cast: Robert Z'Dar (Yamashita), Matt Hammon (Joe Marshall), Janis Farley, Mark

Frazer (Frank Washington), Melissa Moore Cameron (Peggy), Gerald Okamura (Okamura), Cranston Komuro (Fujiyama)

Sometimes a film hits you as perfect. There is a craving that someone didn't know they had that suddenly become fulfilled by a film. *Samurai Cop* is one of those films. Amir Shervan's other films, including *Hollywood Cop*, definitely have their slightly off-kilter charms, odd acting, strange directorial choices made during action scenes, characters that don't really act human and plotting that just doesn't always conform to anyone else's idea of story. But apparently Amir was on some sort of emotional-creative high after that because the follow-up, *Samurai Cop*, takes in rarefied air.

Joe is the cop known as Samurai. He's a white guy with flowing jet black locks that could be a wig in some shots. His partner Frank is a wisecracking African-American who seems like he's in a different cop movie from Joe. Frank is straightforward, pure TV-movie cop. Joe seems to come from some town where everything is a circus and he's the head Clown Cop but he no longer wears the makeup. Joe and his partner get involved in a drug war involving the Katana Gang, run by a man named Fujiyama. Fujiyama's right hand man is played by Robert Z'Dar, sporting a nice beard and bringing on the kung fu. Mixed in with all the not-quite-so-gritty of Los Angeles, there are several lovely ladies. Fujiyama's right hand woman has red hair, very large breasts and can get down and dirty. A blond restaurateur falls for Joe. And there's a cop played by scream queen Melissa Moore who loves innuendo and sex, in that order. The mixture is set. Now it must be stirred.

Shervan stirs it up through his insistence upon everything being shot during the day, as he couldn't afford lights. At times, the characters sound clear as a bell. Other times they sound like they're being recorded in the world's biggest tin can, possibly the one with Prince Albert in it. He shoots car chases, gunfights and fistfights all in the same way: kind of a little too far away and with not enough coverage. There are several moments during fights when it looks like people are practicing instead of fighting properly.

Then, there are the moments that are just weird. A witness is horribly burned. He's covered in bandages in the hospital. His bandages are soaked in blood. He should consider changing those bandages. Z'Dar hides in a dirty linen cart, climbs out, beheads the witness and goes. Melissa Moore's character is very into sex. Joe wears tiny black underpants. The final fight between Joe and Z'Dar is goofy. There is a long, innuendo-laden conversation between Joe and a female doctor. That comes out of nowhere, goes nowhere, but is wonderful. If one watches *Samurai Cop*, one will see about a hundred more things like this.

Place *Samurai Cop* alongside *Rescue Force, Miami Connection, Hell Squad, The Executioner Part II, R.O.T.O.R., The Courier of Death, Kill Squad*. All weird, individualistic films made by wonderful people. Finding films like this is the reason to write a book like this. One wants to spread the love around.

Savage Beach

Director, Screenplay: Andy Sidaris
Producer: Arlene Sidaris
Cast: Dona Speir (Donna), Hope Marie Carlton (Taryn), John Aprea (Capt. Andreas), Bruce Penhall (Bruce Christian), Rodrigo Obregon (Martinez), Michael Mikasa (Japanese Warrior), Michael Shane (Shane Abeline), Teri Weigel (Anjelica)

For fans of the Abilene clan, there is an Abilene here and he is the hunkiest of them all. Even his name, Shane, implies hunkiness. Unfortunately, he doesn't do much. In fact, *Savage Beach* is the point when all the kitchen sink effects of Andy Sidaris's previous two films begin to cause a little trouble. Granted, it's never in the entertainment department. All the shooting, screwing and over-the-top mayhem you want is here. The plot in this one is really straightforward but related in possibly the most over-complicated fashion yet.

Japanese troops steal Filipino gold during World War II. The vessel with the gold sinks somewhere in the Philippines. Now, in

1989, the Japanese government is working with the Filipino government to retrieve the gold. Some of the people involved are not very nice and want the gold for themselves. They didn't take into account that Donna and Taryn might crash land on the island. Plus, they didn't take into account the Japanese soldier who has been living on the island since the end of the war.

The ladies are as beautiful as ever. The guys are hunky. The bad guys are vicious. There is a lot of late '80s computer action. The kind where people say things like, "Okay, let me enter the information from the Star Wars satellite" and they hit four buttons and ENTER. Suddenly, 100 dots appear on the screen off the coast of Japan. "Now, let me enter the info received from Japan and eliminate all non-essential elements." Four buttons. ENTER. Suddenly: "And there is where you'll find the gold that's been missing for 40 years." Hooray for computers! Can modern computers do things like that? The world was still in that vague era where people knew computers should be able to do great stuff but the computers of the time didn't. So watching this is like watching alchemists perform.

Savage Beach doesn't involve a series of encounters and battles like the previous two Sidaris films. The first hour is the set-up to get everyone to the island for about a half-hour of climactic chases and shooting. The giant gears of the plot are almost visible as everyone gradually gets to the island. It's a different sort of film than the others: one big buildup to the climax rather than a lot of chaos throughout. Regardless of where his structure might go, Sidaris has perfected one thing: explosions. Whenever he blows up a vehicle or a person, it is a work of art.

It is nice to see Donna and Taryn again. It was interesting to see Teri Weigel, who is given lines that a really good actress might have trouble with. She is beautiful but seems to be struggling. However, Donna and Taryn get better with each film. And apparently Hope Marie Carlton, who plays Taryn, is a pilot. That's cool.

Shocking Dark aka *The Terminator II*

Director: Bruno Mattei
Screenplay: Claudio Fragasso
Producer: Flora Films
Cast: Christopher Ahrens (Sam), Haven Taylor(Sara), Tony Lombardo (Lt. Franzini), Mark Steinborn (Comdr. Bond)

The Tubular Corporation welcomes you to Bruno Mattei's latest film, which seems a lot like something James Cameron might be able to sue for. It's a bit of *Aliens* mixed with a bunch of *The Terminator*. And it mostly takes place in a couple of stone hallways and large rooms that seem to be in a fallout shelter somewhere. Story-wise, we are in Venice in the year 2000. A group of tough Army folks have been sent under Venice to find whatever is lurking down there.

It's some kind of alien thing. But there's an extra twist that moves the film into the realms of ripping off a different influential film. The whole underground installation, including some very suspect technology, is there because of the Tubular Corporation. I guess if the name is referring to tubes of some variety, then it's a good name. If it's referring to the slang term "Tubular," then there's a whole other thing going on here.

Mattei is no stranger to simply ripping stuff off. For *Hell of the Living Dead*, he stole Goblin's music and footage from a documentary on South American tribes. For *Cruel Jaws*, he stole shark attack footage from other movies. For *Zombie 3*, he took over from Lucio Fulci and ended up ripping off Fulci within a film he made in tandem with Fulci … the man was the best of all possible rip-off artists. One who really didn't seem to care. He made films for around 30 years. Are any of them good? Well, *The Other Hell* certainly has it charms. I saw *Hell of the Living Dead* in a theater and it is fun with a crowd. But Bruno just really did his own thing and went his own way. "His own thing and his own way" involves ripping everyone off but you can't have everything.

Shocking Dark has a young survivor girl,

a la Newt, called Samantha. In a sequence near the end, Sara and Samantha are trying to find one another where they keep yelling each other's names. If you can keep from turning down the volume while these women yell, you are a better person than this reviewer.

A lot like *Robowar*, this film takes great pleasure in not pinning itself down to one specific rip-off. Things are kept fluid. And when the second big rip-off section starts, the sheer audacity of it may make you laugh out loud. This isn't Bruno's best. It is a bit dull. Really, it's just people wandering around corridors shooting. But stay tuned and see what he does next. It's guaranteed nutty.

Shotgun

> *Director, Screenplay:* Addison Randall
> *Producer:* Joseph Merhi, Richard Pepin
> *Cast:* Stuart Chapin (Ian Jones), Rif Hutton (Max Billings), David Marriott (Rocker), Metanel Ryan (Barbara Devlin), Jerry Neal (Lt. Steinbridge)

PM Entertainment strikes again, this time with another thriller-action film that provides a good time. It has a great leading guy with the character name Ian "Shotgun" Jones. Jones kicks ass when he needs to. They call him "Shotgun" because, as a bounty hunter, he totes around a shotgun. In one scene, he shoots a guy in the butt and the guy claims to have been shot in the "asshole." That's good marksmanship.

Shotgun takes all the '80s cop movie clichés and trots them out and, on occasion, fiddles with them. There is a man picking up hookers and then beating them, some almost to death. A suave gent picks the prostitutes up and takes them to a motel room. Then a leather-bound fellow steps out of the bathroom for the beating. They kill Shotgun's sister. The shit hits the fan. Shotgun has a black partner who is much more controlled than he is. (*Lethal Weapon* was out two years before.) And Shotgun gets in trouble with Internal Affairs, "cops who bust other cops." One can sort of guess where the film goes from here.

Shotgun is kind of dull and kind of dumb. It's dumb in the right way. The kind of dumb where the acting is all a little off and everything that happens is very obvious. Shotgun simply looks wrong for all the stuff they're having him do. But it's also dull in the wrong way. The film is only around 85 minutes but it feels much longer. It has that ugly look of many of the late '80s direct-to-video films. Apart from the very end and the bounty hunter moments, it always goes where you expect it to.

If the viewer is in the mood for some PM Entertainment and the goofiest looking action hero since Orson Bean, *Shotgun* will give you exactly what you need. It's too bad that the start of the film is predicated upon violence against women. But Shotgun eventually does take care of the jerks who did it. And, if the story doesn't grab you, you can enjoy some awkward conversations between Shotgun and his partner.

Sinbad of the Seven Seas

> *Director, Producer:* Enzo G. Castellari (Luigi Cozzi)
> *Screenplay:* Tito Carpi, Enzo G. Castellari (Luigi Cozzi)
> *Cast:* Lou Ferrigno (Sinbad), John Steiner (Jafar), Ronland Wybenga (Ali), Enio Girolami (Viking), Alessandra Martines (Alina), Haruhiko Yamanhouchi (Samurai), Cork Hubbert (Midget)

This is the silliest (intentionally) movie in this book. *Sinbad of the Seven Seas* began life with Luigi Cozzi, who had done two Hercules movies with Lou Ferrigno earlier in the 1980s. It ended up being made by Enzo G. Castellarti, director of *The Bronx Warriors* and *The Inglorious Bastards*. From seeing those pedigrees, one might imagine a strange adult fantasy-peplum number that would have weird, colorful moments mixed with violence that will make everyone wince. But, it's actually quite charming and goofy.

Sinbad returns to Basra after one of his voyages. He is big and beefy. Lou Ferrigno's voice is dubbed but he looks like he's having fun here. *Everyone* looks to be having a good time, especially John Steiner as Jafar. This is the hammiest Jafar ever. This is a role to rival the strange witch lady in *Troll 2*. Every few minutes he appears on the screen and he's astoundingly over-the-top. Jafar has stolen the five gems of Basra. Sinbad goes on a voyage to get the gems back and save everyone, including Ali's love, Alina.

The film becomes a series of adventures. Sinbad escapes from a snake pit by tying the snakes together like a rope. They fight zombie soldiers, meet up with sirens, join forces with beautiful women and strange-talking men. It's exactly like the Seven Voyages of Sinbad except (I would imagine) more colorful, possibly a bit less epic and with Lou Ferrigno.

The movie is fun but had a troubled production. One can tell this from the *Princess Bride*-esque framing device. A little girl (dubbed by a grown woman) asks Mom for a story. Mom tells the story of Sinbad. And she tells it and she tells it. Her voice is constantly explaining what is going on in the movie, which seems a bit excessive. She doesn't interject wit like Peter Falk did. She just tells and tells the story.

While the story does have that meandering quality that some people can take or leave, *Sinbad of the Seven Seas* keeps it moving and colorful and fun. It's almost a live-action animated film. The film I thought of while watching was Luigi Cozzi's *Starcrash*, which is another meandering, fun, colorful film about heroes hunting down assorted things. That film is actually a bit more entertaining because of all the wild effects. But this one has a kick-ass dwarf in it.

Snake Eater

Director: George Erschbamer
Screenplay: Michael Paseornek, John Dunning
Producer: John Dunning
Cast: Lorenzo Lamas (Soldier), Josie Bell (The Kid), Robert Scott (Junior), Cheryl Jeans (Jennifer), Larry Csonka (Lt. Boulder)

Lorenzo Lamas plays "Soldier," an ex-member of the Snake Eaters, a very special Marine platoon who are not only very strong but masters at setting traps. But if Soldier is

anything to go by, they have no peripheral vision and can't tell when someone is sneaking up on them. That would seem to be a handicap. But Soldier makes do.

Soldier's sister is kidnapped by a bunch of rednecks and locked in a barn in the woods. Soldier is a cop who engages in a very long disrobing session with a woman at the beginning of the film. He also springs a trap on some mobsters that involves many spikes shooting up out of the floor. When his sister is kidnapped, he heads to the woods to get her back. Those rednecks don't play nice.

Snake Eater has a lot of redneck action in it. Your tolerance for rednecks may determine whether or not you can get through this movie. It's not a terribly exciting film although there is some action. Lamas is fine as Soldier but, really, he gets sneaked up on a lot. It actually becomes kind of amusing seeing how often people creep up on him and belt him one. Or pour beer on him. Or whatever. There's a fight on a dock that seems to consist solely of him knocking one redneck down while another sneaks up on him and hits him. Soldier turns and hits that redneck. Then another redneck sneaks up on him. Apparently wherever the Snake Eaters were stationed, sneaking up wasn't invented yet.

Once Soldier encounters the rednecks, things become pretty entertaining. Violent traps are set and people are hurt in assorted ways. Until then, this viewer did look at the clock a few times. A strain of humor runs through the film. Larry Csonka as Lt. Boulder spends his time goofing. The final sequence involves Ron Palillo in a warehouse, and that's played strictly for laughs. But, surely, this redneck gang of rapists and killers isn't a hoot. Surely the tone should be adjusted somewhat to accommodate the bad guys?

Snake Eater is not great but it's got a tough hunk fighting to the death against a group of pretty gross rednecks. The tough hunk is Lorenzo Lamas. The choice is yours.

Trained to Kill

Director, Screenplay: H. Kaye Dyal
Producer: Arthur Welb

Cast: Frank Zagarino (Matt), Glen Eaton (Sam), Lisa Aliff (Jessie), Chuck Connors (Ed Cooper), Marshall Teague (Vendetta), Arlene Golonka (Martha), Henry Silva (Ace Duran), Robert Z'Dar (Walter)

Trained to Kill is the story of a team of guys who are sent to Cambodia to rescue Sam, the son of a gentleman named Ed Cooper. Sam supposedly has a valuable artifact known as the Red Diamond, which everybody wants. When our heroes find Sam, the Red Diamond is gone. Sam's mom abandoned him and took the Red Diamond back with her to the United States. When Sam returns to the States and meets up with his brother Matt, Hell is waiting for him in the person of Ace Duran and his thugs. Ace wants that Red Diamond. He will kill for it.

The Red Diamond is clearly the McGuffin that drives the story. It keeps Duran and his nasty thugs pestering Ed Cooper. That pestering keeps Sam and Matt in constant scuffles with the baddies. And, luckily for the viewer, their fights are impressive. An exciting displays of fisticuffs, a nicely done car chase, and the requisite explosions and shootouts. The action is enhanced by the presence of Z'Dar, Silva and the great Michael Pataki.

A Red Diamond in the rough.

War Bus Commando

Director: Pierluigi Ciriaci
Screenplay: Dardano Sacchetti
Producer: Alfred Nicolaj
Cast: Mark Gregory (Johnny Hondo), John Vernon (Ken Ross), Savina Gersak (Linda Cain), Mario Novelli, Bobby Rhodes (P.O.W. Mechanic)

The War Bus franchise continues! And ends here. With Johnny Hondo, played by Mark Gregory, as a Green Beret sent into Afghanistan to find a school bus with some important documents in it. Some time ago, Johnny's dad hid them there. Now, Dad is dead and Johnny is going to retrieve the documents, and a few P.O.W.s. But, is he being double-crossed? Does he care if he is?

War Bus Commando is the film that I thought *War Bus* was going to be: a slightly dumb but mostly entertaining war-type film. But *War Bus* was a surprise. It started off feeling like a fairly standard Italian Namsploitation thing but then it got better and it became a really *good* Italian Namsploitation thing. This follow-up or sequel (or probably just a film ripping off *War Bus*, to be honest) is just fun. It's not as good with the action but it moves at a decent pace. Mark Gregory is fine but he was never known for showing too much emotion.

I expected to hear one of the standard group of dubbing artists replacing John Vernon's very recognizable voice. But the dubber they used was the one who plays Weng Weng's boss in *For Y'ur Height Only*. The guy who appears in that James Bond rip-off as M and Q in the same scene. He gives Agent 00 gadgets. ("It's a real humdinger." "You got a bug in your hair?" "I like the way you pay attention.") Seeing Vernon matched up to that voice is quite funny.

Hondo heads into Afghanistan looking for that school bus and the P.O.W.s. It is a silly concept that his dad hid these super-secret documents inside an Afghani school bus. Why not bury them somewhere? It doesn't make sense but, in the movie, it works perfectly so who are we to say? Mark Gregory keeps that one look on his face as he leads a group with their armor-plated bus through lots of Soviet forces.

War Bus Commando is a pretty standard Italian action film that is based on a silly premise. Why have the bus in it at all, apart from using it to make ties with *War Bus*? But *War Bus* had a real reason for having the bus in it, and it was set during the Vietnam War. This is set around the same time *Rambo III* is set. And all that movie did was prove that at that time, Americans didn't really care too much about Afghanistan. Stallone and Gregory tried.

Wizards of the Lost Kingdom II

Director: Charles B. Griffith

Screenplay: Lance Smith
Producer: Reid Shane
Cast: Mel Welles (Cademon), Bobby Jacoby (Tyor), David Carradine (Dark One), Susan Lee Hoffman (Idun), Blake Bahner (Erman)

Mel Welles as the star of a sword-and-sorcery adventure film? Yes, in 1952. In 1989-ish, he looks like an old guy in a bad wig, even if he *has* been called by some spirit to find the Chosen One and defeat three evil lords in a mystical, magical land. *Wizards of the Lost Kingdom II* is goofier than the first one, with which it shares nothing in common, except the general theme of a group of people embarking on a quest. This is pretty fitting as it's directed by Charles B. Griffith, who wrote many of Roger Corman's wittier scripts, including *The Little Shop of Horrors* ... with Mel Welles.

Cademon of Nog (Welles) is asked to find Tyor, an annoying kid. Cademon soon finds him and they go on a journey and meet up with several heroes and some hot ladies who help defeat the evil lords. The quest plot is similar to the first movie, but there are different groups to fight and several different tough heroes, one being David Carradine, to help out. It's less exciting than the first one. That one had a chintzy feel to it here and there

but was able to keep its head above water most of the time. *II* doesn't do so well.

First off, there is the score. It's all synths here. (The first film had a whole bunch of orchestral stuff in it.) The film does reveal the difference between a wizard and a sorcerer. Wizards are smarter and better looking.

The film never quite takes off. It meanders along from one kingdom to another, one hero to another. There isn't all that much shown in the way of Tyro becoming a master wizard. Mel Welles is an acquired taste; he may be best in small doses. And who doesn't have fun dressing up in Renaissance Fair outfits? But it doesn't feel like everyone's trying all that hard, even Mel Welles. Actually, maybe he is and I can't tell.

Index

Numbers in **bold** refer to films that are reviewed in full.